OXFORD THEOLOGICAL MONOGRAPHS

OXFORD THEOLOGICAL MONOGRAPHS

Theory and Theology
in George Herbert's Poetry

'Divinitie, and Poesie, Met'

ELIZABETH CLARKE

CLARENDON PRESS · OXFORD
1997

Oxford University Press, Great Clarendon Street, Oxford OX2 6DP

Oxford New York

Athens Auckland Bangkok Bogota Bombay
Buenos Aires Calcutta Cape Town Dar es Salaam
Delhi Florence Hong Kong Istanbul Karachi
Kuala Lumpur Madras Madrid Melbourne
Mexico City Nairobi Paris Singapore
Taipei Tokyo Toronto Warsaw

and associated companies in
Berlin Ibadan

Oxford is a trade mark of Oxford University Press

Published in the United States
by Oxford University Press Inc., New York

British Library Cataloguing in Publication Data
Data available

Library of Congress Cataloging in Publication Data
Theory and theology in George Herbert's poetry: divinitie, and poesie, met / Elizabeth Clarke.
(Oxford theological monographs)
Based on the author's thesis (D. Phil., Cambridge) under title: Divinitie, and poesie, met.
Includes bibliographical references
1. Herbert, George, 1593–1633—Criticism and interpretation.
2. Christian poetry, English—History and criticism. 3. Theology in literature. I. Title. II. Series.
PR3508.C58 1997 821'.3—dc21 97–9925
ISBN 0-19-826398-8

1 3 5 7 9 10 8 6 4 2

Typeset by Pure Tech India Ltd, Pondicherry
Printed in Great Britain on acid-free paper by
Biddles Ltd., Guildford and King's Lynn

ACKNOWLEDGEMENTS

I would like to thank the supervisors of my thesis, Dr Nigel Smith and the Right Revd Dr Rowan Williams, for their inspirational help and guidance. The readers for Oxford University Press, Dr Paul Fiddes and Dr Judith Maltby, supplied invaluable comment and criticism. Sean Hughes of Trinity College Cambridge and Dr Diarmaid McCulloch of St Cross College, Oxford helped me with the vexed question of early seventeenth-century theology. I am grateful to Dr Timothy Bartel for checking the thesis for theological and editorial errors. Thanks too to Emily's many baby-sitters, especially my mother, without whom this book would not have been finished, and to Jean-Pierre, Alan, and Russell in Duke Humfrey, who have forced me to modify my opinion of librarians. However, I owe most to my husband Matthew Stiff, who has supplied meticulous proof-reading and computer expertise, and has generally kept me sane during the writing of this book.

CONTENTS

INTRODUCTION

Poetry and Divine Motion

Probably the most impressive construction in *The Temple* is the role of the Reformation poet. This book is an exploration of George Herbert's success in creating that role for himself in unpromising seventeenth-century circumstances. Herbert is writing at a key moment in literary history, at the confluence of the Renaissance rhetorical tradition and Reformation theology. This exceptionally creative conjunction gave rise to questions about the authority of sacred discourse, and the validity of poetry itself. Herbert struggled with these issues in *The Temple*, with enormous success in terms of his seventeenth-century readership.

The theologians of the fledgling Reformation in England had not been sympathetic to poetry. Tyndale used the word 'poet' as a term of abuse.[1] There was universal concern that preoccupation with the 'husk' of words could divert attention from the 'kernel' of truth. Richard Rogers scorns those who 'preferre the Case before the Instrument, the Rinde before the Pith'.[2] Savonarola, whose writings were influential in Reformation England, was convinced that the 'shell' which was poetic language would always distract from the truth, because it was essentially self-glorifying to the poet.[3] Versified narrative such as *The Mirror for Magistrates*, where content was clearly primary, and verse paraphrases of the Bible were more acceptable. George Wither distinguished three types of poetry, the first including 'such Conceits as delight Schoolboyes and Pedanticall wits', which is clearly unsuitable for sacred poetry, the second 'necessary Truths . . . couched in significant Parables'. He has chosen to write in the third kind, 'which delivers commodious Truths, and things Really necessary, in as plain, and in

---

[1] See Eiléan ní Chuilleandin, 'The Debate between Thomas More and William Tyndale, 1528–33: Ideas on Literature and Religion', *JEH* 39 (1987), 398.

[2] Richard Rogers, *The Practice of Christianitie* (London, 1618), 345: quoted in Russell Fraser, *The War Against Poetry* (Princeton, 1970), 8.

[3] Jérôme Savonarola, *Apologeticus De Ratione Poeticae Artis*, in *Compendium philosophia et alia* (Venice, 1534), 17ᵛ.

I

as universall tearmes, as it can possibly devise'.[4] Many Christian writers adopted this 'plain style', but, like Wither himself, they did not necessarily escape criticism. A satiric verse 'On a Puritan' copied into several commonplace books of the 1640s notes the Puritan concern that biblical discourse, 'true Geneva characters', should entirely exclude 'the bastarde monument of humane witt'. It is the infiltration of the human into the divine, an inescapable condition of sacred poetry, that is objected to by the Puritan:

> That in his censure each alike gainesayes
> Poetts in Churches: & Scriptures in plaies.[5]

Of course, other Protestants took a less bleak attitude to sacred literature. The Sidney circle, nourished by French influence in the shape of poet-theologians such as Beza and Philippe Duplessis-Mornay, was an enclave where religious poetry could be practised with confidence, although Sir Philip himself was stung by an attack from Stephen Gosson, who had himself been a poet-dramatist, into writing his *Apology for Poetry*.[6] Alex Walsham in her study of these polemics concludes that the commercial demand for the Puritan pamphlets suggests that 'such tracts did not articulate the grievances of an over-scrupulous few'.[7] James Doelman has noted the expansion in publication of religious verse at the accession of James I, whose exploits in the field of sacred poetry encouraged imitation and compliment in that area.[8]

---

[4] George Wither, *Halleluiah or Britans second Remembrancer, bringing to Remembrance (in powerfull and Penitentiall Hymnes, Spirituall Songs, and Morall Odes) Meditations advancing the glorie of God, and the Practice of Pietie and Vertue* (London, 1641), 15–17.

[5] 'On a Puritan', Folger MS V. a. 162, fol. 29. The version in Bodleian MS Tanner 456, fol. 82 has the variant 'Prelates in Churches' for 'Poetts in Churches' but since the context is a literary one the Folger reading seems more satisfactory.

[6] Late sixteenth-century attacks on literature include J. Northbrooke, *Treatise where in vain Plays or Interludes are reproved* (London, 1577); S. Gosson, *A Short Apology of the School of Abuse* (London, 1579); H. Denham, *Second and Third Blast of Retreat from Plays* (London, 1580); P. Stubbes, *Anatomy of Abuses* (London, 1583); G. Whetstone, *A Touchstone for the Times* (London, 1584); W. Rankins, *A Mirror of Monsters* (London, 1587); J. Rainoldes, *Overthrow of Stage Plays* (London, 1599). The main target is the drama, but poetry is guilty by association, as it were. The main provocation for Philip Sidney's *Apology for Poetry* is thought to be Gosson's pamphlet, which was dedicated to him.

[7] A. Walsham, 'Godly Recreation: The Problem of Leisure in Late Elizabethan and Early Stuart Society', in D. E. Kennedy (ed.) *Grounds of Controversy: Three Studies in Late 16th and Early 17th Century English Polemics* (Melbourne, 1989), 24.

[8] For poetic activity at the court of James VI of Scotland, see L. B. Campbell, *Divine Poetry and Drama in Sixteenth Century England* (Cambridge, 1959), 74–83. James I was the author of a version of Du Bartas's *Uranie* and two poetical works, *The Essayes of a Prentise in*

Joshua Sylvester's collected version of du Bartas' *Divine Weekes and Workes*, dedicated to King James in 1605, was hugely popular, but even Sylvester did not escape criticism for treating sacred subjects in verse.[9] Doelman traces the determined efforts of Sylvester, John Davies of Hereford, and John Harington to gain favour with James I.[10] The context of royal solicitation he describes is not conducive to authorial introspection about the role of religious poet. In the preface to his Psalm paraphrases, dated 1607, Joseph Hall, later to be Bishop of Exeter and Norwich, distances himself from his 1603 volume *The Kings Prophecie*, which was grossly flattering to King James:

Indeede, my Poetrie was long sithence out of date, & yielded hir place to graver studies. This worke is holy and strict.

The rest of the preface runs through the familiar arguments in defence of religious verse. The Scripture gives warrant to it; it is profoundly affective; he is writing for the glory of God in a deliberately simple strain. Nevertheless, he mentions 'the wanton Poet of old, who lost his eyes when he went about to turne Moses into verse', the Greek poet Theodectes, clearly a classic exemplar of what happens when divine Word is contaminated by human words.[11] In a contemporary letter to a friend Hall admits 'I have boldly undertaken the holy meeters of *David* . . . there is none of all my labours so open to all censures.'[12] Similarly, John Harington felt that his efforts in religious verse, a manuscript of verse paraphrases of the Psalms presented to James in about 1607, had 'raised . . . a mighty enmitie'.[13] He does not specify the reason for such opprobrium, but James Doelman notes 'by about 1610 straight theology without poetic embellishment was perceived as the best way to attract the king's attention and favour'.[14] The boom in the

---

the Divine Art of Poesie (Edinburgh, 1584) and His Maiesties Poeticall Exercises at Vacant Houres (1591).

[9] See Joshua Sylvester (tr.), *The Divine Weeks and Works of Guillaume de Saluste Sieur du Bartas*, ed. Susan Snyder, 2 vols. (Oxford, 1979), 75.

[10] J. Doelman, 'The Accession of King James I and English Religious Poetry', *SEL* 34 (1994), 19–40.

[11] Joseph Hall, *The Collected Poems of Joseph Hall*, ed. A. Davenport (Liverpool, 1949), 127–8.

[12] Ibid. 271.

[13] John Harington, *The Letters and Epigrams of Sir John Harington*, ed. N. E. McClure (Philadelphia, 1930), 143.

[14] Doelman, 'James I and Religious Poetry', 35.

publication of religious poetry was short-lived. Even William Leighton, who had received a knighthood after the 1603 publication of *Virtue Triumphant*, was apologetic about his far less confident 1613 volume *The Teares, or Lamentations of a sorrowful Soule*, which begins with 'A Declaration by the Author to the religious and devoute':

> I have published these Himnes and spirituall sonnets, not in vaine affection or ostentation of my owne skill, which ingeniously I confesse to be but small and mediocrious: butt onely in an unfeigned affection & earnest desire that the humbled hearts (together with mine) may reape profit and consolation by singing or reading of them.[15]

A positive reception for religious poetry was no longer guaranteed.

Giles Fletcher, in his preface to *Christ's Victorie and Triumph* in 1610, is self-conscious about the status of his project, and the need to justify the writing of a religious poem: 'some . . . thinke it halfe sacrilege for prophane Poetrie to deale with divine and heavenly matters'. 1610 is a significant date for George Herbert, also. Newly arrived at Trinity, Giles Fletcher's college, he was writing two sonnets to his mother announcing his own vocation as a religious poet. It may well have been Fletcher's vigorous defence of sacred poetry which inspired him. Louis Martz finds ideas congenial to Herbert in Robert Southwell's Epistle Dedicatorie to *Marie Magdalens Funerall teares*, but, to an ambitious, academic seventeen-year-old, Fletcher serves much more satisfactorily as a role model than a Catholic priest who was trying to disseminate heretical doctrines in populist poetry.[16] Fletcher claims the same ancestry as Sir Philip Sidney in his *Apology for Poetry*, listing the biblical writers, and taking care to include King James I amongst recent poets and theologians as one 'enamour'd with this celestiall Muse'. Thus bolstered by the example of Scripture, Protestant theologians, and British monarchs, Fletcher concludes with a familiar quotation which Sidney had used to support the divine origins of the poetic gift: 'the heavenly infusion of such Poetry, shoulde ende in his glorie, that had beginning from his goodnes, *fit orator, nascitur Poeta*.'[17] The role of Christian poet as constructed

---

[15] William Leighton, *The Teares, or Lamentations of a sorrowfull Soule* (London, 1613), sig. *1ᵛ.

[16] Although some of Herbert's lyrics follow Southwell's practice of employing popular verse forms: see, for example, 'Submission', 'Dialogue', 'Love (iii)'.

[17] Giles Fletcher and Phineas Fletcher, *Giles and Phineas Fletcher: Poetical Works*, ed. Frederick S. Boas, 2 vols. (Cambridge, 1908), i. 10–12.

by Fletcher must have looked peculiarly attractive to the young Herbert, seeming to promise both spiritual and worldly success. Fletcher's poem was prefaced with commendatory verse by Francis Nethersole, Fellow of Trinity, who was to become a kind of patron to Herbert, and was his predecessor as University Orator.[18] Two years later, both Herbert and Fletcher contributed elegies for Prince Henry to Legge's *Epicedium Cantabrigensis*. In 1613, both men wrote complimentary verse for the Princess Elizabeth and the Elector Palatine in a manuscript volume presented to them shortly after their marriage.[19]

George Herbert was himself not averse to gross flattery of the King: in fact, this was his professional duty for several years. Like other Jacobean poets, he claims inspiration from James in the dedication of *Musae Responsoriae*, written in 1620 or soon after:

> My Muse too was vile mud:
> But now, because of You, she is alive,
> She can creep along, and has the nerve
> To step up where you are the sun.[20]

However, the *Musae Responsoriae* is not a volume of sacred poetry, but a collection of topical Latin epigrams with a political slant, an enterprise well within the terms of Herbert's role as Orator at the University of Cambridge. Far more introspection seems to have been taking place about the other role Herbert was preparing for himself, and one for which he would eventually achieve far more fame, although he could not have foreseen such a thing in the early seventeenth century. In the two sonnets of 1610 Herbert declares his sense of vocation in terms reminiscent of Sidney. Sir Philip Sidney had identified the lack of Christian lyric, and formulated a vision for the Christian poet writing in English, in *An Apology for Poetry*:

other sorts of Poetry almost have we none, but that lyrical kind of songs and sonnet: which, Lord, if He gave us so good minds, how well it might be employed, and with how heavenly fruit both private and public, in

---

[18] See George Herbert, *The Works of George Herbert*, ed. F. E. Hutchinson (Oxford, 1945), 369.

[19] See L. Bradner, 'New Poems by George Herbert: The Cambridge Latin Gratulatory Anthology of 1613', *Renaissance News*, no. 15 (1962), 208–11.

[20] George Herbert, *The Latin Poetry of George Herbert: A Bilingual Edition*, tr. M. McCloskey and P. R. Murphy (Athens, Oh., 1965), 39.

singing the praises of that God who giveth us hands to write and wits to conceive; of which we might well want words, but never matter; of which we could turn our eyes to nothing, but we should ever have new-budding occasions.[21]

George Herbert seems to have taken the hint from his distant relative when he announces his vocation to Christian poetry in similar vein:

> Sure, Lord, there is enough in thee to dry
> Oceans of *Ink*; for as the Deluge did
> Cover the Earth, so doth thy Majesty.[22]

The kind of Christian poetry Herbert specifies in these early poems—'sonnets' and 'layes'—is exactly that suggested by Sidney. This places him firmly within Sidney's third category, 'right poets', as opposed to Fletcher, who is constructing the role of epic poet within Sidney's first category of *vates*. Herbert is articulating his conscious choice of the role of the Christian lyric poet in opposition to the secular love poet:

> Each Cloud distills thy praise, and doth forbid
> *Poets* to turn it to another use.
> *Roses* and *Lilies* speak thee; and to make
> A pair of Cheeks of them, is thy abuse.

This fundamental rejection of secular love poetry is reiterated throughout his poetic career. In the early sonnets, as well as in 'Jordan I' and in 'The Forerunners', he suggests that in choosing to use poetic language exclusively for sacred poetry, he is doing something previously unattempted. In 'The Forerunners' he describes the baptism into Christian poetry of 'sweet phrases' and 'lovely metaphors':

> when ye before
> Of stews and brothels onely knew the doores,
> Then did I wash you with my tears, and more,
> Brought you to Church well drest and clad.

This substitution of sacred poetry for profane is not the straightforward exchange of religious subject-matter for secular envisaged

---

[21] Sir Philip Sidney, *An Apology for Poetry or The Defence of Poesy*, ed. G. Shepherd (London, 1965), 137.

[22] Herbert, *Works*, 206.

by earlier Reformation poets.[23] The anxiety of the pioneer is betrayed in the very number of the poems that contain Herbert's own authorial agonizings, from the determinedly optimistic 'A true Hymne' to the unremittingly pessimistic 'Perseverance', which was finally left out of *The Temple*. However, although these poems raise many of the theological and literary problems for the Christian poet, none of them display unqualified confidence about a favourable outcome. If Isaak Walton's account is to be believed, Herbert himself felt so ambivalent about his efforts that he was willing to consign them to the bonfire.[24] The story forms part of Walton's attempt to canonize his hero: the ideal Christian poet, even as late as 1670, must be willing, in principle at least, to destroy his poetic compositions.

Herbert's seventeenth-century readers, of all theological persuasions, were supremely confident of the status of the poems in *The Temple*. After an initial surge of popularity—there were two editions of *The Temple* in the first year of publication—there were another eight editions within the next forty years, a period in which Walton reckoned more than 20,000 copies had been sold. Nicholas Ferrar, in his preface to the work, had introduced him as holy saint as much as inspired poet, and his readers seemed to have received him as such. This is a typical tribute from Robert Codrington, in 1638:

> Veiw a true Poet, whose bare lines
> Include more goodness then some shrines.
> We'll canonise him, and what er
> Befalls, style him heavens Chorister:
> No Muse inspird his quill, the three
> Graces, ffaith, Hope, and Charitie
> Inflamd that breast.[25]

George Wither in his own volume of hymns and spiritual songs of 1641 specifies Herbert as one of the poets who has changed the opinion of 'some good men' that poetry is 'the Language and

---

[23] See Campbell, *Divine Poetry and Drama*, 5–6 for her outline of 'a movement to substitute divine poetry for secular poetry.' She shows that in the 16th century divine poetry was defined by its sacred subject-matter. In the 17th century, as I hope to show, the concept of 'sacred poetry' was problematic.

[24] Isaak Walton, *The Life of Mr. George Herbert* (London, 1670), 109.

[25] C. A. Patrides (ed.), *George Herbert: The Critical Heritage* (London, 1983), 63.

invention of the Devill'.[26] The most eloquent testimony to the force of Herbert's example as a holy poet is the number of his imitators. Stanley Stewart has gone so far as to suggest that there is an 'identifiable school of Herbert' in the seventeenth century.[27] A number of poets, including major authors such as Crashaw and Vaughan, declare their affinity with Herbert by their choice of title. Ralph Knevet's *A Gallery to the Temple*, composed in the 1640s, is prefaced by a discussion of Herbert's unique status:

I wonder . . . at the inadvertencye of our moderne wittes, who . . . have appeared so barren concerning the production, of this most divine sort of Poesye, that the species thereof might have been number'd among lost Antiquities if our Pious Herbert had not by a religious cultivation, added new life to the withr'd branches, of this celestiall Balme Tree.— whereby Hee hath not onely surpassed those of his owne Nation, but even the haughty Italians, who chalenge a priority in art, as well as devotions.[28]

Herbert is presented as the foremost divine poet, at least in modern times, not only in England but on the Continent. This judgement involves Knevet in sweeping aside the efforts of Dante and Petrarch as not sufficiently dedicated to the glory of God. In a similarly bleak although not as specific poetic history, Henry Vaughan identifies Herbert as 'the first, that with any effectual success attempted a *diversion* of this foul and overflowing *stream*'.[29] The subtitle to Vaughan's 1650 volume *Silex Scintillans* is identical to that of *The Temple: Sacred Poems and Private Ejaculations*. The same subtitle is also adopted by Christopher Harvey in 1640. Before Herbert's volume, no English poet had dared to claim that his work could be labelled 'Sacred Poems'.

Arthur Marotti has recently stressed the significance to lyric poetry of the publication of *The Temple*.[30] Herbert was widely perceived as having achieved the impossible, a genuinely sacred poetry, and as Helen Wilcox has shown, the detailed borrowing

[26] Wither, *Britans second Remembrancer*, 21.

[27] See Stanley Stewart, *George Herbert* (Boston, 1986), 128–56, for details of his 'School of Herbert'.

[28] Quoted in Patrides, *George Herbert: The Critical Heritage*, 65. *A Gallery to the Temple* was written in the 1640s, but not published until 1766. For a longer discussion of Knevet's views see Stewart, *George Herbert*, 129–32.

[29] Henry Vaughan, *The Complete Poems*, ed. A. Rudrum (Harmondsworth, 1976), 142.

[30] A. F. Marotti, *Manuscript, Print, and the English Renaissance Lyric* (Ithaca, NY, 1995), 256–7.

by the imitators, not just for the title of their volumes but for the contents, indicates how closely these poets adopted *The Temple* as a poetic model.[31] Christopher Harvey was perhaps the most successful of Herbert's followers, in the sense that his poetry was actually bound with *The Temple*, and achieved thirteen editions by 1709. John Legate, writing a poem for the second edition of Harvey's *The Synagogue, or The Shadow of The Temple*, seems to have had a very clear view of what was special about Herbert's poetry, in both theological and literary terms:

> *Herbert*! whose every strain
> Twists holy Breast with happy Brain,
>   So that who strives to be
>   As elegant as he,
> Must climb Mount *Calvary* for *Parnassus* Hill
> And in his Saviours sides baptize his Quill;
>   A Jordan fit t'instill
> A Saint-like stile, backt with an Angels skill.[32]

This is one of the few tributes which gives more weight to elegance than holiness, and it does so in terms reminiscent of Herbert's own spirituality. Herbert certainly did attempt to baptize his poetic skill in Jordan, as the two poems of that name testify. Contemporary readers, of all theological persuasions, thought that he had succeeded.

Theological Views of George Herbert

It is not a simple matter to situate George Herbert in the complex theological context of the early seventeenth century. A recent study claims a precise theological placing of Herbert, in 'the exact middle way' of Anglicanism: an ambitious enterprise indeed.[33] The term 'Anglican' needs qualification in the context of the early Stuart Church. Anglicans from seventeenth-century Royalists to nineteenth-century members of the Oxford Movement

---

[31] See H. E. Wilcox, 'Something Understood: The Reputation and Influence of George Herbert to 1715' (Univ. of Oxford D.Phil. thesis, 1984), 40–94.

[32] Poem postfixed to Christopher Harvey's *The Synagogue*, 2nd rev. edn. (London, 1647), sigs. C8ʳ⁻ᵛ.

[33] C. Hodgkins, *Authority, Church and Society in George Herbert: Return to the Middle Way* (New York, 1993).

have chosen in retrospect to declare Herbert's beliefs and practice as constitutive of what it means to be 'Anglican'.[34] However, the word is meaningless before 1642, as Kenneth Fincham points out. He posits four categories within the early Stuart Church of England, defined by beliefs and practice: radical Puritans, moderate Puritans, conformist Calvinists and anti-Calvinists.[35] This book will situate Herbert firmly in the third category. Herbert's attitude to Church authority as expressed in *The Country Parson* is deeply conformist, which is why Barnabas Oley published it in 1652 as an example of ideal Anglican practice: the stress on 'decency' and 'order' in the chapter on church furnishing, and the resonance of the words 'Authority' and 'uniformity' throughout the work, would have endeared him to Laud. Perhaps the most telling section of the work is that which gives advice on how to deal with 'Schismaticks' whose problem was the scandal of corruption in the church. Herbert advises a diligent examination of the problem:

whether, there being two precepts, one of obeying Authority, the other of not giving scandall, that ought not to be preferred, especially since in disobeying there is scandall also: whether things once indifferent, being made by the precept of Authority more then indifferent, it be in our power to omit or refuse them.[36]

Herbert's position here is absolutely clear, and it distinguishes him from those who took so much offence at Laud's enforcement of 'things indifferent' in the 1630s. Conformist he certainly was, and I shall argue strongly in this book that he is unambiguously Calvinist in his doctrine and spirituality. As Kenneth Fincham argues, however, Puritan influence in this period was pervasive, and Herbert shares in a word-centred piety and a concern to purify abuses: like the Puritans, he refuses to baptize on week-

[34] The Keble Lectures in honour of the 200th anniversary of John Keble's birth, entitled 'The Genius of Anglicanism', are an example of an 'Anglican' tradition being constructed which includes such definitive non-Anglicans as Bede, Julian of Norwich, and John Wesley. My own contribution to this series tried to problematize a simple equation of George Herbert's beliefs and practice with what has come to be known as High Anglicanism. See G. Rowell (ed.), *The English Religious Tradition and the Genius of Anglicanism* (Oxford, 1992).

[35] K. Fincham (ed.), *The Early Stuart Church 1603–1642* (London, 1993), 4–6. Patrick Collinson thinks that the term 'Anglican' only acquired meaning in the nineteenth century: see 'A Comment: Concerning the Name Puritan', *JEH* 31 (1980), 485.

[36] Herbert, *Works*, 246, 263.

days.[37] The term of abuse which was the name 'Puritan' was applied fairly indiscriminately, in any case: as Francis Rous complains in 1627, the word, having been applied by King James in *Basilikon Doron* to sectarians, 'is now diverted to Saints, even to those that doe not walke in the broad way of common, and sociable vices, and especially if they goe somewhat higher than civil and naturall Righteousnesse'.[38] This is the reason why the conformist Master of Sidney Sussex College, Samuel Ward, is happy to receive that appellation whilst understanding its political significance:

I hope the States Puritan, and the common Puritan, bee two creatures. For with that staffe the multitude beates all that are better then themselves, and lets fly at all that have any shew of goodnesse. But with that which most call Puritanisme, I desire to worship God.[39]

Herbert, who shares so many of Ward's beliefs and habits of mind, might well have been designated 'Puritan' in the acrimonious climate of the later 1630s, had he lived, despite his attack on Puritanism in *Musae Responsoriae*. Certainly his friend Nicholas Ferrar, whose ecclesiastical practice was much closer to Laudianism than Herbert's, acquired that name.[40] In the troubled period of the Civil War, non-conformists and sectarians alike joined with Royalists in praising the poetry of *The Temple*. Royalists seem to have enjoyed, in the conformist practice represented in *The Temple*, a nostalgic appreciation of the good old days of the 1620s and 1630s. Dudley, Lord North, admits in a poem of his own that in praising George Herbert the Royalists were mourning their own loss:

> Thus living, sing we, (Swan-like singing dye)
> His Panegyrick, our own Elegie.[41]

---

[37] Ibid. 258. Puritans felt that to hold baptisms on weekdays, separate from normal church worship, was to strengthen the impression that it was a ceremony with its own magical saving power.

[38] Francis Rous, *The Onely Remedy, that can cure a people, when all other Remedies faile* (London, 1627), 56.

[39] Samuel Ward, *A Collection of such sermons as have been written and published* (London, 1636), 269.

[40] Barnabas Oley (ed.), *Herberts Remains, Or, Sundry Pieces of that sweet singer of the Temple Mr. George Herbert* (London, 1652), sig. a11ʳ.

[41] Dudley North, *A Forest of Varieties* (London, 1645), 197: quoted in Wilcox, *Something Understood*, 99.

Moreover, the party victorious in the Civil War (however temporarily) seem to have gained both inspiration and ammunition from *The Temple*. Within a few years of Herbert's death, the Ipswich lecturer Samuel Ward based one of his sermons on two lines from Herbert's poem 'The Church Militant'. These particular two lines had given the licensers pause when the first edition of *The Temple* was being prepared.

> Religion stands on tip-toe in our land,
> Readie to passe to the American strand.[42]

The Vice-Chancellor of Cambridge University had finally allowed these lines to stand, remarking drily that although Herbert 'was a Divine Poet...I hope the World will not take him to be an Inspired Prophet'.[43] Later in the 1630s, in an England which was fast polarizing along a religious divide, no such fine distinctions were made. For taking Herbert to be an Inspired Prophet, and thus implying that England would soon be godless, Samuel Ward was arrested and died a lingering death in prison.

This partisan practice of adopting Herbert to support any particular shade of religious opinion is not, of course, limited to the seventeenth century.[44] Within the past thirty years critics have assigned Herbert to every religious and political category from revolutionary Puritan to enthusiastic Laudian. Michael Schoenfeldt's study of Herbert identifies anti-authority sentiment in the rhetoric of *The Temple* and speculates that Herbert 'might have entertained the chance to trumpet the social frustration the monarch had come to represent'.[45] It is a brave critic who would confidently assume that Herbert would have fought on Cromwell's side, but Gene Edward Veith Jr. suggests, humorously, that modern critics have almost re-enacted the Civil War in their opposing convictions about Herbert's theology. He gives a list of modern-day 'Roundheads' (those who claim that Herbert has Puritan tendencies) and 'Cavaliers' (those who read his poetry in

---

[42] 'The Church Militant', 235–6: Herbert, *Works*, 196.

[43] From Walton's *Lives*, quoted in Herbert, *Works*, 547.

[44] See Crys Ambrust, 'Nineteenth-Century Re-presentations of George Herbert: Publishing History as Critical Embodiment', *The Huntington Library Quarterly*, 53 (1990), 131–51 for a revealing study of the reception of Herbert in the Victorian period: the contexts in which Herbert was published show his adoption by the Tractarians as a kindred spirit.

[45] M. C. Schoenfeldt, *Prayer and Power: George Herbert and Renaissance Courtship* (Chicago, 1991), 56.

the light of Catholic devotional practice).[46] Both sides have distinguished scholars in their ranks. Barbara Lewalski and Richard Strier, not to mention Veith himself, find Protestant doctrine deeply embedded in the poetry; Rosamund Tuve, Louis L. Martz, and Stanley Stewart seem convinced that Herbert was a High-Church Anglican with a penchant for Catholic means of devotion. My concern is not merely to establish the precise shade of Herbert's theology. However, I shall be taking the line of Gene Edward Veith in suggesting a way for both sides to be right, in exploring the nature of the early seventeenth-century *via media* which Herbert had praised in his dedication of *Musae Responsoriae* to James:

the . . . *via media* was not in Herbert's day a mere compromise, a golden mean. Rather, it was a balance and an integration, an affirmation of the best of both traditions. In the sense that it was Catholic—in its sacramentalism, its liturgical worship, and in its continuity with the past—it was very Catholic. In the sense that it was Reformed—in its focus on the grace of God, in its Biblicism, in its evangelical liberty—it was very Reformed.[47]

This conception of Herbert's *via media* is a complex synthesis of various elements in the European Christian tradition, rather than a narrow theological position.

Contemporary criticism

Critics of Herbert have varied not only in their religious predilections but in the scope of their studies. On the basis of the poems of *The Temple*, A. D. Nuttall, Gene Edward Veith, and Richard Strier find that Herbert was 'fully Protestant'. Stanley Stewart tries to challenge this conclusion, declaring quite correctly that 'the context within which the Herbert canon is construed' is vital to interpretation: however, he inexplicably focuses on the 'Harmonies' of Little Gidding as the 'key to a historical understanding of Herbert's poetic method'.[48] These wholly unremarkable biblical compilations seem to me unable to yield the hermeneutic Stewart

---

[46] G. E. Veith, Jr., 'The Religious Wars in George Herbert Criticism: Reinterpreting Seventeenth Century Anglicanism', *George Herbert Journal*, 11 (1988), 18.

[47] Ibid. 31.

[48] See also Stewart, *George Herbert*, 60 and 82.

tries to derive from them. Other critics have looked for Herbert's poetic method in a wider sample of spiritual literature, with a higher degree of success. Louis Martz and Barbara Lewalski have applied their insights into theological writing of the period to the activity of writing poetry, although they come to very different conclusions. Martz considers Herbert's poetics in relation to Continental treatises of the Catholic Reformation; Lewalski prefers to locate Herbert in the tradition of home-grown Protestant meditation. Both studies, huge in their scope, are necessarily limited in their treatment of Herbert. For Lewalski, Herbert is deliberately writing within biblical genres of poetry. According to her, every one of his poems is a kind of Protestant meditation, a statement which seems to render the term 'Protestant meditation' so general as to be meaningless in critical practice.[49] Martz represents Herbert as a High Anglican who had an affinity with Catholic devotional techniques. He makes a strong case for Herbert having read two Continental treatises: Savonarola's *De Simplicitate Christianae Vitae* and St François de Sales' *An Introduction to the Devoute Life*. However, Martz's analysis is extremely superficial. He admits that he is dealing with treatises which are not well known, and actually translates six paragraphs from Savonarola's *De Simplicitate Christianae Vitae*, but the work is five books long, and this exercise is necessarily extremely selective. It is clear that Martz is tracing similarities of a most general nature, as when he identifies 'a certain mildness and effortless ease' in the spirituality of both St François de Sales and George Herbert. Martz finds resemblances in imagery and vocabulary, as well as overall tone and style, but is not able to pursue any of these similarities within the framework of his book, which includes several other major poets. In his consideration of Herbert he unaccountably excludes another Continental treatise which we know Herbert to have read: Juan de Valdés' *The Hundred and Ten Considerations*. This treatise is particularly important because Herbert's comments on it are extant, and these comments constitute the only straightforwardly theological writing of Herbert's that survives.

This book builds on the work of Martz, and, to a lesser extent, Lewalski, taking as its object of study the two treatises covered

---

[49] B. K. Lewalski, *Protestant Poetics and the Seventeenth-Century Religious Lyric* (Princeton, 1970), 171.

briefly by Martz, together with Valdés's *The Hundred and Ten Considerations*. Two of these three treatises have been selected because there is textual evidence that Herbert read and valued them. François de Sales's *An Introduction to the Devoute Life* is included because it has become critical orthodoxy, after Martz, to assume its influence on Herbert, and no book on the rhetorical and spiritual context for *The Temple* would be complete without it. The book gives a theological and literary treatment to all three authors: Savonarola, St François de Sales, and Juan de Valdés. Four other books are known to have been in Herbert's possession. The translation of the *Introductio Ad Catechismum* of Ludovicus Carbo seems to have been sent to him for approval in the same manner as *The Hundred and Ten Considerations*: and Herbert actually translated the treatise on diet by Luigi Cornaro, *Trattato de la via sobria*.[50] The work of the Catholic theologian Ludovicus Carbo, who also wrote a volume on Christian oratory, is mentioned in Chapter 1. Cornaro, whose work has rather limited concerns, is referred to wherever relevant. Two books, one of them containing the works of Augustine, were bequests to his two curates. Several studies have already been undertaken on the relationship between St Augustine and George Herbert, and while I will refer to Augustine's work throughout, there is no separate chapter on him.[51] The other book cited in Herbert's will is *In Sacrosancta quatuor Evangelia F. Lucae Brugensis Commentarius*, which is a collection of variant readings of the Scriptures published in 1606. This work, which draws mainly on patristic sources, shows Herbert's concern for accuracy in interpretation of the Bible, and confirms the eclectic nature of Herbert's spirituality.

These are, admittedly, fragmentary examples of what must have been a vast library, but at least it is more than mere speculation that Herbert read them. I believe a study of these authors to be important in a number of ways. First, the very heterogeneity of the theological origins of the three treatises helps to explain the ubiquity of favourable response to Herbert both in the modern

---

[50] See 'The Will of George Herbert', Herbert, *Works*, 382; for the description of the Ferrar–Herbert literary collaborations, ibid. 564.

[51] See R. Todd, *The Opacity of Signs: Acts of Interpretation in George Herbert's 'The Temple'* (New York, 1986); W. H. Pahlka, *Saint Augustine's Meter and George Herbert's Will* (Kent, Oh., 1987); A. Mortimer, 'Words in the Mouth of God: Augustinian Language-Theory and the Poetics of George Herbert', in R. Waswo (ed.), *On Poetry and Poetics* (Zurich, 1985), 31–43.

period and in the seventeenth century. Secondly, each of these authors was both a theologian and a man of letters: in the case of Savonarola and Juan de Valdés there are other works specifically dealing with literary production, whilst François de Sales was a friend of poets.[52] Since Herbert's poetry, as Bacon said, is 'Divinitie, and Poesie, met', the work of authors who were both theologians and rhetoricians is bound to have resonances with the work of the pastor-poet.[53] Given the lack of role models for Herbert at the start of his career, the consideration of various models for Christian discourse as presented in these treatises is important. They represent the range of options available to an author at the confluence of the Reformation and the Renaissance rhetorical tradition.

Issues in Literary Theory and Theology in the Seventeenth Century

Each of these treatises deals explicitly with the nature of the relationship between God and the believer, and offers a different model of sanctification, the process whereby the believer becomes more and more like God. Each writer has a strong theology of the Holy Spirit, and thus a consideration of inspired speech and writing, because words are thought to be the primary way that the divine Spirit expresses himself. Often, the production of discourse is the paradigm for all holy action. Authorship becomes a special case of the way God works to sanctify the ordinary Christian.

In dealing with the treatises, I pursue this connection between sanctification and authorship, and look for the application to George Herbert as a Christian poet. This is a precise point at which Renaissance literary theory and Reformed theology meet, and certain concepts and vocabulary constantly recur. Medieval authorship theory had described authorship in the terms of scholastic theology, which posited a hierarchy of causes culminating in the First Cause, or Prime Mover. The Aristotelian prologue which was used long into the Renaissance described the process of authorship in terms of causation, and the symptom of causation as movement. God was the Prime Mover of the chain of move-

---

[52] Savonarola, *Apologeticus De Ratione Poeticae Artis* (1st pub. Florence, 1492); Juan de Valdés, *Diálogo de las lenguas*, ed. F. Montesinos (Madrid, 1928).
[53] Patrides, *George Herbert: The Critical Heritage*, 57.

ment that resulted in spiritual authorship. The four causes of writing could be summarized under the heading *causae moventes ad scribendum*.[54] The *causa efficiens* was the author, the *causa materialis* his source, the *causa formalis* his choice of form, the *causa finalis* the ultimate purpose of the work. Spiritual authorship was often seen as having a twofold *causa efficiens* in bringing about the *finis* or aim of the writing: God, the Unmoved Mover, and the human author, both moved by God and moving the reader.[55] Aquinas ascribed spiritual growth to the same kind of hierarchy of causes. God, the Prime Mover, planted a principle of grace in the soul that in itself became the cause of the believer's good works. Herbert would have been familiar with this vocabulary: he used it himself on occasions.[56]

In theological discourse of the sixteenth century, the word 'motions' has two distinct meanings. Reformed theology uses it to describe the passions, with a very negative connotation: the natural passions are the enemy of holiness. In both Reformation and Counter-Reformation spirituality they are to be 'mortified.' However, Counter-Reformation spirituality does allow a positive role for the passions: they are 'not wholly to be extinguished ... but sometimes to be moved, and stirred up for the service of virtue' says the Catholic Thomas Wright in his 1601 treatise, *The Passions of the Minde: An Introduction to the Devoute Life* constitutes a detailed manual of how to do just that. Using the Aristotelian model, it is only a short step from a real motivating object to a rhetorically constructed one, which is why *The Passions of the Minde* is so useful to the Christian orator, who 'perfitely understanding the natures and properties of mens passions, questionless may effectuate strange matters in the minds of his auditors'. [57] Robert Southwell in the Epistle Dedicatorie to *Marie Magdalens Funerall teares* suggested a sanctifying function for Catholic poetry: 'Passions I allow, and loves I approove, onely I woulde wishe that men would alter

---

[54] A. J. Minnis, *Medieval Theory of Authorship* (London, 1984), 80.

[55] A. J. Minnis argues that towards the end of the medieval period allowance was made for the individual motivation of the author, and his own talents: in other words, the individuality of the human author was important as a second cause. He concludes: 'The influence of Aristotle's theory of causality as understood by the late-medieval schoolmen helped to bring about a new awareness of the integrity of the individual human *auctor*' (ibid. 84).

[56] See 'Providence', and 'Perseverance': Herbert, *Works*, 116 and 205.

[57] Thomas Wright, *The Passions of the Minde* (London, 1601), 4.

their obiect and better their intent.'[58] In Counter-Reformation spirituality, the task of channelling those emotions was at least in part a literary one.

Reformed theology, however, regarded these kinds of motions as irredeemable. The Authorized Version of 1611 renders Romans 7: 5 in these terms: 'For when we were in the flesh, the motions of sins, which were by the law, did work in our members to bring forth fruit unto death.' St Paul goes on in chapters 7 and 8 to describe what Reformed theologians took up as the solution to the problem of fleshly passions: the believer is to die to his old nature, which is the source of the sinful 'motions', and live by the power of the Holy Spirit: 'For if ye live after the flesh, ye shall die: but if ye through the Spirit do mortify the deeds of the body, ye shall live.'[59] It seems as though the negative, carnal moving principle has been entirely replaced by a divine one. In such a spirituality the use of poetry, which in classical rhetoric worked closely with the passions, is under question.

However, in a Reformed spirituality, the passions are not the only tangible sensations within the believer. The word 'motion' could also in the sixteenth century be used for an impulse from God. The *OED* records the first use of this meaning in Cranmer's 1549 Prayer Book. The collect for the first Sunday in Lent was a new composition, not simply adapted from the Catholic missal, and its terminology is very modern:

Give us grace to use such abstinence, that, our flesh being subdued to the Spirit, wee may ever obey thy godly motions in righteousnesse, and true holinesse.[60]

The implication here is that fleshly passions are to be replaced by a different sort of 'motion'. The referent of 'motion' here is clearly a sense of divine direction that is almost palpable. It shares the same connotation of physical impulse as the 'motions', 'passions', or 'affections' described by Wright in his sub-Aristotelian psychology: the only difference is in its source and character. Since these 'motions' can be perceived only within the inner experience of the believer, differentiating between carnal passions and 'godly' motions is not an easy task.

---

[58] Robert Southwell, *Marie Magdalens Funerall teares* (London, 1594), sig. A2[v].
[59] Rom. 8: 13.
[60] *The Booke of Common Prayer* (London, 1619), sig. D5[r].

These impulses from God were identified by Reformation theologians with the work of the Holy Spirit, God dwelling in human beings. Instead of a causal chain from God to the believer with the divinely created principle of grace as an intermediary, God as the third person of the Trinity is immediately present in the believer and the immediate cause of 'motions'. The Reformers, with their emphasis on felt inner experience and the irresistibility of grace, made these 'motions' the basis for some of their most radical doctrines. Calvin argued fiercely in his *Institutes* that God is the source of all motions towards Him, and that the wills of the elect are not free to disobey.[61] Two of the most controversial doctrines of Calvinism, predestination and the perseverance of the saints, become contingent on these sovereign movements from God, and the experience of 'motions' acquires an awesome significance: it is the mark of the true Christian. Thus Tyndale defined saving faith as 'none opynyon, but a sure felyng', less an emotion than a tangible sensation that could be compared to burning one's fingers.[62] In *Certain Questions on Predestination, Use of Gods Word and Sacraments*, inserted between the Old and New Testaments in the quarto edition of the black-letter Geneva Bible, these sensations are described as the 'motions of spiritual life, which belongeth only to the children of God: by the which that life is perceived, even as the life of this body is discerned by the sense and motions thereof'. The following question in the catechism is about the doctrine of the perseverance of the saints:

Question. Cannot such perish as at some time or other feel these motions within themselves?

The prescribed answer was a resounding 'No'.[63] Since this version of the Bible, produced by the royal printers, was issued in thirty-nine editions between 1579 and 1615, several generations of English Protestants, including Herbert's, would have learnt that the guarantee of salvation from hell, and eternal life, was the inner sensation of spiritual 'motions'. What Herbert's answer to

---

[61] John Calvin, *The Institution of the Christian Religion*, tr. Thomas Norton (London, 1578), II. iii. 10, p. 112.

[62] Thomas More, *The second parte of the confutacion of Tyndale's answere* (London, 1533), ccxli–ccxlii.

[63] C. Eason, *The Geneva Bible: Notes on its Production and Distribution* (Dublin, 1937), 23.

that particular catechetical question was, we shall see later. He was certainly aware of twin spiritual imperatives: the necessity to experience saving 'motions', and the difficult task of differentiating them from other kinds of motion.

Educated Protestants like Herbert would also be exposed to the classical theory of rhetorical 'motions'. The Latin rhetorics ascribe a sense of movement to the figures of speech that in turn move the passions. Cicero describes them as 'gestures' (*schemata*), Quintilian in terms of actions: 'some figures are represented as running or rushing forward, others sit or recline.'[64] It is no wonder that both *motus* and *motio* became used as technical terms in rhetoric. In classical rhetorical theory there is a perceived connection between accuracy of signification and movement, vividness and effectiveness. Aristotle used the term *energeia* to signify the power of the rhetorically constructed object in its closeness to the truth. 'Things are set before the eyes by words that signify actuality [*energeia*].'[65] Aristotle praises Homer for this capacity to signify actuality, and describes it in terms of movement: 'he gives movement and life to all, and actuality is movement.'[66] *Energeia*—actuality—and 'movement' here seem to describe both the rhetorical quality of Homer's verse and the reaction it produces in the reader. Effective communication, it seems, depends on two kinds of movement—that which signifies actuality within the figure of speech, and that caused by the figure of speech within the hearer. In their handbooks for Latin orators, both Cicero and Quintilian focus on rhetorical figures of vividness—*enargeia*—in their instructions for moving the emotions. In the Renaissance, Erasmus' definition of *enargeia* is highly derivative of Quintilian:

We use *enargeia* whenever we do not explain a thing simply, but display it to be looked at as if it were expressed in colour in a picture, so that it may seem that we have painted, not narrated, and that the reader has seen, not read.[67]

---

[64] Cicero, *Brutus*, tr. G. L. Hendrickson (London, 1939), 65. Quintilian, *Institutio Oratoria*, tr. H. E. Butler, 4 vols. (London, 1921), i. 293.

[65] Aristotle, *Rhetoric* iii. 11.

[66] Ibid.

[67] Erasmus, *Opera Omnia*, ed. J. Frobel (Basle, 1540), i. 66. Quoted in T. Cave, *The Cornucopian Text: Problems of Writing in the French Renaissance* (Oxford, 1979), 28. Cf. Quintilian, *Institutio Oratoria* iii. 437.

Terence Cave notes that *enargeia* became confused with Aristotelian *energeia* in the Renaissance, so that vividness and dynamism became linked.[68] Sir Philip Sidney, working to promote a Protestant poetry in England, integrated the two concepts into a defence of poetry based on its ethical effectiveness.[69] Sidney suggests, on rational if audacious grounds, the superiority of the poet to the philosopher:

There is a second activity, 'moving', of more use to moralist and Christian alike: and that moving is of a higher degree than teaching, it may by this appear, that it is well nigh the cause and the effect of teaching. For who will be taught, if he be not moved with desire to be taught? and what so much good doth that teaching bring forth (I speak still of moral doctrine) as that it moveth one to do that which it doth teach?[70]

However, poets only have power in as much as they themselves are moved, and can convince the reader that

in truth they feel those passions, which easily (as I think) may be betrayed by that same forcibleness, or *energeia* (as the Greeks call it) of the writer.[71]

Sidney criticizes the love poets for their failure to achieve *energeia*, by contrast with Christian poets. The Christian poet has access to a *copia* of subject-matter, the infinite God, and the sincerity of his emotions will naturally produce *energeia*. Since Sidney has earlier attributed to the true poet the ability to imagine a pre-fallen state, and ascribed that power to 'the force of a divine breath', there is a composite but strong image of the potential Christian poet built up throughout *An Apology for Poetry*. The Platonic 'furor' combines with Renaissance rhetoric and psychology to produce a new vision of the Christian poet: inspired directly by God, or moved by his own love of God, the Christian poet will achieve an *energeia* in his writing which will move his readers to virtue.

This role model for the Christian poet sketched out in the terms of classical rhetoric must have been attractive to Sidney's distant relative, George Herbert, especially as it was similar to the Augustinian synthesis of Horatian, Ciceronian, and Platonic rhetorical theory.[72] It allows a more direct role to the Divine Mover than

---

[68] Cave *The Cornucopian Text*, 28 n.
[69] See Sidney, *An Apology for Poetry*, 86.
[70] Ibid. 113.
[71] Ibid. 138.
[72] See Geoffrey Shepherd's introduction to Sidney, *An Apology for Poetry*, 71.

that of the Aristotelian prologues: God can be the immediate cause of writing, instead of the First Cause in a chain of secondary causes. This change from the scholastic model of causation in authorship is ascribed by Ullrich Langer to the rise of nominalist philosophy in Europe, which effectively eliminated the causal chain. Nominalist philosophy, which seems to have influenced both Luther and Calvin, posited that God could intervene at any point: He is the immediate cause of everything. Reformed spirituality and authorship, with its emphasis on the work of the divine Spirit within the believer, fits in well with nominalist theory.

However, the other legacy of nominalist philosophy to Reformation theology, and potentially the more relevant to authorship, is the attitude to merit in the believer. In scholastic theology the principle of grace implanted in the believer produced tangible results that were good in themselves. The believer, then, was capable of real holiness. However, Duns Scotus' maxim, that the value of an offering is determined solely by the divine will, became adopted into the late medieval nominalist tradition, which influenced both Luther and Calvin.[73] 'Good' is the name for whatever God wills: this is the philosophical basis of 'justification by faith'. God has pronounced all the 'motions of the flesh' to be evil: holiness is whatever God wills it to be. Discerning God's will becomes the prime occupation of Reformation spirituality. Gone are the natural laws of the universe, and the common judgement of what 'goodness' is. In this bleak moral landscape it is no wonder that the 'motions' of the Holy Spirit acquired such prominence in Reformation spirituality: they were the only certain guidance for what God truly willed. The implications for authorship are potentially devastating.

At this point, however, Aristotelian psychology and rhetoric could threaten even this last shred of certainty. As John Hoskins had declared in 1599, rhetoric was 'the directest means of skill to describe, to move, to appease, or to prevent any motion whatsoever'. Presumably this could include a spiritual motion. The link between rhetoric and internal 'motion' is made by Sir Francis Bacon in *The Advancement of Learning*, which Herbert helped to

---

[73] See A. McGrath, *The Intellectual Origins of the European Reformation* (Oxford, 1987), 70–122, particularly 104–5.

translate. Bacon defines rhetoric primarily in terms of movement within the mind:

The duty and office of rhetoric is to apply reason to imagination for the better moving of the will.[74]

In the 'negotiation within ourselves', rhetoric works by means of rational persuasion on the imagination, which subsequently moves the will. His model potentially replaces both divine 'furor' and human emotion as the source of the perceived movement within the mind: the movement is that of rational persuasion rather than instinctive emotion. By 1640, Edward Reynoldes in *A Treatise of the Passions and Faculties of the Soule of Man* had formulated a rational explanation for the poetic 'furor':

Its assistance to the Understanding, is principally in matter of Invention, readily to supply it with varietie of objects whereon to worke, as also to quicken and rayse the Minde with a kind of heat and rapture.[75]

The catalyst for this powerful reaction between Reason and Imagination is the first part of rhetoric, Invention. This combination of imagination, rhetoric, and understanding Reynoldes identifies with 'the *Poets* Divine Raptures'. Even the ecstasy of divine inspiration, it appears, could be produced by the mechanics of rhetoric.

Spiritual and Rhetorical 'Motions'

At the beginning of the seventeenth century, then, Herbert was formulating his role as a Christian poet within a nexus of influences whereby assurance of salvation, the inspiration of authorship, the sinful passions of the flesh, and the power of effective rhetoric are all signified by internal impulses, or 'motions'. In practice, it is almost impossible to separate the discourse of theology from the discourse of rhetoric in this period. The production of discourse is inevitably related to the Spirit of God, even in an apparently secular work such as Henry Peacham's *The Garden of Eloquence*. He is somewhat triumphalist in his claims for rhetoric: the orator 'may lead his hearers which way he list, and

---

[74] Francis Bacon, *The Advancement of Learning*, ed. A. Johnston (Oxford, 1974), 139.
[75] Edward Reynoldes, *A Treatise of the Passions and Faculties of the Soule of Man* (London, 1640), 18.

draw them to what affections he wish'.[76] In the second edition Peacham became even more enthusiastic: the orator is 'in a maner the emperour of men's minds and affections, and next to the omnipotent God in the power of perswasion'.[77] Theological treatises on the working of God within the soul inevitably refer to the production of discourses as one of the prime foci of the Holy Spirit's activity. All the devotional writers considered in this book consider the production of discourse as a kind of blueprint for the operation of the redeemed human consciousness. The close quarters at which the discourse of theology and rhetoric were required to operate, together with the similarities in concept and vocabulary, tended towards a conflation of the two discourses. All the spiritual writers considered here believe theoretically in the importance of keeping them apart: however, their practice as represented in the treatises reveals the impossibility of such an endeavour. I would like to suggest that, despite the attempt to separate them, these two discourses finally collapse into one master discourse, which is used to describe both authorship and spirituality. At one end of the spectrum, this produces a particularly strong model for literary spiritual authorship, assigning spiritual phenomena such as faith to the effects of rhetoric: at the other, it would tend to make spiritual authorship of a literary kind impossible, because of the overwhelming nature of the experience of divine inspiration. I hope to show that these treatises, and Herbert's poetry, take up various places on one spiritual–rhetorical continuum.

There is no discourse of literary theory separate from that of theology in the early seventeenth century. Even a rhetorical treatise such as Henry Peacham's *Garden of Eloquence* is saturated with theological terms, whilst works of academic theology deal with issues that to a twentieth-century reader would seem to be the province of literary theory, such as authorship and signification. No study of Herbert has yet taken proper account of this fact. Most of those critics who take Herbert's theology seriously have limited their discussion to themes in the poetry rather than the process by which the poems were composed: as I have indicated, Martz and Lewalski, who are concerned with poetics,

---

[76] Henry Peacham, *The Garden of Eloquence* (London, 1577), sig. Aiii^r.
[77] Ibid., 2nd edn. (London, 1593), sig. ABiii^v.

have not taken their respective investigations very far. One critic who has taken seriously the implications of a particular theology for Herbert's poetics is Stanley E. Fish, and I shall be building on some of his ideas later in the book. As I hope to show, a seventeenth-century readership applied their comprehensive understanding of theological ideas to produce a sophisticated reading of Herbert's poems, which included a judgement of the method of composition of *The Temple* as well as its content. This deeply theological reading gave rise to literary judgements about Herbert's poetry, establishing him as the most influential Christian poet of his period.

1

Herbert and Savonarola:
The Rhetoric of Radical Simplicity

Savonarola's *De Simplicitate Christianae Vitae*, first published in 1496, deserves detailed consideration by scholars of Herbert, as it is one of the few books that we know Herbert to have possessed and loved. 'Sauonorola in Latine he hath of the Simplicity of Chr. Religion and is of great esteme wth him' wrote Arthur Woodnoth in a letter to Nicholas Ferrar.[1] Herbert was not the only reader of the Dominican monk in Protestant England. Short of Protestant heroes, Foxe enlisted him in his widely available *Booke of Martyrs*. In London, where in 1500 the printing industry was as yet embryonic, Savonarola was one of less than fifty authors printed that year, and an English translation of one of his works was bound up with the first prayer book in English. Savonarola was thus an important influence on a developing Protestant devotional literature, and we shall be considering this in more detail in Chapter 3. The writings of Savonarola treat many of the theological controversies of the sixteenth century, and were used to further both the Reformation and Counter-Reformation in Europe. From his death in 1496 onwards, printing presses in Paris, Antwerp, and Cologne churned out an astonishing number of Savonarola's sermons, treatises, and meditations. Savonarola's works were placed on the Index because he bypassed the hierarchy of devolved authority in the Catholic Church, a heresy which endeared him to the Reformed community. According to him, the Christian can experience intimate communion with God outside of the external ceremonies of the Church, beyond the scope of the office of the priesthood: in the holy place that is his heart. Moreover, his attack on the externals of religion extended to a derogation of the use of rhetoric in religious discourse: for

---

[1] In Nicholas Ferrar, *The Ferrar Papers*, ed. B. Blackstone (Cambridge, 1938), 268.

him the highest experience of the sacred need not be expressed in words.[2]

Savonarola is famous for his attacks on rhetoric, which makes him a surprising favourite of the one-time lecturer in rhetoric, and Orator at Cambridge University, George Herbert. In his *Apologeticus De Ratione Poeticae Artis* of 1492 he attacked the humanists of the court of Lorenzo the Magnificent who had originally welcomed him to Florence, men like Pico della Mirandola and Lorenzo Valla. Armed with Aristotelian logic, he rejected the all-embracing claims for rhetoric formulated by Cicero and taken up by the Renaissance humanists.[3] According to Savonarola, the humanist scholars' claim that poetry is identical with theology was based on the fact that much of the discourse of the Bible is metaphorical.[4] Savonarola is unimpressed, and replies with the argument that Scriptural poetry is merely a decoration for truth. The ornaments are not the temple, he argues, in an image that George Herbert could have used of his own volume. Poetry is merely wisdom's 'handmaid': the biblical authors, it seems, used rhetoric only as a kind of sop to the weak-minded. This grudging attitude to poetry is similar to Augustine's attitude to rhetoric in *De Doctrina Christiana*:

since there is some comparison between eating and learning, it may be noted that on account of the fastidiousness of many even that food without which life is impossible must be seasoned.[5]

---

[2] Savonarola's views on meditation are particularly audacious, as shown in his two tracts on mental prayer: *Trattato primo devoto et tutto spirituale, in defensione et commendatione della oratione mentale* and *Trattato secondo della oratione*. For further discussion see Massimo Petrocchi, *Storia della spiritualita italiana I* (Rome, 1978), 117–23. In *De Savonarola à Louis de Grenade*, RLC 16 (1936), 31, M. Bataillon shows that Luis de Granada made extensive use of Savonarola's writings: the first editions of his *Libro de la Oracion*, *Guia de Pecadores*, and *Manual de diversas oraciones* were prohibited for manifesting illuminist errors, and offering a way of perfection outside of the accepted paths of monastic vows and ordination. The profound inwardness of this spirituality was called 'illuminism' or 'Lutheranism' by Grand Inquisitor Valdés in 1559 when he placed the works of Luis de Granada on the Index of Prohibited Books. The revised 1566 editions of Granada's works, which had such an impact on St François de Sales, showed no trace of such Savonarolan tendencies.

[3] Cicero, *De oratore*, tr. H. Rackham, E. W. Sutton, Introd. 2 vol. (London, 1952), ii. 61–2. 'Eloquence is so potent a force that it embraces the origin and operation and developments of all things.' Savonarola cites this argument sarcastically and proceeds to attack it. See *Apologeticus De Ratione Poeticae Artis*, in *Compendium philosophia et alia* (Venice, 1534), 16ᵛ.

[4] Ibid. 16: 'quod Scriptura metaphoris & similitudinis utitur, quemadmodum & ars poetica: quo inquiunt evidenter apparet ipsam nihil aliud esse quam theologiam.'

[5] St Augustine, *On Christian Doctrine*, tr. D. W. Robertson Jr. (New York, 1958), 136.

This excuse for composing in poetry—that it will attract readers who would otherwise not profit by holy writing—was used by English religious poets in the late sixteenth and early seventeenth centuries. Henry Lok in 1593 felt the need to raise the question of why he wrote in poetry. In the preface to his *Sundry Christian Passions* he admits 'I find manie oftentimes... to reade books rather for the affection of words then liking of matter'.[6] Thomas Winter in the dedication to Prince Henry of his translation of du Bartas' *Third Day* expressed the same hope that poetry would, as Herbert put it, became 'a bait of pleasure':

when the reader thinks peradventure but to tickle his eare, with the sweete measure and delicate cadence of a majestical verse; he finds that both Divinity and Philosophy do steale upon him unawares.[7]

George Wither in 1624 defended his Biblical poetry for a similar reason:

since god in mercie hath provided and permitted us meanes to assist our weaknesses, let not such as are strong enough to be without them, condemne the use of such helpes in those, whoe beeing not so able, must have their affections weaned by degrees from their childish in-clynations.[8]

George Herbert was not, of course, able to write an apologetic preface to his volume of poems, but the first stanza of the first poem in *The Temple* expresses his version of this doctrine as if to ward off criticism:

> A verse may find him, who a sermon flies,
> And turn delight into a sacrifice.

In the seventeenth century these became the most frequently quoted lines from *The Temple*, as Herbert's successors, including Edward Benlowes, Samuel Crossman, and Nahum Tate, sought to provide justification for their own poetic efforts.[9] Richard Whitlock formulated the dilemma about poetry in 1654:

---

[6] Henry Lok, *Sundry Christian Passions Contained in two hundred Sonnets* (London, 1593), sig. A5^v.

[7] Guillaume de Saluste du Bartas, *Third Day*, tr. Thomas Winter (London, 1604), sig. A2^r, quoted in A. L. Prescott, 'The Reception of Du Bartas in England', *Studies in the Renaissance*, 15 (1968), 171.

[8] George Wither, *The Schollers Purgatory, discovered in the Stationers Common-wealth* (London, 1624), 61.

[9] See R. Ray, 'The Herbert Allusion Book: Allusions to George Herbert in the Seventeenth Century', *Studies in Philology*, 83 (1986), 46, 77, 148.

although it may seem to *rob Truth* of her *best Ornament, Nakednesse* (as is commonly objected to *Poetry*) yet it furnisheth her with an advantageous *Dresse* of taking *Pleasure*, even to those that care not so much for *Truth* it self.[10]

Whitlock concludes his argument with Herbert's couplet, which he obviously considers authoritative.

Savonarola has two main quarrels with poetry, both to do with authorship. The first is its source: most poetry is pagan, and therefore inspired by the Devil. However, there is also something in the nature of the public production of words that is in itself deeply suspect, and self-publicizing.[11] As Herbert would have put it, the self becomes woven into the sense.

Like Herbert, however, Savonarola's suspicions of poetry did not put a stop to his own composition of poems. His own poetic activities seem to have inspired the Italian poet, Marcantonio Flaminio, who sympathized with Reformed doctrine, and acknowledged Savonarola as one of his spiritual forerunners.[12] George Herbert perhaps found *De Simplicitate Christianae Vitae* so valuable simply because he, like the author, was a Christian poet with a deep suspicion of poetry: Savonarola suggests ways of avoiding the pitfalls they both perceived so well.

Simplicitas: *Moving from the Inner Principle*

De Simplicitate Christianae Vitae was not published in England in the sixteenth century, although it was issued in Venice, Paris, and Cologne.[13] However, even a cursory reading of *De Simplicitate* will reveal much with which Herbert would have been deeply in sympathy.[14] Herbert's work itself has often been seen as

---

[10] Richard Whitlock, *Zootomia: Observations on the Present Manners of the English, or A Morall Anatomy of the Living by the Dead* (London, 1654), 469.

[11] Savonarola, *De Ratione Poeticae Artis*, 17–17ᵛ: 'Nihil enim habet humilitatis, quae est omnium virtutem fundamentum. Cuius signum, manifestissimum est, quia poeta cum necdum carmina sua ad finem perduxerit, in publicum ea producit, omnibus quibus potest ostendit, ore proprio laudat, ab aliis laudes expectat'.

[12] Marcantonio Flaminio, 'De Hieronymo Savonarola', in *M. Antonii Flaminii Carminum Libri III* (Florence, 1552), 128 (really 228).

[13] See L. Giovannozzi, *Contributo all bibliografia delle opere del Savonarola: Edizioni dei secc. XV e XVI* (Florence, 1953), 34–6.

[14] Louis Martz noted this and treated the topic briefly in *The Poetry of Meditation: A Study in English Religious Literature of the Seventeenth Century*, rev. edn. (London, 1962), 282.

'simple',[15] but this stylistic sense of the word is an incidental and unnecessary effect of *simplicitas*, which in Savonarola's writing is a comprehensive principle affecting the whole person. This brief definition of *simplicitas*, given in Book V, seems to articulate many of Herbert's preoccupations:

Simplicity: that is to say, Sincerity or purity of heart, integrity of conversation, together with neglect or renouncing of whatsoever is superfluous.[16]

This formula, embracing as it does inner purity, sincerity of words and deeds, and frugal lifestyle, represents a distillation of Books I, II, and IV of *De Simplicitate Christianae Vitae*. It could also be seen as a summary of the chapter in *The Country Parson* called 'The Parson's Life'. Savonarola's rather more lengthy work goes into some detail as to the theological and psychological framework for his prescriptions for the Christian life. However, Herbert's prose work contains detailed instructions very much like those of Savonarola's writing, and it is possible to trace a similar conceptualization of verbal inspiration, although Herbert, I think, finally rejects the Savonarolan model.

The first book of Savonarola's work is concerned with a theological expression of the distinctive nature of the Christian life. This is the kind of theological writing that has not survived of Herbert's works, if indeed he ever produced any. Much of Book I, which expresses an evangelical and Augustinian doctrine, could be accepted by any moderate Puritan, particularly as it shows a high regard for Scripture. However, Conclusion 1 would not have been endorsed by any Calvinist, including Herbert, without qualification: it shows Savonarola's insistence on the trustworthiness of the outward signs of a Christian. He is a realist in that he defines a Christian life as the imitation of Christ, distinguishing between true Christians and their counterfeit—*simulati christiani*—on the basis of Christlike deeds. The following Conclusion immediately balances this external criterion with an inner one—purity of heart. This is much more congenial to a Reformed spirituality.

---

[15] This is the general assumption of Joan Bennet's study of Herbert in *Five Metaphysical Poets* (Cambridge, 1971) and Patricia Beer's *An Introduction to the Metaphysical Poets* (London, 1972).

[16] Taken from the English translation of Book V: *The Felicity of a Christian Life by Hierome Savonarola*, in *Five Treatises* (London, 1651), 72.

No one can begin to approach God without inner purity, a criterion which is reminiscent of Herbert's warning in 'Superliminare', where *The Church* is not to be entered except by those who are 'holy, pure, and cleare'. Typically, Savonarola's definition of purity is a radical one, which goes beyond Herbert's. His purity is elemental, 'unmixed with any other inferior substance', whereas Herbert allows for an imperfect mixture of human and divine: if your heart is not 'holy, pure, and cleare', but only 'groneth to be so', you may still approach. However, the two writers agree that 'mortification' is the way to achieve purity. For Herbert, this process is 'the stupefying and deading of all the clamorous powers of the soul'.[17] Savonarola stresses the subjection of body to spirit, and an 'alienating of the will from the love of creatures'. As we shall see in Chapter 4, what the two authors mean by 'mortification' is actually quite different: but the practical results, as described in these two works, are almost indistinguishable. Thus the Christian will offend no one in any of his actions, a result which is important to both writers, for whom piety has a crucial social dimension. The concern with good works might seem hostile to a proper emphasis on grace: however, most of this first book is taken up with proving that the source of these 'works' is entirely divine, a theological point very important to Calvinist England.

Savonarola rejects other possible causes of piety in human beings—philanthropy, the imagination, the influence of the stars—including human reason, which Herbert also rejects in the poem 'Divinitie' as the 'staffe of flesh', useless on the journey to heaven. Conclusion 8 states that 'The root and ground of the Christian life is the grace of God', a divinely implanted principle within the soul. Savonarola's definition of grace is very similar to the Protestant conception of the Holy Spirit:

something similar to the Deity, through which something is freely given to the spirit, making it conform to the Divine nature, and in a measure united to the divine ineffability.[18]

This supernatural gift produces assurance of faith, and love and unity between Christians. This formulation is very different from

---

[17] George Herbert, *The Works of George Herbert*, ed. F. E. Hutchinson (Oxford, 1945), 227.
[18] Savonarola, *De Simplicitate Christianae Vitae* (Strasbourg, 1615), 37. Book V of *De Simplicitate Christianae Vitae* exists in an anonymous seventeenth-century English translation (see n. 16). Translations from Latin are my own, unless otherwise stated.

the orthodox *habitus* of grace conceived by Thomas Aquinas.[19] In the Aristotelian language such as Aquinas used for the same concept, Savonarola claims that it also moves Christians to supernatural good works, above and beyond those which ordinary people are able to do by virtue of the fact that God moves all things as Prime Mover. Given the divine efficacy of this gift, it is not surprising that the latter part of Book I is taken up with ways to conserve and increase the gift of grace. Chapter 10 of Book I is concerned with harmonizing the relationship between the Prime Mover and the moving cause of good works, including discourse, within the believer. I shall be dealing with this important chapter later.

Herbert and Simplicitas

Book II of *De Simplicitate Christianae Vitae* seeks to clarify the idea of *simplicitas* as presented in Book I. The first conclusion establishes the principle on which the rest of the conclusions are based: that spiritual things are understood through corporeal. This is a theme that Herbert returns to in *The Country Parson* when he is dealing with the teaching of the people. Both authors note that Scripture uses many parables and similitudes, Herbert stressing that Christ used illustrations drawn from the natural world so that 'by familiar things he might make his Doctrine slip the more easily into the hearts even of the meanest'.[20] There is an inevitable hierarchy of knowledge implied here: the parson 'condescends even to the knowledge of tillage and pastorage' for use in teaching. Savonarola, however, is constructing a hierarchy on a much grander scale. While Herbert is employing 'things of ordinary use' as metaphors to explain the catechism to his less intelligent parishioners, Savonarola is subscribing to a belief in Neoplatonic cosmology.

Savonarola begins with the *forma*, or Platonic idea of a natural thing: this is the only entity which is truly *simplex*. When the form is materialized it becomes mixed, or composite in nature. 'Only

---

[19] Alister McGrath points out Luther's Reformed hostility to the Thomist concept in *The Intellectual Origins of the European Reformation* (Oxford, 1987), 116: 'if the concept is to be retained in any form, it should be understood to refer to the bond of love which unites God to man—in other words, the uncreated grace of the Holy Spirit.'

[20] Herbert, *Works*, 261. See also 257, and 228.

God is truly and absolutely simple,' claims Savonarola.[21] Savonarola's second way of defining *simplicitas* is in opposition to *duplicitas*, which is a lack of consonance between words and deeds. Those who are *simplex* are called so because heart and words and deeds are in harmony.[22] This is a moral definition of an integrity of character that is attainable by unbelievers, but with great difficulty. It is, however, the natural fruit of grace. In the third mode of Savonarola's *simplicitas* this concord within the individual psyche expands to become the principle by which the universe is held together, a harmony of power and motion between all the heavenly bodies. In Book II, Conclusion 4 the variety and complexity of the stars becomes for Savonarola a vivid illustration of the richness of *simplicitas*. The closeness to God of those with the starlike gift of inner *simplicitas* guarantees an even closer correspondence between thought, word, and deed. The inner workings of *simplicitas* are reinforced as the fire of God, the purest state of the purest element, is approached. It is very important for Savonarola that this sophisticated concept is not confused with the first mode of *simplicitas*: simple ignorance (*stulta simplicitas*). He goes to great lengths to stress in Conclusion 6 that 'the simplicity of Christians does not exclude wisdom, but always includes it'. God, the most truly *simplex* of beings, has all knowledge. This is the solution to the biblical riddle—'be ye therefore wise as serpents, and harmless as doves'. Knowledge and wisdom do not take away *simplicitas*, but perfect it.[23]

The second and third modes of *simplicitas* have an affinity with much of Herbert's work, and it is easy to see why Herbert was so drawn to this treatise. The concept of integrity is a very potent one in Herbert's writing, and is one of his first principles for the country parson. Herbert's expression for it is 'hearty', a word that in the seventeenth century signified the consonance between inner and outer contained in the modern word 'heartfelt': the

---

[21] Savonarola, *De Simplicitate*, 56: 'solus Deus est vere & absolute simplex.' There follows a hierarchy of the four Platonic elements—earth, water, air, and fire—according to the proportion of form to matter in their composition. In a further twist of the Platonic plot these mostly composite elements—only fire being truly *simplex*—become elemental 'simples' of which all other things, and people, are composed: and there are degrees of *simplicitas* which correspond to the four elements.

[22] Ibid. 58: 'simplices dicuntur: quia cor & verba & facta eorum concordant.'

[23] Ibid. 62: 'Scientia ergo & prudentia, non tollit simplicitatem, immo perfecit.'

parson is 'hearty, and true in all his wayes'.[24] The most important test of sincerity is in discourse: 'the Parson is very strict in keeping his word . . . neither will they beleeve him in the pulpit, whom they cannot trust in his Conversation.'[25] This looks like the pragmatism of the classical orator, for whom an honest reputation was an essential strategy for effective rhetoric.[26] Ludovicus Carbo in his *Introductio Ad Catechismum* poses lack of integrity as the reason why preaching has lost its power as a two-edged sword. 'Teaching without good works creates arrogance' he says, in a sentiment reminiscent of Herbert's 'The Windows'.[27] In Herbert's advice to preachers the criterion for sincerity approaches the depth of Savonarola's second mode of *simplicitas*:

dipping and seasoning all our words and sentences in our hearts, before they come into our mouths, truly affecting, and cordially expressing all that we say; so that the auditors may plainly perceive that every word is hart-deep.[28]

'The Windows' advocates the same conjunction of 'doctrine and life' for effective preaching. But the only explicit mention of 'simplicitie' in Herbert's work is in the poem 'A Wreath', a poem which works to undermine its complex form. The convention is that each line begins with the words that end the previous line. Herbert employs a similar form in 'Sinnes round', which is about a Satanic coincidence of thought, word, and deed which eventually builds Babel. As so often with Herbert, the self intervenes in the intended sense, which then undermines the form of the poem. It starts affirmatively enough, however: this is to be 'a wreathed garland of deserved praise' like, perhaps, the classical laurel. However, the focus soon shifts from God to the poet, and the form begins to be subverted. At the mention of 'my wayes' at the end of line 3 the poet feels he has to give additional information, and the next line begins 'My crooked winding wayes'. The form is going awry at the same time as the poet's life. Even a simple concept such as the end of line 4, 'wherein I live', has to be radically qualified at the beginning of line 5: 'wherein I die, not

---

[24] Herbert, *Works*, 253.
[25] Ibid. 228.
[26] Quintilian, *Institutio Oratoria*, tr. H. E. Butler, 4 vols. (London, 1921), i. 9.
[27] Ludovicus Carbo, *Introductio Ad Catechismum, sive Doctrinam Christianum* (Venice, 1596), 22: 'doctrina sine moribus arrogantem facit'.
[28] Herbert, *Works*, 233.

live'. The whole purpose of the wreath comes into question: is this really a garland of praise for God, or a funeral wreath for the sinful poet? However, the poet's focus turns back to God just in time, and the poem recovers its form and purpose at the same time: it literally straightens out.

> life is straight,
> Straight as a line, and ever tends to thee.

The end of this tortuous eight-line sentence is approaching, and as it does, we see that this complex poem actually has something to do with simplicity:

> To thee, who art more farre above deceit,
> Then deceit seems above simplicitie.

The connection between 'deceit' and the complicated form of this poem is inescapable at this point. The new sentence begins 'Give me simplicitie'—a difficult request, as the poet is committed to a complex form, where the first words of each new line have to echo the last words of the previous one. However, the remaining four lines of the poem have the effect of unravelling a tangled mess: there are no qualifiers, no parentheses, and although the complex form is strictly adhered to, the sense of the sentence is much more easy to comprehend. The judgement of the final line is that the poem is a 'poore wreath', and judging by the original proposal for the poem, it is indeed a failure: there is very little praise in the poem at all. The prescription of the last sentence for a better and more appropriate poem—'a crown of praise'—is that the discourse should have the support of a godly life. Complexity is no substitute for sincerity, or in the terms of this poem, 'simplicitie'.

With the help of Savonarola's third definition of *simplicitas* it is possible to expand the conception of 'simplicity' usually associated with Herbert into something which does justice to his sophistication. Herbert's Country Parson is a simple, but knowledgeable man, and chapters 4 and 5 of the work enumerate the things he should know. Chapter 4 begins promisingly 'the Countrey Parson is full of all knowledg'. Nothing is beyond the scope of the parson's mind, it seems: he is to know everything from farming to the writings of the Schoolmen. In Herbert's vision, Truth is a unity with Knowledge. It is important not to ignore the wisdom of previous ages either, for spiritual truth throughout the ages forms a consonant whole:

> God in all ages hath had his servants, to whom he hath revealed his Truth, as well as to him; and that as one Countrey doth not bear all things, that there may be a Commerce; so neither hath God opened, or will open all to one, that there may be a traffick in knowledg between the servants of God, for the planting both of love, and of humility.[29]

This wholeness also encompasses the individual Christian. Chapter 23, 'The Parson's Completeness', announces dauntingly that 'the Countrey Parson desires to be all to his Parish, and not onely a Pastour, but a Lawyer also, and a Phisician'. Herbert gives recommended reading for both these disciplines. The first book on the Parson's reading list is of course the Bible: 'the book of books, the storehouse and the magazene of life and comfort.' One of the methods Herbert uses is 'a diligent Collation of Scripture with Scripture' and the reason for this practice is that 'all Truth [is] consonant to itself, and . . . penn'd by one and the self-same Spirit'. Various books of the Bible are 'diverse' but not 'repugnant'. In this view of Scripture Herbert is very close to Savonarola, who sees in the Bible the working out of his principle of *simplicitas*, unity in diversity:

> how admirable, how ravishing is that variety we meet with in them [the Scriptures], of Histories, of senses, of Types, of Figures? and yet a most exquisite harmony between them all, All the parts, All the Books of the Old and New Testament, exactly consenting in one, and pointing to the same generall and supream verity or end, which is the love of God and our neighbour: of which while they treat sometime historically and plainly, sometime more mystically and profoundly.[30]

It was from a very similar conviction that the Harmonies, or Concordances, were produced at Little Gidding, showing how the Gospel writers could be combined into one master-narrative, and how Chronicles could be harmonized with Judges. Herbert, who loved the Harmony that was sent to him, celebrates this very concept in the second of his sonnets on 'The H. Scriptures'. His metaphor for the profound unity of the Bible is very reminiscent of Savonarola: it is the same principle as orders the stars.

---

[29] Herbert, *Works*, 229.   [30] Savonarola, *The Felicity of a Christian Life*, 47–8.

Oh that I knew how all thy lights combine,
  And the configurations of their glorie!
  Seeing not onely how each verse doth shine
But all the constellations of the storie.

Not only is Scripture consonant with itself: it also 'rhymes' with the believer's life, so that the Christian takes his place in a vast harmony of Scripture, nature, and redeemed humanity. It is in these very terms that Anne Southwell, defending her own religious lyrics, argued with her friend the Lady Ridgeway in 1627:

the first father, was God; whose never enough to bee admired creation, was poetically confined to 4 generall genusses, Earth, Ayre, water & fire: The effectes wch give life unto his verse; were, Hott, Cold, Moist & Drye, wch produce Choller, Melanchollye, Bloud & Flegme: By these iust proportions, all thinges are propagated. Now beeing thus poetically composed: How can you bee at unitye with yourself, & at oddes with your owne composition?[31]

Of course, Herbert's name for the principle which ensures the continuing consistency of truth throughout the pages of the Bible and the history of the Church, within the individual believer and between groups of Christians, is the Holy Spirit: Savonarola calls it the *forma*, infused by the grace of God, of *simplicitas*. But in Conclusion 5 of Book II he admits that the two entities are one and the same: the *forma Christiani* is the grace of the Holy Spirit.

Book II of *De Simplicitate Christianae Vitae* ends with a comprehensive but conventional survey of what *simplicitas* means in the individual psyche. Savonarola uses the medieval categories of the rational soul to enumerate what perfect *simplicitas*, union with God, will involve. The *intellectus* should perceive or contemplate nothing but God. Everything loved by the *voluntas* must be chosen and loved by God. The *memoria* will always retain God and his mercies. The imagination will constantly picture the Cross: and the net result is 'that the whole clean man may be made the sanctified temple of God'.[32] There is no need to elaborate on the attraction that this mode of *simplicitas* would hold for George Herbert.

---

[31] Folger MS V. b. 198, fo. 3. There is a reproduction of this letter in J. C. Cavanaugh, 'Lady Southwell's Defence of Poetry', *ELR* 14 (1984) following p. 284. She dates it as 1627.

[32] Savonarola, *De Simplicitate*, 65: 'ut homo totus mundus efficiatur templum Dei sanctificatum'.

The Effective Experience of Prayer: Divine Motion

Savonarola's theory of the perfecting of the human soul is characteristically streamlined, and is the key to his conception of spiritual rhetoric. He takes a radical and slightly iconoclastic attitude to the sacraments that are the traditional means of grace, prepared to sacrifice all of the sacraments except for those of baptism and the Eucharist. He recommends frequent partaking of the Eucharist, as does Herbert: however, it is probable that Herbert did not share the Catholic view of the Eucharist as a means of imparting grace directly into the soul.[33] Savonarola's tenth Conclusion states that the best way to conserve and augment grace is prayer. There is no doubt that Herbert would have been in agreement with that statement, but for rather different reasons.

Prayer for Savonarola has a dynamic quality: it actually brings the soul closer to God. Prayer is defined as the elevation of the mind to God, and the proximity to the source of grace is the means of strengthening the gift within. Savonarola elaborates in Book II a traditional order of ascendancy for souls, in Neoplatonic terms. There are four stages of ascent, corresponding to earth, water, air, and fire. The purest and highest stage is fire, and the soul must transcend its earthly nature and rise in spiritual purity to union with God. Despite the argument of Gene Edward Veith Jr., who correctly identifies patterns of ascent with Catholic spirituality and thus stresses the patterns of descent in Herbert's poetry, there is some evidence that Herbert shares Savonarola's conceptualization.[34] The terms Herbert uses have much in common with Savonarola's Neoplatonic scheme. His most common complaint is that of 'Dulnesse':

> Why do I languish thus, drooping and dull,
> As if I were all earth?

[33] George Herbert, *The Country Parson*, ch. 22: Herbert, *Works*, 259. Critics have disagreed over Herbert's view of the Eucharist: in fact, Herbert presents apparently different views of its significance in the two poems entitled 'The H. Communion', one in the W manuscript, one in *The Temple*. For the argument that Herbert's doctrine on the Eucharist is a perfect example of his *via media*, see Donald R. Dickson, 'Between Transubstantiation and Memorialism: Herbert's Eucharistic Celebration', *George Herbert Journal*, 11 (1987), 1–14.
[34] G. E. Veith, Jr., 'The Religious Wars in George Herbert Criticism': Reinterpreting Seventeenth-Century Anglicanism; *George Herbert Journal*, 11 (1988), 25.

Coldness is linked with the heaviness of earth, and the failure to compose poetry, in poems like 'Employment (ii)'. In contrast to man's plight as a constant reminder of what he has lost are the stars, a potent symbol in Herbert's poetry. The 'silly soul' in 'Vanitie (ii)' never looks up:

> Poore silly soul, whose hope and head lies low;
> Whose flat delights on earth do creep and grow;
> To whom the stars shine not so fair, as eyes.

The poem 'The Starre' helps to explain the attraction of stars for Herbert, and the frequency with which they appear as symbols in his poetry. He longs to share the 'trinitie of light, | Motion, and heat' enjoyed by stars, along with their proximity to the face of Christ: this would entail his being purged from earthly elements such as 'sinne and sicknesse'. Sin keeps the soul earthbound, as is poignantly expressed in the poem 'Miserie':

> sinne hath fooled him. Now he is
> A lump of flesh, without a foot or wing
> To raise him to a glimpse of bliss.

Although Herbert's aspirations are heavenward, the reality for him is that he cannot lift himself towards God: it is only on the divine wings that he can get off the ground, as 'Easter-wings' makes clear. However, prayer is the exception to this rule. In 'The Storm', the fervent human prayer is able to join the stars and make an effective petition from its privileged position. One of the advantages of 'groaning' in prayer is expressed in terms of upward movement in 'Sion', and it also seems to have implications for the successful writing of poetry:

> grones are quick, and full of wings,
> And all their motions upward be;
> And ever as they mount, like larks they sing;
> The note is sad, yet musick for a King.

Although Herbert's words, or rather wordless prayers, may ascend to heaven, he himself seems firmly earthbound: the aspirations, couched in Neoplatonic imagery, remain aspirations. For Savonarola, the ascent to heaven through prayer, although entirely spiritual, is a reality, which leads to sanctification and results in practical holiness. The reality of this experience is emphasized by a change from Neoplatonic terms to Aristotelian vocabulary with its concrete terms. Savonarola is trying to explain why prayer is so effective, and he does this in terms of cause and effect. First of all he establishes the Aristotelian dogma that the completion of any effect is dependent on its cause, and that the more the influence of its cause, the more perfect the result. For the Christian, perfection is achieved by drawing near to the cause of the grace within him: and since the cause is God, infinitely far above all his creation, the closer a man approaches to Him, the more perfect he will become.[35] Savonarola seems to want to elide the causal chain, reducing the number of linked secondary causes, and making all the Christian's actions the effect of the First Cause.

The adoption of Aristotelian terminology leads Savonarola to think about exactly how the closeness of God achieves perfection in the believer, and he introduces the concept, familiar from Aquinas, of 'divine motions'. In prayer a believer opens himself to the influence of God moving in him, and thus strengthens the grace which is already there. At this point he abandons the interior model of inspiration—'motions' from the divinely implanted source of grace within—for an exterior and very forceful model. Quoting 2 Corinthians 3: 5, 'our sufficiency is of God', Savonarola claims that the responsibility of the Christian is simply to receive the motivating power of God: 'the task is, that a man well align himself with this kind of divine motions.'[36] Prayer is thus supremely effective in that it raises the soul to God, thus allowing the divine Mover more access to do His work in the soul. This is a very different model of subjectivity to that presented in Herbert's 'The H. Communion', where grace has no such overwhelming power. However, Aquinas, adapting Aristotle, had suggested this kind of psychological model in the *Summa Theologiae*.[37] For Aristotle, of course, the soul was characterized by motion: the only debate was over the source of the

---

[35] Savonarola, *De Simplicitate*, 43–4: 'effectus quilibet quanto magis subiicitur influentiae suae causae, tanto magis perficitur, cum tota eius perfectio dependeat a causa sua... Praeterea, perfectio effectus est per assimulationem seu appropinquationem ad causam. Et ideo quanto magis effectus appropinquat causae suae, tanto efficitur perfectior. Cum ergo prima causa sit Deus, qui est in infinitum elevatus super omnes creaturas; quanto homo magis appropinquat ei, tanto efficitur perfectior.'

[36] Ibid. 46: 'opus est quod homo bene se disponat ad huiusmodi motiones divinas.'

[37] Aquinas, *Summa Theologiae* IaIIae. 109. 10.

motions. For his model of the workings of divine grace, Aquinas
had distinguished between two different kinds of 'motions'. One
emanated from the divinely infused gift of habitual grace,
implanted by God at conversion, and very similar to Savonarola's
supernatural principle of *simplicitas*. The second type of 'motion',
however, was directly from God, and necessary to ensure perseverance in the faith. The need for motions of this type kept the
believer dependent on God. Savonarola's comments on this direct
type of motion are also in the context of perseverance, but his
vision for the effectiveness of the Christian life goes far beyond
that of Aquinas. Savonarola's original definition of prayer in
terms of closeness to God suggests possibilities for the soul of
rising to be joined to the Prime Mover, rather than simply waiting
to receive influences from on high. The metaphor of fluidity—the
'influx' of the inspirations into the soul—is replaced by a mechan-
ical image as the soul attaches itself to the great Motor:

it is fitting that a man does not withdraw himself from this influx but
rather shows himself worthy of the continuation of motions of this sort,
and this becomes strongest through prayer; which joins his spirit
through all his powers to the Prime Mover, and adapts to His motion.[38]

The undermining of separate subjectivity is complete: not only is
the Christian moved by the inspirations which 'pour' into his
being, but through prayer he is able to transcend his humanity
and become integrated into the divine machine.

This is a very satisfying and reassuringly solid model for Christian perfection. The implication is that the believer, thoroughly
'locked in' to the divine source through prayer, will be able to use
that power in every area of his Christian life. Savonarola chooses
to make the production of discourse the paradigm for the production of all holy actions. The implications for rhetoric within this
framework are radical.

Simplicitas *and Rhetoric*

Having established the internal workings of *simplicitas* in Book II,
Savonarola moves on in Book III to consider the working out of

[38] Savonarola, *De Simplicitate*, 47: 'Oportet etiam quod homo non se subtrahat ab hoc
influxu, sed magis se semper habilem ad huiusmodi continuationem motus exhibeat, & hoc
maxime per orationem fiat: quae ipsam animam cum omnibus potentiis suis primo motori
coniungit, & ad motum habilitat.'

this principle in visible and external form. Although several quite complex models of the working of God in the soul had been set out in Books I and II, a consistent psychological model is put forward throughout Book III. At times in Books I and II the original definition of *simplicitas* as an infused principle of grace in the soul is almost forgotten, as Savonarola employs other models to describe the working of God, based on Neoplatonic ideas of 'closeness to God' and 'ascent', linked with a Thomist concept of the 'motions' of God in the soul. The dominant conceptualization of *simplicitas* in Book III is also Thomist: it is close to the 'infused gift of habitual grace' given by God at conversion, which is the source of an impulse to do supernaturally good works.[39] Such a conceptualization could be happily accommodated to the Reformed idea of the Holy Spirit: and as we have seen, Savonarola himself equates *simplicitas* with the Holy Spirit at times. Thus the consistent mode of functioning of *simplicitas* is as an inner principle giving rise to outer signs and works which are consonant with it, in the same way as the seed of a vine eventually produces grapes. 'From the inner form of *simplicitas* nothing can proceed outwardly but *simplicitas*' declares Savonarola.[40] Again we are back with the law of cause and effect: effects, such as words and deeds, will be consonant with the moving principle which causes them. In Book III the production of spiritual rhetoric is used as the paradigm for the production of 'all other works and motions', whilst the other focus for his study of *simplicitas exterior* is clothing, which has inescapable associations for rhetoric.

In line with Aquinas, actions and words spring from the moving principle implanted in the human being by the Prime Mover. Conclusion 1 states 'We say that which is external simplicity proceeds from the interior principle from God, whether naturally or supernaturally imparted, and does not show the invention of art.' The key word here is 'natural'. Savonarola also uses the word 'natural' to describe the motions of the supernatural principle, *simplicitas interior*, which result in congruent external words, *simplicitas exterior*. The point is that for the Christian the supernatural

---

[39] Aquinas, *Summa Theologiae* IaIIae. 109.

[40] Savonarola, *De Simplicitate*, 16 (actually the page following p. 67, after which the pagination in this edition goes awry; after this page, numbered 16, it begins again from p. 62): 'A forma ergo simplicitate interiori non potest exterius procedere, nisi simplicitas.'

has become natural. Perhaps a better word in this context would be 'spontaneous', because Savonarola wants to stress the ease with which *simplicitas exterior* is produced, just as physical motions occur by natural instinct. By contrast, the production of art is a struggle. Savonarola posits two manners of speaking, 'natural' and 'artificial'. The classical orator's mode of operation is, of course, unnatural: 'when he...struggles to imitate speech which is alien to him, or eloquence, he is said to speak according to art.' This distinction is used by Savonarola to illustrate the difference between spiritual talk and that which is merely human. The spiritual man speaks without effort from the principle of *simplicitas* within him. Because he is allowing that principle to express itself freely with no obstruction in the form of human effort, he is said to speak by the Spirit of God. This model for speech, says Savonarola, is the pattern for all external 'works and motions'.[41]

Savonarola's treatment of the rules of rhetoric is very Augustinian. Augustine warns against acquiring a vast knowledge of the rules of rhetoric.[42] Savonarola states that the rules of art and the structures of invention are superficial and human sources for speech, compared with the deeper and divine principle of *simplicitas*. 'Works of art are those which proceed immediately from human invention' says Savonarola. Much more effort is involved in this 'artificial' speech. The orator struggles for eloquence, and then struggles to hide his art and appear to be speaking 'naturally'. The vocabulary of Augustine and Savonarola for consciously rhetorical discourse is similar: studied eloquence is laborious and distracting. This, for Savonarola, is the language of *duplicitas*, that deceitfulness which is anathema to the Christian spirit.

In Savonarola's terms, rhetoric is bound to fail because its cause is duplicitous human effort. His proof is in the words of children, which, he says, always please the hearers because there is no art or *duplicitas* involved in their simple utterances. Savonarola's concern is to eliminate the human intermediary between divine cause and external effect. Simple works, says Savonarola,

---

[41] Savonarola, *De Simplicitate*, 66 (the first of the two pages in this edition numbered 66): 'Quando...conatur imitari alterius loquelam vel eloquentiam, dicitur loqui secundam artem. Similiter qui in gratia Dei & charitate plenus est, sit verba sua prosert, prout ab illa forma, id est a gratia & charitate subministrantur: dicitur loqui a spiritu Dei non artificialiter.'

[42] Augustine, *On Christian Doctrine*, 119.

are the works of God. Not surprisingly, this type of divine action is supremely effective: 'the Apostles, and all preachers who utter their words from the Spirit of God, convert the whole world.'[43] Augustine's models for inspired speech in *De Doctrina Christiana* are as potentially effective as Savonarola's, and similarly reduce the role of the human intermediary to a passive channel. It is by the use of such Spirit-inspired rhetoric that Augustine claimed to have stopped a civil war.[44] In fact Savonarola refers to *De Doctrina Christiana* in his treatise on poetry, *Apologeticus De Ratione Poeticae Artis*, to support his conclusions about the power of spiritual discourse compared with that of classical rhetoric. The Scriptures are the best example of divine rhetoric, expressing God's mysteries in the optimum way, not distracting readers by the shell of truth which is the words, but taking them straight to the kernel. The kernel is the *finis* or aim of the discourse according to medieval authorship theory: yet again Savonarola is collapsing the causal chain, preferring to make God the immediate cause of all good words and works. 'Secular eloquence', by contrast, 'feeds the ears, and scarcely ever leads to the final goal. Thus, even the fathers of eloquence, who have written brilliantly against vices, and praised virtues with the greatest study and sweetest eloquence, and that most effectively, and have caressed the ears of the people throughout their speech with the flattery of words, will leave neither themselves nor others persuaded, in the sense that they will be able to lack vice.'[45]

In *De Simplicitate Christianae Vitae*, Savonarola attacks those who do not discern the working of the Spirit, and so reverse the categories, seeing rhetoric as profound and the Scriptures as trivial.

They never, or rarely, read the Scriptures, or reading they do not understand, or understanding, they do not taste: therefore they say, our mind is disgusted with this trivial fare. Who will let us hear the

---

[43] Savonarola, *De Simplicitate*, 68: 'Sed Apostoli & alii praedicatores, qui verba protulerunt per Spiritum Dei, totum Mundum converterunt.'

[44] Augustine, *On Christian Doctrine*, 160.

[45] Savonarola, *De Ratione Poeticae Artis*, 17ᵛ–18: 'Eloquentia enim secularis pascit aures, & raro vel nunquam ad finem intentum perducit. Unde & ipsi patres eloquentiae, qui contra vitia luculenter scripserit, & virtutes summa studio ac facundia suauissima laudauerunt efficacissimeque: perorantes verborum lenociniis aures populi demulserunt, nec alios nec seipsos unque ita persuasos relinquerit, ut vitiis carere potuerint.'

eloquence of Cicero, and the resonant words of the poets, and the sweet speech of Plato, and the subtleties of Aristotle? For this Scripture is simple, and food for mere women: preach to us subtle things.[46]

These people misuse the word 'simple' and use the language of *duplicitas*: sweetness, resonance, subtlety, eloquence. In Augustine and George Herbert, these are also epithets for the seductive power of rhetoric.

The denunciation of rhetoric in *De Simplicitate Christianae Vitae* would appear to apply even more to poetry than to rhetoric, so that it is a surprise to find Savonarola writing what he describes as a 'defence' of poetry in *Apologeticus De Ratione Poeticae Artis*. Savonarola follows Aristotle in believing that poetry, in terms of its logical status, is essentially example. He seems to envisage a poetry of things, not words: poetry is a branch of *scientia*, wisdom, the branch whereby specific *exempla* are quoted in order to enliven a philosophical argument, and make it more effective. Sidney used this defence in his *Apology for Poetry*. Thus the poet is essentially a philosopher.[47] Savonarola, like Sidney, also follows Aristotle's dictum that metre and rhyme are merely an ornament of poetry, and not essential to it. Unlike Sidney, however, he overturns the accepted genealogy of sacred poetry, declaring that books of the Bible generally held to be in verse form (he includes the Gospels in this category) should actually be read less often than the others! It is not clear from this treatise what kind of poetry Savonarola does consider to be acceptable, although he does mention 'the songs of the prophets', who 'do not practise the great study of arranging words, but of telling the truth'.[48] The reluctance to accommodate any rhetorical or verbal elements in the discussion of poetry in *De Ratione Poeticae Artis* is symptomatic of a similar reluctance to allow for the human and practical links in the chain of causation which runs from the moving principle of *simplicitas* through to its *finis* in another man's soul. However, it is very difficult to identify in practice what kind of poetic discourse would meet Savonarola's requirements for a 'natural' art.

---

[46] Savonarola, *De Simplicitate*, 53, tr. Louis Martz, in *The Poetry of Meditation*, 283.

[47] This is argued at some length in Savonarola, *De Simplicitate*, 15ᵛ.

[48] Savonarola, *De Ratione Poeticae Artis*, 17ᵛ: 'prophetarum carmina...Non enim magnum studium verbis componendis sed veritatis dicendae adhibuerunt.'

Models for Composition in George Herbert's Writing

Such a severe judgement on the art of rhetoric would not seem to be helpful to a Renaissance poet, but there are many ideas in *De Simplicitate Christianae Vitae* which have parallels in George Herbert's poetry. The preoccupation with subject-matter rather than words would resonate with the poet who constantly reaffirms his superiority to profane poets in terms of the truth of his subject. 'Jordan (i)' seems to hint at a poetry of true things: even a chair must be 'true', not 'painted'. It is in truth, not words, that the beauty of the poetry consists: the words that describe the true things must be clear in order that their beauty will shine through. 'Jordan (ii)' was originally called 'Invention', the word which for Savonarola was most characteristic of *duplicitas*. 'Invention' is often used by Herbert to suggest just that mixture of artificiality and human effort that so repelled Savonarola. 'Invention' was essential to the composition of poetry in Renaissance literary theory, and thus became a focus for Herbert in his reformulation of the role of Christian poet: the efforts of the love poets are called 'poor invention' in the second sonnet from Walton's *Lives*. 'Invention' was always the first section in the manuals of rhetoric, and concerned the subject-matter for the discourse to be undertaken. The recommended method was usually to analyse the inventions of others, and use the topics, or *loci communes*, which were conventionally associated with a subject. In the original meaning of the term, as a 'finding out', the word could be used with or without connotations of effort. However, it soon came to be used to signify 'fabrication', with its suggestions of the effort to deceive. In the seventeenth century four uses of the word were available: rhetorical 'invention', 'fabrication', 'original contrivance', and 'the faculty of mental creation'. These uses of the word cover a wide spectrum of human motivation and activity from spontaneous discovery to laborious deception.

Herbert's sonnets 'Love (i)' and 'Love (ii)' discuss both the corruption and redemption of invention. The first sonnet envisages invention as a worldly partnership between 'wit and beautie' that is entirely superficial and carnal. It is necessary to sacrifice the inventive faculty in order to purify it:

> Then shall our hearts pant thee; then shall our brain
> All her invention on thine Altar lay
> And there in hymnes send back thy fire again.

The Christian poet may expect to write with sincerity, and even with divine inspiration, but only if he is prepared to subject his creative faculty utterly to God, to the extent that he is prepared for it to be extinguished. This is why the first poem in *The Church* is 'The Altar', the site of sacrifice. The second couplet of the poem apparently denies any human art in its composition:

> Whose parts are as thy hand did frame;
> No workmans tool hath touch'd the same.

Ernest B. Gilman notes Herbert's fear that to use human invention in sacred poetry 'is to violate the biblical prohibition of craftsmanship in Deuteronomy 25: 2–8, the verses alluded to in "The Altar's" denial that any "workmans tool" has touched this carefully tooled artifact.'[49] The verse alluded to is in fact Exodus 20: 25, 'if thou wilt make me an altar of stone, thou shalt not build it of hewn stone: for if thou lift up thy tool upon it, thou hast polluted it.' This poem shows the complex dilemma of the author who can only use some kind of 'human invention'. Herbert makes two apparently contradictory claims, the first that the poem is God's workmanship, the second that it is a 'broken altar'. We shall be looking at this paradox in Chapter 4. Of course there is another unseen altar in the poem, which is 'made of a heart': but the altar which is the poem is clearly not broken, as its form is visibly perfect on the page.

It is no coincidence that the early poems of *The Church* are concerned with sacrifice: after 'The Altar' comes 'The Sacrifice', then 'The Thanksgiving' and 'The Reprisall', both of which enact a sacrifice of human reason and discourse. Some of Herbert's poems show a specific sacrifice of his poetic art. In 'The Posie' Herbert is dealing with the fashion of composing witty mottoes for use on all kinds of occasions, a practice which became a competition for those who wanted to pit their wits against each other. Herbert rejects the competition and the effort involved in it:

> Let wits contest,
> And with their words and posies windows fill.

---

[49] E. B. Gilman, *Iconoclasm and Poetry in the English Reformation: Down Went Dagon* (Chicago, 1986), 56.

He also rejects the internal effort of 'invention' and rhetoric:

> Invention rest,
> Comparisons go play, wit use thy will.

Herbert's eventual choice of 'posie'—*Less than the least of all God's mercies*—is entirely derivative and needs no human invention at all in composition. Another of Herbert's poems is entirely focused on the problematic concept of invention. The re-christening of 'Invention', the original title of 'Jordan (ii)', mirrors the baptism of the poetic process of invention as described in the poem. The activity described in Herbert's poem involves enormous human effort, and in the end traps the poet into the disjunction between *res* and *verba* characteristic of *duplicitas*:

> Curling with metaphors a plain intention,
> Decking the sense, as if it were to sell.

The product of this artificial process is a corrupt adulteration of 'sense' with 'self', the self-publicizing process described in *De Ratione Poeticae Artis*. *Simplicitas* has been lost: in the midst of the 'bustle' a 'friend' condemns this activity specifically because it manifests *duplicitas*, and suggests quite another model for poetic composition:

> *How wide is all this long pretence!*
> *There is in love a sweetness readie penn'd:*
> *Copie out onely that, and save expense.*

The spontaneous discovery of divine love and the passive act of copying it would have been recognizable by both Savonarola and St Augustine as a model for inspired discourse. The *res* of divine love is located elsewhere than in the poet's faculty of 'invention', and when it is truly found it becomes the natural source of words, produced with very little effort or 'expense'. The other use of the phrase 'ready penn'd' in Herbert's work is to describe the composition of sermons, in *The Country Parson*. Herbert's title for the chapter 'The Parson's Library' is a deliberate irony to which the first sentence draws attention: 'The Countrey Parson's Library is a holy Life.' The whole chapter is anti-intellectual: the preparation for a sermon is not study, but living as a Christian.[50] Thus the parson's own

---

[50] See R. Strier, *Love Known: Theology and Experience in George Herbert's Poetry* (Chicago, 1983), 198–9, for an excellent discussion of this chapter.

victories over temptation with the aid of the Holy Spirit become 'sermons ready penn'd'. In both sermons and poetry, then, the words simply copy out what is already written on the heart, a process of which Savonarola would have thoroughly approved.

However, Herbert did not find the formal model for his poem in his heart, but in the work of Sir Philip Sidney. The final lines of the first and third sonnets of *Astrophil and Stella* contain this conceit. Sonnet 1, like 'Jordan (ii)', is about poetic invention. Sidney represents the would-be poet studying the 'inventions' of others, as recommended in the handbooks of rhetoric. This turns out to be unhelpful not because invention itself is a spurious process but because these inventions are not his own: 'others' feet still seemed but strangers in [his] way.' Sidney's conception of invention is personal and natural, and unrelated to the effort of study: 'Invention, nature's child, fled step-dame study's blows.' The resolution of the dilemma with the intervention of Sidney's muse is famous: 'look in thy heart, and write', a formulation consistent with Savonarola's *simplicitas*. The process by which Herbert adopts Sidney's inventions for his poetry, however, might not have been viewed with approval by Savonarola. Sidney's Sonnet 3 is like an amplified version of Herbert's 'The Posie'. It describes with contempt the strange and difficult activities of contemporary poets.

> Let dainty wits cry on the sisters nine...
> Ennobling new-found tropes with problems old.

The poet's self-ironizing stance is that he is simply too stupid to participate in this process. Instead, he will adopt the role of scribe:

> in Stella's face I read
> What love and beauty be; then all my deed
> But copying is, what in her nature writes.[51]

Rather than look within to his love for Stella for inspiration, the poet is now looking outside himself to the ultimate source—Stella herself. This, again, is a 'natural' process: he is simply transcribing what nature has already written.

The adjective 'natural' is not without ambivalence for Herbert, however. As a theological term in his writing it is used as the

---

[51] Sir Philip Sidney, *Selected Poems*, ed. Katherine Duncan-Jones (Oxford, 1973), 118.

antithesis of 'spiritual' ('Affliction (i)'), and it goes most easily with vices such as 'concupiscence', as his comment on Valdés' sixth Consideration makes clear. In fact the subject of Philip Sidney's love poetry could be described as exactly such 'Inflammation of the naturall'.[52] Herbert's poem 'Nature' does not celebrate created beauty but laments the passions of the unregenerate soul. The rewriting of Sidney's sonnets is not a commitment to a natural faculty for love poetry but a dedication to an alternative source of inspiration. The original title, 'Invention', drew attention to Herbert's redefinition of this traditional source of the poet's wit.

Although Herbert and Savonarola would agree about the cause of Christian poetry, Savonarola's conclusions about poetic form would seem to make any kind of spiritual 'art' a contradiction in terms. In George Herbert's work, 'art' is also an ambivalent quality. Very often it is used of Satanic invention, such as 'sinnes force and art' in 'The H. Communion', and Sinne's hardening activities in 'Grace'. Both Sinne and Satan 'use much art' to conquer God's territory in 'Decay'. By contrast there is God's art, a marvellous phenomenon which can accomplish anything from the creation of the world to improving the performance of a song in 'Easter'. Herbert's own contribution to the art of that same poem is described as a 'struggle', a characteristic of all art in *De Simplicitate*. Rhetorical art is referred to coyly, in 'Grateful-nesse', as a tactic which has to be confessed to because God cannot be manipulated. As we have seen, Savonarola is extremely reticent about what kind of words a non-rhetorical Christian poetry might use. George Herbert has a go at supplying the answer in 'A true Hymne'. Here, he tests Savonarola's proposition that the spontaneous utterance characteristic of *simplicitas* is the best rhetoric. 'My joy, my life, my crown', the first line of the poem, is the utterance under discussion. It is clearly a 'natural' expression of the principle in the heart, a 'motion'. Is this a 'true Hymne', or not? The criterion advanced by Herbert on which to judge this issue is exactly that of Savonarola:

> The fineness which a hymne or psalme affords,
> Is, when the soul unto the lines accords.

[52] Herbert, *Works*, 308.

This poem sheds light on the kind of poetry Herbert is writing, and its audience. God is the judge, as Herbert says elsewhere in 'The Forerunners': 'if I please him, I write fine and wittie.' It is God who will complain 'if the words onely ryme', just as Savonarola spelled out in *De Ratione Poeticae Artis*. It seems that something else is supposed to rhyme: not word with word, but 'motion' with word. Such a total integration of the truly virtuous and learned man is described by Anne Southwell, who possessed a volume of *The Temple*:

> his treuth with retorick is surely graced
> his thoughts a grammer of congruitye
> all logicks arte is in his reason placed
> his actions bound as rules of poetrye
> his moods, tropes, figures, deeds of charyty.[53]

This is the kind of spiritual 'rhyming' described in 'Deniall', where God's intentions 'chime' with man's. There, as here, such spiritual harmony is posited as producing verbal euphony by supernatural means: the rhyme is 'mended' in 'Deniall', the 'scant' metre is supplied in 'A true Hymne'.[54] The message of both poems actually goes beyond Savonarola's already supernatural vision of poetry: if the utterances truly spring from *simplicitas*, God will intervene to supply the rhetorical elements necessary to write good poetry in human terms.

However, the positive answer of 'A true Hymne' raises another question. Since the poet has chosen not to finish the poem after the first line which is the spontaneous utterance—'My joy, my life, my crown'—does he not contradict the conclusion of the poem? Or are we to believe that the resulting poem is actually an example of God's supernatural art in changing everything into poetry? Is the poem itself 'A true Hymne' or is it merely about a true hymn? The real problem is the dual audience for Herbert's poetry. Although it is God's approval that he seeks, he cannot be writing for God alone: if he were, the spontaneous utterance would be all that was necessary. Thus the poem has to be rhet-

---

[53] Folger MS V. b. 198, fo. 42. I am grateful to Victoria Burke for drawing the poetry of Anne Southwell to my attention.

[54] See W. H. Pahlka, *Saint Augustine's Meter and George Herbert's Will* (Kent, Oh., 1987), 32, where he points out that Thomas Buck, the 1633 printer (not God!), supplied a syllable missing from a line in the last stanza, which read in B: 'Although verse be somewhat scant'.

orically, as well as spiritually, successful. Savonarola also assumed a human audience for poetry, but he envisaged a rhetoric which did not need to be effective in terms of words, which are the 'husk' of poetry: something supernatural about the message, the 'kernel', would guarantee its effectiveness in an indefinable way. Herbert's God seems to care about human standards, and use human means of communication, in a way that Savonarola's does not.

Language Theory in Herbert and Savonarola

Savonarola assumes the accuracy of language to reflect *simplicitas* in the soul. The process of mediation as Savonarola sees it is charted in Book V of *De Simplicitate*:

Writing, in its own nature, is but the sign of words spoken, as speech is of conceptions or thought.[55]

There is as little sense of inadequacy of sign-system in Savonarola's thinking as there is in this statement from Augustine's *De Doctrina Christiana*:

Our thought...assumes the form of words by means of which it may reach the ears without suffering any deterioration in itself.[56]

There is no reason, therefore, why the communication of *simplicitas* in human words should not be an easy process. In Augustine's suggested prayer before the sermon the preacher should envisage himself as a channel for the Spirit of God, who will pour forth into the world unmediated by reason or rhetoric, or by anything except accurate words:

When the hour in which he is to speak approaches, before he begins to preach, he should raise his thirsty soul to God in order that he may give forth what he shall drink, or pour out what shall fill him.[57]

Augustine and Savonarola can posit the same model for the divine inspiration of Scripture as the mundane production of ordinary speech. Even the divine authors merely transmit their own thoughts in words. It is merely a question of difference of degree, in that the thoughts of the Biblical writers are directly moved by God:

[55] Savonarola, *The Felicity of a Christian Life*, 42.
[56] Augustine, *On Christian Doctrine*, 14.
[57] Ibid. 140.

Because our thoughts do alwayes proceed from some interiour light or illustration of the mind, by how much that light is greater and more excellent, so much the greater also and more perfect must the Scriptures be, and the speech consequently more powerfull, and the writing, wherein that speech is represented, more admirable and profound.[58]

The superiority of the *res*, or the source of the rhetoric, guarantees the superior effectiveness of the *verba*, the words of Scripture. The attraction for both Augustine and Savonarola is that on this model it is possible to share in the effectiveness of such divine rhetoric. Success or failure is judged on the degree to which the moving cause of the discourse is revealed or obscured. The humble style of *simplicitas* gives accurate signification to the divinely inspired meaning, which is then able to function as God's word in the world.

Savonarola is himself in danger of collapsing the two discourses of theology and rhetoric, but with the opposite effect to that which he is attacking. Instead of assigning spiritual power to poetry, he gives rhetorical effectiveness to the Holy Spirit. In the ideal relationship of unity with God, infallible, inspired discourse such as the Holy Scriptures is a result of a motion from God. The role of the human author is merely to deliver accurate signification, a rhetoric of humility which is subservient to the truth it encapsulates.

George Herbert's prayer before the sermon assumes a very different model for mediation of God's word to that of St Augustine.

Lord Jesu! teach thou me, that I may teach them: Sanctifie, and inable all my powers, that in their full strength they may deliver thy message reverently, readily, faithfully, & fruitfully.[59]

The inspiration does not flow through the preacher in an effortless flood. The intellectual powers of the divine orator are at full stretch to understand the divine message, and then to convey it adequately, in a two-stage process. This language implies a full engagement of intellectual activity and rhetorical ability in mediating divine discourse. All the orator's skill is to be used, and as ex-University Orator at Cambridge, Herbert's own skills must have been formidable. Moreover, in his advice on preaching in

---

[58] Savonarola, *The Felicity of a Christian Life*, 42.   [59] Herbert, *Works*, 289.

The Country Parson, Herbert's first dictum is to use 'all possible art'. Although the 'art' in question does not appear to involve much technical rhetoric, there is no doubt that the process of preaching as Herbert envisages it (and apparently practised it) would have been classed as 'artificial' by Savonarola. Apart from the rhetorical strategies used, the hard work involved smacks of the struggle associated with *duplicitas* in *De Simplicitate Christianae Vitae* III. I. To 'inflame or ravish' a congregation (the common aim of Augustine, Savonarola, and Herbert) the preacher must compose 'a set, and laboured, and continued speech'.[60] In Herbert's description of his congregation the awareness of the effort involved in preaching to them Sunday by Sunday is almost palpable:

Countrey people . . . are thick, and heavy, and hard to raise to a poynt of Zeal, and fervency, and need a mountaine of fire to kindle them.[61]

The techniques recommended to move this audience bear a close resemblance to the Protestant 'grand style' of Bartholomew Keckermann, the most influential of the seventeenth-century rhetoricians.[62] Keckermann sees the sluggishness of his congregation, and the consequent need for a passionate rhetoric, as the result of the Fall. Rational argument is less effective than, as Herbert puts it, 'moving and ravishing', which is an expressive and dramatic enterprise, during which the church is turned into a theatre, as the cosmic drama between God and the souls of men is played out. The techniques Herbert recommends also consciously dramatize the preacher and his function:

He often tells them, that Sermons are dangerous things, that none goes out of the Church as he came in, but either better, or worse; that none is careless before his Judg, and that the word of God shal judge us. By these and other means the Parson procures attention.[63]

As attention-gaining strategies, Herbert's are very powerful: he is setting a stage on which God is to be chief actor, and there is to be audience participation. Thus Herbert employs all Keckermann's recommended figures of prosopopoeia, dialogue, apostrophe, and hypotyposis. Where Keckermann will sometimes halt abruptly, 'as

[60] Ibid. 257.
[61] Ibid. 233.
[62] According to Debora K. Shuger, *Sacred Rhetoric: The Christian Grand Style in the Renaissance* (Princeton, 1988), 91.
[63] Herbert, *Works,* 233.

if transgressing the boundaries of human speech', Herbert will threaten to do so.[64] All Herbert's techniques are recommended as effective signs of sincerity and holiness. After one particularly blood-curdling example of the 'urging of the presence and majesty of God' the lapse back into the humble, discursive style of *The Country Parson* is almost bathetic:

Oh let us all take heed what we do, God sees us . . . he sees hearts, he sees faces: he is among us . . . And he is a great God, and terrible, as great in mercy, so great in judgement: There are but two devouring elements, fire, and water, he hath both in him; *His voyce is as the sound of many waters, Revelations 1*. And he himself *is a consuming fire, Hebrews 12*. Such discourses shew very Holy. The Parsons Method in handling of a text consists of two parts.

There could be no clearer illustration of Savonarola's concept of *duplicitas*. Herbert's example of sermon rhetoric is entirely 'artificial' in Savonarola's terms, yet it is intended to signify holiness. Even when at his most sincere, in prayer, Herbert's parson has to pay attention to the signs he is using: 'lifting up his hands and eyes, and using all other gestures which may expresse a hearty, and unfeyned devotion.'[65] In *simplicitas exterior* as Savonarola conceives of it, such a contrived signification could not possibly be effective.

Herbert does not use metaphors of fluidity. For him, the pipes which carried the current of authentic inspiration have been broken with the martyrdom of the Apostles:

> But since those pipes of gold, which brought
> That cordiall water to our ground,
> Were cut and martyr'd . . .
> Thou shutt'st the doore, and keep'st within;
> Scarce a good joy creeps through the chink.[66]

Not only has the link been broken but dividing structures—doors, walls—have been thrown up, which militates against any flow of inspiration. Herbert never really expects any more in the way of liquid refreshment than the one drop he begs for in the poem that follows this 'Whitsunday', 'Grace'.

---

[64] Bartholomew Keckermann, *Rhetoricae ecclesiasticae sive artis formandi et habendi conciones sacras, libri duo* (Hanover, 1616), 39; Herbert, *Works*, 233.
[65] Herbert, *Works*, 231.
[66] Ibid. 59.

There is one extant poem by Herbert, however, which sets out a model for discourse entirely different from any others in his writing. The poem is the last of *Musae Responsoriae*, the collection of Latin verses and epigrams written against the Puritan Andrew Melville. Entitled simply 'Ad Deum', unlike the witty and sometimes forced titles of the other poems in the sequence, it celebrates what appears to be the poet's experience of divine inspiration. I quote the poem, in its English translation, in full.

(To God)

Once you, great God, bless
With sweet dew him who writes,
No futile labour makes it
A painful time for him: no aching
Fingers bother him for being bitten, no head
Aches, no quill is sad:
But in the pure body verse's
Ripe élan and vein are master,
Even as the Nile, unaware
Of dikes, overflows,
Lovely in its flooding. O sweetest
Spirit, you who fill up minds
With holy groans pouring
From you, the Dove, the writing
That I do, the pleasure that I give,
If I give it, is all from you.[67]

All the Savonarolan elements of inspired discourse are represented here. The poet is pure, surrendered to the power of the Spirit and the power of the verse, and experiences no effort in composition. Metaphors of fluidity abound. There are no pipes to contain the inspiration—the whole being of the poet is awash with the motion of the Spirit and the movement of the verse, which appear to be one and the same thing. There is a powerful sense of physical motion, which helps to emphasize that the source of the poetry is the Holy Spirit within the poet: hence his claim that it is God, not himself, who is the active participant. This would appear to be supremely effective poetic composition on the

---

[67] George Herbert, *The Latin Poetry of George Herbert: A Bilingual Edition*, tr. Mark McCloskey and Paul R. Murphy (Athens, Oh., 1965), 61.

model of *simplicitas*: personal, heartfelt verse, flowing spontaneously from the God-given grace within.

However, it is doubtful whether Savonarola would have
approved it as such. He would have recognized the echoes of
the Horatian Ode of which some of the lines are a copy. He would
have recognized the conventions of the Latin form in which
Herbert was writing, as decorously and as artificially as in the
other poems of the *Musae Responsoriae*, some of which are of a very
different tone, and flaunt their self-conscious wit. He would very
probably have also realized the political capital to be gained out
of a dedication to God of a set of polemic verses, and even more
audaciously, of an assertion that God Himself was the author of
them. 'Ad Deum' may be a description of *simplicitas* in poetry, but
as far as can be judged (one can never be certain!) it is not an
example of it.

External Simplicitas*: The Human, Visible Signs of a Divine, Hidden Principle*

Only those with spiritual light can judge whether rhetoric par-
takes of *simplicitas exterior*, as Conclusion 6 of Book III states.
Moreover, the external signs of *simplicitas* will not be the same
for everyone (Conclusion 5). Of course, this abolition of all external standards gives absolute authority to Savonarola's own
judgement of the genuine signs of *simplicitas*. To produce the
appropriate signs is a matter of some importance, for there is an
imperative for the believer to produce the necessary and congruent signs of *simplicitas*: 'Anyone who does not love *simplicitas exterior*
cannot live the Christian life' (Conclusion 3). A vine cannot bear
olives, nor can the principle of *simplicitas* give rise to anything
which smacks of *duplicitas*: there is, apparently, no room in Savonarola's model for a mixture of human and divine, *duplicitas* and
simplicitas. Yet the signs of *simplicitas exterior* that Savonarola does
describe are entirely socially constructed.

In Conclusion 7 Savonarola tries to present his prescriptions for
simplicitas in dress convention as those of Scripture, using the third
chapter of the first epistle of Peter, and 1 Corinthians 11. He does
manage to extract some general principles from these passages on
the dress and behaviour of women: however, it is not clear from
where the detailed prescriptions of the rest of the book are drawn,

except from contemporary practice and Savonarola's ideas of how his citizens should behave. It is particularly intriguing that his suggestions are almost entirely about manner of dress, although dwelling and diet are also mentioned briefly. His suggestions to queens and duchesses, for example, are as specific as Elizabethan sumptuary laws. They should not wear too much gold and silver, which is an unsurprising suggestion, as this is traditionally associated with ostentation and worldly pride, but silk clothing is compatible with *simplicitas* in a noblewoman.[68] Linen should also be worn, as a good example to the lower classes, as long as it is the best sort of linen, congruent with an exalted status. Anything less expensive would be a sign of ostentatious holiness, and therefore smack of *duplicitas*.

The involvement of the community does save Savonarola from complete solipsism. Savonarola insists that *simplicitas exterior* is a matter of natural instinct, and then defines 'natural instinct' as the ideas current in his community, modified by himself. This is perhaps the kind of thinking one would expect from the prophetic leader of a theocracy. But when it comes to social dress conventions we are a long way from *simplicitas*. The overriding preoccupation of this section of the book seems to be with reputation. Scandal is to be avoided at all costs.[69] The seventeenth-century editor is obviously slightly puzzled by this emphasis on outward phenomena when the primacy of *simplicitas interior* and the difficulty of judging *simplicitas exterior* has already been established. He glosses this section with a rationale that Savonarola does not supply: 'the inner man is known from external things.'[70] Dress conventions alone, however, cannot signify *simplicitas*. By virtue of *simplicitas exterior* dress can correctly signify status, and it is accuracy of signification that is itself a sign of *simplicitas interior*. Clothes are the principal sign of rank in society (III. 5) and Savonarola's concern in this book is to ensure congruency between rank and sign of rank. He condemns both extravagance and deliberate meanness of attire as 'ostentation', an attempt to display misleading signs, instead of the 'natural' signs of rank. Savonarola's refusal to theorize the human and practical side of *simplicitas*

---

[68] Savonarola, *De Simplicitate*, 70.
[69] Ibid. 73.
[70] Ibid. 75: 'Ab externis cognoscitur homo interior.'

allows him to consider a socially constructed dress code, or even his own prejudices, to be 'natural'.[71] The tension between the natural and the artificial in Savonarola's thought is never resolved.

Savonarola does devote some time to elaborating his definition of 'natural' speech. The type of discourse 'natural' to a speaker is that which he learnt in his youth. Thus 'natural' rhetoric includes habitual practices, within the context of the individual's native society. The implication is that the individual has developed a style which is personal to him, but at the same time formed under the influence of the communal discourse: it is both idiosyncratic and derivative.[72] The divine impulse takes on human conventions when it expresses itself in words, a fact that Augustine himself stressed in *De Doctrina Christiana*, to mitigate the excesses of those advocating an extreme view of inspiration: 'those who exult in divine assistance ... should remember that they have learned at least the alphabet from men.'[73] Augustine's divine orator has learned more than the alphabet, and uses the rules of eloquence 'naturally': he will have absorbed them by much reading of eloquent literature. Savonarola, in fact, defends Augustine's rhetorical style in *De Ratione Poeticae Artis* by arguing that it is natural to him because he was well read in secular literature prior to his conversion. It is clear that Savonarola's term 'natural' can mean anything he chooses. One conclusion to his reasoning is that anyone can compose poems without previous study: a conclusion so compelling that Savonarola feels the necessity to raise the issue. Afraid that this reasoning will allow even women to be poets, orators, and logicians, Savonarola is quick to intervene, hurriedly resorting to the odious conception of 'human invention':

---

[71] George Herbert shows himself to be capable of the similar confusion of conventional and spiritual, in the matter of correctly adorning a church. In ch. 13 of *The Country Parson* he manages to interpret two extremely general Biblical texts (I Cor. 14: 26, 40) in a highly specific way, even commenting enthusiastically on their exhaustiveness: 'they excellently score out the way, and fully, and exactly contain, even in externall and indifferent things, what course is to be taken.' However, it is very difficult to see the logical step between the text 'let all things be done decently and in order' and the detailed prescriptions for church furnishings laid out by Herbert.

[72] Concl. 7 of Book III warns against living a solitary life for that reason: the social aspect of *simplicitas exterior* is crucial.

[73] Augustine, *On Christian Doctrine*, 4.

but it is mad to say this when the art of poetry is a part of philosophy and numbered amongst the liberal arts, and although it has its beginning from nature, it achieves perfection from human invention.[74]

This answer comprehensively contradicts the logic about ends and causes, beginning and perfection, in *De Simplicitate.*

When Savonarola comes to write his own poetry, there is very little obvious difference between this—presumably the product of *simplicitas*—and other poetry of the period, including George Herbert's. There are poems of Savonarola's extant from 1472 onwards, beginning with 'De Ruina Mundi', which, according to Donald Weinstein, is 'laced with Petrarchan expressions'.[75] His later poetry, although more austere in rhetoric than the early poems, is almost as complex in metre and rhyme as that of George Herbert. His stanza forms vary, using short and long lines in different combinations in a way reminiscent of Herbert's use of form. The number of external constraints is unexpected in a poet whose theories emphasize the natural production of words. It is clear that the theory of *simplicitas exterior* is inadequate as a basis for judging—or producing—human rhetoric.

'Decorum' in Augustine, Savonarola, and Herbert

Herbert is the poet of external constraints *par excellence*, to the extent that he incurred the mockery of later seventeenth-century critics for the artificiality of his emblematic poems. He does not seem to agonize over this particular aspect of his poetry: in fact, even the apparent freedom of that most agonized of poems, 'The Collar', is carefully designed to signify the conflict and its eventual resolution, as many critics have shown. However, it is possible to see the careful correspondence between subject and form that characterizes Herbert's poetry as an example of *simplicitas*, the principle of integrity that can draw together complex elements such as typography, form, and meaning into harmony. Herbert's concept of integrity in discourse seems to have extended even to

---

[74] Savonarola, *De Ratione Poeticae Artis*, 15^v: 'Sed qua hoc dementis est dicere cum ars poetica sit pars philosophiae rationalis & inter artes liberales connumeretur, que etsi initium habeant a natura perfectionem tamen ab humana inventione accaeperunt.'

[75] Donald Weinstein, *Savonarola and Florence: Prophecy and Patriotism in the Renaissance* (Princeton, 1970), 78.

handwriting, and the layout of poetry. The form of a poem such as 'H. Baptisme (ii)' is designed to signify the 'narrow gate' of baptism that it describes. In all printed versions, no effort has been made to reproduce Herbert's intended effect. In both manuscripts, the end of each line is against the right margin: this emphasizes the shortness of the first and last lines of each stanza, suggesting the narrowness of the entrance into life, a narrowness to which the Christian must return in continually dying to himself. A similar stanza shape is chosen for 'Aaron', and this has the effect of drawing attention to the last word of each line, an effect that is entirely lost in the 1633 edition. In the version of the poem in the Bodleian manuscript it is obvious to what feature the layout is calling attention. Not only is there the same rhyme scheme throughout: the words which constitute the rhyme scheme in the first stanza—'head', 'breast', 'dead', 'rest', 'drest'—are repeated in each successive stanza. To keep to this extraordinarily strict limitation over a poem of five stanzas is an amazing feat of virtuosity. However, the handwriting of these last words tells another story, one that mirrors the narrative of the poem. The first stanza describes the garments of Aaron, the first priest, from Exodus 28. The second, in pathetic contrast, describes the clothing of the 'poore priest' who is the poet: and there is a corresponding difference between the lettering of the last words of the first stanza and those of the second. Joseph Moxon's seventeenth-century printing manual includes clear instructions on how to 'dress' words in the physical medium of typography: '*Capitals* express Dignity wherever they are *Set*.' The letters of the second stanza have lost all their dignity. However, hope returns with the first line of the third stanza: another priest appears, who has dignity. And as the poet perceives the possibility of putting on Christ in the fourth stanza, he more than recovers the status of Aaron: the final words are now even larger. Moxon explains what that means:

if conveniently he can, he will *Set* a *Space* between every *Letter*, and two or three before or after that Name, to make it shew more Graceful and Stately. Space and Distance also implies stateliness.[76]

---

[76] Joseph Moxon, *Mechanick Exercises: or, the Doctrine of Handy-works Applied to the Art of Printing*, 2 vols. (London, 1962: 1st pub. 1683), ii. 212.

Dignity and stateliness are thus conferred on the final stanza, in a visual confirmation of the priest's newly assumed authority and robes.

Such contrived frameworks for discourse as the complex forms of Herbert's poetry do not seem to be in the spirit of *simplicitas* as Savonarola conceived it. However, Savonarola's prescriptions for dress are just as contrived, in the sense that they spring from pragmatic, external considerations, rather than a consistent inner logic. Decorum, rather than nakedness, is the principle of *simplicitas* in Savonarola's discussion of clothing, if he had cared to analyse it: and to be consistent, he should have applied that principle to rhetoric. Of course, the stock Renaissance image for rhetoric was of language as the clothing for thought. Quintilian had begun the sartorial metaphor when talking of figures of speech in terms of statues:

Some figures are represented as running or rushing forward, others sit or recline, some are nude, others clothed, while some again are half-dressed, half-naked.[77]

However, the image of dress as opposed to nakedness implies conscious choice rather than spontaneity. Decorum is one of Augustine's concerns in Book IV of *De Doctrina Christiana*, although his enthusiasm is reserved for the plain style. Both Augustine and Herbert show a kind of nostalgia for the kind of divine simplicity Savonarola insists on, but they are aware of the power of human rhetoric, and cannot ignore it or dismiss it. St Augustine displays a certain amount of embarrassment about his advocacy of the grand style, and is at pains to show that in teaching, a humble style is often more appropriate: 'Of what use is a gold key if it will not open what we wish? Or what objection is there to a wooden one which will?'[78] This is very much in the spirit of Herbert's praise of the subdued style and humble subject-matter of the Scriptures, in a work which is itself an example of *humilis*: *The Country Parson*.[79]

Like Augustine, Herbert acknowledges the need for different styles for different purposes. This subdued style, although useful for teaching, cannot 'inflame or ravish'. He would have agreed with Augustine's prescriptions for sermon rhetoric:

[77] Quintilian, *Institutio Oratoria*, i. 293.
[78] Augustine, *On Christian Doctrine*, 136.
[79] Herbert, *Works*, 257.

delight has no small place in the art of eloquence. But when that has been added it is not sufficient for the obdurate who have profited neither from understanding what was said nor from delighting in the manner in which it was taught...It is necessary therefore for the ecclesiastical orator, when he urges that something be done, not only to teach that he may instruct and to please that he may hold attention, but to persuade that he may be victorious.[80]

At times the 'gilded and bejeweled sword' of the grand style should be brought into play. Although Herbert sometimes lays down the sword of rhetoric, the sermon is one context in which he takes it up, seeing it as the sword of the Spirit. The pulpit is the parson's 'throne', where he performs the definitive vocation of 'The Priesthood':

> fain would I draw nigh,
> Fain put thee on, exchanging my lay-sword
> For that of th'holy Word.[81]

Although part of the sermon is to 'Inform', its distinctive function is to 'Inflame'—and 'that must be done by a set, and laboured, and continued speech'.

Herbert's poetry also approaches the plain style of the Scriptures, and could be described in the same terms:

it condescends to the naming of a plough, a hatchet, a bushell, leaven, boyes piping and dancing; shewing that things of ordinary use are not only to serve in the way of drudgery, but to be washed, and cleansed, and serve for lights even of Heavenly Truths.[82]

Nearly all these objects are named in Herbert's own poetry, along with buckets, bags, anvils, and screws. The purpose of using such homely objects is to make clearer sacred doctrine by illustrating it—the essential function of poetry, according to Savonarola. St Augustine's term for this plain style differs from Cicero's. He calls it *submissus*, rather than *humilis*, and Herbert's poem 'Submission' is, I think, a comment on the character and style of *submissus*. The attitude expressed there is one of complete resignation to God, even of the key power of eyesight, which is a metaphor here for all the intellectual powers, including rhetoric. The simple ballad form and straightforward diction are absolutely characteristic of

---

[80] Augustine, *On Christian Doctrine*, 138.   [81] Herbert, *Works*, 160.
[82] Ibid. 257.

submissus, and of course the decorum of the poem is faultless: a resignation of intellectual powers to God is best expressed in a spare and simple style. However, it is not just the 'things of ordinary use' that Herbert baptizes for the Christian poet's use, but the 'lovely enchanting language' of love poetry. Herbert has a clear sense of the distinct purposes of discourse, and of the different rhetorical styles necessary for each. Decorum is an instinctive principle: Herbert is the poet who described prayer as 'man well drest', and 'lovely enchanting language' as a 'broi-der'd coat'. Rhetorical 'nakedness' is forced on him, in 'The Forerunners': the metaphors and phrases desert him for an unworthy cause. This is a violation of decorum, which dictates that 'beautie and beauteous words should go together': and the naked truth that remains is not effective with others, although it sustains the inner life.

Savonarola's vision for Christian rhetoric, that the principle of *simplicitas* will produce effective utterance without too much con-sideration for the actual words, is entirely lacking in Herbert. In any case, the criticism of rhetoric as 'artificial' would not have had any weight with one trained in the Jacobean rhetorical tradition. In *De Doctrina Christiana* St Augustine claims that rhetoric was not 'instituted', but 'discovered':

> Men did not themselves institute the fact that an expression of charity conciliates an audience, or the fact that it is easy to understand a brief and open account of events, or that the variety of a discourse keeps the auditors attentive and without fatigue.[83]

There is also a strong sense in sixteenth-century thinking about language that rhetoric is not only naturally derived, but helps to improve fallen nature. Something of the sort is suggested by Sidney when he declares of nature that 'Her world is brazen, the poets only deliver a golden.' Herbert would have been famil-iar with George Puttenham's 1589 work, *The Arte of English Poesie*, where the poet is seen as practising the most natural of all the arts, more natural even than gardening:

> there be artes and methodes both to speake and to perswade and also to dispute, and by which the naturall is in some sorte relieved, as th'eye by his spectacle, I say relieved in his imperfection, but not made more perfit

---

[83] Augustine, *On Christian Doctrine*, 71.

then the naturall, in which respect I call those arts of Grammer, *Logicke*, and *Rhetorick* not bare imitations ... but by long and studious obseruation rather a repititio or reminiscens naturall, reduced into perfection, and made prompt by use and exercise. And so whatsoever a man speakes or perswades he doth it not by imitation artificially, but by observation naturally (though one follow another) because it is both the same and the like that nature doth suggest.[84]

The metaphor of the 'spectacle' as an aid to vision is that used by St Augustine and Calvin to describe the healing power of the Holy Spirit to correct man's fallen understanding, very much as Puttenham envisages that nature is 'in some sorte relieued in his imperfection' by rhetoric. The Calvinist divine William Pemble, writing in the early seventeenth century with an extremely severe view of the potential of rhetoric to become artificial and merely decorative, nevertheless found it necessary to write an *Enchiridion Oratorium*, a handbook for orators, simply because of the healing and restoring properties of rhetoric in revealing truth. In the treatise Herbert himself translated, Luigi Cornaro in his discussion of the cures for dietary disorder declares that 'the faults of Nature are often amended by Art'.[85]

The concept of a natural art which has redeeming potential is an attractive one for a poet, and there is some indication in Herbert's writing that rhetoric can be used to mitigate the consequences for language of the Fall and Babel. Herbert's very injunction to employ 'all possible art' in a sermon implies the potential of rhetoric to overcome 'natural' and 'sinful' characteristics such as sloth and hardness of heart. Herbert does not make the connection explicit, as Keckerman does. Yet one of Herbert's Latin poems appears to be about Babel and the possibility of at least mitigating its effects. It contains all the elements from *De Simplicitate Christianae Vitae*—dress, modesty, rhetoric, and giving to the poor. The second poem in the series *Memoriae Matris Sacrum*, Latin poems in memory of Magdalen Herbert, celebrates the linguistic practice of the one who 'taught [him] to write'. The poems were published in 1627, so this description of optimum language use is presumably the product of Herbert's mature

---

[84] George Puttenham, *The Arte of English Poesie*, ed. Gladys Doidge Willcock and Alice Walker (Cambridge, 1936), 307.
[85] Herbert, *Works*, 292.

reflection on this topic. The real Magdalen Herbert was apparently a sophisticated and witty speaker, but I would argue that Herbert has taken the opportunity to superimpose his ideal for a Christian user of language on the identity of his dead mother. Magdalen Herbert was apparently very aware of the curse of confusion put on language at Babel, in a way that Savonarola, it seems, was not. As represented in this poem, she takes great thought over her words. She chatters very little. In fact, idle talk, ostentatious dress, and elaborate hairstyle are linked sins to be avoided: hairstyles can share in the height and pride of the notorious tower.

> She did not deck herself so grandly she
> Wasted time that glides away, nor did she
> Pile up her hair as high as pride,
> Then the day's remainder spend
> In idle talk (language being chaos since
> The time of Babel).[86]

However, the spiritual dangers inherent in both hairdressing and speaking do not force Magdalen Herbert to be dishevelled and silent. On the contrary, she gives all the more care to both dress and discourse. Her hairstyle is 'simple', as befitting a virtuous woman. The use of the word *integra* for Magdalen Herbert underlines the fact that this sentiment is entirely in harmony with Savonarola's dictates for *simplicitas*. Her speech also shares in the effectiveness that Savonarola envisaged for *simplicitas exterior*. Her prayers are 'sharp and fiery'—pure enough and pointed enough to penetrate the heavens. The grace of her speech is like a storm, with all the connotations of passionate effectiveness explored in Herbert's poem by that name. This effectiveness consists of a mixture of wit and wisdom, a recipe that implies a mastery of *verba* as well as a deeper knowledge of *res*. Like the classical orator, she can talk wisely on any subject, even hunting and cattle. Her speeches are oracles, and her writings are renowned throughout the world. So how does Magdalen Herbert overcome the curse of Babel? The secret is in a close conformity between thought, word, and even graphical representation of that word: her skill in chirography (as *artifex*) is celebrated along with the more usual

---

[86] *The Latin Poetry of George Herbert*, 125.

elements in discourse. These elements add up to a consistently beautiful whole—'beautiful the shell, most beautiful the kernel'. Savonarola would have approved of the priority of the 'kernel' of truth in her speaking, and of her generosity to the poor. But the process of production of speech would have seemed to him artificial and unspontaneous. It is clear that Magdalen Herbert took as much care in her speech and writing as she did to dress appropriately and soberly every morning. She tackles everything with 'skill and clear calculation', and although her wise discourse eases her through the twists and turns of her daily duties, her rhetoric is one of considered maxims rather than spontaneous utterance. Even for a Magdalen Herbert, the struggle to over-come the curse of Babel is hard work.

Simplicitas *and Herbert's poetry*

In some ways the principle of *simplicitas* is useful for understanding Herbert's rhetoric. There is a relative simplicity in Herbert's dic-tion, combined with an integrity of meaning, form, and style. Both Herbert and Savonarola are supremely concerned with truth and honesty. Nicholas Ferrar's presentation of *The Temple*—'in that naked simplicitie, with which he left it, without any addition either of support or ornament'—suggests the Protestant attitude to the Scriptures, as Arthur Marotti points out: 'plain words suffice'.[87] However, Herbert is prepared to work at the external features of *simplicitas* in a way that Savonarola is not, and the differences between Herbert and Savonarola are most appar-ent in their consideration of preaching. Savonarola talks of divine discourse as transmitting light: in this enterprise the principle of *simplicitas* means that the human medium should be as transpar-ent as possible. Herbert, however, rejects 'pure' transparency in his poem 'The Windows': the light transmitted into the church by such preachers is 'watrish, bleak, & thin'. Unexpectedly, it is stained glass that is the preferred medium for God's message. The light is refracted through 'colours' (with an unmistakable connotation of rhetorical colours) and through the life of the preacher, so that it is a mixture of divine and human elements that is most compelling:

[87] A. Marrotti, *Manuscript, Print, and the English Renaissance Lyric* (Ithaca, NY, 1995), 256.

> then the light and glorie
> More rev'rend grows, & more doth win:
> Which else shows watrish, bleak, & thin.

Herbert does not share Savonarola's mechanistic vision of the workings of God in the soul. Savonarola's Neoplatonic theories work towards an elimination of the human elements in the Christian life. For Herbert, such perfection is not possible, nor really desirable, although he may make gestures towards it. He is more concerned with the human face of God than the divine nature of the soul. However, the human being has to work very hard to fulfil his responsibility, which is to find human words that are worthy of the Word:

this word of thy rich peace, and reconciliation, thou hast committed, not to Thunder, or Angels, but to silly and sinful men: even to me.[88]

Just what this responsibility involved we shall see in the next chapter.

It is not clear that Savonarola would have entirely disapproved of George Herbert. His ideas about decorum indicate that, like Herbert, he has a profound concern with human actions and words, even if he attributes it all to the divine principle of *simplicitas*.[89] As if he feels he has taken too radical an attitude to rhetoric, his stance softens towards the end of *De Ratione Poeticae Artis*. Allowing a place to the genuinely Christian poet, he finishes the treatise with this plea:

therefore I urge you, O poet, to look to higher things, and not to wish always to dwell among children. Escape the vain superstition of idols, and fly to the cross of Christ, and receive eternal glory from him.[90]

Both Counter-Reformation writers and Reformed poets such as Herbert were to respond to the call to purify poetry in the cause of

---

[88] Herbert, *Works*, 289.

[89] Herbert himself was not above equating a sense of decorum with the prompting of the Holy Spirit: see *Works*, 272: 'the Godly have ever added some houres of prayer.... as they think fit, & see cause, or rather as Gods spirit leads them.'

[90] Savonarola, *De Ratione Poeticae Artis*, 24^v: 'Hortor igitur vos o poete ad superiora conscendere, and ne velitis semper inter pueros commorari. Vanissimam idolorum superstitionem fugite, and ad christ crucem, ac simplicitatem humilitatemque conuolate, & gloriam ab eo percipietis aeternam.'

Christ. However, it was the poets of the Reformation who were to gain the most inspiration from Savonarola's writings. The response of Counter-Reformation poets to the reforming project of the Council of Trent will be dealt with in the next chapter.

2

An Introduction to the Devoute Life
and *The Temple*: 'The Poetry of Meditation'
or 'Private Ejaculations'?

i. The Poetry of Meditation: St François de Sales and The Temple

St François de Sales is at first glance a more plausible model for
Herbert than the austere, fanatic monk of Florence: at least many
critics have thought so, following the magisterial work of Louis L.
Martz, *The Poetry of Meditation*. A bishop of the Catholic Church,
François de Sales had a close personal involvement with poetry
and poets. Under his auspices the Academie florimontane was
founded at Annecy in 1607, an informal gathering of scholars who
met to discuss a range of disciplines from arithmetic and cosmo-
graphy to rhetoric and philosophy. A co-founder of the Academie
florimontane, and close friend of de Sales, was a devotional poet,
Antoine Favre, the leading jurist of Savoy. Favre's *Centurie première
de sonets spirituels de l'amour divin et de la pénitence* of 1595 was
dedicated to François de Sales, with a suggestion that the work
was inspired and facilitated by de Sales himself.[1]

Despite the fact that François de Sales' classic of Counter-
Reformation spirituality, *An Introduction to the Devoute Life,* is a prose
treatise, it was placed firmly in the tradition of Biblical poetry by
the author of *Defensio Ecclesiae Anglicanae*, William Nicholls. He
edited de Sales' work as *An Introduction to a Devout Life* in 1701, and
in his preface surveyed the use of Catholic devotional treatises in
England. He notes 'the good Reception which Devotional Books
have found in this Nation for some Years last past'. Obviously there
is something attractive about Catholic devotional writing, as
Nicholls grudgingly admits: 'it must be confessed that some of
their Books this way are well wrote, with a great deal of Warmth
and Affection.' He attributes this positive quality to the heritage of

---

[1] T. C. Cave, *Devotional Poetry in France c.1570–1613* (Cambridge, 1969), 81.

affective writing beginning with the poetic books of the Bible: Job, Psalms, the Song of Songs, the genealogy familiar from Sidney and others. Continuing with St Augustine, Nicholls includes in his history of devotional works all those which achieve affective power by literary techniques. The secret of Augustine's success, apparently, is his use of the figure of antithesis. Anselm is commended for his flawless imitation of Augustine, as much in rhetorical style as in content. St Bernard receives faint praise, for although his style resembles Augustine's, it is 'mixed with more affectations of a quibbling Wit'. St François de Sales' treatise has been chosen for publication on stylistic grounds: 'natural and pretty similes, and apposite Examples, together with a peculiar Tenderness and good Humour in the Expression.'[2] The undisputed piety and elegant rhetorical style of St François de Sales would seem to make him an inspirational figure for George Herbert.

Louis Martz was the first to identify *An Introduction to the Devoute Life* as a possible origin for Herbert's *The Temple*. He based his conclusions on a study of similarities in style, vocabulary, and spirituality in the two texts, and he went no further than to speculate that 'it seems likely... that Herbert would have known and admired the writings of St François de Sales'.[3] This judgement was based on Herbert's professed admiration for French culture, and Martz suggests that *An Introduction to the Devoute Life* may have been one of the books George Herbert asked his brother Henry to send him.[4] However, Herbert would certainly not have needed to ask his brother to send him a copy from Paris, as the book was available in England, and indeed seems to have been intended for the English market.[5] It was one of the books bound at Little Gidding, as Alan Maycock points out in his biography of Nicholas Ferrar.[6] St François de Sales was revered at Little Gidding, and the Ferrar family's Little Academy may

---

[2] François de Sales, *An Introduction to a Devout Life, Translated and Reformed from the Errors of the Popish Edition, To which is prefixed [sic] A Discourse, of the Rise and Progress of the Spiritual Books in the Romish Church*, ed. William Nicholls D. D. (London, 1701), A1ᵛ.

[3] L. L. Martz, *The Poetry of Meditation: A Study in English Religious Literature of the Seventeenth Century*, rev. edn. (New Haven, 1962), 250.

[4] George Herbert, Letter to Sir John Danvers, in *The Works of George Herbert*, ed. F. E. Hutchinson (Oxford, 1945), 366.

[5] See H. C. White, *Devotional Literature (Prose) 1600–1640* (Madison, 1931), 111 for the success of the first 1613 edition, which she claims was aimed at recusants in England.

[6] A. L. Maycock, *Nicholas Ferrar of Little Gidding* (London, 1938), 283–4.

well have been set up in imitation of the Academie florimontane. Between the Ferrar family and George Herbert there was a well-established correspondence, of books as well as letters. John Ferrar describes an intimate and comprehensive relationship between the two men: 'as N. F. [Nicholas Ferrar] communicated his heart to him, so he made him the Peruser, & desired the approbation of what he did.'[7] This remark is in the context of close co-operation over the translation and publication of European texts.

The publishing activities of the Ferrar–Herbert partnership show clearly that Herbert was familiar with Counter-Reformation spirituality, and felt that publication of key texts could enrich the spiritual life of English Protestants. Herbert translated Luigi Cornaro's *Treatise of Temperance* for the volume *Hygiasticon*, published in 1634 on Nicholas Ferrar's initiative. John Ferrar says that Herbert was closely consulted over the publication of the title treatise, by Leonard Lessius. He also mentions another work by a Counter-Reformation theologian, Ludovicus Carbo, *Introductio Ad Catechismum*, which was one of two texts that Nicholas Ferrar sent to Herbert for approval, in a translation by himself. According to John Ferrar, Herbert 'well approved' the text. However, the Cambridge licensers thought differently, and the work was never published.[8] By the 1630s *An Introduction to the Devoute Life* had also become controversial: all copies of the 1637 edition were burnt.[9] If

---

[7] Nicholas Ferrar, *The Ferrar Papers*, ed. B. Blackstone (Cambridge, 1938), 59, quoted by Hutchinson in Herbert, *Works*, 564.

[8] Amy Charles has made an uncharacteristic error in identifying *Introductio Ad Catechismum* with the third treatise in the 1634 volume of *Hygiasticon*. See *A Life of George Herbert* (Ithaca, NY, 1977), 187–8. Even she has to note the discrepancy between the comment of T. S. that the third treatise is 'a banquet of Junkets after a solid Feast' and the fact that Carbo's treatise is obviously serious in import. Anyone comparing the two treatises will see at once that the great length of *Introductio Ad Catechismum* precludes such an identification. Barnabas Oley's comment in the preface to *Herbert's Remains* should settle the issue: speaking of the translation of Carbo's work, he says 'the Authority at Cambridge suffered not that Egyptian jewell to be published': Barnabas Oley (ed.), *Herberts Remains, Or, Sundry Pieces of that Sweet singer of the Temple Mr. G. H.* (London, 1652). Charles's mistake might have arisen from John Ferrar's comment: 'as N. F. communicated his heart to him, so he made him the Peruser, & desired the approbation of what he did, as in those three Translations of Valdezzo, Lessius & Carbo. To the first Mr Herbert made an Epistle, To the second, he sent to add that of Cornarius temperance, & well approved of the last': Herbert, *Works*, 564. However, as Valdés's treatise was definitely published separately, it is hard to see why she felt the second two must have been published together.

[9] See William Laud, *The History of thee Troubles and Tryal of the Most Reverend Father in God, and Blessed Martyr, William Laud, Wrote by Himself* (London, 1695), 363.

the Ferrar family were working with the text of *An Introduction to the Devoute Life* before Herbert's death, Nicholas Ferrar would no doubt have discussed the treatise with him.

Louis Martz's analysis of the similarities between *An Introduction to the Devoute Life* and *The Temple* has been extremely influential in Herbert criticism, despite the lack of certainty that Herbert actually read de Sales' treatise. The basic thesis of *The Poetry of Meditation* is that 'the qualities developed by the "art of meditation"... are essentially the qualities that the twentieth century has admired in Donne, or Herbert, or Marvell.'[10] I hope to challenge the orthodoxy established by Martz that Counter-Reformation meditation is the rhetorical and spiritual mode adopted by Herbert. I will be showing that the attitude to religious language represented in *An Introduction to the Devoute Life* is actually alien to Reformation spirituality, and to much of Herbert's poetic practice, although there are superficial similarities in style, tone, and occasionally, form.

The Collusion of Spirituality with Rhetoric

Herbert was convinced of the necessity of the techniques of rhetoric in preaching to a congregation, as we saw in the last chapter:

there being two things in Sermons, the one Informing, the other Inflaming... [inflaming] must be done by a set, and laboured, and continued speech.[11]

However, the justification for using rhetoric in preaching, in terms of practical necessity, does not necessarily apply to poetry. As we have seen, Savonarola found it difficult to find a spiritual use for poetry even when attempting to defend it. Herbert may well have found relief from this asceticism in the European tradition of devotional rhetoric, the *utile-doux*, within which François de Sales was writing.[12] Herbert's admiration of French culture, which Martz noted, seems to have been focused on a regard for French eloquence, as he declares in a letter to his brother, then resident in Paris:

[10] Martz, *The Poetry of Meditation*, 2.
[11] Herbert, *Works*, 257.
[12] On the subject of the *utile-doux* in French devotional writing see Cave, *Devotional Poetry in France*, 59–62.

You live in a brave nation, where, except you wink, you cannot but see many brave examples. Bee covetous, then, of all good which you see in Frenchmen, whether it be in knowledge, or in fashion, or in words; for I would have you, even in speeches, to observe so much, as when you meet with a witty French speech, try to speak the like in English: so shall you play a good merchant, by transporting French commodities to your own country.[13]

It is tempting to argue that Herbert tried his hand at a similar import venture, 'transporting French commodities' in the form of translations of French eloquence. There was certainly a rich fund for a devotional poet such as Herbert to draw on. Devotional poetry had flourished in France during the second half of the sixteenth century, both in Calvinist and Catholic circles, in Latin and in the vernacular. At the time of this letter to his brother Henry, George Herbert was an aspiring young lecturer in rhetoric. Louis Martz argues that the books Henry bought for him were devotional treatises: but it is at least as likely that they were volumes of French poetry.[14]

An Introduction to the Devoute Life represents merely the summit of a vast European spiritual tradition which clearly affirms religious poetry. Poetry was profoundly integrated into the practice of Counter-Reformation devotion, as Terence Cave has demonstrated.[15] Unlike Savonarola, St François saw no incompatibility between the poetic muse and the Holy Spirit. His letter of encouragement to a would-be poet is whole-hearted in its praise of the poetic endeavour:

this learned piety which makes you so happily transform the Pagan into Christian muses, taking them from that old profane Parnassus, and putting them on the new sacred Calvary.[16]

Even when the poetry springs from Helicon rather than Jordan, it is not automatically rejected. François de Sales' friend, the Bishop

---

[13] Herbert, *Works*, 366.

[14] Martz, *The Poetry of Meditation*, 250. *An Introduction to the Devoute Life* had been available in England for several years by 1618, so it is unlikely to have been in the precious parcel of books which are described specifically in this letter as 'those Books which were not to be got in *England*'.

[15] Cave, *Devotional Poetry in France*, 203 and *passim*.

[16] St François de Sales, *Letters to Persons in the World*, Library of St. Francis de Sales, i, tr. H. B. Mackey, OSB (London, 1882), 185.

of Belley, describes a visit to a monk's cell, where St François was struck by some lines of poetry written on the wall:

our Blessed Father read and re-read these lines several times, thinking them so beautiful that he wished to engrave them on his memory, believing that they had been written by some Christian poet, perhaps Prudentius. Finding, however, that they were composed by a pagan, and on a profane subject, he said it was indeed a pity that so brilliant a burst of light should only have flashed out from the gross darkness of heathenism. 'However,' he continued, 'this good Father has made the vessels of the Egyptians into a tabernacle.'[17]

Even pagan poems may become the vehicle for the sacred, it seems. The monk who reverently engraved the poem on his wall transformed pagan poem into sacred text. The attention to context as the locus for the sacred in de Sales' writing, rather than source, as in Savonarola's vision, makes the sacred contingent upon exterior and variable conditions rather than interior motivation.

There was another, Protestant, devotional rhetoric developing in Europe, however. The Latin verse collections of such prominent Reformed poets as Marcantonio Flaminio and Theodore Beza, displaying a remarkable virtuosity of form in treating both sacred and profane subject-matter, testified to the validation of poetic discourse by European Protestants.[18] Beza's *Poemata*, edited by the Scottish scholar George Buchanan and published in Paris in 1576, a formidable feat of typography, contained Greek and Hebrew poems as well as classical Latin forms such as *Sylvae*, *Elegiae*, and *Epigrammata*. There were Latin paraphrases of the Psalms, a Greek and Latin paraphrase of the Song of Songs, and Latin elegies on famous Protestant reformers such as Calvin, Luther, Peter Martyr, and Melanchthon. The collection also contained a French verse tragedy, *Sacrifice d'Abraham*, and a few poems in the vernacular such as his sonnet on the death of Calvin. Such a comprehensive mixture of classical and contemporary, pagan and Christian, verse-forms, adapted for Reformed purposes, even the acrostic poem, 'NIHIL', is very much in the spirit

---

[17] St François de Sales, *The Spirit of St François de Sales, by his friend Jean Pierre Camus, bishop of Belley*, tr. J. S. (London, 1910), 337.

[18] Thomas Heywood, for example, translated epigrams by Beza, Marcantonio Flaminio, and other French and Italian poets. See his *Pleasant Dialogues and Dramma's, selected out of Lucan, Erasmus, Textor, Ovid* (London, 1637), 272–9.

of Herbert's own experimentation with both English and Latin genres of poetry. In Beza's anthology there are several *Carmina*, including one addressed to the French Protestant poet du Bartas, acknowledging an explicit debt to du Bartas' conscious annexation of the classical muse for Protestant poetry, a *divine fureur* to replace a poetic frenzy, in the 1574 publication of *La Muse Chrestienne*. Beza's concern to relate genre and spirituality is shown in the Latin version of his Psalms published in London in 1580, in which he gives a lengthy introduction to each Psalm, justifying his choice of genre and stanza form. This is precisely the kind of activity congenial to Herbert, as we shall see: the poet who valued Calvinist orthodoxy and classical scholarship might well have been inspired by a tradition which provided both.

Counter-Reformation Devotional Poetry and Herbert's Poetic Practice

Louis Martz links the lyrics of *The Temple* with Ignatian meditational practice through one of St François' recommended preparations for meditation in *An Introduction to the Devoute Life*. This 'interiour lecture' is seen by de Sales as distinctive of his own brand of spirituality, 'not common unto all sorts of meditations':

This is nothing els, but to represent unto thy imagination, the summe and substance of the mysterie which thou wilt meditate, and to paint it out in thy thoughts so livelie, as though it passed reallie and verilie in thy presence.[19]

As with the words of the set prayer, the task of the meditator is to activate the written word, not for the benefit of others, but for himself. The element of immediate experience has to be recovered: in 'interiour lecture' imagination supplies the immediacy which will provoke the emotion which is the stamp of effective prayer. With set prayer and biblical passages the reader has to appropriate the words and use them as if they were his own, very much in the way Herbert suggests to his own reader, who should 'thrust his heart | Into these lines'.[20] The aim of meditation on a text is that the reader will enter into it, not just as a spectator of events, but as a participant in the sacred drama: François de Sales

[19] St François de Sales, *An Introduction to the Devoute Life, composed in Frenche by the R. Father in God Francis Sales, bishop of Geneva, and translated into English by I. Y.* (Douai, 1613), 138.
[20] Herbert, *Works*, 105.

envisages conversation with 'persons represented in the mysterie which we meditate'.[21] This is exactly the stuff of Counter-Reformation devotional poetry, and of Herbert's Latin verse cycles. In *Lucus*, for instance, the poet addresses such Biblical figures as Martha, Luke, Doubting Thomas, and Simon the Magus, as well as Christ himself.

The neo-Latin branch of this French literary tradition, often ignored in modern criticism, is likely to have been of great interest to Herbert, particularly in his days as University Orator at Cambridge, when his interest in neo-Latin wit would have been a professional one. There is evidence, through epigrams copied into commonplace books, that Herbert circulated his Latin verse within an intellectual community.[22] At least one epigram, the anagram 'ROMA', reached Cardinal Maffeo Barberini, at some point before or during 1620. He wrote a reply, which Herbert must have read in the 1623 edition of Barberini's *Poemata*, after he became Urban VIII.[23] Herbert's two sacred Latin collections, *Lucus* and *Passio Discerpta*, are directly in the Continental neo-Latin style, as is the only work to be published in Herbert's lifetime, *Memoriae Matris Sacrum*. Both show the experimentation with metre and stanza form typical both of French collections and of Herbert's own English poetry. The Latin cycle *Passio Discerpta* displays many of the features of Counter-Reformation devotional poetry. The subjects of the epigrams, with the concentration on the more physical and macabre elements of the Passion, are typical: 'On the bloody sweat', 'On the pierced side', 'On the whip', 'On the crown of thorns', 'On the slaps', 'On the poisoned garments', 'On the nails', 'On the bowed head'. The *Théorèmes* of Jean de la Ceppède, a long series of sonnets on the events of the Passion, published in 1613, contain many verbal parallels with Herbert's collection which may be little more than the coincidence of subject-matter. However, the similarity between certain of Ceppède's sonnets and Herbert's epigrams is striking. For

[21] Sales, *An Introduction to the Devoute Life*, 153.

[22] See R. Ray, 'The Herbert Allusion Book: Allusions to George Herbert in the Seventeenth Century', *Studies in Philology*, 83 (1986), 2–4 for evidence of Herbert's Latin poetry appearing in commonplace books before 1630.

[23] W. H. Kelliher, 'The Latin Poetry of George Herbert', in J. W. Binns (ed.), *The Latin Poetry of English Poets* (London, 1974), 139. Hutchinson obviously did not know this edition and thinks Herbert may have written the Pope's reply himself.

instance, epigram 16 of *Passio discerpta*, 'Ad Solem deficientem', shares the same conceit of Ceppède's sonnet 65: the sun shows himself a good servant by depriving himself of the light, just as his Master has been. Ceppède's sonnets are elaborately typological, and the wittiest of them exactly match the tone of Herbert's epigrams. The central conceit of one of the most anthologized of Ceppède's poems, the so-called 'red' sonnet, is the same as the conceit that Herbert uses in his epigram on the 'red' robe of Christ, and that Crashaw uses in 'Upon the Body of Our Blessed Lord, Naked and Bloody'.[24] There are links too with the poetic practice of Robert Southwell, the English Jesuit, whose poem on 'Christs bloody sweat' involves elaborate Ignatian 'composition of place', and extreme rhetorical conceits. In his series of poems on the Passion, including the epigram 'On the bloody sweat', which is similar to Southwell's, Herbert never indulges in composition of place.[25] He is more concerned with wit, drawing a spiritual significance out of his punning and metaphorical discourse. The treatment of the subjects is ostentatiously rhetorical, with every kind of wit displayed, and rhetorical ingenuity which sometimes verges on the distasteful. Odette de Mourges characterizes this kind of poetry as 'baroque', and concludes 'such motifs and metaphors ... are part of a ritual and not the metaphorical expression of the poet's inner experience'.[26] Herbert's first biographer, Barnabas Oley, makes a similar kind of negative judgement. In the Latin poetry, he says, Herbert 'made his ink with water of Helicon': the English poetry, 'these preparations prophet-icall', however, were 'distilled from above'. Spelling out what he sees to be a difference in inspiration, Oley concludes: 'in those are the weake motions of Nature, in these Raptures of Grace.'[27] The very closeness of the imitation of Counter-Reformation rhetorical mode in *Passio Discerpta*, which was never published, indicates an

---

[24] O. de Mourges (ed.), *Anthology of French Seventeenth-Century Lyric Poetry* (Oxford, 1960), 70. See also sonnet 62, in F. Ruchon (ed.), *Essai sur la vie et l'œuvre de Jean de la Ceppède*, (Geneva, 1953), 58. Compare Herbert's epigram, 'In Arund. Spin. Genuflex. Purpur.', *Works*, 405.

[25] A. D. Cousins, *The Catholic Religious Poets from Southwell to Crashaw: A Critical Study* (London, 1991), 52.

[26] O. de Mourges, *Metaphysical, Baroque and Précieux Poetry* (Oxford, 1953), 81.

[27] Barnabas Oley (ed.), *Herberts Remains, Or, Sundry Pieces of that Sweet Singer of the Temple, Mr. G. H., sometime Orator of the University of Cambridge, Now exposed to Public Light* (London, 1652), sig. b7ʳ.

experiment with this mode of Christian rhetoric that was ultimately rejected.

Herbert's cycles of Latin verse were completed before the final
version of *The Temple*, as their inclusion in the Williams manuscript makes clear, and it seems that the neo-Latin rhetoric and
the echoes of Counter-Reformation spirituality were not the final
choice for his brand of Christian poetry. Herbert's own use of the
Continental devotional tradition in *The Temple* illustrates the
difference between Catholic rhetoric and his own Protestant
poetry. Herbert's 'The Sacrifice', as Louis Martz has pointed
out, *pace* Rosamund Tuve, is clearly as much in the European
meditative tradition as in the medieval lyric tradition.[28] This
poem is unusual in Herbert's English poetry in that it attempts
to place the reader directly at the scene of the Cross. However, in
comparison with Continental models Herbert's visualization of
the scene of the Passion is remarkable for its restraint. The simple
dignity of the direct address, the telling of the Passion narrative in
bare detail, and the stark stanza form throw emphasis on the
saving truths to be assimilated inwardly by the readers. In fact,
there is scarcely any visual detail in the poem. In the Protestant
world, no imaginative effort is needed to approach the figure of
the suffering Christ, only a belief that the combination of sacred
word and Holy Spirit can cover the distance in time and space so
that the Son of God can speak directly from the pages of a book.
'The Sacrifice' uses the 'O vos omnes' topos, written down by
Jeremiah in 580 BC, which in Herbert's hands becomes an
address from the eternal God directly into the world of the
seventeenth-century believer, via the first-century Passion.

Herbert is fond of dramatizing such mysteries as 'Redemption'
and 'Judgement': and his poem 'Love (iii)' is perhaps 'interiour
lecture' at its most 'lively'. It is possible to view some of Herbert's
lyrics—'The Bag', for example—as examples of just this imaginative meditation. However, as the exercises in *An Introduction to the
Devoute Life* demonstrate, Counter-Reformation meditation is a
vehicle for the Christian to push his way into the crowd of

---

[28] See Martz, *The Poetry of Meditation*, 91–6; R. Tuve, *A Reading of George Herbert* (London,
1952), 19–99. Terence Cave has traced the history of the 'O vos omnes' topos in creating a
locus compositus for meditation on the love of Christ as revealed in the Passion. See Cave,
Devotional Poetry in France, 262–3.

spectators at any biblical event. His life and the divine story meet only in the imaginative spaces of the text. In a Protestant view of Scripture, however, the Christian reader does not have to 'thrust' his way into the sacred text—he is already there. This profound participation in the text is described in Herbert's sonnet on the Bible, 'The H. Scriptures (ii)':

> Such are thy secrets, which my life makes good,
> And comments on thee: for in ev'ry thing
> Thy words do find me out, & parallels bring,
> And in another make me understood.

There is a mutual hermeneutics going on here. Not only is Herbert's life made sense of by the biblical story, but in some way his own experience helps to interpret the biblical text. In many ways, the text is about him. The sacred text, like its author, knows no limits of space, time, or influence: every believer in every epoch is a potential character in the story.[29] For Protestants, the experience of participation in the biblical text is not a product of the imagination, as François de Sales appears to believe: the living Word is able to speak directly to the believer.[30]

Herbert's poems make use of literary devices in an aggressive application of biblical narrative to the life of the seventeenth-century Christian: 'Christmas' takes place in a Jacobean inn, whilst 'Redemption' describes a seventeenth-century rent crisis. However, this is only an imaginative realization of what the sacred text already does. Calvin maintained that the distance in time and space between first-century Palestine and sixteenth-century France is covered through the biblical literary devices such as symbol and metonymy, guaranteed as true and of immediate application by the Holy Spirit.[31] The Protestant vision

---

[29] Augustine articulates this notion of the universal particularity of the Scriptures in *De Doctrina Christiana*. See Augustine, *On Christian Doctrine*, tr. D. W. Robertson Jr. (New York, 1958), 102.

[30] I think it can be demonstrated that 'interiour lecture' does not have the same status for St François as it would have for Protestants. In a telling comment from his letter on preaching he warns that any imaginary dialogues with biblical characters produced in meditation should not be shared with the congregation in a sermon: *Œuvres de Saint François de Sales: Édition complète*, 12 vol. (Annecy, 1912), xii. 313.

[31] See John Calvin, *The Institution of the Christian Religion*, tr. Thomas Norton (London, 1578), IV. xvii. 10, p. 572 on the Lord's Supper. The symbol with its congruity of sign and signified mediates the presence of Christ through the power of the Holy Spirit, which 'knitteth in one those things that are severed in places'.

is that the language of the Scriptures moves towards the believer in his own situation, whereas St François' Counter-Reformation spirituality involves the imaginative effort of meditation. The role of the visual imagination, however, is less crucial to a Protestant spirituality and poetics. The Protestant in meditation can bypass the visualization process because the text will speak to him where he is, without any possibility of misinterpretation. He does not need the stimulation of the use of the imagination, or its concomitant restraints. The result is a less rhetorical spirituality than that of de Sales, and a poetics that concentrates less on the visual description of a biblical event, and more on its significance for a modern reader. The poetry of Protestant meditation as practised by Herbert has a rather different set of characteristics from that of Counter-Reformation spirituality.

Invocatory Discourse: Self-Persuasion, or the Presence of God?

It is true that in claiming the influence of de Sales on Herbert, Louis Martz concentrates less on visual meditative techniques than on an intimate conversational tone which he finds in both writers. Martz's chapter is entitled 'In the Presence of a Friend', a description of de Sales' familiar and emotional spirituality which Martz proceeds to apply to Herbert. However, the notion of 'presence' actually draws attention to one of the main differences between de Sales and Herbert. Martz finds in *An Introduction to the Devoute Life* a precise description of Herbert's *Temple*: 'our spirit once giving itself entirelie to the companie, hant and familiaritie of his God, must needs be all perfumed, with the odiferous ayre of his perfections.' However, having found some poems which support this statement Martz quickly finds himself dealing with exceptions to the rule, such as 'Deniall'.[32] St François, with other Counter-Reformation writers, starts from the position that God is always present to the believer. Martz describes this as a basic assumption of post-Ignatian meditation: 'that man, whether he will or not, lives in the intimate presence of God, and that his first duty in life is to cultivate an awareness of that presence.'[33] The task of meditation is to produce the emotions appropriate to

---

[32] See Martz, *The Poetry of Meditation*, 254–5.
[33] L. L. Martz, *The Poem of the Mind* (New York, 1966), 34.

the presence of God, and the ideal tool for producing the correct emotions is rhetoric. Herbert, however, pays only lip-service to the doctrine that God never leaves the believer. He mentions it only in parenthesis in a poem which strongly realizes the sense of absence, 'A Parodie':

> Souls joy, when thou art gone,
> And I alone,
> Which cannot be,
> Because thou dost abide with me,
> And I depend on thee.[34]

Since it is a theological truth that God is always with the believer, real absence has to be reformulated as felt absence.

> Yet when thou dost suppresse
> The cheerfulnesse
> Of thy abode,
> And in my powers not stirre abroad,
> But leave me to my load:
> O what a damp and shade
> Doth me invade!

Herbert sees the sensation of absence as God's responsibility. The natural emotional response of the believer to God's presence is deliberately removed—suppressed—by God. He refuses to move the emotions that are the evidence of His presence. The resulting effect is no different from that of actual absence. Sinne, therefore, has fertile ground for his insinuation that God has deserted the believer, although the truth is apparently that God's presence is felt 'lesse cleare'. However, the argument, although not the battle, is conceded to Sinne in the resolution of the poem.

> I half beleeve,
> That Sinne says true: but while I grieve,
> Thou com'st and dost relieve.

There is no difference between felt absence and real absence, as the active word 'com'st' of the final line betrays. In other poems, such as 'Home', 'The Search', 'Longing', and 'The Temper (ii)' Herbert does not even try to qualify the sense of abandonment with any theological truisms. Rhetoric is not the answer, as it can

---

[34] Herbert, *Works*, 183.

have no power with God: and only God can 'stirre' the sensations of presence.

This fundamental difference in approach to God gives Herbert's writing a rather different character to that of de Sales'. The second of the 'poynts of preparation' suggested by de Sales, although it figures large in the work of Herbert, fulfils a rather different function. It is a form of address that is traditionally powerful, and potentially performative: invocation.[35] 'Invocation' was used in the early seventeenth century to describe the act of calling upon God in prayer, a speech act without inevitable associations of the performative. However, alongside the Christian use of the term there had always been the pagan sense, 'to summon'. This is a classically performative act as defined by J. L. Austin. The act of reciting the correct incantation produces the presence of the spirit thus invoked. It is no wonder that invocation of God was often used in specific reference to requesting his presence. As François de Sales uses the term, in the established context of realizing God's presence, it cannot fail to have associations of 'summoning'. Herbert, with his Calvinist sense of the overwhelming sovereignty of God, cannot finally believe that God has limited himself to any rhetorical convention: but that does not prevent him trying every verbal formulation available.[36]

As would be expected from one whose emotional state and general well-being depends on a sense of presence, Herbert's poems are often invocatory, whether in the assured incantatory rhetoric of 'The Call' or the more desperate pleas of 'Longing'. St François, however, has already assured Philotheus of God's constant presence. Thus the invocatory words he recommends from the Psalms have a strangely negative direction. It would be

[35] 'Invocation' appears to have been regarded as a performative by J. L. Austin, in that he conceived of 'misinvocation' occurring. See *How To Do Things With Words* (Oxford, 1962), 17. However, it is not easy to see how the presence of God can be seen as a 'conventional effect' of a set of conventional words. Certainly neither François de Sales nor Herbert conceive of the effect of words as automatic in this way, but both of them make gestures towards harnessing the performative associations of invocation, i.e. that the use of a certain style of address may have an effect upon God.

[36] See 'Artillerie', where the poet uses the argument that God has limited himself by his promise to answer prayer, only to reject it in the final stanza. Richard Strier describes this as 'an assertion of the Nominalist terror at the core of Calvinist piety': see *Love Known: Theology and Experience in George Herbert's Poetry* (Chicago, 1983), 104.

inconsistent to summon a God who is already present: instead he asks that God will not become absent.

Cast me not (O God) from thy face: take not from me the favour of thy holy spirit. Suffer thy face to shine upon thy seruant.[37]

It is strange that St François recommended any kind of invocation at all, and it is hard to escape the conclusion that his kind of invocation is entirely self-referential. If Philotheus consciously uses the traditionally powerful form of invocation, he is more likely to believe in the subsequent presence of God. The utterance described here uses many of the conventions of the performative speech act of invocation: but it may be that it is performative only of self-persuasion, in that Philotheus needs to believe in the power of his own prayer.

To ensure success, de Sales recommends 'short and inflamed words'.[38] This is the only time St François mentions a stylistic criterion, and he does it in order to exploit the performative associations of such short words in invocation. St François probably knew *The Cloud of Unknowing*, and this seems to be a nod towards it.[39] The imagery of love and fire, and the concept of the soul, inflamed with love, expressing itself to God in powerful words, are common to both works, and to other mystical writers of the sixteenth century such as Louis de Blois. The short prayer pierces heaven because the whole soul is concentrated into it:

whi peersiþ it heue*n*, þis lityl schort preier of o litil silable? Sikirly for it is pr*e*yed wiþ a fulle spirite, in þe heiȝt & in þe depnes, in þe lengþe & in þe breed of his spirit þat pr*e*ieþ it.[40]

However, the short prayer of *The Cloud of Unknowing* is really short: 'þis lityl schort preier of o litil silable.' The brevity of St François de Sales' prayers is relative. His short prayer of invocation takes up seven lines, and there is nothing particularly 'short' about the words he uses, although being quoted from the Psalms of David, they would probably have been considered 'inflamed'. The two authors are speaking from roughly opposite positions. The author

---

[37] Sales, *An Introduction to the Devoute Life*, 136–7.

[38] Ibid. 136.

[39] This is the opinion of René Tixier, a French scholar who works on *The Cloud of Unknowing* (personal communication). No published work on the dissemination of *The Cloud of Unknowing* in France exists.

[40] *The Cloud of Unknowing*, ed. P. Hodgson, Early English Text Society (Oxford, 1957), 75.

of *The Cloud* is suspicious of all images, and sensual detail, and his suspicion extends to words. The overwhelming tendency of *The Cloud of Unknowing* is towards wordless, imageless experience: its author allows the short prayer lest he should seem to fall into the heresy of separating body and soul.[41] The Counter-Reformation devotion represented by François de Sales embraces the world of the senses, including pictorial representation and rhetoric, as a way of reaching the soul, envisaging no gulf between body and spirit.[42] The recommendation of 'short and inflamed words' is more a gesture towards the mystic tradition of powerful, silent prayer than a manifestation of suspicion towards rhetoric. The speaker of an invocatory prayer is more likely to have faith in its performative power if he uses the conventional discourse of invocation. This annexation of a major mystical insight for stylistic purposes is typical of de Sales' eclectic and rhetorical spirituality.

Herbert's suspicion of rhetoric is real if intermittent, as we have seen. He literally uses 'short and inflamed words', in both invocatory moods, the desperate and the confident. 'The Call' is a formal invocation, and seems well adapted to use by others: it focuses less on an individual's emotion and more on generalized truth. It is absolutely regular in metrical and rhetorical structure, and extraordinary in that all the words (apart from 'killeth' in the first stanza) are monosyllabic. The repetition of syntactical units perfectly matched with the line divisions gives the hypnotic effect of an incantation: certainly the remorseless regularity of the poem presents a smooth surface into which it is hard to ask the questions that are so explicitly raised in 'Longing'. Despite being identical in form, each stanza has a slightly different movement which is not obvious at first. The first stanza rehearses the three names of Christ as revealed by the Lord Himself in John 14: 6, then takes each one and adds more conceptual content to it. The discourse is limpidly clear and the thought very simple, so that there is no distraction from the direction of the poem, which is primarily a prayer for God's presence.

Stanza 2 is slightly different in structure. The pattern of summoning God by three different names is repeated, but they are not the more obvious and well-known ones of stanza 1. These epithets are more idiosyncratic, and need more explaining: 'my

[41] *The Cloud of Unknowing*, ed. Hodgson, 90.
[42] Cave, *Devotional Poetry in France*, 6.

Light, my Feast, my Strength.' The personal nature of these descriptions is illustrated in the following three lines: each of these is shown to interact in a relationship of love and presence with the believer. The Light shows the believer the feast that has been prepared for him; the spiritual Feast improves as time goes on; the strength of God which maintains the endless feast also turns the believer into a guest. These are not obvious or simple steps in reasoning, but the ease with which the metre moves on lures the speaker into a declaration of the reality of the presence he is seeking. By the end of stanza 2 the structures of the syntax have already made God present, and turned the speaker into a guest at God's banquet. The divine presence is confirmed by the fact that the rest of the poem, although apparently continuing the invocatory form, is an intimate celebration of the emotional affect of the immediate presence of God.

> Come, my *Joy*, my *Love*, my *Heart*.
> Such a *Joy* as none can move:
> Such a *Love* as none can part:
> Such a *Heart*, as joyes in love.[43]

There is no shadow of parting envisaged at the end of this poem. Its success depends partly on its traditional invocatory mode (a rhetorical technique which presumably has more impact on the speaker himself than on God) and partly on the fact that there is no sense of absence at the start. The invocatory words have achieved less than one might have expected. The lack of a real sense of invocation is betrayed by the last three lines of each stanza, which are certainly not for God's benefit, since each of the lines describes an attribute of His, and presumably He knows all about these already. The fact that the poem could begin so lovingly and confidently reveals that God was present at the

---

[43] I have chosen the typographical layout and punctuation of the B MS here. I agree with Mario di Cesare that B represents Herbert's intentions better than the first edition of 1633. See George Herbert, *The Bodleian Manuscript of George Herbert's Poems*, ed. with introd. by A. M. Charles and M. A. di Cesare (New York, 1984), xxx. Mario di Cesare finds that Thomas Buck, the editor of the first edition, regularizes excessively: 'his notions were clear and well-defined, but there is no evidence that these notions were well-suited to the subtle workings of a major poet.' In a comparison with the Bodleian manuscript (see Herbert, *Works*, 156) I think it will be seen that Buck has over-punctuated to emphasize the syntactic units. I think that the punctuation and emphasis of B is much more effective here in recreating the very personal and emotional tone of stanza 3.

beginning: what the poem has achieved, by providing the speaker with a more definite image of the God he is invoking, is a deeper sense of that presence. This is the type of invocation envisaged by St François de Sales, one that is optimistic about two crucial factors: the constant reality of God's presence, and the power of rhetoric to bring about the experience of that reality.

'The Call', however, represents the one example of formal invocation in the collection of lyric forms that is *The Temple*, and the fact that it is exceptional shows that the tone of Herbert's spirituality is essentially very different from that of de Sales. Herbert's other, more frequent kind of invocation conjures up a sense of devastating absence.

> Wilt thou deferre
> To succour me,
> Thy pile of dust, wherein each crumme
> Sayes, Come?[44]

The stanza form of 'Longing' consists of three short lines and two long ones, designed to throw even greater emphasis onto the last and shortest disyllabic line, which contains the force of the prayer: 'No end?'; 'And heare!'; 'No key?'[45] The poem rehearses a series of theological and emotional arguments which should invoke the presence of God. The unbearable suffering of the believer without God is described in the strongest terms. The absolute compassion of God and his express redeeming purpose in Christ's first coming to earth is appealed to. Everything that is known about God indicates that He should answer the plea of the believer whose privileged title has acquired a bitter irony:

> yet am I stil'd
> Thy childe.

The disjointed stanza form combines with the urgent, broken exclamations to produce a sense of spontaneous expression of the very emotion that is the name of the poem: 'Longing'. In

[44] Herbert, *Works*, 149.

[45] Barbara Lewalski (*Protestant Poetics and the Seventeenth-Century Religious Lyric* (Princeton, 1970), 242) has noted the similarity between this mode of Herbert's poetry and Sidney's version of the 13th Psalm, on the same theme of absence. This is the first stanza. Note the frequent questions emphasized by the short exclamations, and the alternation of long and short lines: 'How long (O Lord) shall I forgotten be? | What? ever? | How long wilt thou thy hidden face from me | Dissever?'

fact, despite the apparent aim of the poem, to achieve the presence of God, this poem does not function as an invocation at all; its success is due to its expression of a sense of absence, rather than its expectation of a sense of presence. Such negative emotion, as we shall see, is well outside the spectrum considered appropriate for Counter-Reformation meditation.

Meditation and Preaching: Human Rhetoric or Spiritual 'Motions'?

In *An Introduction to the Devoute Life*, meditation proper, 'the acte of our understanding', follows 'the acts of imagination', and turns out to be profoundly word-centred, although not necessarily text-centred or literary. St François defines it as

one, or many considerations made by our reason, to stirre up our affections to God, and Godly things.[46]

It is clear from the examples de Sales gives in Book I that a Consideration contains one aspect of the subject for meditation, written briefly in pithy language. These Considerations are not necessarily spontaneous compositions by the meditating Christian. François de Sales sets out a series of meditations in Book I, to be followed in detail.[47] As Louis Martz comments, de Sales' method of meditation is 'deeply indebted to the Jesuits but less rigorous, less fearsome, less intellectual'.[48] He finds six poems in *The Temple* which follow de Sales's looser meditative structures.[49] However, since de Sales' structures follow the familiar pattern of classical rhetoric, such similarities are not surprising. 'Interiour lecture', for example, the rehearsing of biblical events *sub oculos*, is the same activity as is involved in the rhetorical figure *enargeia*, represented by Quintilian as being one of the most effective ways

---

[46] Sales, *Introduction to the Devoute Life*, 141.

[47] Ibid. 64. Here, for example, are the Considerations in a meditation on creation: '1. Consider that there are but so many years past, when thou wast not yet come into the world, & thy being was a iust nothinge. Where were we (o my soule) in that time? The world had then lasted so many ages, and yet there was no newes of us. 2. God hath caused thee to be hatcht of this nothing, to be this somethinge which now thou art: without having any maner of neede of thee, but moved therunto by his only bountie. 3. Consider the being that God hath given thee, for it is the chiefest and most excellentst in the visible worlde: capable to live eternally: and to unite thy selfe perfectly unto his divine maiestie.'

[48] Martz, *The Poetry of Meditation*, 56.

[49] 'Life', 'Man', 'The Crosse', 'Affliction (v)', 'Confession', 'Grieve not the Holy Spirit'.

of moving the emotions of an audience.[50] The enumeration of the various aspects of the subject for meditation is very similar to the process of *inventio* in rhetoric. The purpose is to produce 'good motions in our will, or the affective part of our soule', just as the aim of classical rhetoric is to move the passions. The 'devout motion' has the effect of inflaming the affections, which is exactly the result intended by Herbert in his preaching.[51] The techniques suggested by St François de Sales turn out to be adaptations of the most powerful devices of affective rhetoric. Meditation is a kind of preaching to oneself, in which all the strategies of ecclesiastical oratory are employed.[52] A 'poetry of meditation', then, rather than following a precise meditative structure, would employ the same rhetorical strategies as preaching in order to annex affective power.

Reformed theologians also adopted the strategies of classical rhetoric for their sermons. In 1577 a manual of sermon rhetoric was published in England: a translation of a work by the Protestant Andreas Hyperius, entitled *The Practise of preaching, otherwise called the Pathway to the Pulpit*.[53] The work is a scholarly and thorough adaptation of classical rhetoric for preaching purposes, and it includes advice on meditation. As Herbert was to do in *The Country Parson*, Hyperius takes as his starting-point the necessity for the pastor of 'vulgar people' to use all the techniques of affective rhetoric to make any impression on his unresponsive audience.[54]

---

[50] Quintilian, *Institutio Oratoria*, tr. H. E. Butler, 4 vols. (London, 1921), iii. 437.

[51] Herbert, *Works*, 233, 257.

[52] See Lewalski, *Protestant Poetics*, 152–4 for the similarity between sermon and meditation in Protestant theory.

[53] See also Nicholas Hemminge, *The Preacher, or Methode of preaching*, tr. I. H. (London, 1574), which adopts a similar position to that of Andreas Hyperius.

[54] The similarities between preaching and meditation characteristic of Hyperius' treatise are apparent in de Sales' letter on preaching. Most of the examples of sermon plans enumerated by him are based on Scriptural stories, and he suggests various ways of involving the congregation in the drama. The preacher may concentrate on the various characters and their responses to the events in the text. He may make considerations of the same kind as those featured in his meditations: what we can learn which builds hope, what will inflame our love, what there is to imitate. Everywhere is stressed the aim of preaching, which is to make the congregation love and practise virtue, whilst hating and resisting vice. This affective and practical end is described as 'la maistresse ... de toutes choses', including the form and language of the sermon, so it is no surprise that the first half is to be given over to instruction, and the second half to moving of the congregation. The pattern is very close to that set out for meditation in *An Introduction to the Devoute Life*: first is a reading of the text, then the forming of rational considerations, then the use of similitudes, and finally practical examples from saints' lives. See St François de Sales, *Œuvres* xii. 303, 319. The

The section on meditation is included in advice on how 'to styrre up the motions of the minde' of the congregation, an effect which is the primary aim of all Protestant preachers. The principle adopted is the time-honoured one of Cicero and Quintilian, that the orator should stir up emotions in his own mind before he tries to evoke them in others.

> Before all things it is very necessary that hee which speaketh doe conceyve such lyke affections in his mynde, and rayse them upp in himselfe, yea, and others, as hee coveteth to be translated into the myndes of his auditors.[55]

The words of the sermon are simply the vehicle for an emotional state, 'translating' the speaker's consciousness into that of his hearers. This ability to transfer the contents of the orator's mind to those of his audience constituted the very definition of 'eloquence' for Quintilian.[56] The production of a state of internal holy emotion is thus a vital preparation for preaching. Hyperius recommends four procedures for producing it, of which the second exactly resembles St François de Sales' 'interiour lecture':

> by a vehement imagination or fantasy, when a man with most attentive cogitation apprehendeth, and depaynteth to himselfe the formes and simylitudes of the thinges whereof he entreateth, which afterwards he so fixeth & setleth in his minde, as if his owne private cause were in handling, and as though he should perpetually muse uppon that thinge alone.[57]

This is just the combination of concentration and imagination that François de Sales requires for effective meditation. St François also suggests meditation immediately before the sermon.[58] The meditating individual finds personal space within the biblical text: the job of the preacher is then to mediate that sense of particularity to his congregation, in the way that George Herbert also describes.

---

function of similitudes, which, as Louis Martz notes, includes 'any kind of parable, allegory, simile or metaphor', is particularly vital for the co-operation of God and preacher in moving the congregation. See Martz, *The Poem of the Mind*, 36.

[55] Cicero, *De oratore*, tr. E. W. Sutton (London, 1952), 335; Quintilian, *Institutio Oratoria* iii. 431; Andreas Hyperius, *The Practise of preaching, otherwise called the Pathway to the Pulpit*, tr. John Ludham (London, 1577), 43.

[56] Quintilian, *Institutio Oratoria*, iii. 185.

[57] Hyperius, *The Practise of preaching*, 43^r.

[58] Sales, *Œuvres*, xii. 323.

When he preacheth, he procures attention by all possible art...with particularizing of his speech now to the younger sort, then to the elder, now to the poor, and now to the rich. This is for you, and This is for you; for particulars ever touch, and awake more then generalls.[59]

The desired effect of preaching, as portrayed by Hyperius in *The Pathway to the Pulpit*, is described in terms of internal 'motion'. Hyperius' list of motions is very similar to St François', recounting the affections to be excited in a responsive congregation: 'care of obteyning salvation', 'sorrowe for offences committed', 'lothsom-nesses & hatred of sinnes', 'loue of vertue', 'feare of gods iudge-ment', 'compassion and love towards our neighbour'.[60] Hyperius' treatise is a strange mixture of the spiritual and the pragmatic, sandwiching Christian prayer for inspiration between two expli-citly classical methods in his recipe for success in oratory.[61] George Herbert's ideas about preaching show evidence of similar eclecticism. For him, too, the most important element of the sermon is the wordless communication of God which is 'motion':

Oh my Master, on whose errand I come, let me hold my peace, and doe thou speak thy selfe; for thou art Love, and when thou teachest, all are Scholers.[62]

As we have seen, however, this public threat to cease speaking is also a technique of oratory, and it would be difficult to distinguish the results of an answer to this prayer from the effect on the congregation of its powerful rhetoric. Indeed, it is hard to escape the suggestion here, as in Hyperius' treatise, that the 'moving' impact of rhetoric and the 'motion' of the Holy Spirit are ident-ical in nature. The similarity of the vocabulary defining the nature and function of each implies that the first is almost a highly effective substitute for the second. Hyperius is at pains to stress, with Augustine, that the rhetoric will not work 'unlesse God by his interior grace, governe and worke in the harte'.[63] However, he finds it difficult to distinguish between the motions produced by the Holy Spirit and the affections stirred up by efficient oratory. The most crucial ingredient for the Christian preacher is 'spirit or

---

[59] Herbert, *Works*, 233.
[60] Hyperius, *The Practise of preaching*, 41[r].
[61] Ibid. 44[r].
[62] Herbert, *Works*, 233.
[63] Hyperius, *The Practise of preaching*, 43[r].

power in teaching', which resembles nothing so much, in Hyperius' treatise, as the rhetorical ability to move the emotions of the congregation.[64] Any rhetorical strategy is permissible in order to produce spiritual 'motions': 'all cunning may be used in moving to truth & constancy', he declares, with little scruple about ends and means.[65] By contrast, Herbert seems to want to reserve the word 'motion' for the effect of the moving of the Holy Spirit, never claiming sacred status for his own words. In 'Artillerie' a 'motion' is a direct, silent communication from God, as it is in Herbert's comments on Valdés' forty-ninth and sixty-second Considerations.[66] In 'The Method' a motion can also be a holy impulse from within the believer, as in 'Lent'. Hyperius, however, in *The Practise of preaching*, seems to use 'motion' and 'affection' interchangeably.[67]

The Priority of Words over Silent 'Motions' in François de Sales' Writing

Despite the attention given to human words in *The Practise of preaching*, the most important part of both preaching and prayer is a supernatural silence, and the same is true of meditation in *An Introduction to the Devoute Life*. The rhetorical strategies in *An Introduction to the Devoute Life* outlined so far are merely the preparation for the climax of meditation that follows the making of Considerations. This element is called, variously, 'affections', 'spiritual acts', or 'motions'. Meditation 'poureth out abundance of good motions' says de Sales. As well as the imitation of Christ and desire of Paradise, he mentions zeal of salvation of souls, hatred of sin, confidence in God, fear of hell, shame for the past, compassion, and joy.[68] These are very similar to Hyperius' list of 'motions': not quite ordinary human 'emotions', but those feelings which are specifically useful in a sacred context (shame, compassion, joy) and most likely to lead to discourse and behaviour which is appropriate to Christians. This is a highly sophisticated

---

[64] Ibid. 6ʳ.

[65] Ibid. 42ʳ. See Barbara Lewalski's account of Joseph Hall's *Arte of Divine Meditation*: 'he declares any manner of analysis acceptable which can achieve the primary end of meditation—as also of the Protestant sermon—the stirring of the heart': Lewalski, *Protestant Poetics*, 153.

[66] Herbert, *Works*, 139, 313, 316.

[67] Hyperius, *The Practise of preaching*, 42ʳ. Notice, however, that he does insist on a difference between the types of emotion stirred up by orators and preachers: see p. 41ʳ.

[68] Sales, *Introduction to the Devoute Life*, 143.

development of the role of the affections in meditation: as the *Dictionnaire de spiritualité* puts it, in de Sales' work 'the affections appear primarily as a necessary intermediary between ideas and acts of the will, an indispensable preparation for true and effective resolutions.'[69] These 'motions', like those in Savonarola's text, are the source of change in the Christian's behaviour. However, Savonarola's 'motions', as we have seen, are wordless impulses directly from the Holy Spirit: in *An Introduction to the Devoute Life* they are generated from within the Christian psyche by the tried and tested means of classical rhetoric, which Savonarola repudiated.

In theory, if not in practice, François de Sales can consider leaving verbal meditation unfinished. Even at the very start of meditation, in that most unmystical activity of reciting vocal prayers, the soul may experience the direct prompting of God, and this is not to be ignored, insists de Sales: 'refuse not to go where this good motion inuiteth thee, but let thy spirit decline faire and softly on that side.'[70] After the three points of preparation, it is even more likely that God will take over.

Many times immediately after preparation, thy affection wilbe altogether fired, and inflamed, with devotion to God: and then Philotheus, thou must lett go the bridle to thy affections: that they may runne freely after the inviting of Gods spirit, without keeping that method which I haue set downe. For although ordinarilie, considerations ought to goe before affections and resolutions: yet nevertheless, when the holy Ghost poureth foorth devout affections, and holy motions in to thy soule without discourse and consideration, thou must not then spend time in discourcing the points of thy exercise; for those discources serue for no other end, but to stirre up good affections, which in this case the holy Ghost graciously stirreth up, and therefore need no discource at all.[71]

However, this passage from *An Introduction to the Devoute Life* reveals the true relationship between words and 'motions' as François de Sales conceives it. Words are only necessary in the absence of God's Spirit, to produce 'motions' rhetorically. De Sales uses the word more associated with rhetorical effect, 'affections', interchangeably with 'motions'. The interaction of spiritual power

[69] *Dictionnaire de spiritualité*, 1022: 'les affections apparaissent d'abord comme un intermédiare nécessaire entre les idées et les volitions, une préparation indispensable aux résolutions réelles et efficaces.'
[70] Sales, *Introduction to the Devoute Life*, 129.
[71] Ibid. 151.

and rhetorical techniques is taken for granted: indeed, the rhetorical strategies of *An Introduction to the Devoute Life* are everywhere presented as devotional.

For William Nicholls, publishing his edition of *An Introduction to a Devout Life* in 1701 in a more rationalistic age, François de Sales allows too much priority to spiritual 'motions':

He advises his Reader to *Mental Prayer*, and placing ones self in the *Presence* of God, which in the Mystical Cant signifies to divest our Mind of all kind of thought and desire, and to leave the Holy Ghost to inspire into the Mind what he thinks fit.[72]

Nicholls is being unfair to de Sales here. At no time is the Christian instructed to 'divest [his] Mind of all kind of thought and desire'. On the contrary, the mind of the meditator is thoroughly prepared, as we have seen, by words, images, and appropriate emotions. The range of emotions expected by de Sales leaves very little scope for the Holy Spirit, and the imagination is firmly restricted to the text for meditation. This is hardly the same 'Mystical stuff' as the writings of Julian of Norwich, Teresa of Avila, or other radicals (mostly women) of whom Nicholls thoroughly disapproves. The preference for verbal constructions over mystical experience in *An Introduction to the Devoute Life* is shown by the speed with which St François quickly returns to psychological terminology and to the need for human words, after designating the central experience of meditation as a silent, supernatural one. He stresses the dangers implicit in the wordless power invoked in meditation. The imaginative, affective experience of meditating on a virtue could be substituted for the practice of it:

for virtues meditated, and not practized, do puffe up the mind, and make vs overboldlie presume that we be such in deed, as we resolued, and purposed to be.[73]

Although the aim of meditation has been to provoke a flow of spontaneous emotion, St François advises his pupil not 'to be

---

[72] Sales, *An Introduction to a Devout Life*, ed. Nicholls, A1ᵛ. Note that later 17th-century Protestants were often sceptical of 'mental prayer' for the same reason as Nicholls. John Owen, for example, stresses the need for words in prayer. See G. S. Wakefield, *Puritan Devotion: Its Place in the Development of Christian Piety* (London, 1957), 88.

[73] Sales, *Introduction to the Devoute Life*, 148.

content with these general affections, be they never so fervourous and holy'. Even the moving of the Holy Spirit, it seems, is not as effective as human will-power. Specific resolutions must be made which will affect behaviour when the emotion of meditation is past. Words are indispensable at this point, for it is essential that key elements of the experience are remembered, and the recording of experience necessitates words. St François de Sales uses the rhetoric of the senses to describe the experience of God's presence, but it is an experience mediated through the use of words. The nearness of his presence is sensed through taste, but the memory of that presence needs to be encapsulated in words. Then the words will become a perfume which reminds the believer of the sweetness of the experience. Along with the resolutions is advised the writing of a 'nosegay of deuotion' or 'spiritual posy'. This is the collection of

one or two points which we have found most pleasing to our tast, and most agreeable to our understanding, upon which we might busie our mind, and as it were mentally smell thereon all the rest of the day.[74]

Words are employed in reifying the spiritual experience of meditation. The concrete imagery with which St François describes verbal production contrasts strikingly with his description of 'motions', which is extremely vague and abstract. The images used about this part of meditation stress the palpable effect of a 'motion': swelling with air, running free from restraint. These verb formations give a very different impression from the noun clauses used in the description of words. They are also far from ambivalent in value. 'Swelling' may lead to being 'puffed up', presumably with pride, and there is a place for restraining and confining the emotions. Motions are described in a metaphor which emphasizes their insubstantial nature as compared with words: as precious liquid in a porcelain bowl, to be treasured.[75] In this metaphor, it seems, the words, 'faire porcelain', both preserve and contain the experience, the 'pretious liquor'. Any damage to the container will spill the liquid: it is essential to remember the words. 'Motions' almost disappear under the weight of all this verbiage. It is clear that Louis Martz is also unconvinced about the importance of this central, wordless act of meditation, for in

[74] Sales, *Introduction to the Devoute Life*, 148.
[75] Ibid. 149.

comparing Herbert's poems to de Sales' meditation he completely omits any discussion of 'motions': the poetry of meditation should 'first compose the problem, then analyze its parts, and end with resolutions and petitions in colloquy with God.'[76]

Perhaps it is not surprising that what is apparently the most important part of meditation is not considered in Martz's attempt to construct 'a poetry of meditation'. Whilst it is just credible that the aim of all the human words in meditation or preaching is to achieve the silent, wordless communication of God, it is harder to imagine the kind of poetry that would create a silence in which God could speak. Even in Herbert's advice on preaching, as we have seen, rhetorical plenitude is delivered where the *aporia* of silence is signalled, and the highly finished discourse of poetry is even more crafted than that of preaching.[77] However, in the poetry, human *aporia* is often signified by an interruption of the established rhetoric of the poem, so that the human author appears to stop speaking. Indeed, in 'A true Hymne', that poem about the possibility of a legitimate Christian poetry, the *aporia* in the human discourse is a precondition for the intervention of the divine voice which stamps the poem as 'a true Hymne':

> Although the verse be somewhat scant,
> God doth supplie the want.

In the Bodleian manuscript the verse is literally 'scant': the syllable 'the' in line 1 is missing. All Herbert's editors have played God and supplied this particular want. In doing so, however, they have merely followed Herbert's normal poetic mode, which is not *aporia*, no matter how strongly a 'want' is indicated, but plenitude. The last line of the poem appears to be a good example: the poet 'stops', and God steps into the breach to complete the poem. However, an example is exactly what this last line is. Herbert is merely indicating the manner in which God usually works. There is no indication that the final syllable of the poem, '*Loved*', really is God's contribution. There is no evidence in Herbert's other poems, either, of human lack supplied by divine rhetorical

[76] Martz, *The Poetry of Meditation*, 61.

[77] See C. Hodgkins, *Authority, Church and Society in George Herbert: Return to the Middle Way* (New York, 1993), 95: 'Even in Herbert's poetry his sudden silences and fragmented sentences can be classified as rhetorical devices with their own Greek names: *aporia, aposiopesis, parenthesis, anacoluthon.*'

abundance, despite the rather heavy-handed metaphors for God's intervention in poems like 'Deniall'. In the highly finished, seamless discourse which is poetry, and particularly Herbert's poetry, there could be no trace of God's presence: if God had successfully completed the human poem, the reader would not be able to see the join. However, the silencing of the human voice is the key to the audibility of the divine voice in 'Jordan (ii)' and 'The Collar': and in 'The Collar', the sense of silence created by the sudden end to the poem seems, in the psychology of the poem, to indicate God's 'motions' in the persona, and perhaps creates a space for God to move the reader, also.

George Herbert acknowledges a limitation for human words, and his poetry is full of rueful references to that limit.[78] Although the discourse of preaching and meditation appears to be oriented towards the divine motions which will render the words unnecessary, François de Sales is less concerned about the limitations of human words. It is no surprise that St François de Sales is particularly convinced of the power of human words harnessed in poetry. His own terminology celebrates the masterful, controlling nature of poetry: 'it is a marvel how words marshalled by the laws of verse have power to penetrate hearts and subdue the memory,' he comments, in a letter to a would-be poet.[79] This quality of psychological penetration had been ascribed to poetry since the publication of du Bartas' *La Muse chrestienne* in 1574. This poem consciously adopts the Muse of poetry, Urania, as patron of religious (and in particular, Protestant) verse, in a manner which equates the inspiring function of the Muse with the Holy Spirit. These lines describe the power of poetry, whether secular or sacred:

> Ainsi que le cachet dedans la cire forme
> Presque un autre cachet, le Poète sçavant,
> Va si bien dans nos cœurs ses passions gravant,
> Que presque l'auditeur en l'auteur se transforme.
>   Car la force des vers, qui secrettement glisse
> Par des secrets conduits, dans nos entendemens
> Y empreint tous les bons & mauvais mouvemens,
> Qui sont representez par un docte artifice.[80]

---

[78] See e.g. 'The Forerunners', and 'Jordan (i)'.
[79] Sales, *Letters*, 186.
[80] G. du Bartas, *L'Uranie ou Muse Céleste de G. de Saluste, Seigneur du Bartas* (London, 1589), 10.

It is easy to see how attractive this power is to a Christian poet, a power which can almost transform the listener into the image of the author. The idea of imprinting on the heart would have resonated for both Herbert and de Sales, and as we have seen, sacred poetry is conceived of by de Sales as just this kind of transforming discourse. However, for Herbert the power of transforming and engraving is reserved for the sacred text. These lines from Herbert's Latin poem, 'In S. Scripturas', describe the intimate interaction between sacred text and human subject. They are very close in content to du Bartas' poem, which had been published in England with a Latin translation in 1589. The penetration of poetry into the secret places of the heart described by du Bartas is closely echoed in Herbert's description of the workings of Holy Scripture.

> Sacratissima Charta, tu fuisti
> Quae cordis latebras sinusque caecos
> Atque omnes peragrata es angiportus
> Et flexus fugientis appetitus.
> Ah, quam docta perambulare calles
> Meandrosque plicasque, quam perita es!
>
> (Most Holy Writ, it's you who've travelled through
> All the dark nooks and hidden pleats
> Of the heart, the alleys and the curves
> Of flying passion. Ah, how wise and skilled you are
> To slip through these paths, windings, knots.)[81]

Both poets describe a mysterious force, skilled in the secret passageways of the heart, making its way through into the deepest places of consciousness. Du Bartas' Muse is *docte*, learned, as the Holy Scripture, for Herbert, is *docta*: however, the Scripture is wise in a very special sense. Herbert's poem concludes 'Quae vis condidit, ipsa nouit aedes': 'the spirit that built the dwelling knows it best.' Scripture can penetrate where no other text can because its author actually created the structures of human consciousness, and can bypass the responses to rhetoric. Herbert never allows to poetry the power that French religious poets give it, reserving this power for Scripture. His own theory of poetry has more in common with another different model for the production of

---

[81] Herbert, *Works*, 411; *The Latin Poetry of George Herbert*, tr. Mark McCloskey and P. R. Murphy (Athens, Oh., 1965), 85.

discourse, also described in *An Introduction to the Devoute Life*, but very different in its origin and implications: the style of prayer called ejaculation.

ii. *'Ejaculations':* An Introduction to the Devoute Life *and a Subtitle for* The Temple

In chapter 13 St François de Sales describes another kind of spiritual discourse which is apparently even more important than meditation: 'without it, we cannot well lead a contemplative life, and but badly performe the active life.'[82] This special language is given the name of 'iaculatorie prayer', and it would appear to be a very different kind of discourse from that of meditation, which is carefully and consciously composed in the manner of classical rhetoric, as we have seen. François de Sales cites St Augustine as his source for this particular concept, and indeed in *Epistola CXXX ad Probam* Augustine describes the prayer style of the Desert Fathers as *jaculatas*, 'darted'. *Iaculere* is to throw a weapon, and these prayers come arrowlike, thick and fast: very brief, very sudden, and not to be broken.[83] As Augustine conceived it, the intensity of mental effort, the expression of love kindled in the heart, is what is important in ejaculatory prayer: too many words can defuse the emotion, and blunt the force of the prayer, which is seen as a weapon. Whereas meditation needs special conditions and careful verbal preparation, ejaculatory prayer is spontaneous, and uses the minimum of words. Michel de Certeau contrasts ejaculatory prayer with the operations of the discourse of meditation, which is essentially inward, imaginative,

---

[82] Sales, *Introduction to the Devoute Life*, 179.

[83] St Augustine, *Opera* (Paris, 1688), ii. 389 ff.: 'Dicuntur fratres in Ægypta crebras quidem habere orationes, sed eas tamen brevissimas, & raptim quodam modo jaculatas, ne illa vigilanter erecta, quae oranti plurimum necessaria est, per productiores moras evanescat atque hebetetur intentio. Ac per hoc etiam ipsi satis ostendunt, hanc intentionem, sicut non est obtundenda, si perdurare non potest, ita si perduravit, non cito esse rumpendam. Absit enim ab oratione multa loquutio, sed non desit multa precatio, si fervens perseverat intentio. Nam multum loqui, est in orando rem necessarium superfluis agere verbis. Multum autem precari, est ad eum, quem precamur, diuturna & pia cordis excitatione pulsare. Nam plerumque hoc negotium plus gemitibus quam sermonibus agitur, plus fletu quam affatu. Ponit autem lacrymas nostras in conspectu suo, & gemitus noster non est absconditus ab eo, qui omnia per Verbum condidit, & humana verba non quaerit.'

and rhetorical, and is how the speaking subject is 'born'. 'Ejaculations', as he describes them, are attempts to realize something of
the speaker's deepest sense of identity in the outside world.[84]

Louis Martz, who claims that Herbert's poetry is of the nature of
meditational discourse, also claims that there is a connection
between these 'iaculatory prayers' and Herbert's 'ejaculations',
recognizing no difficulty in reconciling the discourse of Salesian
meditation with that of Augustinian ejaculatory prayer.[85] However, the title of chapter 13 of *An Introduction to the Devoute Life* already
redefines ejaculations in a distinctively Salesian way: 'Of aspirations, iaculatorie prayers, and good thoughts.' The addition of two
other, apparently synonymous terms already weakens the sense of
urgent communication that is present in de Sales' sources. The
Dictionnaire de spiritualité notes the close relationship between 'ejaculations' and 'aspirations' and their physiological origin, but characterizes these movements as a vague manifestation of the need of
the human organism to express the divine soul within. The term
'jaculatory prayer' in de Sales' writing denotes a discourse that
effectively expresses the self: it has 'efficacie to content and satisfie
the hart'. It is the source of the prayer in interiority that is valuable:
ejaculation externalizes the private discourse of 'good thoughts', in
a movement similar to that which Michel de Certeau describes.

St François de Sales is optimistic about the capacity for human
speech to express the divine soul. He is not worried about any
negative effect of words, because he is not primarily concerned
with the power of ejaculatory prayer to persuade God. Despite its
sacred context, de Sales' 'iaculatory prayer' has already become
the more general and secularized 'ejaculation' in the modern
sense of 'hasty emotional utterance'. For a modern reader familiar
with this sense of 'ejaculation', the choice of subtitle for *The Temple*
immediately raises another question. Are the *Sacred Poems* the
same kind of writing as the *Private Ejaculations*, or does this subtitle define two different genres? In the early 1630s the choice of the
word 'Ejaculations' for a collection of poetry was innovatory. The
OED cites the rhetorical sense of the word as developing well after
its original meanings of ejecting sperm (1603) and hurling missiles

---

[84] M. de Certeau, *The Mystic Fable. Volume I: The Sixteenth and Seventeenth Centuries*, tr. M. B.
Smith (Chicago, 1992), 196.
[85] Martz, *The Poetry of Meditation*, 254.

(1610). Sense 4b of the word 'ejaculation' is more applicable to Herbert's lyrics: 'A short prayer darted up to God. A short, hasty emotional utterance.' The first occurrence is cited in a sacred context, Thomas Gokins's *Hallowed be Thy Name* of 1624: 'Thou takest recreation...in one ejaculation.' The modern, entirely secularized use of 'ejaculation' as 'any brief expression of emotion' seems not to occur until later in the century: Pepys used it in 1666. The religious overtones of the first rhetorical uses of the term betray a link with the French term *oraison jaculatoire*, as sense 3b of the word, recorded as first occurring in 1635, makes explicit: 'the putting up of short earnest prayers in moments of emergency; the hasty utterance of words expressing emotion.' The English translation, 'jaculatory prayer', a specific adaptation of the word 'jaculatory' from the verb meaning 'to dart or throw', first occurs in the 1620s, according to the *OED*. However, as we have seen, the translator of *An Introduction to the Devoute Life,* John Yatesley, used the expression in his 1613 version of the title of chapter 13. This is a very early use of the term in English, unrecorded in the *OED*, and it is tempting to follow Martz in assuming a connection between Yatesley's coinage of the term and the subtitle of *The Temple*. It is not clear whether Herbert chose his own subtitle for *The Temple*: it does not appear in either of the manuscripts. However, if Herbert did not choose it, it is most probable that it is the choice of Nicholas Ferrar, who bore the main burden of publishing the work, and who wrote the preface. This would suggest a more secure link between the choice of subtitle and St François de Sales' 'iaculatory prayer': for as we have seen, *An Introduction to the Devoute Life* was well known at Little Gidding. However, the word 'ejaculation' had already been adopted by English devotional writers such as Elnathan Parr, who defines the word in his 1618 treatise on prayer thus:

sudden liftings up of the heart to God, upon manifold occasions occurring every day.[86]

In his 1619 treatise *The Arte of Happiness* Francis Rous suggests 'ejaculations' as a cure for spiritual dryness, as a temporary substitute for ordinary prayer:

---

[86] Elnathan Parr, *Abba Father, or a Plaine and Short Direction Concerning Private Prayer* (London, 1618), 9.

if God yet delaies us (for he seldome finally denies us) let us cast up short eiaculations, desiring God to accept our desires to pray.[87]

Both these writers are Puritan in outlook, as is Gokins. Rather than being associated with Counter-Reformation spirituality, the English use of the word seems to be characteristic of a Reformed doctrine of prayer. This impression is confirmed by an extremely guarded comment, in parenthesis, in John Cosin's controversial volume of set devotions for private prayer, which employs Counter-Reformation symbolism and terminology: 'all sudden and godly iaculations are not to be condemned'.[88] Such a suspicion of unpremeditated impulse is not surprising in a volume which attacks 'all extemporall effusions of irkesome and undigested Prayers', but it does mark a different attitude from that of Puritan writers, who found the concept of ejaculatory prayer deeply congenial.[89] The connection between *An Introduction to the Devoute Life* and *The Temple* remains unproven, and I hope to show that the difference between the Counter-Reformation spirituality of St François de Sales and the Reformed piety of George Herbert makes any significant link unlikely.

Ejaculations, Louis de Blois, and Luis de Granada

There is a fundamental problem with assuming *An Introduction to the Devoute Life* as any kind of source for *The Temple*, and that is the complex origin of St François de Sales' treatise in a deliberate intertextuality. The author intended it as a convenient replacement for the many translations which had been the foci for both Catholic and Protestant spirituality in the sixteenth century.[90] Originality is not possible, nor desirable, in this synthetic enterprise: on the contrary, the greater number of authorities he can cite, the greater authority his treatise will possess.

---

[87] Francis Rous, *The Arte of Happiness* (London, 1619), 327.

[88] John Cosin, *A Collection of Private Devotions or The Hours of Prayer* (London, 1627), sig. A6ᵛ. For Cosin's Arminianism see N. Tyacke, *Anti-Calvinists: The Rise of English Arminianism c.1590–1640* (Oxford, 1987), 119.

[89] Cosin, *Private Devotions*, sig. A5ʳ⁻ᵛ.

[90] For example Luis de Granada, *Le Vray chemin*, tr. F. de Belleforest (Paris, 1579); Diego de Estella, *Livre de la vanité du monde*, tr. G. Chappuys (Paris, 1587): explicitly recommended by François de Sales. See Sales, *Introduction to the Devoute Life*, 191.

I cannot therefore, neither ought I, or would I, in any sort write in this introduction, any thing but that, which hath been alreadie published by our learned predecessors concerning this matter; they be the self same flowers that I present unto thee (gentle reader) which divers before me haue offered unto thy view but the nosegay which I have framed of them, is of a different fashion from theirs, as being handled in another forme.[91]

The compendious nature of this work, however, means that on several crucial issues it is ambiguous, or even inconsistent, and the treatment of 'jaculatory prayer' is a case in point. There are elements in the concept of 'jaculatory prayer', especially as expounded by other sixteenth-century authors, which seem deeply at odds with the kind of spirituality developed in the rest of *An Introduction to the Devoute Life*. There is evidence that François de Sales has taken the concept from his sources and transformed it into the kind of rhetorical exercise more appropriate to his distinctive brand of spirituality.

The French author who had used the term most recently in his spiritual writing was Louis de Blois. His account of *oratiunculae jaculatoriae* in the *Canon Vitae Spiritualis* of 1539 has much in common with that of François de Sales. The chapter on ejaculatory prayer follows those on formal meditation, which is obviously similar to that laid out by de Sales, although the method is not described in so much detail. However, Louis de Blois' description of ejaculatory prayer is even less indebted to Augustine than that of François de Sales: essentially it is just another kind of spiritual exercise, to be prepared for in advance.

Have ever in readiness certain efficacious words, as it were little darts of prayer, whereby thou mayest recall and lift up thy soul to God.[92]

Louis de Blois has obligingly provided various examples of ejaculatory prayers, or 'aspirations', taken from various sources, although he does accept that it is preferable to compose individual prayers, the product of 'one's own feeling and the grace of the Holy Spirit'. The rhetoric of François de Sales' ejaculatory prayer is similar to that of Louis de Blois, although his description of its purpose is rather different. 'Ejaculations' for Louis de Blois are

---

[91] Sales, *Introduction to the Devoute Life*, 12.
[92] Blosius, *The Manual of the Spiritual Life* (London, 1871), 50.

placed firmly in the context of mystical individual experience of God: they are seen as the foundation of mystical theology. In the attempt to reach God, ejaculatory prayer is supremely effective: 'aspirations effectively penetrate and overcome everything that separates God from the spirit.'[93]

One difference between Louis de Blois' theory of ejaculatory prayer and François de Sales' treatise is the anti-intellectualism of the *Canon Vitae Spiritualis*. Louis de Blois, like Bonaventure in *Itinerarium spiritualis*, states that those who achieve successful union with God are *'simplices'* and *'idiotae'*. This anti-intellectualism, the common requirement of mystical spirituality, is not present in *An Introduction to the Devoute Life*: human reasoning and human words have a very important part to play in the spirituality described there. Louis de Blois goes much further into mysticism than St François de Sales, although he too is aware of the need for safeguards. He relies on the regulation of the impulse or motion that inspires prayer: the source of ejaculations should not be an overpowering impulse, but a gentle one.[94] However, the Christian should still be open to the leading of the Holy Spirit. The strong implication is that the Holy Spirit only communicates within a particular emotional spectrum, a supposition which St François de Sales appears to share. Despite the stress that St François lays on the affections, his rewriting of earlier texts retains a residual suspicion of strong, and particularly negative, human emotion.

Luis de Granada's writing is obviously a very important source for *An Introduction to the Devoute Life*, and Herbert's use of 'ejaculatory prayer' seems to reflect Luis de Granada's treatment of *oraison jaculatoire* rather than St François' adaptation of it. Herbert may have had access to the French editions of Granada's treatises, or have read one of the many editions of Granada's work published in the late sixteenth century in English.[95] Francis Meres, translating *Granados Devotions*, had stopped short of coining the term 'jaculatory prayer', although the phenomenon he was describing is identical. The reference is again to Augustine's description of the prayers of the Desert Fathers:

---

[93] Blosius, *Opera Omnia* (Antwerp, 1638), 307: 'huiusmodi aspirationes efficaciter penetrant ac superant omnia media quae sunt inter Deum & animam.'

[94] Ibid. 306: 'faciens hoc non quidem cum immoderatu impulsu. . . . sed placide.'

[95] For example, these three works, all translated by Francis Meres, and published in London in 1598: *Granados Devotion, Granados Spirituall and Heavenlie Exercises, The Sinners Guyde*.

these short and succinct prayers, which for this cause are called darting, because as it were are the darts of a loving soule, which with great celerity are shot forth, and do wound the heart of God.[96]

Granada's definition develops the hint in Augustine: the force of the word 'iaculatory' is that the prayer is effective with God. This original military sense of the word was not forgotten by the man who described prayer as 'engine against th'Almightie', as we shall see. It is possible that Herbert's understanding of this type of prayer is drawn entirely from Augustine, whose works he knew extremely well. However, in the use of 'ejaculation' to maintain constant contact with God, and in the imagery connected with this type of spirituality, Herbert's rhetoric shows an affinity with Luis de Granada's account of ejaculatory prayer. Like Herbert, de Granada describes the devotionless world as 'cold', and ejaculatory prayer is a strategy for keeping warm:

the darts of a loving soule, which with great celerity are shot forth, and do wound the heart of God: by force of which, the soule is stirred vp, and is more enflamed with the love of God.[97]

The initiator here is the human being: the stirring and inflaming of the soul is not the stimulus to discourse, as in *The Cloud of Unknowing*, but the result of it. The prepositional phrase, 'by force of which', could apply either to the power generated by the utterance of the prayer within the human being, or to the power generated by the penetration of the heart of God. The phrase 'the love of God' is also ambiguous: is it human love for God that is stirred up, or is the divine love of God implanted in the soul? There is certainly a sense of God responding to the prayer, and of the human being responding in turn. Herbert's *Ejaculations* are also his expression of a divinely initiated relationship with God: a more personal and intimate generation of speech than the naturally fruitful intercourse of God and Nature described by de Sales, but at a much higher cost.

'Iaculatory Prayer' and Herbert's Ejaculations

For François de Sales, unlike Louis de Blois or Luis de Granada, the originating emotion of ejaculatory prayer is a reaction to an

---

[96] Luis de Granada, *Granados Devotion: Exactly Teaching how a man may truely dedicate and devote himselfe vnto God: and so become his acceptable Votary*, tr. Francis Meres (London, 1598), 70.
[97] Granada, *Granados Devotion*, 70.

event in the external world. A 'good thought', as he conceives it, is produced by the interaction of a signifying world with a mind filled with love towards God: in fact it is the love of the creator in His creation, both human and non-human, that ensures such communication. Citing Augustine, St François suggests a world that testifies of God.

All things in this world speak unto us with a kind of language which though dumbe, in that it is not expressed in words, yet intelligiblie enough in regard of their love: for all things provoke us and give us occasion of good & godlie thoughts, from whence afterward do arise many motions and aspirations of our soule to God.[98]

He quotes many illustrative examples from the lives of the saints, several of which, as concerning such distinctively un-reformed figures as Francis of Assisi, Francis Borgia, and St Francisca, are censored from the Reformed edition printed in London in 1616. Such 'non-verbal' messages from the natural world seem to have come to Gregory of Nazianzen watching the tide sucking the sea-shells back and forth, to St Anselm of Canterbury watching the anguish of a leveret trapped by hounds, and to other saints via rivers, stars, orchards, and chickens. Much of the content of this chapter on ejaculatory prayer is very familiar to readers of Her-bert, and Martz makes the most of the similarities. There is a distinct echo of the poem 'The Odour' in the equation of the presence of God with a sweet perfume. 'Place him in thy bosome like a sweet-smelling posie' is de Sales' instruction, recalling the Pomander which for Herbert is the name of Christ:

Our spirit . . . must needs be perfumed, with the odoriferous ayre of his perfections.[99]

An orchard prompts thoughts of futility similar to those of 'Employment (ii)': 'ay me wretch that I am, wherfore am I alone without blossom or budd in the orchard of holy churche?' The spiritual relationship between the heavens and the earth discovered by 'one [female] devout soule' looking at the stars is identical to that expressed in 'The Foil'. 'The Rose', two poems later, has much in common with de Sales' anecdote of St Basil, who, seeing a rose, declared that 'it seemeth to make [an] exhortation

[98] Sales, *Introduction to the Devoute Life*, 171–2.   [99] Ibid. 169.

to men'. The rose speaks to Basil of the mixture of joy and sorrow that is earthly life: the joy that children bring is tempered by worry, marriage inevitably leads to widowhood, disgust follows indulgence in delicious food. The contradictions inherent in the physical make-up of the rose—thorns and flower, perfume and emetic—spell out much the same message for Herbert.

> So this flower doth judge and sentence
> Worldly joyes to be a scourge:
> For they all produce repentance,
> And repentance is a purge.[100]

Not only the content, but the rhetoric of de Sales' emotional outpourings is reminiscent of the opening exclamations of many Herbert lyrics. The illustrative anecdotes in chapter 13 are structured to mimic the immediacy of the reaction. The immediate context for the 'good thought' is described in the past tense. The utterance which results, the 'iaculatory prayer', is expressed in direct speech. The time represented by the change in tense is the space of the silent 'good thought', unarticulated because the value of the final utterance is in its presumed identity with the thought. François de Sales signifies the unity of thought and word by delaying the verb of saying until halfway through the utterance, and then inserting it parenthetically. St Francis was inspired by the sight of a lamb being eaten by a hog.

Ah little seely Lambkin (sayd he weeping for compassion) how lively dost thou expresse the death of my Saveour?[101]

Juxtaposed with the originating event, the utterance gives the illusion of being the initial 'good thought': the parenthetical verb only half-corrects that impression. Immediacy and emotion is also communicated by the initial form of words, which functions less as an apostrophe than as an 'ejaculation' in a grammatical sense. One nameless female saint was inspired to utterance by the sight of the starry sky: 'O my God (sayd shee) these self same stars shall one day be under my feet.' In other instances the 'good thought' is written into the text as a wordless emotional reaction, followed by or contemporaneous with its verbal expression: 'Anselm answered weeping and sighing'; 'he sighed and

---

[100] Herbert, *Works*, 178.   [101] Sales, *Introduction to the Devoute Life*, 175.

said'; 'sayd he weeping for compassion'. The non-verbal expressions of emotion are at least as important, it seems, as the words themselves.

Such a stress on the immediacy of a verbal reaction, and its faithfulness to the originating emotion, is more characteristic of Herbert's poetry than the meditational structure Martz also claims for it. The more memorable openings of Herbert's lyrics read like ejaculatory prayers. 'Affliction (iii)' describes a strength and spontaneity of reaction that is completely unconscious: the verbal utterance is analysed afterward as if spoken by another. 'The Glimpse' captures the immediate disappointment at the loss of a sense of God's presence:

> Whither away delight?
> Thou cam'st but now; wilt thou so soon depart?

The opening of 'The Collar' depends for its effect on the simultaneous verbal and non-verbal expressions of emotion: 'I struck the board, and cry'd, No more.' However, these *Ejaculations* spring from a very different context to that of the ejaculatory prayer of François de Sales. It is usually an inner impulse which initiates Herbert's prayer, as opposed to a response to an event in the created world, and this 'motion' is often a negative one. Although the opening of 'The Collar' achieves the combination of immediacy and force described by de Sales, the sentiment is un-Salesian in its violence: 'I struck the board, and cry'd, No more.' 'The Temper (ii)' begins with an emotional reaction to a very recent deprivation:

> It cannot be. Where is that mightie joy,
> Which just now took up all my heart?

These openings create the sense of an immediate response to 'inner weather', as Aldous Huxley describes the variation in Herbert's emotions.[102] The stimulus to utterance in de Sales' description of ejaculatory prayer is the reception of suggestion from the outside world, which will interact with the presence of God within. The result will, apparently, engender spontaneous, unselfconscious language, although in practice it is hard to describe any of François de Sales' examples in these terms.

---

[102] A. Huxley, *Texts and Pretexts* (New York, 1933), 13.

Herbert's poetic openings often create a rhetorical impression of spontaneous response, but they are usually not expressive of the 'good and godlie thoughts' exclusive to ejaculatory prayer in *An Introduction to the Devoute Life*. That of 'The Collar' is characteristic of a sinful human reaction. In 'The Temper (ii)' the response is at the least ambivalent: only in 'Affliction (iii)' does the content of the utterance, rather than the strength of the emotion, declare its origin to be God.

> My heart did heave, and there came forth, *O God!*
> By that I knew that thou wast in the grief.[103]

Where the stimulus is apparently outside the subject, as in 'The Crosse', Herbert encounters it as a symbolic entity rather than as a physical object in the real world, and his initial response—'What is this strange and uncouth thing?'—is anything but godly. The opening of his poem 'Nature' is certainly not a 'good thought':

> Full of rebellion, I would die,
> Or fight, or travell, or denie
> That thou has ought to do with me.

'Nature' for Herbert is the sinful constitution of the human heart rather than the created world that speaks so clearly of God. Characteristically, Herbert gives these negative reactions their full weight, apparently doing nothing to diminish their intensity. What happens in these poems is that the speaker sooner or later turns to address God, thus bringing the emotional reaction under divine control. But this is not a spontaneous process: it involves some wrestling with himself and with God. This is a deeper acknowledgement of God's interest and presence in all circumstances of life than the happy interaction of God's natural creation and God's human creation described by de Sales.[104] It is human consciousness, both sinful and redeemed, that speaks most often in *The Temple*, and which is the stimulus to utterance.

Even Herbert's use of natural analogy springs from different premises and is different in effect. Nature does not speak directly to him: nature, for Herbert, is dumb, as 'Providence' makes clear.

---

[103] Herbert, *Works*, 73.
[104] See J. E. D'Angers, *L'Humanisme chrétien au XVIIe siècle: St. François de Sales et Yves de Paris* (The Hague, 1970), 3 for the triumph of optimism about human nature in the work of St François de Sales.

Beasts fain would sing; birds dittie to their notes;
Trees would be tuning on their native lute
To thy renown; but all their hands and throats
Are brought to Man, while they are lame and mute.

Speech, and the power of conferring signification, is the distinctively human gift, as Herbert has learned from a long line of classical rhetoricians. Thus he, like Adam, confers signification on nature, as in 'The Rose': nature has no power to speak to him of its own accord. The landscape, or rather architecture, of *The Temple* is a spiritual and inward one. Every aspect of the spiritual life—Church services, church buildings, the church calendar—provokes a prayer-meditation to God in exactly the way that the natural world functions as a stimulus in *An Introduction to the Devoute Life*. Even the humble 'Church-floore' is eloquent in a way that for Herbert, the natural world is not. The yearly festivals of 'Easter' and 'Christmas' both provoke 'aspirations, iaculatory prayers, and good thoughts', as do the daily services of 'Mattens' and 'Even-song'. The sphere of *The Temple* is not the world of nature, or even the physical fabric of the church, as 'Sion' makes clear: 'all thy frame and fabrick is within.' It is the architecture of human consciousness that is the real subject-matter of Herbert's poetry, and the poems show how it feels for a human being to be reconstructed as the temple for the Holy Spirit. Thus Herbert refers—and usually defers—to God in all the vicissitudes of a spiritual life: actual circumstances are not mentioned unless they have a direct bearing on spiritual well-being, such as the Affliction and Employment poems.

Herbert's *Ejaculations*, then, have a different context and a much wider scope than François de Sales' 'jaculatory prayer'. However, it is in the perceived purpose of ejaculatory prayer that the two writers reveal fundamentally different conceptions. Augustine's audience for the original ejaculatory prayer had been God, who alone can hear the clamour of silent emotion. For him, conscious verbalizing is not important, and is in fact less effective than non-verbal exclamation. God does not need to hear human words, and too many words will diffuse the force of the emotion behind the utterance. Elsewhere Augustine makes his own recommendation of a suitable 'ejaculation': *Deo gratias*.[105] His most effective ejaculations, however, are absolutely silent:

[105] See Augustine, *Epistle*, 41.

there is a hidden groaning which is not heard by man . . . there is another
way of praying, interior and unbroken, and that is the way of desire . . .
love's glowing ardour is the clamour of the heart.[106]

It is obvious that de Sales, by contrast, is envisaging a primarily
human audience, who will need to hear coherent audible words.
Even those speakers wandering solitarily by rivers and sea-shore
must have had at least one hidden auditor to report back to St
François de Sales. The neat allegories contained in the prayers,
transparent to a moral interpretation, need a complex syntax
rather than a brief exclamation, and are directed horizontally
rather than vertically. The aim of continuous spontaneous ejaculatory prayer in *An Introduction to the Devoute Life* is described in
the picturesque terms of a lover carving the name of his beloved
on every available tree, as if the experience of natural life were
to be continually sanctified as a testimony to all passers-by.
The desire of fervent Christians is actually for a deeper sort of
carving:

Yf it were possible, they would grave the sacred name of our Lord
IESVS, upon the brests of all the men in the world.[107]

This is certainly a penetrative rhetoric, but of a rather different
kind to that of ejaculatory prayer. This kind of holy persuasion is
represented by St François as effective human oratory. In this
reading, the relationship of feeling to words perceived as characteristic of ejaculatory prayer becomes Cicero's formulation for
effective oratory. The evangelizing purpose of St François de
Sales has annexed the Godward and devotional activity of ejaculatory prayer for the human-centred end of teaching.

Louis Martz's determination to find as much similarity as
possible between *An Introduction to the Devoute Life* and *The Temple*
is seen in his description of Herbert's lyrics in terms of both
meditational discourse and ejaculatory prayer. He apparently
sees the origin of many of Herbert's lyrics in François de Sales'
'colloquies', noted down as St François suggests:

---

[106] Augustine, *Enarrationes in Psalmos* xxxvii. 13–14, my translation. 'Est enim gemitus
occultus qui ab homine non auditur. . . . Est alia interior sine intermissione oratio, quae est
desiderium . . . flagrantia caritatis, clamor cordis est' (*Corpus Christianorum Series Latina*
(Turnhout, Belgium, 1956), xxxviii. 391).
[107] Sales, *Introduction to the Devoute Life*, 171.

Amid these affections and resolutions, it is good to use colloquies, or familiar talke, as it were somtime with God our Lord, somtime with our blessed Ladie, with the Angels, and persons represented in the mysterie which we meditate, with the Saints of heaven, with our selves, with our owne hart, with sinners, yea and with insensible creatures: as we see that holy David doth in his psalmes.[108]

These are the same lyrics which Martz elsewhere describes as of the nature of ejaculatory prayer, but the careful prescriptions of *An Introduction to the Devoute Life* rule out an equation of the two. The discourse of the colloquy is not to be repeated to others: it remains firmly in the imaginative and imaginary realm of meditation.[109] By contrast, ejaculatory prayer is reliable to the extent that it is used by God for evangelistic purposes. François de Sales' account of the phenomenon of ejaculatory prayer is dominated by his concern to see the results of spiritual exercises in something more tangible than a sense of unity with God: in his scheme, ejaculatory prayer, which is always audible, fulfils a kind of evangelistic function.

Ejaculations and Sincerity

Although Herbert is also concerned for the didactic worth of his poems, he does seem primarily interested in engraving the name of Jesus on his own heart. The 'ejaculation' of the poem 'Nature' is an urgent request for God to write His law on the sinful human heart that is ready to self-destruct. This is a prayer repeated in poems such as 'Good Friday' and 'The Sinner', with the sense that such a carving will be deeply painful, an activity far removed from the playful engraving of a lover's name in bark. A. D. Nuttall, in *Overheard by God*, comments on the grimness of Herbert's determination. 'Let us hear no more of the serene and tranquil country parson,' he exclaims: 'Herbert's thoughts are indeed ... "a case of knives".'[110] However, Nuttall questions the sincerity of such prayer poetry, which demands a human readership for its private communications with God.[111] Although both

---

[108] Ibid. 153. See Martz, *The Poem of the Mind*, 37.
[109] Sales, *Œuvres* xii. 313.
[110] A. D. Nuttall, *Overheard by God: Fiction and Prayer in Herbert, Milton, Dante and St. John* (London, 1980), 32.
[111] Ibid. 9.

François de Sales' ejaculatory prayer and Herbert's 'ejaculations' are addressed specifically to God, there is always a human audience present to eavesdrop on both conversations.

François de Sales is happy for his 'ejaculations' to have two apparent audiences, human and divine, but it is difficult to see how Herbert's discourse of ejaculatory prayer can attain the spontaneity and authenticity to which it aspires, in the presence of two audiences with differing demands.[112] After all, the 'ejaculations' of *The Temple* are hardly 'private'. Henry Lok, whose *Sundry Christian Passions* so nearly mirror Herbert's 'Ejaculations' in scope, confronted the issue in the preface to his volume, aware that to write public poems about private spiritual transactions could appear disingenuous.[113] For Michael Schoenfeldt, Herbert achieves a sense of integrity through a discourse which constantly questions the authority—God—to whom he speaks. However, the demand of that authority, as Herbert sees it, and as the Protestants of the sixteenth century interpreted the Psalms, is not the articulation of orthodoxy but a discourse that represents as far as possible the true feelings of the speaker, no matter how inappropriate or unorthodox they might be.[114] In fact, that authority is willing to go to some lengths to extract a genuine account from the speaker, as the poem 'Confession' somewhat gruesomely recounts. Any resort to 'fiction' in the speaker's self-revelation will be punished by 'affliction': not the random sequence of ordinary misfortune but torture designed specifically to unlock the lips of each individual.

> No scrue, no piercer can
> Into a piece of timber work and winde,
> As Gods afflictions into man,
> When he a torture hath designed.

Under these circumstances it is unlikely that Herbert will embark on the systematic campaign of subversion detailed by Michael Schoenfeldt. The discourse of resistance to authority which he

---

[112] M. C. Schoenfeldt, *Prayer and Power* (Chicago, 1991), 52–3.

[113] Henry Lok, *Sundry Christian Passions Contained in two hundred Sonnets* (London, 1593), sig. A5ᵛ.

[114] Strier, *Love Known*, 176 notes 'the insistence that he does not have to suppress or deny anything he is feeling in order to address God'. William Pahlka, quoting St Augustine, argues in *Saint Augustine's Metre and George Herbert's Will*, 187, 'it is his duty to say what he thinks in his heart, whether it be true or whether he only think it to be true'.

notes in *The Temple* is, in fact, a feature of the inspired text of the Psalms. It is not a deliberate strategy, but an honest articulation of a rather dangerous position. However, as the poem 'Confession' makes clear, honesty is less dangerous than concealment. In this poetics the imperative is genuine self-expression.

In the poems of *The Temple* Herbert also represents himself as being constantly concerned with his own sincerity. 'Jordan (i)' tries to establish a new kind of poetry divorced from any kind of duplicity.

> Who sayes that fictions onely and false hair
> Become a verse? Is there in truth no beautie?

Of course, Herbert is concerned here about the subject-matter for poetry, but he is also establishing his concern for truth in all things. In 'Confession' Herbert shows a ruthless procedure of self-exposure in operation, and finally is able to boast that his breast is more transparent than any diamond. However, we have to take any transparency of the discourse of the poetry on trust: we have no access to the poet's inner thoughts and intentions. In *The Temple* Herbert constructs a persona who is continually making distinctions between good verbal practice and bad: between true and false naming (in 'Frailtie'), between effective and ineffective prayer (in 'The Method'), between successful and unsuccessful preaching ('The Windows'), and fundamentally between truth and lies (in 'Assurance'). All these judgements, like Savonarola's, are based on the criterion of accurate signification: but we have to take his word for it, as we have no access to the signified. However, the nature of the persona created in *The Temple* is of an author whose constant preoccupation is legitimate use of language. The most compelling conclusion for a reader is that an author who represents his own consciousness in this way is most likely to resemble his rhetorical creation.

The discourse of ejaculatory prayer, according to Michel de Certeau, is archetypally 'sincere', in that it allows the inner self to exist in the outer world:

the (masculine?) gestures of 'throwing' outside a *fragment* of oneself, an expelled, ejaculated object, which becomes the irreducible exteriority of being to itself.[115]

---

[115] Certeau, *The Mystic Fable*, 196.

In this sense an 'ejaculation' is a good model for a sacred poem in that it externalizes the internal spiritual holiness which is the essence of Reformed piety, and which is so difficult to represent rhetorically. Chapter 38 of *The Cloud of Unknowing* describes the power of the ejaculatory prayer in terms of its ability to represent the essential identity of the soul, because 'it is pr*e*yed wiþ a fulle spirite, in þe hei3t & in þe depnes . . . of his spirit þat pr*e*ieþ it: In þe hei3t it is, for it is wiþ al þe my3t of þe spirit. In þe depnes it is, for i*n* þis lityl silable ben contyned all*e* þe wittis of þe spirit.'[116]

The essence of ejaculatory prayer is motion, not rhetoric, and as such it would seem to be inimical to a poetry of meditation. The function of ejaculatory prayer as Augustine conceived it was to be effective with God: such prayer gains its power from the very fact that 'a fragment of oneself' has been realized in words. This is the ultimate discourse of sincerity. It is not surprising that the lyrics of a poet who both valued sincerity and wanted answers from God are called 'Ejaculations'. Part of that sincerity seems for Herbert to be encapsulated in Augustinian gestures towards the redundancy of human words.

'Private Ejaculations': Sighs, Groans, and Tears

Those writers who share St Augustine's concern for effective prayer, including Herbert, lay emphasis on the power that wordless emotion has with God, simply because it is seen to be the most authentic type of prayer. Sir John Hayward describes 'sorrow, sighes, groanes and teares' as 'the only armour of defence, the onely weapons of advantage, by which wee atchieve true victorie and triumph'.[117] It seems that the main protagonist against whom these weapons are to be exercised is God:

My teares have overcome the Omnipotent, the voyce of my tears hath vanquished the invincible. These like warme droppes haue quenched Gods anger, qualified his iustice, recovered his mercie, wonne his loue. True teares are the language of heaven; they speake strongly to God, hee heareth them well. No voyce hath more free and familiar accesse unto him; none is more acceptable, none better understood. He who often regardeth not the voyce of the tongue, will alwaies heare the voice of our teares. The voyce of the tongue is framed in the mouth, but the

---

[116] *The Cloud of Unknowing*, 75.   [117] John Hayward, *David's teares* (London, 1622), 3.

voyce of teares proceeds from a heart, surprised either with ioy or with griefe. He who regardeth only the heart, doth much regard this language of the heart. Therefore in all the anguishes of my soule, I will use few words heereafter, but powre foorth my sorrow in silent teares... Teares are too mighty Orators to let any suit fall.[118]

All the topoi associated with tears are gathered together here. Tears are valuable because they are the 'language of the heart' rather than the less trustworthy 'voyce of the tongue'. They are closer to the inner impulse, which is more valid because unpremeditated. Like ejaculatory discourse, tears are a way of speaking the inner self: 'the voyce of teares proceeds from a heart.'

The subtitle of Herbert's volume indicates his claim to the inwardness and spontaneity that imply authenticity, and establishes the profound link with emotion of the *Private Ejaculations*. However, even if Herbert had in mind the most emotional and least rhetorically complex of his poems when he used this title, he is actually referring to highly sophisticated verbal artefacts. This apparent paradox is underlined by the fact that he is quite happy to write five stanzas' worth of words in the tradition of French penitential poetry and call his composition 'Sighs and Grones'. In Augustine's sign system, non-verbal cries and expressions of emotion occupy a special status. He separates them from the conventional signifiers of speech, placing them in a category of their own, close to natural signs such as facial expressions.[119] Natural signs have the advantage of possessing an integral connection with the signified. Thus Herbert's titles point beyond the poetry to the emotion which is primary.

Herbert, in the sophisticated verbal artefacts which are called 'Ejaculations', acknowledges the power of wordless exclamations to prevail with God, and repeats the commonplaces about the effectiveness of tears. 'Grones are quick, and full of wings, | And all their motions upward be' says Herbert.[120] His poem 'The Search' describes his use of various non-verbal artillery with God.

> I sent a sigh to seek thee out,
> Deep drawn in pain,
> Wing'd like an arrow: but my scout
> Returns in vain.

---

[118] Ibid. 65.   [119] Augustine, *On Christian Doctrine*, 34–5.
[120] Herbert, *Works*, 107.

> I turn'd another (having store)
>   Into a grone;
> Because the search was dumb before.

A groan is wordless, yet eloquent, rather like the tears in 'The Familie', which cry loudly in God's ear. As St Augustine comments on Psalm 3: 4, 'such a prayer is termed a cry by reason of its burning intensity': it is actually silent to the ears of men. Psalm 56: 8 shows how precious tears are to God, and how effective. Herbert paraphrases this Psalm text in 'Praise (iii)':

> when I did call
>   Thou heardst my call, and more.
> I have not lost one single tear:
>   But when mine eyes
> Did weep to heav'n, they found a bottle there
>   (As we have boxes for the poor)
> Readie to take them in.

The storing of tears represents God's intent to answer the prayer, if not immediately then at some point in the future. But the most persuasive argument for the force of tears occurs in 'Ephes. 4.30. *Grieve not the Holy Spirit, &c*'. This poem starts with an ejaculation of astonishment provoked by a message from God via the Scriptures. Herbert suddenly realizes that in response to his sin 'Almightie God doth grieve, he puts on sense'. The non-verbal expressions of grief from God are certainly effective with Herbert, who vows to weep for ever in repentance for his sin.

> Lord, I adjudge my self to tears and grief,
>   Ev'n endlesse tears
> Without relief.

The consequence of ceasing to grieve would be to die spiritually, and this poem communicates powerfully the fear of offending God which has suddenly struck Herbert's soul. The poem is full of questions, and disjointed exclamations: but it finishes with the realization that it is not within the human being's power even to continue to grieve. Exhausted by the effort to prolong this frenzied emotion, Herbert throws himself on the mercy of the one who sweat blood for him, confident that those 'tears' will be far more effective than his own.

Herbert's *Ejaculations* are intended to be 'engine against th'Al-mightie' as well as sincere expressions of deep emotion. And this is what characterizes Augustinian ejaculatory prayer as opposed to mere 'ejaculations': there is a concern for effectiveness towards God as well as for powerful self-expression. Written in to the discourse, as well as 'pathetical ejaculations', will be a sense of answers to prayer: the eventual and almost inevitable calm with which the writing ends will not be merely that of 'passion spent' but of God intervening to calm and to soothe. This is the mode of the Psalm poetry, and Herbert, unlike François de Sales, attempts to reconcile poetic power and emotional sincerity using this model.

As we have seen, St François de Sales also exploits the link between emotion and spontaneity of discourse in his account of ejaculatory prayer. However, St Augustine's statements about prayer leave no room for words at all: 'groans are more effective than words, weeping than speaking.' If it is only the intensity of the impulse that is necessary, why use words? It is clear that what attracts François de Sales to ejaculatory prayer is the same element that attracts him to the Psalms: both types of discourse have affective power. Using a Ciceronian model for effective eloquence, St François finds in this emotional discourse an effective tool for his primarily moral purpose. In the best tradition of the *utile-doux* he employs the most powerful form of human words, the poetry of sacred emotion, in his mission to evangelize and teach. Invoking the authority of Augustine allows de Sales to try to have it both ways, and imply the effectiveness of a non-verbal groan for poetic discourse: essentially, however, St. François has turned what was originally an anti-literary mode of divine communication into a literary trope.

Ejaculatory Prayer: 'Artillerie'

Herbert's most specific treatment of ejaculatory prayer is in the poem 'Artillerie'. At first glance, 'Artillerie' seems the poem in *The Temple* most reminiscent of a Salesian anecdote. It begins in narrative mode with an apparently natural phenomenon—a shooting star. This is one occasion on which natural creation does appear to speak to the poet, and the poet responds correctly, 'turning to my God, whose ministers | The starres and all things are' and directing the appropriate 'good thought' at Him. This soon turns into an aspiration: 'I will do, or suffer what I ought.' 'Thus', says François de Sales, 'are iaculatory prayers made.'[121]

However, the poem does not finish with the morally correct prayer, as St François' anecdotes invariably do. Instead, Herbert begins to reflect on the whole mode of communication between man and God. There is no place here for the medium of the natural world, although the imagery is of stars. In fact, it looks very much as though the shooting star of the first verse is simply a communication from God—a 'good motion'. This suspicion is confirmed when the poem shifts into military imagery, and the star (except for its significance as a 'shooter') disappears. It seems that God communicates directly with human beings: the poet merely has to open himself up to such communication, as he does later in the poem. However, such communication does not necessarily involve words. It is evident that the original 'motion' was not verbal, and only broke into speech because it was the only way to gain the poet's attention. The equivalent of the star, or motion, for a human being is 'tears and prayers': human communication to God has both verbal and emotional content, it seems. The possibility of mutual communication via 'motions' is open, but it is more like a battle than a conversation. By the end of the poem the difficulties of negotiating with Almighty God overwhelm the poet, and he surrenders. This no-holds-barred argument, this acknowledgement of the power of emotional prayer, and the concern with its impact on God is utterly characteristic of Protestant spirituality. But the poem that started in the manner of Salesian ejaculatory prayer has ended in a mode utterly alien to it, with the restoration of the weapon element of the original Augustinian definition.

Luis de Granada's use of the Augustinian concept of 'jaculatory prayer' functions far more satisfactorily as a likely 'source' for Herbert's poem than de Sales, or even Augustine himself. The aim of the 'shooters' of 'Artillerie' is to wound the heart of God, as is that of Luis de Granada's darts: there is also, as in *Granados Devotions*, the sense of two-way communication, or a mutual wounding. 'Shunne not my arrows, and behold my breast' pleads Herbert. However, the end of the poem does not resolve with the assurance of mutual love, so taken for granted by de Granada.

---

[121] Sales, *Introduction to the Devoute Life*, 169.

The formula for ejaculatory prayer has failed simply because God has not responded to the poet's 'arrows'. It seems that the most penetrating human discourse can be resisted by God. Even the invoking of God's own promise to answer the prayers of the believer does not work. In Herbert's Protestant universe God is absolute sovereign: even his own Word cannot bind him. This is an example of what Richard Strier described as 'the Nominalist terror at the core of Calvinist piety': God's thoughts are ultimately unknowable.[122]

The Poetry of Tears

The problem with an easy identification of Counter-Reformation spiritual rhetoric and *The Temple* is shown in Louis Martz's discussion of Herbert's enlarged sonnet 'Grief' as an example of Counter-Reformation 'poetry of tears'.[123] St François is writing within a French Counter-Reformation tradition which specialized in the 'poetry of tears'. The subject of such devotional poetry was usually the events of Christ's Passion, and the focus was the grief of Christ himself or those surrounding him. It combines an emphasis on the physical and visual aspects of the Passion with a thoroughgoing adoption of sensual rhetoric. The result is an indulgence in emotion for the pleasure of the reader: Counter-Reformation meditational practice carried to extremes. The success of Malherbe's *Larmes de Saint Pierre*, published in 1587, a version of Tansillo's *Le Lagrime di San Pietro*, was followed by a spate of poems by minor poets, entitled *Les Larmes* or *Les Pleurs*. This poetry, with its emphasis on rich description and stunning verbal effects, is typical of the 'baroque' period in French writing. The elaborate description of the beauty of tears, and the adoption of secular Italian models, calls into question any religious purpose. Robert Southwell, fresh from the Jesuit College at Rome, was in on the beginning of this phenomenon with his prose work *Mary Magdalens Funerall Teares* and his poetic cycle *Saint Peter's Complaint*.

---

[122] Strier, *Love Known*, 104.

[123] Louis Martz argues (*The Poetry of Meditation*, 202) that Herbert adopts some of the 'poetry of tears' conventions in his poetry, and chiefly in this sonnet. I would agree that Herbert's description of tears in 'Praise (iii)' owes something to this tradition: but I think Martz has missed the irony to which the inversion of the Petrarchan sincerity topos draws attention.

Both works were highly popular and spawned several imitations in England at the very end of the sixteenth century. The nearest equivalent in English poetry is Richard Crashaw's 'Saint Mary Magdalene, or, the Weeper', but on the whole the 'baroque' style seems alien to English sensibility.[124]

The focus of the poem 'Grief' is indeed the poet's lachrymal ducts, and there are several somewhat extravagant visual images to describe them: 'two shallow fords, two little spouts | Of a lesse world.' There is no internal reason suggested for this emotional state. Rather, the poet seems to be indulging every technique of rhetoric, and displaying an uncharacteristically superficial wit. The sonnet turns on the paradox that the poetry he is writing is the wrong vehicle for expression: 'Verses, ye are too fine a thing, too wise | For my rough sorrows.' This reminds the reader of a Petrarchan commonplace even as Herbert inverts it. The conventional sincerity topos has the poet unable to write good poetry under the force of love: in this sonnet Herbert is writing rather too well about another strong emotion. The outrageous and elaborate puns on the 'feet', 'running' in his verse and to his eyes, and the smooth-'running' line which supports the witticism, gives the lie to the sincerity of the 'rough sorrows'. Only the final inarticulate gasp—the more powerful because of its contrast with the urbane poetry that precedes it—has any sense of authenticity. Up until this final line, far from breaking 'measure, tune, and time', Herbert has kept it rather too well. I am not suggesting, however, that this is a miscalculation on his part. Rather, the heavy-handed use of the conventions of the poetry of tears draws attention to the disjunction between the professed sincerity of the emotion and the artificiality of its supposed expression. The apostrophe of the first four lines smacks of parody.

> Come all ye springs,
> Dwell in my head & eyes: come clouds, & rain:

---

[124] See A. Boase, *Poètes anglais et français de l'époque baroque* (Lille, 1948), 184. However, in Herbert's cycle, *Passio Discerpta*, which is the closest to Counter-Reformation devotional mode of all Herbert's writing, there are many examples of such 'baroque' wit. 'Christ on the cross' is characteristic of the sensual and rhetorical treatment of emotion in Counter-Reformation 'poetry of tears': 'Here, where the healed world's | Smooth balm distilled, | On the welling up of the blood, | I, joyous, and my mouth open wide, | Am driven to the drenched cross' (*The Latin Poetry of George Herbert*, 71).

> My grief hath need of all the watry things,
> That nature hath produc'd.[125]

Such hyperbole from the pen of Herbert would make us look twice, even if we knew of no models for Herbert to be satirizing. In fact, however, the opening question closely mirrors the first line of a sonnet by Jacques de Billy, a poet writing both in French and Latin. De Billy was known in England: the Bodleian copy of his *Anthologia Sacra* was owned by another poet who wrote in English and Latin, the Christ Church man Richard Edes.[126] The French version, in sonnet form, of his poem 'De tristitia spirituali' begins in a way almost identical to Herbert's 'Grief':

> Qui me donra de l'eau pour mon chef miserable
> De larmes pour mes yeux un ruisseau tout entier?[127]

However, it is not necessary to trace a specific model for Herbert's poem. The concentration on the outward and physical effects of emotion, without regard to the inward cause, is so foreign to Herbert that it alerts us to the irony, a double irony in that he is invoking a version of the sincerity topos. The hidden message is that poetry is not a good medium for spontaneous overwhelming grief, and the poet would do better to call upon God in his distress, rather than describe his outward physical (and even poetic) symptoms. The 'ejaculation' of the last line is of more worth than the elaborate rhetoric of the previous fourteen. The final irony is that it is only possible to confer this kind of rhetorical value on an ejaculation within a highly poetic structure.

The 'Ejaculatory School' in Seventeenth-Century English Poetry

Given such an awareness of the antithetical nature of the two types of utterance it is hardly likely that Herbert himself gave his poems the subtitle *Sacred Poems and Private Ejaculations*. Whoever did clearly hit on a formula with a powerful attraction for aspiring religious poets. There was no lack of followers in what Stanley Stewart has called 'a school of Herbert', all cashing in on what had been a winning title: according to Walton, 20,000 copies of

---

[125] Herbert, *Works*, 164.
[126] Jacobus Billius, *Anthologia sacra* (Paris, 1575), 43ᵛ.
[127] I. D. McFarlane (ed.), *Renaissance Latin Poetry* (Manchester, 1980), 99.

The Temple were sold in forty years. Cardell Goodman's *Sacred Meditations and Private Ejaculations, digested into Verse* was composed in manuscript sometime before 1648. Christopher Harvey in the heavily Arminian *The Synagogue: or Sacred Poems and Private Ejaculations* of 1640 was aware of the paradoxical nature of the title, as his opening poem, 'A stepping stone to the threshold of Mr. Herbert's Church-porch', makes clear:

> And if I say grace gave all, wit straight doth thwart
> And saies, All that is there is mine: but Art
> Denies, and saies, There's nothing there but's mine:
> Nor can I easily the right define,
> Divide.

Harvey does not agonize about the status of his own poetry, but is happy to bask in the reflected glory of an imitated ejaculatory mode. That he did not understand the origins of ejaculatory discourse in extemporary prayer is illustrated by his poem in celebration of The Book of Common Prayer.

> The spirit of grace
> And supplication
> Is not left free alone
> For time and place,
> But manner too. To read, or speak by rote,
> Is all alike to him, that praies
> With's heart.

If God really does care about the heart's impulse alone, then the words do not matter at all: set prayer is as spiritually acceptable as ejaculation. However, such an attitude is a long way from Herbert's concern over the correct mode of spiritual praise in 'A true Hymne'. It is ironic that a wide, if Royalist, readership thought that Herbert's and Harvey's ejaculations were of the same kind: the joint issue of *The Temple* and *The Synagogue* went into many editions until 1787. Harvey was sometimes quoted by mistake for Herbert, an understandable error in view of the close association of the two volumes.[128] In an Arminian theology of the church which validated Old Testament models, the synagogue seemed a

---

[128] John Flavel, *Husbandry Spiritualized: Or, The Heavenly Use of Earthly Things* (London, 1669), 264. This was noticed by Robert Ray in 'The Herbert Allusion Book: Allusions to George Herbert in the Seventeenth Century', *Studies in Philology*, 83 (1986), 83.

natural annex to the temple.[129] Herbert, of course, had made clear his Reformed view of the Old Testament temple in his poem 'Sion': 'now... all thy frame and fabrick is within.' God's preference is for one heartfelt ejaculation, 'one good grone', above all the external splendour of Solomon's temple.

Henry Vaughan in the 1655 edition of *Silex Scintillans: Sacred Poems and Private Ejaculations* described his debt to Herbert in effusive terms, announcing him the founder of a new kind of poetry. Vaughan decried those who had previously followed in Herbert's footsteps on the basis of their lack of 'perfection', a term that applies less to the quality of their poetry than to their mode of spirituality. Vaughan often borrows directly from Herbert's poems in ejaculatory mode, showing that he understands what makes the poems of *The Temple* holy.[130] When lesser poets followed the formula, the disjunction between title and content was more obvious. Jeremiah Rich in his 1650 volume makes clear his perception of the link between poetry and ejaculations: *Mellificium Musarum: The Marrow of the Muses. Or, An Epitome of Divine Poetrie, Distilled into Pious Ejaculations and Solemne Soliloquies.* The soliloquies here are in prose, and it seems that the essence of divine poetry for Rich is in 'Pious Ejaculations'. Unfortunately, the poetic contents of the volume are a disappointment after the rather promisingly coherent logic of the title. Francis Quarles's son John annexed 149 'Divine Ejaculations' to his *Gods Love and Mans Unworthiness* of 1651. He invokes a heavenly deity for aid, but the divine Muse apparently speaks consistently in six-line stanzas of iambic tetrameter, a metre which resists all sense of ejaculatory mode. However, the apotheosis of ejaculatory poetry is Nicholas Billingsley's *A Treasure of Divine Raptures*, promising *Serious Observations, Pious Ejaculations and Select Epigrams* in 1667. These alphabetical Raptures, composed by a self-styled 'chaplain to the illustrious and renowned Lady URANIA', work methodically through from Abba to Axel tree, Babel to Byway, and Cabinet to Cynosure. Clearly Billingsley's readership did not consider the poems as divinely inspired, for there is no record of a subsequent volume of

---

[129] See P. Lake, 'The Laudian Style: Order, Uniformity and the Pursuit of the Beauty of Holiness in the 1630s', in K. Fincham (ed.), *The Early Stuart Church, 1613–1640* (Oxford, 1993), 165.

[130] For details, see Ray, 'The Herbert Allusion Book', 34–6.

Raptures from D to Z despite his promises to produce one if there were to be a demand.

There is some evidence that Herbert's supremely popular volume of 'Ejaculations' actually changed the Arminian perception of ejaculatory prayer. In the 1637 edition of Cosin's *Private Devotions* the strict prescription of set prayer is modified somewhat:

these Prayers are *chiefly* allowed and recommended unto us (wee say *chiefly*; for all kind of ejaculations, or sudden, devout, and holy praiers, are not to bee condemned).[131]

Cosin has changed his mind about the status of ejaculatory prayer. The 'ejaculatory' poets were of the same political persuasion as Cosin: I would suggest that Herbert's lyrics offered them an alternative model of divine inspiration to the disturbing spontaneity of radical 'inspired' discourse in the Interregnum. Detaching the term from its Augustinian source, much as François de Sales did, they were able to exploit the identification of 'ejaculation' with holy discourse without feeling the need to replicate its rhythms or authenticate its sources. Herbert, however, constantly feels the need to validate poetry against the claims of the nonverbal exclamation, favoured by Augustine, or the non-rhetorical 'plain intention' which often surfaces as divine discourse in *The Temple*. This chapter has charted the strategies by which Herbert produced a sacred poetry that could at the same time be read as 'private ejaculations'. It is part of his success that imitators pounced on *The Temple* and reproduced its style, using a title which had come to signify its status as holy discourse.

[131] John Cosins, *A Collection of Private Devotions Or The Houres of Prayer* (London, 1637), sig. a3ᵛ.

3

'Ejaculations' and the Poetry of the Psalms: Herbert's Role as Contemporary Psalmist

In the last chapter I argued for a particular kind of relationship between Herbert and the European devotional tradition which François de Sales' rhetorical spirituality represents, suggesting that Herbert knew this Continental poetics, and even experimented with it, but felt the need to separate his lyrics from the excesses of Counter-Reformation piety and rhetoric. After the Council of Trent Counter-Reformation poets concentrated on producing a poetry of the senses in order to manipulate the emotions of the reader. François de Sales is writing at the height of the fashion for the *utile-doux*, consciously appropriating the 'dépouilles d'Égypte' in the form of rhetorical sweetness, for an audience with literary taste.[1] The 'mildness' noted by Martz is as much a feature of the rhetoric of *An Introduction to the Devoute Life* as of its theology. Both aim to create a serene space in which the imagination can work to bring the Christian into the presence of God. François de Sales' purpose is to incite the emotion appropriate to devotion, from a controlled basis of serenity. His language for the detachment from violent emotion emphasizes strongly the sense of a delineated place in which the presence of God operates:

Examin often every day, at least morning & evening, whether thy soule be in thy hands, or some passion of unquietnes hath robbed thee of it. Consider whether thou have thy hart at commandement, whether it be not escaped and fled away from thee, to some unrulie affection of love, hatred, envie, covetousnes, feare, ioye, sadnes: and yf it be wandred astray, seek it out presently, and bring it back againe gentlie to the presence of God.[2]

---

[1] See Ch. 2 n. 12.
[2] Francis de Sales, *An Introduction to the Devoute Life* tr. I. Y. (Douai, 1613), p. iv, p. 45 (pagination starts again from the beginning of p. iv).

Jesuit poetic theory also stressed the need for the poet to remain
tranquil. Like St François de Sales, Counter-Reformation poets
such as Robert Southwell were aware of the power of the imagination, and concerned to keep it within proper bounds.[3] The
Jesuit literary theorist Jacobus Pontanus articulated the disjunction between poetic composition and emotion when he warned
that 'the poet must carefully refrain from indulging in those
emotions which he tries to awake in others': a reversal of classical
formulations for rhetorical effectiveness.[4] Counter-Reformation
poets, such as Alabaster, are concerned with elaborate verbal
techniques that create a *locus* for the sacred in the imagination
and the senses. According to Anthony Cousins, this is an exten-
sion of Ignatius' attempt in his *Spiritual Exercises* to 'sanctify and
control' the imagination, using meditation as 'a localized ordering... of the entire personality'.[5]

Herbert's Protestant conception of the scope of the subject-
matter for sacred poetry is less limited and rather more robust
than that of the Counter-Reformation tradition, *pace* Martz, who
sees 'a certain mildness and effortless ease' in the writing of both
Herbert and François de Sales.[6] George Herbert's Protestant God
is able to meet him in any psychological or rhetorical condition
known to the Psalmist David, including the rather rough waters of
'The Collar', and the anything-but-sweet rhetoric of 'Deniall': he
often chooses to work from an initially unstable situation of very
inappropriate emotion. According to Isaak Walton, Herbert
represented his own poems in this negative light, as 'a picture of
the many spiritual Conflicts that have past betwixt God and my
Soul'.[7] If Walton is accurate, Herbert would not be the first
Protestant poet to describe his poetry in terms of negative emotional experiences. Henry Lok's concept of his sonnet cycle *Sundry
Christian Passions* is identical:

[3] A. D. Cousins, *The Catholic Religious Poets from Southwell to Crashaw: A Critical Study*
(London, 1991), 70.
[4] Jacobus Pontanus, *Jacobi Pontani Societate Iesv Poeticarun Institutionum* (Ingolstadt, 1594).
Quoted in M. Jeanneret, *Poésie et tradition biblique au XVIe siècle* (Paris, 1969), 121.
[5] See A. D. Cousins, *The Catholic Religious Poets From Southwell to Crashaw: A Critical Study*
(London, 1991), 52, 33. Francis de Sales's language is often reminiscent of Ignatius: he
instructs his readers, beginning a meditation with a *compositio* of place, in this way: 'shutt vp
thy mind and thought within the bounds, and limits of the subiect' (*An Introduction to the
Devoute Life*, 141).
[6] Louis Martz, *The Poetry of Meditation*, rev. edn. (New Haven, 1962), 148.
[7] Isaak Walton, *The Life of Mr. George Herbert* (London, 1670), 109.

I ... have thought good to set downe these abrupt passions of my passed afflictions, as witnesses of the impediments most stopping me in my Christian pilgramage, and testimonies of my evasion hitherto.[8]

William Leighton in the preface to *The Teares of Lamentations of a sorrowfull Soule* of 1613 professes to be in a turmoil about the whole enterprise of publicizing his spiritual conflicts:

Gentle Reader, the unfained zeale, and dutie I owe unto the most free, and honorable service, and glory of almighty God, hath bred a restless desire & doubtfull dilemma in my troubled thought, so that every sence stands a mazed with doubt whether I were better to make knowne the best part of my unfained and true repentance, and mine experience of afflictions.[9]

As with Lok, and Herbert, the decisive factor in deciding to publish is represented as the possible benefit to a reader.

As we shall see in this chapter, the maintaining of the link between poetry and the motions of the heart is crucial to a Protestant poetics, which regarded this link as having been sacralized by the Psalmist David. One text in the tradition of Christian poetics which has been established as important to *The Temple* is the book of Psalms.[10] St François de Sales linked his concept of ejaculatory discourse with the biblical Psalms. His own writing, however, reveals the discontinuity between such a discourse and Counter-Reformation poetics, which is deeply committed to rhetorical artifice, as we have seen. However, Protestant poets were also familiar with the idea of the Psalms as 'ejaculations'. John Harington's comment on his own Psalm paraphrases of 1607 describes them as 'darts', a formulation close to the etymological root of 'ejaculation':

For as the fathers call these psalms darts to drive away devills, so I have been an instrument to sharpen up som of them that seem'd to bee dull poynted, and overgrown with rust.[11]

---

[8] Henry Lok, *Sundry Christian Passions Contained in two hundred Sonnets* (London, 1593), sig. A5^r.

[9] William Leighton, *The Teares or Lamentations of a sorrowfull Soule* (London, 1613), sig. *2^r.

[10] B. K. Lewalski, *Protestant Poetics and the Seventeenth-Century Religious Lyric* (Princeton, 1970); C. Bloch, *Spelling the Word: George Herbert and the Bible* (Berkeley, 1985); and R. Zim, *English Metrical Psalms: Poetry as Praise and Prayer 1535–1601* (Cambridge, 1987) have all established the importance of the Psalms for George Herbert's poetry.

[11] John Harington, *The Letters and Epigrams of Sir John Harrington*, ed. N. E. McClure (Philadelphia, 1630) 143.

The Protestant use of the Psalm text seems more congenial to Herbert's practice of ejaculatory poetry, which, as we have seen, preserves the Augustinian sense of prayerful emotion as 'Engine against th'Almightie'. The genre of Psalm meditation, which seems to have developed within Reformed contexts, is particularly illuminating for a reading of Herbert, who was considered by seventeenth-century readers to be a new Psalmist.

French Readings and Rewritings of the Psalms

The Protestant wing of French literary culture is well represented by the theologian and poet Théodore de Bèze, who was well known in England. Beza's greatest influence on the lyric form and popular spirituality alike was through his collaboration with the vastly popular and innovative poet Clément Marot on the Marot–Bèze Psalter, which was adopted by Calvin for use in services at Geneva. Marot's contribution to the Psalter consisted of the first forty-nine Psalms, written in forty-one different forms, with many differing combinations of metre, stanza form, and rhyme scheme. The only controlling factor is that each form should be well adapted for singing: in Ronsard's formula for the lyric, 'mesurée a la lyre'. One of Ronsard's colleagues in the Pléiade, Joachim Du Bellay, had the grace to admit that Marot had beaten them to their goal of finding a vernacular lyric form.

dès le même tens que Clément Marot (seule lumière en ses ans de la vulgaire poésie) se travaillait à la poursuite de son Psaulter, et osai, le premier des nostres, enrichir ma langue de ce nom, Ode.[12]

The success of the Psalter is measured by the fact that it was translated into twenty-two languages, including a translation back into the original Hebrew. The vision of Protestants across Europe united by the same tunes and the same verse forms inspired François Perrotta, the translator of the Marot–Bèze Psalter into Italian, to poetry:

> L'Angleterre, la Flandre; ensemble et l'Alemagne,
> Comme d'un mesme son ce sainct chant accompagne
> Chant, qui la terre au ciel, et l'homme unit à Dieu.[13]

---

[12] Joachim Du Bellay, *La Deffence et Illustration de la Langue Françoyse* (Paris, 1948), ii. 4. Quoted in Jeanneret, *Poésie et tradition biblique*, 74.

[13] François Perotta, 'Dedication, *À l'Italie*', in *Settantacique Salmi* (n.p., 1581), quoted in Jeanneret, *Poésie et tradition biblique*, 111.

The inclusion of England in this verse makes it all the more surprising that there is no extant English translation of the Marot–Bèze Psalter. Donne expresses a lack in rueful terms, perhaps thinking of the clumsy Sternhold and Hopkins version which was current in England,

> these Psalms are become
> So well attired abroad, so ill at home.[14]

The poem from which this lament is taken is written in praise of an English version of the Psalms with close affinities to the work of Marot and Beza. It circulated in manuscript in the early seventeenth century, and the first editor of the work, in 1823, speculated that in its handsome manuscript form it had been prepared for Prince Henry.[15] Donne, Jonson, Daniel, Fulke Greville, and Joseph Hall certainly read it and the most recent editor speculates that Herbert probably read it.[16] Its authorship is not surprising: Philip Sidney had already shown an attraction to this growing French Protestant literary tradition, translating a work by Philippe Duplessis-Mornay and perhaps du Bartas' *La Semaine* at the same time as working on his own paraphrases of the Psalms.[17] It has recently been suggested that many of the unusual stanza forms in the Sidney–Pembroke version were close copies of the Marot and Bèze paraphrase of the Psalms.[18] Ringler finds that four Psalms are direct translations from the French, whilst others are influenced by French phrases. Eight duplicate wholly or in part the metre and rhyme scheme of the corresponding French Psalm, while six others use the metre and rhyme scheme of other Psalms from the French collection. This leaves considerable scope

---

[14] John Donne, *John Donne: The Complete English Poems*, ed. A. J. Smith (Harmondsworth, 1971), 333.

[15] *The Psalmes of David, translated into divers and sundry kindes of verse more rare and excellent for the Method and Varietie than ever yet hath been done in English. Begun by the noble and learned Gent. Sir Philip Sidney, KNT, and finished by the right honourable the Countess of Pembroke his sister*, ed. S. W. Singer (London, 1823), p. x.

[16] Mary Sidney and Sir Philip Sidney, *The Sidney Psalms*, ed. R. E. Pritchard (Manchester, 1992), 18.

[17] Sir Philip Sidney, *Selected Poems*, ed. K. Duncan-Jones (Oxford, 1973), p. xv.

[18] J. H. Summers, 'Sir Calidore and the Country Parson', in E. Miller and R. DiYanni (eds.), *Like Season'd Timber: New Essays on George Herbert* (New York, 1987), 209. R. E. Pritchard states confidently, 'demonstrably, the Sidneys were influenced by this volume' (*The Sidney Psalms*, 11), but does not demonstrate this: if he means the general scheme of the work, 'the wide range of verse-forms, rhyme-schemes and metres', this is certainly the case.

for Sidney's own metrical invention, although he seems to have gained inspiration from the metrical innovation of Marot and Beza.[19] However, there are certain features common to both works: the use of very short lines, particularly for a strong final effect; the tendency to rhyme lines of differing length; and the carrying of rhyme schemes across separate stanzas. These features are immediately recognizable as being common to the work of that other Protestant poet, George Herbert.[20] Perhaps Herbert's stanza forms owe some of their virtuosity and effectiveness to this French rendering of the Psalms in lyric form: if not through direct contact, then mediated through the pen of his relative, Sir Philip Sidney. At least two prominent critics have asserted the kinship of the two works, and Rivkah Zim finds in the Sidney–Pembroke Psalter the foundation of an English spiritual genre: 'thereafter, the English archetype of devotional poetry was the Sidneys' idea of a psalm.'[21]

François de Sales' emphasis on emotional expressions of devotion and the usefulness of the language of the Psalms should have led him to welcome the Marot–Bèze Psalter. Instead, he attacked it with a ferocity unusual for the man who urged gentle treatment for Huguenots. He called Marot 'this ignorant rhymester' and criticized the Psalter for the very reason Calvin liked it: it is singable, and memorable. 'In the temples publicly, and everywhere, in the fields, in the shops, they sing the rhymes of Marot as Psalms of David'. His criticism has two main thrusts. He has theological objections to Marot's paraphrase, as in his version of Psalm 8, but also seems to envisage an inherent contradiction between the sacred text and poetry. The demands of poetry and the strict translation that is the only appropriate vehicle for transmission of the sacred text are incompatible.

[19] Sir Philip Sidney, *The Poems of Sir Philip Sidney*, ed. W. A. Ringler (Oxford, 1962), 306–8.

[20] Barbara Lewalski describes the Sidney–Pembroke psalter as 'a secure bridge to the magnificent original seventeenth-century religious lyric in the biblical and psalmic mode' and goes on to note similarities with George Herbert's lyrics: see *Protestant Poetics*, 241–4. She thinks they were probably known to Herbert: those who definitely saw them included Donne, Fulke Greville, Joseph Hall, and Sir John Harington (45). Louis Martz traces stylistic similarities between Herbert's lyrics and Sidney's Psalms: *The Poetry of Meditation*, 273–8. He concludes that 'Sidney's translation of the Psalms represents, I believe, the closest approximation to the poetry of George Herbert's *Temple* that can be found anywhere in preceding English poetry.'

[21] Zim, *English Metrical Psalms* (Cambridge, 1987), 202. She assumes the connection proved, stating of Sidney 'his influence on *The Temple* (1633) is well known'.

The measure and restrictions of verse make it impossible that the sacred meaning of the Scripture words should be followed; he mixes in his own to make sense, and it becomes necessary for this ignorant rhymester to choose one sense in places where there might be several.[22]

In fact, Marot is very careful to keep close to his original, working within an early sixteenth-century reverence for an ancient text, and a determination to reproduce it as strictly as possible.[23] The absolutist view of sacred text represented here is very different from that implied by de Sales' advice on the use of Scripture in *An Introduction to the Devoute Life*, where he places other texts and discourses on a level with the Bible, and it is also inconsistent with his attitude to poetry as a whole.[24] In fact, François de Sales had annexed the language of sacred poetry for his conception of ejaculatory prayer.

True it is that there are certain words, with [*sic*] have a particular force and efficacie to content and satisfie the hart in this behalf: such are the daintie sighes, and passionate complaints, and loving exclamations that are sowed so thick in the psalmes of Dauid; the often invocation of the sweet & delightfull name of IESVS; the lovely passages which be expressed in the Canticle of Canticles; and spirituall songs also do serve for this ende, when they be song with attention.[25]

After his description of the production of individualistic, unself-conscious, 'inspired' language, the recommendation of poetic discourse—non-spontaneous, highly complex, and pre-composed by other authors—is a surprise. Again, the explanation for the lack of consistency may be in de Sales' sources for his account of ejaculatory prayer, which, as we have seen, differ in their represent-ation of the importance of spontaneity. François de Sales' concern is that both forms of language, spontaneously generated or prepared in advance, 'content and satisfie the heart': the expression of emotion is what is important here. That is why complex verbal artefacts such as the Psalms are described as 'daintie sighs' and 'loving exclamations': these incoherent emo-tional responses are used by de Sales as names for the working-out of emotions in the poetry of the Psalms.

---

[22] St François de Sales, *The Catholic Controversy: Treatise Written to the Calvinists of the Chablais*, Library of St. Francis de Sales, iii, ed. H. B. Mackey OSB (London, 1886), 133.
[23] Jeanneret, *Poésie et tradition biblique*, 60.
[24] Sales, *Introduction to the Devoute Life*, 191.   [25] Ibid. 170.

The Psalms and Human Emotion

Like de Sales, Luis de Granada declares the all-sufficient source for the language of prayer to be the Psalms of David, which provide the words to express all the affections of the human heart.

> Very many verses of *David* are profitable & conducent unto this purpose, which a man ought alwaies to have in readines, that by them he may be lifted up unto God: not alwaies after the same manner, least the assiduity of the same wordes breed wearines, but with all variety of affections, which the holy Ghost doth stirre and rayse up in his soule; for hee shall finde convenient and meete verses for all these in this heavenly seminary of Psalmes.[26]

This linking of Psalm language with ejaculatory prayer, common to both de Granada and de Sales, involves an adaptation of the Augustinian text. Augustine's comment at the end of his description of ejaculatory prayer does not recommend the language of the Psalms, but wordless exclamation: 'groans are more effective than words, weeping than speaking.'[27] St François de Sales rewrites this passage thus: 'the daintie sighes, and passionate complaints, and loving exclamations, that are sowed so thick in the psalmes of David.' The alternative to spontaneous Spirit-inspired discourse, it seems, is not wordless exclamation, but the poetry of the love lyric. Martz finds a perfect parallel in Herbert's poetry: 'The sighs and groans and tears of the afflicted lover form the ground-tone of the Psalms, as of the *Temple*.'[28]

Louis de Blois shares François de Sales' view of 'the sweetness and gracious peace' of the Book of Psalms, an attitude to be expected in a writer so suspicious of strong emotion.[29] Calvin's comment on the Book of Psalms shows a very different reading, one which has a bearing on the difference between Catholic and Protestant spirituality:

> Not without cause am I woont to terme this book the Anatomy of all the partes of the Soule, inasmuch as a man shal not find any affection in himselfe, wherof the Image appeereth not in this glasse. Yea rather, the

---

[26] Luis de Granada, *Granados Devotion*, tr. Francis Meres (London, 1598).

[27] Augustine, *Epistolarum* x. 20, PL xxxiii. 502: 'Nam plerumque hoc negotium plus gemitibus quam sermonibus agitur, plus fletu quam affatu.'

[28] Martz, *The Poetry of Meditation*, 280.

[29] Blosius, *The Manual of the Spiritual Life* (London, 1871), 42. For advice on avoiding strong emotions such as perplexity and sadness see p. 41.

holy Ghost hath heere lyvely set out before our eyes, all the greefe, sorrowes, feares, doutes, hopes, cares, anguishes, and finally all the troublesome motions wherewith mennes mindes are wont to be turmoyled.[30]

This view of the Book of Psalms as an epitome of all human emotions is typical of Protestant theologians, as Barbara Lewalski has shown.[31] Because the sacred Scripture deals with every emotion known to man (even the 'troublesome motions') it is possible to validate those emotions by reference to the text. The correct source for holy discourse is the human heart: and any 'motion' within it is appropriate for expression, because it has already been mentioned in the inspired words of Scripture. François de Sales' description of the useful language of the Psalms already implies selection: as Calvin knew well, the sighs of the Psalmist are not always 'daintie', the exclamations certainly not always 'loving', and the complaints not always those of the passionate lover. As his catalogue of authorized biblical discourse, including the Song of Songs, makes clear, St François' idea of poetic discourse suitable for ejaculatory prayer is limited to the love lyric. His rewriting of 'motion' as 'good thought' in chapter 13 already represents a radical self-censorship. Not just any interior 'motion' will do: the stimulus to ejaculatory prayer, which is the primary language of devotion, is limited to one particular, positive kind of emotion.

In fact, François de Sales' view of the Marot–Bèze Psalter is consistent with his ideas about holy discourse in *An Introduction to the Devoute Life*: it requires special treatment, including sequestration from the distraction of ordinary life and emotions. It is the mixture of sacred and profane discourse to which St François primarily objects: 'Is it not good to hear cooks singing the penitential Psalms of David, and asking at each word for the bacon, the capon, the partridge!', he asks, ironically.[32] It seems that even the blasphemous version of the Psalms by Marot shares in the holiness of the original text. The belief that correct utterance of sacred words requires that the speaker 'make exterior demonstration of the reverence which the very words he is uttering demand' is far from the spirit in which the Reformers had envisaged

---

[30] John Calvin, *The Psalmes of David and others*, tr. Arthur Golding (London, 1571). Quoted in Lewalski, *Protestant Poetics*, 43.
[31] Lewalski, *Protestant Poetics*, 42–9.   [32] Sales, *The Catholic Controversy*, 135.

ploughboys and spinners singing Psalms in their own language at their work.[33] It is also removed from the logic of 'iaculatory prayer' as de Sales himself presents it, which appears to allow for any daily event as the stimulus for sacred utterance. However, at the end of his discussion in chapter 13 St François makes clear that his context for ejaculatory prayer, despite its apparent spontaneity, is actually 'an exercise of spirituall retyring', as opposed to the pressures of a busy secular life, which was Augustine's original context.[34] It is tempting to conclude that for François de Sales, genuine 'iaculatory prayer' is limited to persons of leisure such as saints or moneyed ladies who were free to wander in natural environments and to cease from their activity to give the prayer its necessary context of reverence. Herbert's Protestant ideal of devotion is less aristocratic.

Herbert's theology and poetic practice is in profound sympathy with the Marot–Bèze Psalter, both in its execution and perceived function. Herbert actually instructs the Country Parson to ensure that his parishioners sing Psalms at their work. Far from desacralizing the Word of God, using the holy text in this way sanctifies the task:

> they labour profanely, when they set themselves to work like brute beasts, never raising their thoughts to God, nor sanctifying their labour with daily prayer.[35]

This for Herbert is the reason why the biblical text so often uses illustration from Nature. Its author thereby makes possible a sacralizing of ordinary human experience:

> that labouring people (whom he chiefly considered) might have every where monuments of his Doctrine, remembring in gardens, his mustard-seed, and lilyes; in the field, his seed-corn, and tares: and so not be drowned altogether in the works of their vocation, but sometimes lift up their minds to better things, even in the midst of their pains.[36]

This interaction between the natural creation and human beings is very different from François de Sales' conception of a world

[33] See L. B. Campbell, *Divine Poetry and Drama in Sixteenth Century England* (Cambridge, 1959), 31 for the context of this famous remark by Coverdale and its source in Erasmus.
[34] Sales, *Introduction to the Devoute Life*, 179.
[35] George Herbert, *The Works of George Herbert*, ed. F. E. Hutchinson (Oxford, 1945), 247–8.
[36] Ibid. 261.

that speaks directly of God. Herbert's world can only speak if signification is conferred on it by the sacred text: and it is the reference to the sacred text that sanctifies the working man's task and environment. In Protestant thought, sacred meaning is conferred by the sacred text rather than implicit in the natural creation. However, this extends rather than diminishes the potential for sanctification of human experience. As we have seen, in a Protestant view the events in the Scriptures were seen to refer, typologically, to the individual lives of Christians in any period. The Bible deals in depth with the inner world of human experience, which is far more extensive than its geographical and temporal setting, the *locus* for Catholic meditation.

In St François' scheme of devotion, 'troublesome motions' are not to be articulated. His model of the human psyche is one where emotions can be suppressed, or even produced at will:

Finally make a thousand sorts and diuersities of motions in thy heart to enkindle the love of God within thee.[37]

Since 'motions' precede speech, only positive emotions will reach the stage of expression. This coincides with Jesuit poetic theory, which required a physical and imaginative environment for meditation that distanced the subject from his immediate problems and 'troublesome motions'.[38] To make the object of meditation the 'troublesome motions' themselves is utterly foreign to post-Tridentine spirituality: yet this is the distinctive characteristic of Protestant meditation, including George Herbert's religious lyrics. Roland Greene has recently argued that many lyric cycles, from Petrarch onwards, are examples of the rhetorical figure *variatio*. Successive poems illustrate differing or even conflicting aspects of the state of love, such as Petrarch's sonnet 230: 'I wept, now I sing' which follows 229: 'I sang, now I weep.'[39] Christian lyric cycles such as Herbert's are theologically justified by the immensity of the character of God, which can only be enumerated by attributes.[40]

---

[37] Sales, *Introduction to the Devoute Life*, 169.

[38] See P. Janelle, *Robert Southwell the Writer: A Study in Religious Inspiration* (London, 1935), 121.

[39] R. E. Pritchard suggests that Mary Sidney was adopting the Petrarchan model of a variety of protagonists and moods for her versions of the Psalms: *The Sidney Psalms*, 18.

[40] R. Greene, *Post-Petrarchism: Origins and Innovations of the Western Lyric Sequence* (Princeton, 1991), 115.

Herbert's poems are not about God as an entity outside of the subject: they are set, however, in the only place God can be known, the temple where He dwells and is worshipped, which is the human heart. *Variatio*, in terms of God within, involves the enumeration of the differing emotions produced by His work in the Christian soul. Henry Lok, in his 1593 sonnet cycle *Sundry Christian Passions*, had expressed just this view of the purpose of his Reformed poetry:

in which (as in a glasse) may be seene, the state of a regenerate soule, sicke with sinne, sometimes (Ague-like) shivering with cold dispaire, straight waies inflamed with fervencie of faith and hope. One while yeelding under the burthen of sinne to eternall death, and presently incouraged to runne cheerfully forward the appointed course of this his pilgramage, and like a practized traveller, used to the change of companie, diet, heate, cold, paine, pleasure, plentie, and want, not to amaze himselfe long with anie change.[41]

This model, clearly derivative of Calvin's view of the Psalms as a compendium of 'troublesome motions', is observable in the lyrics of *The Temple*, which seem to be deliberately ordered so as to illustrate shifting and contradictory moods. Herbert's sonnet 'Josephs coat' imitates the shift of mood between Petrarch's sonnets 229 and 230, within the short space of one lyric: but it contains an affirmation of human emotions that is characteristic of the poets of the Reformation and also of the Psalmist.

> I live to shew his power, who once did bring
> My *joyes* to *weep*, and now my *griefs* to *sing*.

This concluding couplet not only expresses the vagaries of the emotional state of the lover of God, but also the absolute power that God has over the lover's emotions: as Calvin had declared, 'the wittes of men are in the hand of God to rule them at every moment'.[42] The corollary of this theory is that the Christian's emotional moods are significant, borne out by Herbert's (and the Psalmist's) frequent questionings of the source of the mood, as in 'Dulnesse': 'Why do I languish thus, drooping and dull?' Since God communes with man in the seat of the affections, the heart,

---

[41] Lok, *Sundry Christian Passions*, sig. A5^r.

[42] John Calvin, *The Institution of the Christian Religion*, tr. Thomas Norton (London, 1578), II. ii. 17, p. 101.

an emotion could turn out to be a prompting from God, as we shall see in the next chapter.[43]

The sacred text, then, sanctifies the expression of human emotion. It is a short step from this position towards the legitimization of new writing by reference both to human emotion and the sacred text. Erasmus set out this interaction of Scripture and individual heartfelt experience as the most truly Christian form of creativity.

Make your own heart the library of Christ himself. Like the provident father of a family, draw out from him as from a store-room either new or old materials as the situation demands. What you produce from your heart like living things will penetrate the minds of your listener far more vividly.[44]

As Terence Cave comments, 'the scriptural text is absorbed, made consubstantial with the reader and is then re-uttered in a speech-act grounded in the living presence of the speaker, a process which achieves its end in that vivid penetration of the listener's mind which is a mark of authenticity.'[45] This rewriting of Scripture involves true 'writing on the heart', an intimate interaction of biblical text and human psyche, sacred word and human emotion. Another of God's utterances, at the end of 'Jordan (ii)', with its echo of Sidney's 'Look in thy heart, and write', acquires a new meaning in the light of this model for Christian creativity:

> There is in love a sweetness readie penn'd:
> Copie out onely that, and save expense.

The Christian poet can copy Love because it has already been written on his heart, and become that *copia* which Erasmus envisaged for the Christian writer, a plenitude produced by dynamic inward imitation of Scripture, a living library.

Thus a reworking of a Psalm in the context of immediate new emotion and experience can be regarded as a kind of sacred text itself, as in Donne's description of contemporary Psalm versions:

---

[43] Note that the emotional prayer which is the *Artillerie* is conceived of as inspired, or at least prompted from above: 'But I have also starres and shooters too, | Born where thy servants both artilleries use. | My tears and prayers night and day do wooe, | And work up to thee.'

[44] Erasmus, *Opera Omnia* (Basle, 1540), 111.

[45] T. Cave, *The Cornucopian Text: Problems of Writing in the French Renaissance* (Oxford, 1979), 79.

The songs are these, which heaven's high holy Muse
Whispered to David, David to the Jews:
And David's successors, in holy zeal,
In forms of joy and art do re-reveal.[46]

The formula of emotion and rhetoric, 'joy and art', is important
for a Protestant poetics. Any composition which was seen to
partake of that formula within a Christian context was received
as a kind of contemporary Psalm. The use of Biblical tropes, or
merely Biblical forms such as the lyrics of the Psalms, enabled the
reader to link his experience securely with events in the Biblical
story. This is why so much of Calvinist poetry, like Savonarola's,
is concerned with particular events or persons. A nineteenth-
century collection of Calvinist poetry by P. Tarbé commemorates
certain occasions and attacks specific Catholic personages such as
the duc de Guise and Charles de Lorraine, Archbishop of Reims.
If the stanza form of any particular Psalm in the Marot–Bèze
collection were used, all the resonances of that Psalm could be
employed in the interpretation of that event: in this way Psalm 137
was applied to the plight of the Huguenots besieged at Lyons.
Another example is a song in the mood and in the form of Marot's
translation of Psalm 79, composed in 1588, in solidarity with a
Protestant neighbour, on the defeat of the Spanish Armada.[47]
The connection with Holy Scripture, via a translation with
which the poem has nothing in common except metrical form,
is made through the vengeful emotion expressed in both the new
poem and the Psalm. In England at least one Protestant polemi-
cist followed in this French tradition. John Vicars, who specialized
in polemical verse, added a paraphrase of Psalm 123 entitled '*King
Iames against the Antichristians*' to his 1631 volume *England's Hallelu-
jah*. His model is confirmed by the inclusion of two poems by Beza
on the defeat of the Armada, which Vicars renders into English.[48]
The influence of the metrical innovation of the French Psalter on
a very mediocre poet results in a poetic style not unlike that of
Sidney's Psalm paraphrases, or Herbert's lyrics.

[46] Donne, *The Complete English Poems*, 333.
[47] Jeanneret, *Poésie et tradition biblique*, 117–18.
[48] John Vicars, *England's Hallelu-jah or, Great Brittaines Gratefull Retribution, for Gods Gratious Benediction In our many and most famous Deliverances, since the Halcyon-Dayes of ever-blessed Queen Elizabeth, to these present Times. Together, with divers of Davids Psalms, according to the French Metre and Measures* (London, 1631), sigs. F2ᵛ-F3ʳ.

Savonarola and Psalm Meditations in English

The Biblical texts which most stimulated literary production in Renaissance England contained exactly those 'troublesome motions' identified by Calvin. The Penitential Psalms had been translated into English poetry by Thomas Wyatt while he was in prison between 1536 and 1541, following, often closely, an Italian text.[49] These particular seven Psalms were those that received most devotional and literary attention in the sixteenth century, and spawned a kind of writing which became popular well into the seventeenth century: the Psalm meditation, loosely based on the gloomier Psalm texts. Among the very first works printed in England, by Caxton's assistant, Wynkyn de Worde, in 1500, was Savonarola's prose meditation on the thirty-first Psalm, in its Latin version. Luther showed his approval of Savonarola's meditations on Psalms 31 and 51 for a Protestant audience by reprinting them.[50] As a result, an English version appeared in the first English Prayer Book.[51] In 1563 *Foxe's Booke of Martyrs*, after a hagiographic account of Savonarola's death, particularly recommended his meditation on the thirty-first Psalm to English readers. In France, translations were published as part of the 1584 edition of the Protestant Philippe Duplessis-Mornay's *Discours de la vie et de la mort*. The association of these texts with significant documents in the emerging Protestant spirituality sanctioned this particular mode of expression for increasing numbers of English, German, and French Christians: given the widespread dissemination of these meditations in the vernacular throughout Europe it is fair to assume that they helped to form the conception of an emerging Protestant devotional literature.

These Psalm meditations take the form of inner dialogues, in the manner of much Protestant devotional writing that followed. Like the Psalms they comment and elaborate on, the Psalm meditations are powerful expressions of turbulent emotion, which is not surprising, as the meditation on Psalm 31 was composed during a period of torture and imprisonment: execution intervened to prevent its completion. It takes the form of an

---

[49] Pietro Aretino, *I Sette Salmi de la Penitentia di David* (Venice, 1536).

[50] See R. Ridolfi, *The Life of Girolamo Savonarola*, tr. C. Grayson (New York, 1959), 302.

[51] Appended to *A Prymer in Englyshe, with certeyn prayers & godly meditations, very necessary for all people that understonde not the Latyne tongue* (London, 1534). In this first edition the author is unacknowledged.

internal dialogue between hope and despair. The debate is sanctioned by the close link between Savonarola's writing and the biblical text with which it interacts. Both 'voices' in Savonarola's meditations adopt biblical language, and like many other texts based on the Psalms, his models follow a dialogic pattern. To begin with the two voices represent changes of mood within the writer's consciousness, as in the original Psalm, but gradually separate identities emerge. 'Hevyness' is personified as a formidable woman, and her intervention as the meditating individual is rehearsing the rhetoric of hope can produce an immediate shift of mood:

I am replenyshed with ioy bycause I truste in the, therfor I shall nat be confounded for evermore. Heavynes cometh agayne with great purveyaunce she is returned, with swerdes and speres on every side she is defended, standying without she commaunded silence, and a farre of she spake saynge.... Where is the conforte? what haue thy teares profyteth the?[52]

Fortunately, another protagonist is introduced, whose voice is more strongly represented than that of the original writer. 'Hope' is characterized as a male, addressing the writer as 'Sonne', and his rhetoric is very close to that of God in Jeremiah 1: 8, although there is nothing like it in Psalm 31.

Wherefore hope cam shining with a certeyne divine bryghtnes, and smylyng sayd, O soudyer of Christ...fear thou nat, this evyl shal nat take ye, thou shalt nat peryshe lo I am with the to delyver the.[53]

This highly individualistic interpretation of the Psalm text, and its acceptance as devotional literature alongside the Prayer Book, assumes a radical and personalized use of Scripture. The individual Christian is authorized to add to Scripture, and reassign utterances—in fact, to rewrite it. Michel Jeanneret comments on the distance from the original text that writers of Psalm meditation often travelled in order to incorporate their own particular experience.[54] This is the ultimate expression of the Protestant engagement with Scripture expressed by Herbert in his sonnet, 'The H. Scriptures (ii)'. It is a Protestant article of faith that

---

[52] Jérôme Savonarola, *A meditacyon of the same Jerom upon the Psalme of In the Dne spoeravi whiche preventyd by death he coulde nat fynyshe*, in *The Englysh Primer* (Paris, 1538), sig. fii^r.

[53] Ibid. sig. fiii^v.   [54] Jeanneret, *Poésie et tradition biblique*, 401, 417.

Scripture is about the Christian's experience: the interpretation of the sacred text involves finding Scriptural parallels for his own circumstances, so that experience acts as a commentary on the text. This is exactly the function of Psalm meditation in English Reformation spirituality.

Perhaps the earliest example of this phenomenon is the sonnet sequence on Psalm 51 attached to the translation of Calvin's sermons on Hezekiah by Anne Lok, published in 1560. It encompasses all the features of Psalm meditation identified so far, including a separate voice for the personified figure of Despeir. Each sonnet appears securely attached to the originating Psalm by a marginal reference to the text, but this does not stop the writer digressing in the final sonnet from the context of personal penitence to a vision of a godly community that is clearly Protestant England.[55] Ros Smith has identified this volume as part of a body of texts produced in Calvin's Geneva by the expatriate English community designed to have an admonitory function for their new monarch. The exemplary figure of Hezekiah, who did not carry his kingdom's reformation far enough, recurs in these texts as a warning to Elizabeth to extirpate all traces of Popery from her church administration. This sonnet sequence is an extremely early example in English of the Psalm meditation, and its ability to carry political meaning: it could not, I think, have been produced outside of the French literary and religious context exemplified by the Marot–Bèze Psalter.[56]

Another such rewriting of two of the Penitential Psalms, Psalm 6 and Psalm 32, was published in London in 1622: Sir John Hayward's *Davids teares*. Psalm 32 is notable for its many changes of mood, and for its change of speaker. Verse 8 appears to be spoken by God in reply to the prayers of the first seven verses. Hayward supplies his own version of God's words, although he introduces them tentatively as a voice he thinks he hears. The change of speaker is indicated by a change of typeface.

[55] John Calvin, *Sermons of John Calvin, upon the songe that Ezechias made after he had bene sicke, and afflicted by the hand of God, conteyned in the 38. Chapiter of Esay*, tr. Anne Lok (London, 1560), sig. H7ᵛ.

[56] See ' "In a mirrour clere": Anne Lok's "Miserere mei deus" as Protestant Admonitory Text', in Danielle Clarke and Elizabeth Clarke (eds.), *'The Double Voice': Gendered Writing in Early Modern England*, forthcoming.

And now (me thinke) this heavenly voyce perpetually soundeth in mine ears.

Feare not, beholde, as I have infused a soule into thy body, so will I infuse my spirit into thy soule, to guide all the actions and motions thereof.[57]

Later, perhaps growing bolder, he abandons the tentative approach and the need for a Biblical text as model and improvises some words of God, for which he demands the respect due to divine authority.

Heare me whom experience hath taught; Or rather heare the LORD himself: listen well what hee sayth unto you.... Come unto me, thou miserable man.[58]

Three pages later he himself responds to his original composition as if it were holy discourse: 'O sweete wordes!' In this way, Psalm meditation was seen as 'a conversation with God'. As Tessa Watt notes, 'the invention of non-scriptural speeches for God or Christ was a dubious exercise for Protestants, with their emphasis on biblical authority.'[59]

Paradoxically, however, it is the Protestant mode of appropriation of Scripture which allows for such daring on the part of authors. The act of reading as a two-way conversation demands both a profound identification with the original writer and a belief that the words spoken by God in those original circumstances could be annexed, no matter what the gap in space and time, by a Christian individual in similar circumstances. Both these ideas were inherent in the Protestant reading of the Biblical text, which, as Herbert asserts in 'The Bunch of Grapes', is about the modern Christian reader every bit as much as the ancient Jews. It seems that this basic freedom in interpretation of the text could be expanded to elaboration on the biblical words: not only could the human element be expanded, but new words of God could be invented. The genre of Psalm meditation established a strong tradition for assuming that God will speak to the believer in the same tone and manner as the biblical text, but not necessarily in the same words. This is one literary context for George Herbert's religious lyrics, which freely invent dialogue for God.

---

[57] Sir John Hayward, *Davids teares* (London, 1622), 241.   [58] Ibid. 234.
[59] T. Watts, *Cheap Print and Popular Piety, 1550–1640* (Cambridge, 1991), 105.

The Healing Power of the Psalms

Having translated Savonarola's Psalm meditations, Duplessis-Mornay had occasion to compose one of his own. In grief for his son, killed during the wars of religion in an attack on Geldre, he wrote and published a prose meditation which has many affinities with Savonarola's style. Jeanneret sees Duplessis-Mornay's style as typical of the emerging Protestant genre of Psalm meditation in the 1570s, and attributes it to the all-pervasive influence of Savonarola:

mêmes groupes syntaxique brefs, même rythme hâché, même concision, à l'opposé exact des balancements de la période cicéronienne; il y a plus: l'auteur se plait à jouer avec les mots, il cultive les points et les paradoxes, il affectionne les artifices rhétoriques...les mêmes recettes servent à la recherche d'une même expressivité.[60]

Other French writers who shared in this style of Psalm meditation included Beza, Sponde, and d'Aubigné, who were also the most prominent French religious poets. It is no coincidence that this description exactly fits the 'ejaculatory' style as it was to develop in English prose and poetry in the seventeenth century, perhaps as a direct result of the widespread reading of Savonarola, or of the powerful influence of French Protestant authors. Duplessis-Mornay's meditation, based on Psalm 39, was published in English in 1609, as *Philip Mornay, Lord of Plessis, his Teares for the death of his Sonne*. It takes the form of an internal argument, as the author maintains a taut balance between grief and restraint. The language used by Duplessis-Mornay—embottelling, venting, channelling—as well as his overall concern for what is psychologically healthy shows that he too is using his meditation as a purging of his grief through expression, although the writing is not poetic or particularly literary. The dedication by the translator John Healey claims the work as a model for Protestant reaction to grief. What is striking about this text is its constant interrogation of its own legitimacy. Duplessis-Mornay refers constantly to Psalm 39, which questions the lawfulness of certain kinds of utterance, and begins with a declaration of future silence: 'I said, I will take heed to my ways, that I sin not with my tongue:

---

[60] Jeanneret, *Poésie et tradition biblique*, 415.

I will keep my mouth with a bridle.' However, the Psalm charts the impossibility of silence under extreme suffering, as does Duplessis-Mornay's *Teares*. Lest he give voice to utterances which are offensive to God, he takes refuge in the inspired and therefore legitimate words of the Psalm.

Oh my LORD! I feele a rebellious battell within me! keepe down my tongue, let it loose to no language, but these sounds of the Psalmist: *I am dumbe: and do not open my mouth, because thou hast done it. But thou Lord, laye thine hand upon my mouth,* that my redoubling dolour burst not out into outragious murmure.[61]

The apparent quotation from Psalm 39 is actually adapted for the writer's purpose. The tense of verse 9 is changed from past to present, and the italics which indicate direct quotation include a prayer of the author's own. The author's meaning is seen as close enough to the Biblical text to partake of its sacrality. However, the adoption of sacred words does end Duplessis-Mornay's search for a legitimate discourse which fully expresses his emotion. Later in the work one biblical text, which is an almost exact quotation from Job 32, actually cracks under the pressure of the emotion within, and is fragmented by brackets, exclamation marks, and the powerful physical imagery of suppressed grief:

I am dumb—then But thou (LORD) keepe a bridle within my mouth, be sure (LORD) that thou doest see, that my lips be not let loose to impute uniustice unto thee: oh no but let them ever oppose iniquity...Ah! but (my gracious Lord) I am full of (dolorous) matter: my spirit swells within me, and compells mee! Behold, my belly is as the wine that hath no vent, & wanting vent, resembles the embotteled wine that breakes through all that bindeth it in. Therefore I wil speake (I think it bee best) that I may take some breath, against this abundant excesse of sorrowe.[62]

The author decides in favour of a psychologically healthy way to deal with grief, and continues with a delicate balance of restraint and indulgence. Grief must be expressed but not luxuriated in: 'stoppe it too soone, it spoiles us: stay it too long, it kills us.'[63]

---

[61] Philippe Duplessis-Mornay, *Philip Mornay, Lord of Plessis, his Teares for the death of his Sonne. Vnto his wife Charlotte Baliste,* tr. John Healey (London, 1609), sigs. A8ʳ⁻ᵛ. See Herbert's poem 'Affliction (i)'. In accusing God Herbert is staying within the boundaries of Psalm discourse, where a frequent refrain is 'Thou hast done it': all misfortune is seen as attributable to God.

[62] Duplessis-Mornay, *Teares,* B4ʳ.   [63] Ibid. A4ʳ.

However, the author also has biblical precedent for this procedure. Psalm 39 does not conclude with the stated intention of
silence. In fact, that promise is placed firmly in the past. The
Psalm traces the breaking of the promise in verse 3, and continues
to demonstrate by its own discourse that such a promise is
unrealistic and unnecessary. God does not, in the end, require
silent suffering. Thus Duplessis-Mornay concludes, in an epilogue
addressed to his wife,

> wee may weepe lawfully thus, as long as the streames that raine from our
> eyes, do not make the river of our griefes overflowe their bankes, so
> then, keeping this channell, let them droppe from our cheekes eternallie:
> let us make pearles of them, which no bloud, no vinegar may ever
> dissolve.[64]

The lawful channel of expression for their grief is not in the actual
words of the Psalms but in the tone and form of the holy discourse. The constant reference to the authorizing text enables a
legitimate expression and purging of grief very much in the way
John Reading had envisaged in *Davids Soliloquie*. Thereafter these
'tears' may be read alongside the holy text, as was recommended
by James Howell in his *Instructions for Forreine Travell*: Philippe
Duplessis-Mornay's writings are good Sunday reading because
of his 'pathetical ejaculations'.[65] It is a comment on the human-
centred and psychological nature of this type of discourse that it
could easily be secularized and adapted for any type of lament,
such as the elegiac volume published in 1625 after the deaths of
the Earl of Southampton and his son, *The Teares of the Isle of Wight*.

John Reading, a Calvinist with Royalist sympathies, tried to
theorize some of the perceived power of the Psalms in a way that
did justice to their status as poetry. In a series of sermons given
during his appointment as chaplain to Dover Castle, which were
published as *Davids Soliloquie conteining many comforts for afflicted minds*,
he describes two functions for Psalm language, both concerned
specifically with its literary qualities. His description of the Psalms
as a 'soliloquie' is qualified in his early definition of them as
'Colloquies and secret Conferences with God'. However, it
seems that God is present in these conferences only as an obser-

---

[64] Ibid. E2ᵛ.
[65] James Howell, *Instructions for Forreine Travell* (London, 1650), 21.

ver. All the talking is done by the human being, whether silently or audibly: God, of course, can hear both discourses, so the audible words are purely for the benefit of the person praying,

to stirre up the affections, and to leave a more firme impression in the mind then those slender and unuttered thoughts could have done.[66]

In fact, Reading's explanation of the power of the Psalms remains entirely on the human and psychological plane. The Psalms contain healing for every state of mind: and much of this curative power is located in the poetry itself. God deliberately ordered that the content of the Psalms should be 'taught to runne in smooth numbers, ordered feete of divine Poesie'. He concludes that sung poetry is the most powerful of all:

When wee heare not onely voyces but words, and these spirituall and heavenly, I know not how, the affections, reason and deepest sense of the soule are so moved, as that there appeareth the most excellent use of Psalmes and singing.[67]

Reading then attempts an explanation of this mysterious poetic power, a discussion taken straight from sixteenth-century Italian debates about the usefulness of poetry. The most important use of the Psalms, he says, is 'to pacifie & calme ungoverned affections'. This is the classic Aristotelian defence against the Platonic claim that poets should be banished from the commonwealth.[68] Defenders of poetry in Christian Italy argued that poetry purged the passions which could be harmful to the individual and to the state. Reading also wants to annex Plato for his promotion of the spiritual use of Psalm poetry, however. The second reason for reading the Psalms is Platonic in content and terminology: 'to stirre up and awaken the affections, to carrie up the minde to an higher flight.' Both functions of the Psalms, as perceived by Reading, operate within the context of ordinary human emotions. The Psalms 'heal' therefore, by soothing some passions and arousing others, the classical functions of poetry.

---

[66] John Reading, *Davids Soliloquie conteining many comforts for afflicted minds* (London, 1627), 102.

[67] Ibid. 15. In *Saint Augustine's Meter and George Herbert's Will* (Kent, Oh., 1987), William Pahlka argues that the musical power of poetry has the effect on the rational faculty that St Augustine describes in *De Musica*; see pp. 32–4.

[68] B. Weinberg, *A History of Criticism in the Italian Renaissance* (Chicago, 1961), 347.

The terminology in which the second aim is described is very reminiscent of Herbert's language when he is looking to poetry as a release from spiritual torpor. A Psalm can 'greaten and give more vigour to good passions, make the minde more active and quicke'. A Psalm 'sequestreth the mind from the earth, lifeth up the thoughts, and maketh them light and high flying'. The Psalm must be earnestly appropriated: 'What were our hearing with drowzie, unmoved attention? What fruit could wee expect from devotion so cold?'[69] Cold, drowsy, earthbound as opposed to quick, active, flying: this is the language for devotion and creativity in 'Dulnesse', 'Employment (ii)', and 'The Answer'. The poetic, holy discourse of the Psalms, when used in 'an inward speaking of the soule within it selfe', has the power to arouse the useful passions of love and devotion.

The Aristotelian half of the equation, in which unwelcome passions are removed, is a rather different process. The 'emptying of the heart' which occurs in the use of the Psalms happens through the appropriation of the biblical words as self-expression. 'How moovingly doe men sing their owne grief, true sorrowes?' comments Reading. Yet, apparently, there is no audience present to move. As Reading makes clear, the function of the negative Psalm discourse is not to persuade others of the rightness of the cause, as in Ciceronian forensic oratory, but simply to expend negative energy: 'His [the Psalmist's] purpose is to show, that the most iust grief and disquiet of mind, must be moderated.' The usefulness of Psalm language as opposed to ordinary human language is that it is authorized by nature of its direct inspiration from God, and therefore can represent no sinful attitudes:

The afflicted man is comforted, when following the dearest saints of God in their conditions, and in their words, he thinketh, and is resolved, no tentation hath overtaken him, but such as belongeth to the beloved sonnes of G O D.[70]

The Psalms function as a sort of safety-valve for the 'troublesome motions' which affect all human beings. According to Isaak Walton, Nicholas Ferrar described *The Temple* in the same terms as the

---

[69] Reading, *Davids Soliloquie*, 20.   [70] Ibid. 27.

book of Psalms: 'a harmony of holy passions.'[71] Herbert's lyrics were received as divinely inspired, perhaps because they were seen as a version of the biblical compendium of emotional discourse that is the Psalms.[72]

The Lyrics of The Temple and the Poetry of the Psalms

In English devotional literature of the Reformation 'ejaculations' seems to denote a language in which biblical text and the emotional experience of the writer combine to produce a highly individualized, emotional text that is perceived as biblical. The function of the holy lyrics of the Psalms is seen by Protestants throughout the period as a language in which to express every emotion of the human heart. It is not essential that this language is literary.[73] The Psalms show themselves open to use on several different models. The human-centred discourse which John Reading describes stresses its rhetorical effectiveness for use on a psychological level. Herbert's The Temple has its fair share of 'troublesome motions', which, as we have seen, were perceived by Protestants if not by Catholics as the very stuff of ejaculatory prayer. He seems to feel no embarrassment about recording the most rebellious and violent feelings, as in 'The Collar', 'Nature', or 'Affliction (i)'. Despite his tendency to chart the 'mildness' of Herbert's lyrics, Louis Martz has noted the major influence of the Penitential Psalms on Herbert's poetry.

Most important of all [the Psalms] are the psalms of affliction, for this word, which gives a title to five poems in The Temple and occurs in nine more, is used (including verbal forms) thirty-five times in the King James version of the Psalms, more often than in any other book of the Bible.[74]

[71] Walton, Life of Herbert, 109.
[72] See, for example, the comments of Robert Codrington, Ralph Knevet, and Daniel Barker, in C. A. Patrides (ed.), George Herbert: The Critical Heritage (London, 1983), 63, 64–5, 140.
[73] However, Rivkah Zim, in surveying English metrical Psalm-translation of 1535–1601, concludes that the Psalms led directly to the growth of a literary tradition: 'Because metrical psalms were poetic expressions of devotion to God's truth, they lent credence to other personal expressions of emotional intensity in different forms of English secular poetry. The reader could feel more comfortable with expressions of emotional intensity in such poetry, since he knew that in the Psalms they had been sanctioned by religious experience mediated through a divinely inspired model' (English Metrical Psalms, 205).
[74] Martz, The Poetry of Meditation, 280.

All the Penitential Psalms bar one begin in abject misery: doubt, despair, potential rebellion. These are indeed 'troublesome motions', and there are plenty of Herbert's lyrics which begin similarly. After the ejaculatory beginning, the pattern which the subsequent discourse takes varies from Psalm to Psalm.

Of the seven Penitential Psalms, one, Psalm 38, does not resolve on a more positive note. There are flickers of optimism, as the possibility of God answering is considered, but the final position is one of consciousness of the immediate presence of enemies, and resulting anxiety. Herbert's poem 'Longing' has this structure. The 'sick and famisht eyes', the 'doubling knees and weary bones' of the start of the poem are very reminiscent of Psalm language, as at the beginning of Psalms 38 and 102. Focusing on the power of God to hear and to save produces momentary lightening of tone but at the end of the poem the arrows of God still 'stick fast' in the poet's heart, as they do in verse 2 of Psalm 38. Most of the verses in 'Longing' have the same ejaculatory, emotional force with which the poem began: no progress has been made, no kind of answer has been received, and the initial event of the poem is simply repeated in various formulations. The tone of the poem continues frantic, the punctuation exclamatory and interrogative. However, this is a rare event in *The Temple*: the poem in which there is no progress is the exception. Very common is the pattern represented in another Penitential Psalm, Psalm 143, which is equally divided between the expression of grief and the petition to God. The change of direction from self-centred to God-centred discourse is indicated by a formal pause, after which the tone is far more peaceful. The reason for the change in tone seems to be that the writer's suffering is objectified by reference to another, supreme, being, who has the power to change the writer's circumstances for the better.

In Herbert's poetry, the mere mention of God, or at least the turning towards him of the speaker, is often sufficient to resolve the poem on a more positive note. More often than not, a turning towards God reminds the speaker of what God can do for him, and this in itself strikes a note of hope, as we see in Psalm 143. 'Nature' is a vivid example of this movement. The first three lines express ultimate rebellion, kept in check only by the appeal to God in line 4. Verse 2 threatens disintegration again, and only the appeal to God of verse 3 saves the speaker from complete dissolution. The imagery for the rebellious heart changes that of corrupting flesh to dry rough stone, at least a more stable material, and one that God specializes in as a craftsman. The accusation of the second verse, that God is allowing this destructive state of affairs, is dropped by verse 3: the implication is that it is a shift in the speaker's attitude which is part of the answer to his own prayer. As Chana Bloch comments, 'Herbert's complaints, for all their bitterness, are typically not just a grieving but a lifting of the eyes. That motion initiates a mood of certainty in which these poems come to rest.'[75]

The movement of Psalm 102 is again linked to the mood of the writer: the dark tone is relieved as he shifts his gaze to the omnipotence of God. This time it is objective consideration of God's attributes, such as His faithfulness towards His followers, that opens the way to a new, less self-centred prayer.

I said, O my God, take me not away in the midst of mine age: as for thy years, they endure throughout all generations... thou art the same, and thy years shall not fail. The children of thy servants shall continue.[76]

'Whitsunday' expresses exactly the sentiment of Psalm 102. The comfort is in the continuing tradition of God's worship, even if the individual himself does not survive. The possibility of comfort hardens into a fully imagined future by the end of Psalm 51. Verse 13 assumes God answering the petition of verse 12 at some point in the future: from that point on the discourse inhabits an imaginary, happier time.

Then shall I teach thy ways unto the wicked; and sinners shall be converted unto thee... Then shalt thou be pleased with the sacrifice of righteousness.[77]

The writer of Psalm 51 seems to locate his eventual relative optimism in hope for the future. There is a similar focus in Psalm 130, where the very strength of the expression of hope seems to create it.

I look for the Lord; my soul doth wait for him: in his word is my trust. My soul fleeth unto the Lord: before the morning watch, I say, before

[75] C. Bloch, *Spelling the Word: George Herbert and the Bible* (Berkeley, 1985), 278.
[76] Ps. 102: 24, 27–8. All Psalm quotations in the rest of this chapter are from the Coverdale version, which Herbert would have known from the Prayer Book.
[77] Ps. 51: 13, 19.

the morning watch. O Israel, trust in the Lord: for with the Lord there is mercy: and with him is plenteous redemption. And he shall redeem Israel: from all his sins.[78]

Herbert's 'Affliction (iv)' is a very poignant example of this model. The poem begins in complete disintegration and despair, again with the added twist that God is responsible.

> Broken in pieces all asunder,
> Lord, hunt me not.

By verse 4 the speaker has been able to turn from the contemplation of his own misery and frame a prayer to God: between verses 4 and 5 he is able to conceive an image of God's healing power,

> As the sunne scatters by his light
> All the rebellions of the night.

This imaginative rendering of the potential power of God almost creates its reality in Herbert's mind, at least in terms of hope for the future.

> Then shall those powers, which work for grief,
> Enter thy pay
> And day by day,
> Labour thy praise, and my relief;
> With care and courage building me,
> Till I reach heav'n, and much more, thee.

By the end of the poem the speaker has reached God, at least in the terms of the poem. The tone, language, and pace of the poem has been utterly transformed: what was expressive of desperation is now redolent of peaceful hope.

In all of the Psalms that we have been analysing so far there has been a psychological and thus rhetorical reason for the change of tone or mood. However, the reason for a shift in tone is not always supplied in the Psalm lyrics. In Psalm 6 there is a sudden change of tone before verse 8. The first seven verses have been laments and pleas for God's mercy. In verse 8 the speaker suddenly feels as if he has been answered: so much so that he rouses himself to attack all his enemies.

---

[78] Ps. 130: 6–8.

Away from me, all ye that work vanity; for the Lord hath heard the voice of my weeping. The Lord hath heard my petition: the Lord will receive my prayer. All mine enemies shall be confounded and sore vexed: they shall be turned back, and put to shame suddenly.[79]

And 'suddenly' is the way things happen in this Psalm. There is no audible voice which indicates to the reader that the Lord has answered. Everything takes place within the writer's consciousness. It is left to the reader to speculate on what has happened. George Herbert's poems occasionally make sudden movements in this way. Perhaps the most sudden is at the end of 'A Parodie', which laments the absence of God, or at least the sense of the absence of God, which is also God's responsibility. As in many of the Psalms, the enemy is ready with accusations, reported in the text of the poem:

> While Sinne doth rave,
> And falsly boast,
> That I may seek, but thou art lost.

The enemy is silenced only by the return of God Himself, which is as sudden, silent, and inexplicable as the answer of God in Psalm 6.

However, Herbert is not usually happy with unexplained silence. 'Assurance' also deals with the accusation of enemies: the familiar one, that the relationship with God is broken. The direction of the discourse is rather similar to that of Psalm 6. We hear half of two separate conversations: in each case, the poet's half. The opening of the poem focuses on the accusation of the enemy, with a correspondingly negative tone and mood. The actual voice of the enemy is not heard: his words are enclosed within the discourse of the speaker, in reported speech. The poem finishes with a triumphant banishment of the enemy very similar to the defiant and contemptuous final verse of Psalm 6. However, what Herbert supplies us with, which the Psalmist does not, is a description of the moves which result in such a victorious conclusion. The movements within this poem are as much physical as psychological, as the speaker turns his back on the accuser and goes to talk to his God: 'But I will to my Father, | Who heard thee say it.' As in other Psalm texts, this change of focus and direction for the discourse immediately results in a positive change in the

---

[79] Ps. 6: 8–10.

state of mind of the speaker. Although Herbert allows no opportunity for God to reply to his address, his own discourse begins to take on some of the content and confidence of biblical rhetoric. The answer from God is not audible, but there is the sense of an external infusion into the poet's consciousness, reflected in the syntax of the penultimate stanza, which piles clause on clause in a confident rhetoric far removed from the fragmentary exclamations of the first three stanzas:

> while rocks stand,
> And rivers stirre, thou canst not shrink or quail:
> Yea, when both rocks and all things shall disband,
> Then shalt thou be my rock and tower,
> And make their ruine praise thy power.

As in Psalm 6, there is a certainty that God has heard the prayer: the petition is successful. However, the reader also knows exactly what has happened, which is not the case with Psalm 6. The discourse of the penultimate stanza has an authoritative quality: it seems to come from elsewhere than the poet's fraught consciousness. The imagery and rhetoric is redolent of the Scriptures. The figures of security, the 'rock' and 'tower', are taken from Psalm 61. Whether mediated through Scripture and the poet's memory, or communicated directly into his mind at the moment of confrontation, this discourse represents God's answer to the supplicant, and it is very clear from whence the speaker found the confidence and authority to belittle the accuser of verse 1, who had appeared so threatening.

Dialogism and Monologism in The Temple

Throughout the Psalms, which John Reading called *Davids Soliloquie*, the voice of the poet is continually heard, although there are sometimes pauses, as we have seen, and occasionally the intervention of another voice. However, much of the discourse is apparently monologic, and this is true for Herbert's lyrics, too. Mikhail Bakhtin designated poetry as the supremely monologic form because of the high degree of control exerted by the poet. However, he admitted that 'even in poetic speech it is possible not to reduce verbal material to a single common denominator'.[80] As

---

[80] M. Bakhtin, *Problems of Dostoyevsky's Poetics*, tr. and ed. C. Emerson (Manchester, 1984), 200.

Herbert J. Levine has argued of the Psalms, it is possible to represent poetry as an internal dialogic discourse. The poet struggles with various voices: the authoritative voice of God; the words of earlier selves he has been; and the statements of 'the wicked'.[81]

The poem in *The Temple* which has an overtly dialogic element is the exception rather than the rule. However, as in 'Assurance', there is usually no need for Herbert to put words into the mouth of God. We recognize the influence of God's words without actually hearing them, in the movement traced by the stream-of-consciousness monologue. As in St François' conception of the way God speaks, the silent divine 'motions' are the most eloquent rhetoric. It is possible for Herbert to simulate a 'motion' within his poetry without embodying that motion in direct speech: in charting the effect upon the speaker's consciousness, the impression of another and rather more eloquent speaker is created. Sometimes it is with the appropriation of the authoritative words of the Bible that the poem changes register, as in 'Nature', where the formulation of the Biblical prayer, with its authoritative image of engraving on the stony heart, actually predominates over the more recent Renaissance imagery of 'bubbles' which describes the poet's predicament at the start of the poem. We have already charted the effect of the 'master image' of Christ as the sun in 'Affliction (iv)': the almost iconic power of that metaphor/pun is elaborated by Herbert in his poem 'The Sonne'. The mere mention of it has the power to bring about an anticipatory dawn in the dark night of 'Affliction (iv)'.

As a poet, rather than an orator, Herbert has many extra resources available with which to signal a change of mood. Some shifts of mood or perspective are enshrined within the disciplines of form itself. The sonnet form, for example, whether in its Petrarchan or Shakespearean form, traditionally located a shift in tone or direction between the octet and the sestet. 'The Sinner' exploits this division for a Christian meditation. It consists of a survey of the contents of the speaker's memory, and the first octet makes damning reading.

> I finde there quarries of pil'd vanities
> But shreds of holiness.

---

[81] H. J. Levine, 'The Dialogic Discourse of the Psalms', paper given at the Literature and Theology International Conference, Durham, 1989.

The second sestet focuses on these 'shreds', to positive effect. The existence of a 'quintessence' among the 'dregs' gives the speaker strength to 'groan' a request to God in terms of the writing on the stony heart in which He specializes. As we have seen, groans are effective with God: this 'groan' is contained in the final couplet of the sonnet, which English poets from the sixteenth century had been perfecting as a powerfully affective closure to the sonnet form.

> And though my hard heart scarce to thee can groane,
> Remember that thou once didst write in stone.

The poem finishes with a verbal event, a prayer, described as a non-verbal but traditionally effective 'groan', and which represents progress in terms of the agonized regret with which the poem began.[82] In fact, Herbert has it both ways, for the benefit of the reader: the content of the ejaculation is articulated, giving a sense of how God might possibly answer the request.

Herbert's mastery of form enables him to exploit all the affective possibilities in a change of metre, rhyme, or stanza form. It could be argued that the subliminal sound effect of an alteration in form most nearly approximates the mysterious, almost subconscious affect of a 'motion': a change in imagery, by contrast, would be a more obvious way of signalling a change in mood, and one more assimilable by the rational faculty. However, Herbert's deviations in form are usually firmly linked to the sense of the poetry. 'Deniall', for example, pivots on the postponement by the poet of a resolution to the poem. The metre and rhyme scheme of the stanzas throughout is calculated to evoke a niggling dissatisfaction: the final line, far from giving each stanza a sense of closure, is tacked on to the end of each stanza with no obvious place in the rhythm or rhyme scheme of the poem. Only in the final stanza does the final line take up its proper role: it forms a rhyming couplet with the penultimate line and echoes the iambic duometer of the second line. Furthermore, in place of the feminine endings which have characterized the final lines of the stanzas, there is a masculine ending. The trochaic tendency in the penultimate stanza resolves into normative iambics in the final stanza, and the resulting sense of harmony and closure is calculated to

---

[82.] The possibilities within the last couplet of the sonnet to reverse the movement of the previous twelve lines are also used by Herbert, most effectively in 'Sinne (i)'.

underline the 'chime' of God's grace and man's needs. This represents a movement of hope in a poem that has been uniformly negative. Herbert boldly draws attention to his technique by positing this future blessing as one which will 'mend [his] ryme' as well as everything else. The restoration of the regular form of the poem functions as the first hint that the deadlock between God and man is broken and that other blessings will follow this one.

A less obtrusive use of the same technique is seen at the end of the poem 'The Collar'. The disruption of the form of this poem is more radical but less explicit. The apparent randomness of the metre and rhyme is accentuated by the carefully disordered layout of the poem, which is so untidy that many editors cannot cope with it, and regularize somewhat. The final four lines pick up the underlying metre and rhyme of the rest of the poem and impose an order and peace which corresponds to the effect of the restraining word from God. Antony Mortimer has pointed out that the crucial words 'Child' and 'Lord' sound so inevitable because 'the "eye" and "or" sounds have been established from the start as the dominant vowels of the poem', but this sound effect is not created by sound alone.[83] The alteration in form, however, actually occurs before the intervention from God: the subject-matter of the first regular line is 'But as I rav'd and grew more fierce and wild'. The sense of change is achieved partly by the regularizing of the form but also by the grammatical shift from direct speech into reported speech and from present tense to past. Of course, it would be impossible for God to impose a four-line stanzaic form in one word, however significantly placed: the whole point of the poem is that God only has to speak one authoritative word to overcome the effect of 221 rebellious ones from Herbert. However, God needs a little help from the poet. Although there is no doubt that one word from God would produce a dramatic effect if spoken directly to the human being, when that movement is mimicked in poetry the resources of syntax, rhyme, and metre have to be employed.

It is in Herbert's experiments with form, then, that we must look for the source of his ability to create movement and life in a poem. Herbert seems to be aware of the affective possibilities of a wide range of stanzaic forms, some conventional, some innov-

---

[83] Mortimer, 'Words in the Mouth of God', 40.

ative. 'An Offering' begins in six-line stanzas of ponderous pentameters. The scenario is that of the Christian offering his heart to
God in a traditional gesture of piety: the interlocutor, however,
casts doubt on the enterprise from the beginning. It seems that the
giver has been rather slow to come forward: but the first stanza,
whilst mirroring this slowness in the pace of the poem, justifies the
giver's reluctance by finding fault with the gift.

> Come, bring thy gift. If blessings were as slow
> As mens returns, what would become of fools?
> What hast thou there? a heart? but is it pure?
> Search well and see; for hearts have many holes.
> Yet one pure heart is nothing to bestow.

The stern moralizing of the speaker, having established the inferior condition of the heart which is the gift, relents only after
three stanzas of this sort of thing to offer some kind of hope. It
seems that to restore the heart to health requires an ointment,
which turns out to be Christ's blood. The giver is advised to defer
his offering until he has found some of this 'All-heal'. At that
future time, says the speaker, not only will the gift be acceptable,
but the giver will be able to praise God in the words of the second
half of the poem. The contrast between the form, tone, and
sentiment of the poem before and after the colon which introduces
the 'hymn' could not be greater. The slow pentameters are
replaced by a skipping rhythm of very short lines: the mood is
carefree as opposed to the anxious interrogation of the worthiness
of the gift in part one.

> Since my sadnesse
> Into gladnesse
> Lord thou dost convert,
> O accept
> What thou hast kept,
> As thy due desert.

'Sadnesse' has been metrically converted into 'gladnesse'. Since
the second part of the poem is still apparently spoken by the
grave interlocutor of the first part the effect is so dramatic as to
be mildly schizophrenic. Herbert obviously wanted to illustrate
the healing effect of the blood of Christ on the whole psyche of
the believer, reflected in the happy lyric of the second half of the
poem. However, the abrupt change in the poem's persona, along

with the fact that the happiness is placed firmly in an as yet unattained future, makes the shift difficult to follow.

There are other poems where it is not clear whether Herbert intended them as two single poems or two halves of the same poem. The layout of the B manuscript serves to confuse the issue by placing two poems on the same subject on facing pages, giving only the first a title. In some cases, such as the two parts of 'Good Friday', this is a change from the practice of the W manuscript, which prints the two parts separately: the second part even has a different title, 'The Passion'. In fact, it is hard to see what these poems gain from being united in this way.[84] The two parts of 'Easter', however, which are separated in W, add an interesting dimension to each other. Part one is a typically Herbertian self-exhortation to sing God's praise. Often, as in 'A Wreath', such poems will end before the actual act of praise has commenced: but having carefully ascertained in part one what the correct formula for praise is—heart, lute, and Holy Spirit in a sacred trio—part two is a plausible result of such composition. In form it is a simple, personal love-lyric, encompassing the Easter imagery of the rising sun. The combined effect is in fact one of resurrection: after the 'struggle' for effective praise in part one, which is explicitly connected with Christ's sufferings on the Cross, the answer to the prayer for the intervention of the Holy Spirit is achieved in the happy sentiments and easy rhythms of part two.

Janis Lull finds the possibility of a similar internal relationship in the two-part 'The H. Communion'.[85] Originally separate poems with different names, the effect of joining the two poems is to offer a different perspective on the same activity. As with 'Easter', and to some extent 'An Offering', the first part is a complex form, containing, as often in Herbert's poetry, a reflective consideration of the implications of standard Christian doctrine. Here it is the implications of the choice of a meal as the central experience of communion with Christ that Herbert is exploring. Having celebrated the straightforward analogy that like the bread, God's grace penetrates the deepest recesses of the

[84] Janis Lull, in *The Poem in Time: Reading Herbert's Revisions of 'The Church'* (Newark, Del. 1990), 24–5, argues persuasively that Herbert 'did not mean to combine the two poems'.

[85] Ibid. 29. J. T. Shawcross, 'Herbert's Double Poems: A Problem in the Text of *The Temple*', in C. J. Summers and T.-L. Pebworth (eds.), *'Too Riche Too Clothe The Sunne': Essays on George Herbert* (Pittsburgh, 1980), 216, argues that they are two different poems.

Christian's being and is made an integral part of him, Herbert goes on to consider in stanzas three and four the unlike poles of the analogy. The physical elements are not like God's spirit in that 'these cannot get over to my soul': and Herbert develops a model of the Christian's interiority that resembles a medieval castle, with outworks, walls, hidden gates, and inner fastnesses. The limit of the efficacy of the bread and wine is the 'outworks', the flesh, at which they affect the enemy as a deterrent: 'carrying thy name, | Affright both sinne and shame.' Actually, for a Protestant, this is quite a long way to go on the question of the efficacy of the elements. However, in true Protestant fashion it is the grace which accompanies the elements that has the real power, which 'Knoweth the ready way, | And hath the privie key'. In this way the grace of the Holy Communion penetrates the deepest places of the soul as well as the body.

The second part of 'The H. Communion' reverses the movement of the first, which had charted the inward movements of the physical elements and the spiritual grace towards the Christian's heart. The poem had started with the external elements and moved gradually to its destination in 'the souls most subtile rooms': in part two the Christian is being drawn out of his earthly habitation in a 'lift' which takes him towards heaven. The walls and locked doors of the fortress have at least temporarily disappeared: the Christian has been restored to the unity with God which Adam experienced.

> He might to heav'n from Paradise go
> As from one room t'another.

Once God's grace has accomplished the intricate process of penetrating the fortress of the heart, a sigh from the heart, inspired by that grace, is able to waft the Christian from earth to heaven. The 'ease' of this process is reflected in the simple songlike metre of this second part. As with the other two-part poems in this series, the meditation of the first part achieves a breakthrough in a relationship with God, which is reflected in poetry that is fluent and confident.

As we have seen, the movement in these two-part poems is achieved by a change in poetic form which almost represents a shift in genre, from meditative poem to lyric. There are other poems in which a sense of movement is generated in similar fashion. 'The Bag' is a poem which turns into a story. It begins with a difficult situation in which the speaker is being tempted to despair. His first strategy is to liken his situation to that of the disciples in the storm on Galilee. Jesus was with them in the boat, but because he was sleeping they thought he was powerless to help. By using this analogy the poet asserts the presence of Christ with him, and His ability to save. The next tactic is to tell a story, a strategy which has the double function of silencing the voices which counsel despair and distracting the poet from the difficulties of his own situation: the equivalent of sleeping in the boat while the storm is raging. The change to narrative mode functions like a change of speaker, as Quintilian noted. He describes prosopopoeia as 'a device which lends wonderful variety and animation to oratory', and then shows how narrative can function as prosopopoeia.[86] The beginning of the story in 'The Bag' is just this kind of case. The story is promised to be 'strange', and strange it is. It begins with the story of Jesus coming to earth, described in terms of disrobing: 'He did descend, undressing all the way.' The homely image is elaborated as we are told which accessories conform to which divine attributes and then the story of redemption continues in terms of the cancellation of a hotel bill. Payment of the bill eventually cost him his life. The 'accessory' metaphor is recovered at the end of the poem when someone gratuitously makes a wound in his side: Christ takes over the discourse of this poem to state in his own terms the convenience of this wound for the believer.

> If ye have any thing to send or write,
>   I have no bag, but here is room:
> Unto my Father's hands and sight,
>   Beleeve me, it shall safely come.

It seems that the communication need not be written, or even verbal: 'Sighs will convey | Any thing to me.' This appears to be the end of the story: Jesus died, and was mutilated, simply so that the believer would have a channel of communication open at a difficult time. Certainly the original speaker of the poem sees this as the solution to his dilemma. Seizing on Christ's final words he brandishes them at Despair, and finally dismisses him. The reader

---

[86] Quintilian, *Institutio Oratoria*, tr. H. E. Butler, 4 vols. (London, 1921), iii. 393, 395.

of the poem has all but forgotten the original problem at this stage. Instead of the internal dialogue that could well have ensued, as in 'A Parodie' or 'Assurance', the narrative genre establishes the tranquillity which the poet needs. In the sense of closure which the end of the story supplies there is the power to dismiss the enemy: in the shift of speaker of the poem to Christ Himself there is the authority to use that power. With the disappearance of the original speaker of the poem, the one who receives the force of the answer is the reader.

The Inner Voice in Herbert's Poetry: Divine 'Motions'

Frequently in Herbert's poetry the words which have the authority to change the poet's state of mind and the direction of the poem actually come from within the poet's mind. The movement here is rather different from the psychological model of a poem like 'Affliction (iv)' where the ability to imagine seems to be the means of grace for the poet, or 'Repentance', where his salvation is the faculty of rationalizing his predicament. The force of the direction is so strong and so specific that it can be channelled into words, just like the verbalized 'motions' of St Francis de Sales' meditations. In fact, 'motion' is Herbert's own term for the phenomenon. We have already seen that Herbert mistook a 'good motion' for a star in 'Artillerie'. The image is significant, for Herbert refers to the Holy Scripture as a 'book of starres'.[87] More specifically, in his Latin poem 'In S. Scripturas' he describes the power of the sacred text upon his inner being in terms of 'swallowing a falling star'.[88] This is identical to the image in 'Artillerie', although Herbert shakes off the star instead of ingesting it. This is the wrong response, and the 'motion' has to speak to him in audible words instead of the profound yet silent engagement with his psyche envisaged in 'In S. Scripturas'.

The most systematic treatment of 'motions' and therefore the most helpful in assessing their nature and significance is in the poem 'The Method'. Here a familiar problem is posed: God appears to be disregarding the prayers of the poet. The situation is analysed rationally. In stanza two the possibility of God being unwilling or inadequate to grant the prayer is entertained and

---

[87] Herbert, *Works*, 58. [88] 'Stellam vespere suxerim volantem': ibid. 411.

quickly dismissed. In stanza three an alternative procedure is suggested: 'Go search this thing, | Tumble thy breast, and turn thy book.' This is not the book of Scripture, but that record of every man's thoughts and deeds, 'ev'ry mans peculiar book' mentioned in 'Judgment'. The writing is very specific, and in this case it refers to two different kinds of 'motions'. The first is a motion from man to God in prayer, in St François' terms an 'ejaculation'. Herbert's sin here was to 'behave me carelessly, | When I did pray'. The poet comments sternly that if the petitioner is indifferent to his own motions, God can hardly be expected to hear them. There is another sort of motion recorded, however: this time a message from God to man, in the 'falling star' category.

> *Late when I would have something done,*
> *I had a motion to forbear,*
> *Yet I went on.*

The sin here is equally heinous. This motion was a communication from God, and if man ignores God he can expect God to ignore him. Having located the problem in the authoritative inner writing, there is an easy solution, and the poem ends with words of blessing put into the mouth of God: the tense is future, but confidence is high. 'Seek pardon first, and God will say, | *Glad heart rejoyce.*' The whole poem has been about the desire to hear God's voice, and the logical remedy, which is to obey what has already been communicated before asking for new messages, is successful. There are at least three methods of communication from God outlined in this poem: the actual words of the final line; the 'motion' from God which was intended to stop the poet from committing sin; and the third kind of motion, which originates in the human consciousness, but which also, it seems, is to be reverenced.

This identification of a voice within which can express divine communication is confirmed in the poem 'Affliction (iii)', which begins with a conscious reflection on an unconscious ejaculation: 'My heart did heave, and there came forth, *O God!*' The second voice has an almost physical force, and speaks, as it were, straight from the heart, without the permission of the rational and self-aware first voice. However, the first speaker welcomes it as evidence of the presence of the Holy Spirit within: 'By that I knew that thou wast in the grief.' All three members of the Trinity inhabit this poem: the voice within is obviously the spirit of Jesus, who is remaining consistent to his life on earth, continuing to grieve over sin and call out to His Father in His role as the indwelling spirit.

> Thy life on earth was grief, and thou art still
> Constant unto it, making it to be
> A point of honour, now to grieve in me,
>   And in thy members suffer ill.

As with many Herbert poems, the text behind this poem is that which inspired Augustine in formulating his concept of prayer language as wordless groans: Romans 8: 26, 'for we know not what we should pray for as we ought: but the Spirit itself maketh intercession for us with groanings that cannot be uttered.'

This is the theology which ultimately underpins the theory of the effectiveness of non-verbal ejaculations. Unconscious expressions, particularly of grief, are likely to be direct signifiers of the interceding presence of the Holy Spirit within. By implication, He is the one who does know how to pray, and thus these wordless exclamations are the most effective prayer language.

Words in the Mouth of the Word

So far in this chapter, various methods have been traced which Herbert uses to give an impression of God speaking. Most of the time, as we have seen, Herbert does not have to assign human words to the Almighty. This is a particular strength of the holy poetry of the Psalms. However, there are poems in which Herbert is not content merely to detail the psychological effect of turning to an all-powerful God and Father, or to suggest by a shift of rhetoric that the poem has been taken over by a different speaker. There are prayer experiences, it seems, which can only be described in terms of dialogue with God. As we have seen, Savonarola and Sir John Hayward also felt the need to invent a separate speaker for God's words, instead of using the stream-of-consciousness technique which the Psalm-writer usually adopts. Mere reportage, as in 'The Parodie', is neither spiritually nor poetically effective. Occasionally, as in 'The Collar' or 'Jordan (ii)', God will speak in audible words to resolve the poet's problem in an immediate and surprising way. A. D. Nuttall finds this prosopopoeia disturbing.

Herbert's poems dramatize one of the most important requirements of the religious temper, which is quite simply that God should be other than oneself. But by that very act of dramatizing (which is a kind of usurpation) they blaspheme it.[89]

The 'usurpation' in Nuttall's comment here is wrongly located. He has not understood that Herbert is writing against a background of 'usurpation' of the Psalm texts. For example, he professes himself shocked by the accusations against God in 'Affliction (i)', apparently unaware that readers familiar with the accusations of the Psalmist in the Penitential Psalms were quite accustomed to the practice of attributing all misfortunes to God.[90] God has authorized the dramatizing of himself as Other in his own inspired text. Psalm 32, uniquely among Penitential Psalms, includes words apparently spoken by God. The sorrow in this Psalm is safely in the past tense, and the discourse charts the successful prayer to God for help, together with the rejoicing afterwards. As if in reward, after a pause, God Himself speaks in promise: 'I will inform thee, and teach thee in the way wherein thou shalt go.' Not surprisingly, this Penitential Psalm ends not in peace, nor even in optimism, but in shouts of joy: 'Be glad, O ye righteous, and rejoice in the Lord.' God's words are effective.

However, as in the Psalms, lyrics which include actual words from God are rare in *The Temple*. As we have seen, there are other more subtle and possibly less daring ways of portraying the relationship between God and man. Occasionally the poems are truly dialogic: God speaks in audible words. The most obvious of these is 'Dialogue', in which Christ enters into lengthy conversation with the poet, even echoing his metrical forms as He does so. The stanza form which both Christ and Herbert use is actually one of the strictest and most distinctive in *The Temple*. The short trochaic lines emphasize the very restricted rhyme scheme; the last four lines of each stanza rhyme with each other to produce a very strong effect. In the verses apparently from Herbert's pen the

---

[89] A. D. Nuttall, *Overheard by God: Fiction and Prayer in Herbert, Milton, Dante and St. John* (London, 1980), 3.

[90] Ibid. 47. See Ps. 39: 9–10, Ps. 51: 8, Ps. 102: 10–11.

design seems to be to make his point particularly strongly. The first stanza is a statement of the hopelessness of the Christian project as far as he is concerned:

> But when all my care and pains
> Cannot give the name of gains
> To thy wretch so full of stains,
> What delight or hope remains?

Christ, it seems, decides to answer the complainant in equally strong terms, choosing the same very definite form and rebuking the speaker for questioning the loving divine purpose. This is very different from the occasional authoritative word which is sufficient to finish an argument or change a situation in most of Herbert's lyrics. Perhaps it is because Christ echoes Herbert so closely—even beginning the stanza with the sort of loving address with which Herbert began his—that Herbert does not feel it necessary to regard this as the last word. Christ simply sounds too much like Herbert here. Thus the argument continues, in presumptuous terms on the part of the human being. In the third stanza God's entire scheme of redemption is rejected: 'I disclaim the whole design.' This would be rebellious enough, but the reason for this great apostasy appears to be simply that Herbert's intelligence is insulted. He cannot see the logic of the divine plan:

> As the reason then is thine;
> So the way is none of mine.

Herbert, of course, is missing the whole point, which is that man is powerless to help himself and needs saving. Far from rejecting Herbert for his ingratitude, however, Christ continues with His patient pleading, turning the poet's words on himself. True 'resignation' is exactly what God wants. It may involve a surrender of human pride and independence; but as Christ points out in the final lines of His second stanza, He 'resigned' a great deal more than that. The persuasive rhetoric of Herbert's stanza form is turned against him, and this time it works. Christ is appealing to Herbert's emotions, and the final line of the poem, which is Herbert's broken-hearted cry, shows that it has worked.

> *That as I did freely part*
> *With my glorie and desert,*

> Left all joyes to feel all smart—
> Ah! no more: thou break'st my heart.

All Herbert has to do is give up his sense of unworthiness: Jesus had to sacrifice the knowledge of His own worthiness. The poetry here is a metaphor for what Jesus is doing in sacrificing His divine status to redeem mankind. As He enters human flesh, He also enters the language world of humanity where His discourse is not automatically performative. The authoritative divine language is one of the things He has 'resigned', and it is a measure of His humility that He is willing to bandy words on Herbert's terms. However, He proves Himself a better poet than Herbert, achieving the end of sacred poetry, which, as we have seen, is to move the reader. Herbert is obviously moved at the end of the poem. Although he just about keeps within the metre he himself has set, the pace is slow and broken, and the vocabulary directly expressive of deep emotion: rhetoric and poetics have been left behind, along with pride and rationalism. Of course, the scheme of this poem is an elaborate metaphor, and Herbert does not repeat this experiment: but the representation of Christ as poet is a rather pleasing one, and a vivid illustration of the implications of incarnation as described in the poem.

'Love (iii)', that most famous dialogue in *The Temple*, also represents God in the form of Christ entering into human language conventions. The same issue is at stake, and it is an issue on which human beings will talk endlessly: whether a Christian can ever merit his salvation. This particular scene is set at a moment of consummation and fulfilment of that saving process, either the service of Holy Communion or that greater marriage feast of the Lamb which takes place in heaven. The arguments on both sides are familiar. The poet protests his unworthiness. Love explains the system of redemption. As in 'Dialogue', it is the cost of his redemption that wins over the speaker. The tone taken by Love— 'sweetly questioning' and 'smiling'—is also similar to the gentle tone of the 'sweetest Saviour' of 'Dialogue'. However, the tone taken by the human speaker is very different. For a start, he does not take the initiative; neither does he establish the language conventions within which they are to communicate. This time, as Michael Schoenfeldt has pointed out, the language conventions set by Love are those of courtly hospitality. This is obviously a

code with which the speaker is very familiar, as he tries to respond
with the appropriately courteous reply to all Love's overtures.
However, he is clearly out of his depth. He is trying to come to
terms with an unthinkable situation: Almighty God is inviting him
to dinner. Michael Schoenfeldt has detailed the various deferen-
tial responses which guests practised before their powerful hosts:
but no guest would go so far as to suggest that he should not be
invited in the first place![91] This is to repeat the miscalculation of
'Dialogue', where Christ points out that to insist upon his own
unworthiness for Christ's invitation is to cast doubts on His good
taste, a strategy that reeks of presumption rather than politeness.
It is also to question the effectiveness of Christ's redemption.
When Love announces, in the speaker's assertion that what he
needs is to be a worthy guest, 'You shall be he', he is not merely
repeating a polite fiction, to be translated 'You shall be considered
as if you were he'. This is the one user of language whose words
are truly performative, who can say 'Thy sins are forgiven thee'
with immediate results. The human speaker, however, chooses to
ignore the fact that he has just been made instantly worthy, and
repeats his declaration of inadequacy in different terms. Love,
with true gentility, ignores the inappropriateness of the responses
and the self-assertion they imply. The problem for the poet is
accepting that all his learnt responses—'the quick returns of
courtesy and wit'—cannot cope with this situation, and in the
end he has to fall silent, something that as a poet and a courtier he
hates to do. Once again, Love never steps out of the role of
earthly host which he has chosen for himself: but neither does
he give an inch by considering for one moment any of the poet's
responses, which, as Michael Schoenfeldt points out, are avoid-
ance techniques. The firm yet courteous command which constitutes Love's last word cannot be disobeyed without straining the
courtly conventions to breaking point. The guest is embarrassed
by his lack of all verbal defences, and has to accept the authority
of his host's instruction. The poem ends with engagement in the
direct experience of the intimate meal which has been set up for

---

[91] M. C. Schoenfeldt, *Prayer and Power: George Herbert and Renaissance Courtship* (Chicago,
1991), 205. He quotes from the *Mirror of Complements*, which in its 1650 edition actually
included extracts from *The Temple* as examples of appropriately pious courtesy.

the poet: the reader is left to surmise whether the experience is one of unalloyed delight or excruciating embarrassment.

God often has the last word in Herbert's lyrics, a pattern which tends to stress the superior status of divine words over human. 'Redemption' includes divine words in the final line of the sonnet, with its effect of closure. Another element in the finality with which the poem ends is the narrative structure. God is here envisaged as entering into the binding words of a land contract. The story is of a search for the divine landlord, in order to re-negotiate the contract: a presumptuous business in a seven-teenth-century context, as Michael Schoenfeldt points out. How-ever, God is not at home, in heaven, where the supplicant expects to find Him. He is away on an extremely important mission. The theologically literate reader immediately understands that the 'purchase' which God has descended to earth in order to make is the redemption of mankind: the storyteller, however, is nothing if not naïve and pursues his relatively insignificant quest to the end. Like the Magi, however, the speaker is looking for his Lord in the wrong place: He is finally found not in a situation appro-priate to His wealth but in a desperate plight. It seems as if He has fallen among thieves. The speaker has no chance to articulate his request even if he felt like doing so:

> there I him espied
> Who straight, *Your suit is granted*, said, & died.

The enigmatic combination of literal 'last words' and an event whose significance is not elaborated seems to leave the storyteller with the wind taken out of his sails. Again, something is being said about the way God enters into human contracts, including the contract of human communication. God is willing, it seems, to play a recognizable role in order to give the human being some guidelines for proceeding: host in 'Love (iii)', poet in 'Dialogue', landlord here. However, there is always a point at which the terms of the contract are no longer valid. Here, the petition that the lessee has travelled so far to present is made redundant. The disquiet caused by the untimely death of the landlord is somewhat allayed by His positive words, but the storyteller is still puzzled: he has no exposition or sequel to tack on to the story, and the reader of the poem is left with the full burden of the interpretative act. The narrative progression, the form of the sonnet, and the fact that these are literally 'last words' give tremendous power to the reading of the last line. The reader is left with the knowledge that in the narrative logic the 'last words' must be significant. The Christian reader, of course, knows that it was by dying that Jesus released humanity from the Old Covenant of the Law and set up the New Covenant, dependent not on fulfilling legal requirements but on free grace, the 'small-rented lease'. The poem is in fact a neat allegory of salvation, which the reader is forced to interpret because of the apparent incomprehension of the storyteller. However, it also says something about divine words as opposed to human words. The human words of petition were not even necessary: the supplicant did not have a chance to frame them. On the other hand, the divine words immediately created the reality to which they referred, and were supported by a validating action. Although God will enter in to our roles and rituals out of compassion for His creatures who do not know how else to approach Him, the overwhelming superiority of the power of divine discourse always puts an end to human speech.

The human storyteller of 'Love unknown', who somehow seems to have ended up talking to an angel, or at least someone intimately conversant with God's purposes, is also naïve. The advantage of using an obviously naïve speaker is that the inadequacy of his interpretation of events immediately draws the reader into an attempt to construe the poem correctly. Indeed, at first the 'friend' is apparently the reader himself, who is brought into the poem via the line 'Deare friend, sit down, the tale is long and sad'. It is obvious that what the storyteller is looking for is an audience, a sympathetic listener. In the reader, that is exactly what he gets: the story is full of pathos and an irony that is calculated to engage a hearer's sympathy. However, the first quiet words from the 'friend', who, it appears, is actually in conversation with Herbert, disappoint that expectation. Far from latching onto the detail which the storyteller emphasizes, that of his sufferings, the 'friend' goes straight for the reason behind the suffering: *'Your heart was foul, I fear.'* Whether deliberately or not, the storyteller has withheld any mention so far of behaviour which deserved this punishment: yet in response to the friend's interjection he immediately confesses to serious sin.

Indeed 'tis true. I did and do commit
Many a fault more than my lease will bear.

However, the (literally) heart-rending story of torment and suffering continues: again, unaccountably, with no mention of desert.
In fact the stress is on the cruelty of the master in allowing the
offered heart to be thrown into a furnace. Again, the friend has to
interject to bring a sense of a moral scheme into the story: and
again, the storyteller is quite happy to have it corrected. He is
even happy to supply the details which reveal that the apparently
cruel treatment was after all necessary: the hard heart needed
melting, so that the dross could be removed. By the third stage of
the story, when the narrator returns from this traumatic experience in order to rest, only to find that his bed has been stuffed
with thorns, the 'friend' and the reader have become totally
alienated. The friend is refusing to respond to the story correctly,
either in terms of literary convention or human politeness. He
refuses to suspend disbelief, and to allow the narrator to control
his own story. The narrator does show a willingness to revise his
story: what started off as a tragedy, with himself as hero, turns
after prompting into a rescue with Christ as saviour. This is not
quite enough for the friend, who takes over the story. In his
mouth, however, it is no longer the same story: it is no longer
'long', nor 'sad', but a cheerful anecdote of kindness and healing.
The suffering is made light of, its rewards emphasized: and any-
way, it appears that the suffering was all self-inflicted. '*All did but
strive to mend, what you had marr'd.*' Both narrator and audience need
to understand that the story was written from the wrong perspective from the beginning. The 'friend' rewrites every episode from
a new perspective, that of God's benevolent purpose. By the end
of the poem, the narrator has effectively disappeared: he is
silenced ten lines from the end, along with his story. What is left
in the dynamic of the poem is the friend confronting the reader
with his conventional theological perspective on the story he has
just heard. The reader needs to hear it, because the poet has
ensured that he has responded in human compassion and sympathy to the subject of the sad autobiography, and it is that which
must be corrected. The Christian's own story—his autobiography—is not even his own to tell. What he gives up to God along
with his heart is the starring role in the one story where everyone

is a hero—his own autobiography. By the end of 'Love unknown' he has become simply another character in God's story, stripped of the dignity of the role of tragic hero or even innocent sufferer.[92]

The movement of dialogue, narrative, and rhetoric in this poem intertwines to produce a complex response. The reader is looking for an answer to the 'friend' and an end to the story. He sees no response from the narrator—because he, the reader, is now in dialogue with the 'friend'. The story is finished, although there is a deep sense of transgression about it being completed by someone else: and the closure is supplied with the sort of confident rhetoric which the narrator has never managed to attain. The lines are end-stopped, emphasizing the authority of the regular pentameters and strict rhyme scheme: the structure is antithetical, contrasting the narrator's sinfulness with God's correcting processes, and the poem ends with an exhortation to praise God, exploiting fully the resources of the three-part list.

> *Wherefore be cheer'd, and praise him to the full,*
> *Each day, each houre, each moment of the week,*
> *Who fain would have you be new, tender, quick.*

Since the storyteller has disappeared from the text, the only available subject for this powerful rhetoric is the reader: presumably the exhortation is addressed out of the text, to us. The sneaking suspicion has been growing throughout that like so many of Herbert's 'friends', this one is divine. It is His story that He is telling, which perhaps explains why He tells it so well. The reader has been drawn into a sympathetic identification with the storyteller, which is why these words can be logically addressed to reader as much as narrator: we also need to be made aware of the divine story. It is by a very clever process of changing the roles within this poem that Herbert finally confronts his reader with God. It is not possible to channel these words only towards the persona of the poem, for he has by now gone silent, which is to cease to exist in terms of the poem: the reader is left with the impact of the words and the burden of interpretation. In the lyrics where the reader seems to end up confronting God, Herbert has simulated the fulfilment of his desire, articulated in *The Country Parson*, for God to take over the discourse

[92] Richard Todd in *The Opacity of Signs: Acts of Interpretation in George Herbert's 'The Temple'* (New York, 1986), 72, describes how the reader's participation here reinterprets the original presentation of God as capricious.

of his sermon: 'Oh my Master, on whose errand I come, let me hold my peace, and doe thou speak thy selfe.'[93] However, it takes all his poetic resources to simulate this phenomenon.

Herbert as Psalmist

In allowing the reader to eavesdrop on his conversation with God Herbert is following a precedent set by the sacred Psalm text, as well as the tradition of Psalm meditation which was well established by the early seventeenth century. Where Herbert is more daring than St François de Sales is in his attempt to represent not only the discourse of ejaculation, the 'motion' from man to God, but also the reverse 'motion', from God to man. St François, as we have seen, never attempts to represent divine communication, preferring to remain silent about the possible content of 'motions'. Herbert develops the hints in both Psalm poetry and Psalm meditation as to how this silent discourse could possibly be charted, through its rhetorical and psychological effect on the speaking subject. In a first-person stream-of-consciousness discourse, the effect of God's 'motions' on the content and rhetoric of the poetry will be discernible, as we have seen.

However, in performing the more daring manœuvres which we have noted in this chapter Herbert is breaking new ground. Those lyrics which do not have their literary origin in the prayer relationship between Herbert and his God need a different kind of rationale. The only sense in which 'The Bag' or 'Redemption' or 'Love unknown' can be said to be 'a picture of the many spiritual Conflicts that have past betwixt God and my Soul' is a highly allegorical one: and allegory is not the main source of power in these poems. The very intratextual relationships, as we have seen, are set up for the moment at the end of the poem when Herbert can make his God speak to his reader, and the power of these endings is entirely literary.

We have already traced the way that spiritual 'motions' collapse into rhetorical motions in the writing of Andreas Hyperius and St François de Sales. Herbert is apparently careful to maintain the distinction between them. His poetry is full of gestures towards the superiority of silence and inarticulate emotion over

---

[93] Herbert, *Works*, 233.

rhetoric. However, it seems that having discovered just how indistinguishable spiritual motions are from rhetorical motions, he cannot help exploiting this resemblance for a didactic purpose. In poems such as 'Love (iii)' Herbert has abandoned his safer role as preacher or Psalmist for the time being, and ventured on one that does not have the authorization of a Protestant poetics behind it. The daring aspect of these true poems of meditation is the extent to which human imagination is employed, in the setting, in the creation of a persona, and most audacious of all, in the words put into the mouth of God. Although Herbert will have found precedent for this practice in the Protestant Psalm meditation, as we have seen, his integration of divine language into poetry raises different kinds of questions. Even Luis de Granada, who partook of the Counter-Reformation optimism about the use of literary language in devotion, warned that any dialogue with God imagined in the course of meditation should not be written down. He was aware of the dubious status of such writing. Within the careful boundaries Granada sets for meditation such imaginary discourse can do no harm. Extrapolated from that context, however, and made available for others to read, the existence of such 'divine' language raises awkward questions about its origins. The Christian world was not yet ready to accept the fruits of the imagination whole-heartedly as from God: the only alternative, and the only acceptable origin for such writing, is that it is divinely inspired. We shall consider this claim further in the next chapter.

Herbert was soon accepted as the Psalmist of his age. Ralph Knevet, writing in the 1640s, judged that 'it was Hee who rightly knew how to touch Davids Harpe'. The first biography of 1652 presented him as the 'Sweet Singer of the Temple', a title which was taken up and made more specific: John Bryan in 1670 and Oliver Heywood in 1672 described him as 'that incomparable sweet singer of our *Israel*'.[94] James Duport in *Musae subsecivae* wrote a poem on *The Temple* in which he declared

> No Lyre sang sacred hymns so graciously as this,
> Save David's only—his, or none's.

---

[94] Oliver Heywood, *Heart-Treasure* (London, 1672), ii. 119. Quoted in H. Wilcox, 'Countrey-Aires to Angels Musick', in Miller and DiYanni, *Like Season'd Timber*, 55.

Samuel Speed, in 1677, placed George Herbert in the tradition of biblical poetry which included the Psalms and the Song of Songs.[95] Although clearly hyperbolic, this placing of Herbert's poems alongside the biblical text demonstrates that he succeeded in creating a poetics which was seen to be truly Christian, and a role for the poet which was conceived as truly godly. The extent of this achievement may be measured by the fate of a similar, yet more conservative poetic project by George Wither in the 1620s. His *Hymns and Songs of the Church* of 1623 was an English paraphrase of much of the poetry in the Bible. The volume, however, never appeared, having been suppressed by the Stationer's Company. Wither had somehow obtained from the King the promise that all copies of the Psalter should have his text appended, a considerable financial benefit given that he held sole copyright. However, the fact that he had also been given the power to search for and seize all Psalters that did not include his hymns probably accounted for the hostility of the Stationers' Company. Wither's resentment is expressed in an illegally printed pamphlet which is said by the author to have been printed in haste, before the 1624 Parliament was dissolved. George Herbert was a member of this Parliament, and probably read Wither's text, which includes arguments in defence of a poetic rendering of biblical poetry. It is clear that one of the criticisms that Wither has encountered is that poetry is not suitable for holy discourse. Wither retorts, angrily, that it is only right that modern versions reflect the fact that the Scriptural text is poetic. Wither is engaging with a two-pronged attack on poetry: first, its tendency to become a set form; second, its problematic status as human rhetoric. Wither is a defender of liturgy, and therefore prepared to accept a human element in divine worship:

humane Traditions & observations discreetly established in the Church do . . . resemble those markes which charitable and skillful Seamen have aunciently sett up to discover dangerous passages and a safe Channell to unskillful Mariners.

He defends his poetic versions on the grounds of decorum and simplicity, declaring of the Song of Songs, 'I fitted the same unto

---

[95] All these judgements may be found in Patrides, *George Herbert: The Critical Heritage*, 65, 135, 136, 12.

our English Lyre, in measures becomming the nature of the subject, in a playne and unaffected Phrase.' It is clear, however, that he feels the force of the arguments against poetry. He resorts to the same argument that Augustine employed in the defence of Christian rhetoric:

since god in mercie hath provided and permitted us meanes to assist our weaknesses, let not such as are strong enough to be without them, condemne the use of such helpes to those, who beeing not so able, must have their affections weaned by degrees from their childish inclynations.[96]

The sheer defensiveness of Wither's pamphlet shows the attitudes which Herbert's Sacred Poems would have encountered.

Perhaps Wither's mistake was to assume that his poems could take their place with the holy discourse of the liturgy. As Horton Davis has shown, neither Laudians nor Puritans could accept metrical poetry into their worship until the very end of the seventeenth century, thanks to 'the conviction that metrical Psalms were the Word of God while hymns were human compositions'.[97] Yet it has been demonstrated that Herbert's modern Psalms were used to change attitudes towards poetry in worship among even the most austere members of the Christian community. Helen Wilcox has shown how one of Herbert's poems was used in a controversial volume of Psalm paraphrases which William Barton tried to get Parliament to authorize for public worship in the mid-1640s. He asserted defiantly that poetry was 'a gift of God', 'very notable to kindle, quicken and enflame affection', but Parliament did not take the point. In 1659 Barton cited Herbert in an address to Parliament prefacing a collection of hymns for congregational singing, *A Century of Select Hymns*. Later authorize for public worship in the mid-1640s. He asserted defiantly that poetry was 'a gift of God', 'very notable to kindle, quicken and enflame affection', but Parliament did not take the point. In 1659 Barton cited Herbert in an address to Parliament prefacing a collection of hymns for congregational singing, *A Century of Select Hymns*. Later in the century poems from *The Temple* played their part in the development of non-Scriptural hymns,

---

[96] George Wither, *The Schollers Purgatory Discovered in the Stationers Common-wealth* (London, 1624), 72, 62, 19.

[97] H. Davis, *Worship and Theology in England from Andrewes to Baxter and Fox 1603–1690* (Princeton, 1975), 255.

to be sung to the old Psalm tunes.[98] Helen Wilcox comments, 'The choice of Herbert's poems as suitable for this daring defiance of scriptural autonomy suggests the closeness of *The Temple* to the Bible in seventeenth-century non-conformist devotional life'. Arthur Marotti points out that the unusual presentation of the first edition of *The Temple*—in handy Prayer Book duodecimo, with nothing but a kind of concordance at the back—reinforced its status as sacred text.[99] George Herbert was sufficiently revered as an author to help break the monopoly of the biblical text in worship, and to make possible a Christian poetry of the imagination.

[98] *Select Hymns Taken out of Mr. Herbert's Temple* (London, 1697). See H. Wilcox, 'Something Understood: The Reputation and Influence of George Herbert to 1715' (Univ. of Oxford D.Phil. thesis, 1984), 334–6.

[99] A. Marotti, *Manuscript, Print, and the English Renaissance Lyric* (Ithaca, NY, 1995) 256–7.

4

Reading Herbert Reading Valdés:
Antinomian Disruption, *The Hundred and Ten Considerations*, and *The Temple*

Like Savonarola, the Catholic reformer Juan de Valdés was incorporated into the Protestant project to construct a pedigree for their Reformed Church, despite the fact that he remained within the Catholic Church throughout his life.[1] In an elegy by Daniel Rogers on the death of Bishop Jewell in 1571 he is praised along with a number of eminent Reformers, including those with whom George Herbert aligned himself in *Musae Responsoriæ*: Calvin, Beza, and Bucer.[2] The first name on both Rogers' and Herbert's lists is Peter Martyr Vermigli, through whom the English people may well have heard of Valdés, for Peter Martyr, as well as being a prominent figure in the English Reformation, had been a disciple of Valdés in his informal community at Naples.[3] Juan de Valdés was a biblical scholar and teacher who had fled from Spain to Italy in the early 1530s. He died in 1540, ten years before his major work was first published, in Basle. *The Hundred and Ten Considerations* reached England in its Italian version in the sixteenth century, but the first English edition was not published until 1638, when a translation by Nicholas Ferrar was finally passed for publication in Oxford. George Herbert's reputation had grown in stature since 1633, when there had been some discussion about whether his own volume of poetry should be

---

[1] See A. Milton, 'The Church of England, Rome, and the True Church: The Demise of a Jacobean Consensus', in K. Fincham (ed.), *The Early Stuart Church 1603–1642* (London, 1993), 187–210 for a discussion of the differences between Puritan and Laudian constructions of the origins of the Church of England.

[2] George Herbert, *The Works of George Herbert*, ed. F. E. Hutchinson (Oxford, 1945) 398.

[3] See P. McNair, *Peter Martyr in Italy: An Anatomy of Apostasy* (Oxford, 1967), 139–79. A recent study controversially claims that Valdés was the disciple of Peter Martyr rather than the other way round: see F. James, '*Praedestinatio Dei: The Intellectual Origins of Peter Martyr Vermigli's Doctrine of Double Predestination*' (Univ. of Oxford D.Phil. thesis, 1993), 216–17.

published.[4] The condition for publication of *The Hundred and Ten Considerations* was that his corrective notes were attached to the text. Affixed to the first edition was a letter from George Herbert to his friend Nicholas Ferrar, who had asked whether such a translation should be published. Herbert's response indicates that he considers Ferrar's translation providential: 'You owe the Church a debt', he says, 'and God hath put this into your hands (as he sent the fish with mony to *S. Peter,*) to discharge it.'[5] Whatever the nature of the 'debt' Ferrar owed—a specific instance, or the general obligation believers owe to the Church—Herbert clearly thought this treatise so important that its publication was a responsibility laid on Ferrar by God.

The Doctrinal Context for The Hundred and Ten Considerations

This was not the first publishing project of the Ferrar–Herbert partnership, as we have seen, although it was probably the last. *The Hundred and Ten Considerations* was part of the Little Gidding project to rectify the dearth of works on spirituality in a newly Protestant nation. The popularity of *The Benefite that Christians receive by Jesus Christ Crucifyed* by Benedetto of Mantua, a follower of Valdés, testifies to the demand for devotional literature of this particular stamp in sixteenth-century England.[6] Although he never left the Catholic Church, Valdés could be claimed for the Reformed Church by reason of his unambiguously Pauline doctrine. George Herbert's first reason for publishing his work, given in a letter of 1632 to Nicholas Ferrar, is that Valdés is part of the continuous, invisible Elect so important to Puritan propaganda,

---

[4] See Herbert, *Works*, 567, for the opinion of Thomas Jackson (then President of Corpus Christi, Oxford) on the subject of publication of the work. The full title reads: *The Hundred and Ten Considerations of Signior Iohn Valdesso. Written In Spanish, Brought out of Italy by Vergerius, and first set forth in Italian at Basil by Coelius Secundus Curio, Anno 1550. And now translated out of the Italian Copy into English, with notes* (Oxford, 1638).

[5] Herbert, *Works*, 304.

[6] Benedetto of Mantua, *The Benefite that Christians receive by Jesus Christ Crucifyed*, tr. A. G. [prob. Arthur Golding] (London, 1573). There appear to have been two more printings of the work by 1577, and a second edition in 1580. Two more editions of the same translation, labelled 'The Third Edition' and 'The Fourth Edition' respectively, appeared in 1633 and 1638. See the introduction and bibliography of 'The "Beneficio di Cristo"', by R. Prelowski, in J. A. Tedeschi (eds), *Italian Reformation Studies in Honour of Laelius Socinus* (Florence, 1965), 23–102. For the lack of devotional literature, see H. C. White, *English Devotional Literature (Prose) 1600–1640* (Madison, 1931), 64 ff.

who had preserved evangelical truth throughout the Catholic centuries:

I wish you by all meanes to publish it, for these three eminent things observable therein: First, that God in the midst of Popery should open the eyes of one to understand and express so clearly and excellently the intent of the Gospell.[7]

Another of Herbert's reasons for recommending publication was the 'many pious rules of ordering our life' expressed in the *Considerations*. Herbert's description of it in terms of rules and observations would seem to indicate that the work is of the nature of a manual of traditional piety, such as Lewis Bayly's *The Practice of Pietie*, hugely popular in the first half of the seventeenth century. But whereas Bayly claims, in his preface to Prince Charles, that he has 'endeavoured to extract (out of the Chaos of endlesse controversies) the *old Practice of true Pietie*, which flourished before these Controversies were hatched', Valdés' treatise is working towards a new definition of piety, the very stuff of which the 'Controversies' were made.

Several critics have claimed that Valdés influenced Herbert's poetry, but that is unlikely, given the tone of delighted discovery in the letter to Nicholas Ferrar written five months before Herbert's death.[8] What is more likely is that Herbert found so much of the work congenial because it has much in common with the spirituality of his own brand of early seventeenth-century English Protestantism. *The Hundred and Ten Considerations* was being written in Naples in the late 1530s at about the same time as the second, authoritative edition of Calvin's *Institutes of the Christian Religion*. There is disagreement about whether Valdés was directly influenced by the Northern Reformers, but all scholars recognize the similarity between Valdés' doctrine and that of Calvin.[9] By the

---

[7] Herbert, *Works*, 304.

[8] See P. Grant, *The Transformation of Sin: Studies in Donne, Herbert, Vaughan and Traherne* (Montreal, 1974), 100. I. Bell, 'Herbert's Valdésian Vision', *ELR* 17 (1987), 303–28 argues for a comprehensive influence of Valdés on Herbert, suggesting that Ferrar might have shown Herbert his copy much earlier (325). She mentions Amy Charles's conjecture that *The Hundred and Ten Considerations* may have been in the parcel of books sent from France by Henry: yet another suggestion for the content of this interesting and perhaps rather large parcel.

[9] Calvin's authoritative second edition of the *Institutes of the Christian Religion* appeared in 1539. José Nieto thinks that Valdés did not borrow the doctrine of total depravity from Calvin, but from Pedro Ruiz de Alcaraz, his only real influence. See J. Nieto, *Juan de Valdés*

time that Herbert saw Valdés' treatise, many of the ideas fundamental to Calvin's *Institutes* were the subject of bitter nationwide
controversy. The Synod of Dort, called to discuss the opinions of
the Dutch Arminians in 1619, had produced orthodox Calvinist
doctrine on five disputed topics: predestination, limited atone-
ment, the total depravity of man, conversion, and perseverance.
These canons, which had been meant to establish Reformed
Protestant doctrine across Europe, were never made legally binding in England, and within a few years were subject to attack by
an increasingly powerful group of divines in the English court.
Richard Montagu claimed royal support for his 1624 publication
A New Gagg for an Old Goose, which argued that the Church of
England was not essentially Calvinist at all, and the new king,
Charles I, was unambiguously hostile to the Calvinist bishops,
who were in the majority on his accession in 1625.[10] The Parlia-
ments of 1625 to 1629 spent a great deal of time debating Armi-
nianism. Charles revived Elizabethan legislation forbidding
Parliament to discuss the Thirty-Nine Articles, a gesture seen by
Kevin Sharpe as irenic; Nicholas Tyacke sees it as part of the
Arminian advance.[11] The fourth edition of Francis Holyoke's
Latin–English dictionary, dedicated to Laud in 1633, contains a
new entry: *praedestinatiani*, defined as 'a kinde of Heretiques'.

---

and the Origins of the Spanish and Italian Reformation (Geneva, 1970), 60–80, for an account of
the life and thought of Pedro Ruiz de Alacaraz, born 1480. However, Carlos Gilly has
shown that Valdés' early *Dialogue on Christian Doctrine* (1527–8) incorporates translations of
one of Luther's early works, the 1520 *Explanatio dominicae orationis*. See C. Gilly, 'Juan de
Valdés: Übersetzer und Bearbeiter von Luthers Schrifte in seinem Dialogo de Doctrina',
Archiv für Reformationsgeschichte, 74 (1983), 257–305. In spite of Gilly's findings, Frank James
thinks that Valdés' doctrine only became truly Reformed after his contact with Peter
Martyr in 1537. See *Praedestinatio Dei*, 359–60.

[10] See Fincham, *The Early Stuart Church*, 37 for Caroline policy on promotion of bishops.
Kevin Sharpe disagrees, but does admit that Arminian bishops had very powerful positions: *The Personal Rule* (New Haven, 1992), 295–6. A contemporary joke went like this:
'What do the Arminians hold?' 'All the best livings in England': C. Carlton, *Charles I: The
Personal Monarch* (London, 1983), 168. Sharpe mentions this joke, but dismisses it as
inaccurate: however, the very existence of the joke demonstrates a public perception on
which the point of the joke depends.

[11] Nicholas Tyacke suggests that in the context of intense Puritan discussion of predestination, this is an anti-Calvinist measure: *Anti-Calvinists: The Rise of English Arminianism
c.1590–1640* (Oxford, 1987) 250–1. Fincham thinks that the implementation of legislation
had an anti-Calvinist bias: *The Early Stuart Church*, 39. Interestingly, William Prynne, no
friend to the administration, sees the ban on discussion of the Thirty-Nine Articles as an
anti-Arminian measure, but this may be a politic gesture. See William Prynne, *The
Perpetuitie of a Regenerate Mans Estate* (London, 1626), sig. **2[r].

Whether this shift is seen as the work of an anti-Calvinist Church hierarchy who had embraced Arminian doctrine, or as a matter of sensible management of the Church of England by its supreme governor, there is no question that, by the 1630s, many Englishmen were talking of 'innovations' instigated by an Archbishop Laud who was leading the Church of England toward reunion with Rome. A general accusation of 'Arminianism' went hand-in-hand with criticism of Laudian policy towards altars, ceremonies, and vestments.[12] Many critics gave up on the old country and the Church of England and sailed to New England to found a purer church.

George Herbert died before the polarization of the Church of England was complete, and he might well have been cited by Kevin Sharpe as one of those who, though Calvinist in doctrine, was concerned for what he considered to be decency and order. The 1620 epigrams *Musae Responsoriae* are dedicated to a king who had promoted Calvinist doctrine at Dort, and their author aligns himself with famous Calvinist theologians: however, they include vehement attacks on Puritans who reject ceremonies such as infant baptism and churching, and defences of the wearing of vestments and using the sign of the Cross. Chapter 13 of *The Country Parson* delineates a variety of external fittings considered necessary 'to keep the middle way between superstition and slovenliness': these include 'a Communion Cloth *of fine linen, with a handsome, and seemly Carpet of good and costly Stuffe*', a stoop, and chalice. Such church adornment was to become deeply controversial: Julia Merritt has identified gifts of fine altar cloths, even in some cases adorned with the IHS symbol, which were treasured by Puritan congregations in the 1620s but considered 'Popish trash' in the 1640s.[13] Like Laud, Herbert wanted all the pews to be uniform, but unlike Laud he was careful to establish that he was not 'putting a holiness in the things'. A measure of the 'middle way' he is consciously espousing here is his strange insistence that the Scriptures he has quoted 'fully, and exactly

---

[12] Sharpe points out that a concern for ceremonial did not go hand in hand with Arminianism: *The Personal Rule*, 360–3. He argues that this 'paranoia' was unjustified, so he does admit to its existence: ibid. 295–7.

[13] This information was given in a paper to the Graduate History Seminar at Oxford University, Michaelmas 1995. She cites the churches of St Bartholomew Exchange and St Giles in the Fields.

contain, even in external and indifferent things, what course is to be taken'. It was a complaint against Laud that he implemented rulings on matters traditionally considered 'things indifferent' as a reinforcement of Church authority: typically, Herbert finds his authority in the Bible, although it is difficult to find, in the verses he has quoted, 'let all things be done decently, and in order' and 'let all things be done for edification', the warrant for his particular style of church furnishing.[14] His friend Nicholas Ferrar used the same text in defence of genuflection and making the sign of the Cross, a practice Herbert presumably approved of, as he sanctioned the publication of Ludovicus Carbo's treatise, which treated the sign of the Cross in detail.[15] Herbert would have been familiar with the doctrinal debate, which had already taken place in the 1620s. As early as 1622 the Parliamentarian Francis Rous had identified key problems with the national Church in *The Diseases of the Time Attended by their Remedies*, where he identifies himself with the derogatory term 'Puritanisme'. At this stage the 'diseases' are seen purely in terms of doctrine. Chapter 7 is devoted to 'aphorisms of Predestination'. The aphoristic style is chosen by Rous because it is simply proclamatory of 'short and evident Truthes':

the revelation of Gods secrets must informe and teach our understandings & iudgements what they are, but our understandings or iudgements must not tell themselves what these secrets are; so we must be passive in a submissive receiving them not active in an inventive contriving of them. Therefore, the reason must lye still, and meerly suffer.[16]

The 'suffering' of Reason in this chapter involves total acceptance of God's arbitrary choice of elect and damned. Predestination has been perceived as the fault-line over which Arminians and Calvinists divided, but as Peter White points out, Arminians did believe in predestination. They even believed in double predestination— predestination to damnation as well as to salvation. The difference was in the perceived grounds for predestination. Arminians hoped for some rational criteria, based perhaps on foreknowledge,

---

[14] Herbert, *Works*, 246.

[15] 'Letter from Edward Lenton to Sir Thomas Hetley', 1634, published by Little Gidding Community Press in *The Arminian Nunnery and other 17th century accounts of Little Gidding* (Little Gidding, 1987), 9. Hutchinson describes the project to publish Carbo's *Introductio Ad Catechismum*: Herbert, *Works*, 564.

[16] Francis Rous, *The Diseases of the Time Attended by their Remedies* (London, 1622), 165.

whereas Calvinists insisted on stressing the arbitrary nature of God's election.[17] Both Calvin and Juan de Valdés enthusiastically espoused double predestination, and it is characteristic of Calvinist rhetoric that the arbitrary nature of God's choice is celebrated in terms of His ineffability, echoing St Paul's *O altitudo* (Rom. 11: 33). Like St Paul, both authors quote the superbly capricious Old Testament utterance of Romans 9: 13: 'Jacob have I loved, but Esau have I hated.'[18] It is not surprising that another characteristic of predestinarian rhetoric is the injunction to human beings to refrain from curiosity, the kind of curiosity into 'high speculative and unprofitable questions' which, says Herbert, is 'a great stumbling block to the holinesse of Scholars'.[19]

It would have been extraordinary if Herbert did not believe in double predestination. Certainly, he did not comment adversely on Valdés' extreme version of reprobation, although he does note that this doctrine 'needeth discreet, and wary explaining'.[20] There has been some speculation as to whether Herbert's poem 'The Water-course' celebrates double predestination. In fact, in the late 1620s or early 1630s, when the poem was probably written, an explicit consideration of predestination would have been politically daring. Christopher Hodgkins notes that in 1631 John Davenant, Herbert's bishop at Salisbury, had been harshly rebuked for discussing predestination and election in a court sermon.[21] Hodgkins claims that the poem 'explicitly affirms double predestination', but in fact it does not mention any kind of predestination at all. The final line '[He] gives to man as he sees fit' refers only to a future Day of Judgement, not to a predestinating moment in the past. To a reader of seventeenth-century theology the poem appears to support double predestination because it shares a predestinarian rhetoric with theologians like William Perkins, dichotomizing the eventual destinals of mankind in a Ramist-like diagram and implying that the grounds for salvation

---

[17] P. White, *Predestination, Policy and Polemic: Conflict and Consensus in the English Church from the Reformation to the Civil War* (Cambridge, 1992), 29.

[18] Mal. 1: 2–3. See John Calvin, *The Institution of the Christian Religion*, tr. Thomas Norton (London, 1578), III. xxi. 6, p. 384; Juan de Valdés, *Juan de Valdés on the Epistle to the Romans*, tr. J. T. Betts (London, 1883), 225.

[19] Herbert, *Works*, 238.   [20] Ibid. 314.

[21] C. Hodgkins, *Authority, Church and Society in George Herbert: Return to the Middle Way* (New York, 1993), 21.

or damnation are entirely in the arbitrary and inscrutable will of
God:

> That so in pureness thou mayst him adore,
>
> Who gives to man, as he sees fit $\begin{cases} \text{Salvation.} \\ \text{Damnation.} \end{cases}$[22]

Calvinist theologians' insistence on double predestination was
part of an obsession with the dependence of the believer on
God in which the central issue was absolute divine causality.[23]
Double predestination is often referred to as 'The Decree', but
this initiating act of will by God extends beyond the act of
predestination to embrace the whole of a Christian's life and
conduct:

> the Decree is God willing the Futurition; ie The future being of all
> things. The external Efficiency of God, is Gods working all that he hath
> willed, according as he hath willed.[24]

Hence the Calvinist concern with the believer's perseverance and
sanctification, which also have to be considered as the sovereign
work of God. Charles Lloyd Cohen has declared that scholars
have overstressed the importance of predestination in Calvinist
thought. He argues for the pre-eminence of justification and
sanctification, and it was sanctification that became the focus for
controversy in the Arminian–Calvinist debate.[25] However unpal-
atable, it is easy to formulate the doctrine of predestination as a
sovereign act of will by God without reference to human beings.
Even justification by faith, the saving act of God irrespective of
human merit, is easier to grasp than the Calvinist doctrine of
sanctification, which demands that the holy actions of a believer
are regarded as the work of God. God's exclusive causation of all
the believer's 'good works', from justification to sanctification,

---

[22] See J. C. Hunter, 'Herbert's "The Water-Course": Notorious and Neglected', *Notes and Queries*, 34 (1987), 310–12 for claims that 'The Water-course' echoes Calvinist predes-tinarian rhetoric in other ways, also.

[23] See R. A. Muller, *Christ and The Decree: Christology and Predestination in Reformed Theology from Calvin to Perkins* (Durham, NC, 1986), 1–2.

[24] John Norton, *The Orthodox Evangelist or a Treatise wherein many Great Evangelical Truths (Not a few whereof are much opposed and Eclipsed in this perillous houre of the Passion of the Gospel) Are briefly Discussed, cleared, and confirmed. As a further help, for the Begeting, and Establishing of the Faith which is in Jesus* (London, 1654), 101.

[25] C. L. Cohen, *God's Caress: The Psychology of Puritan Religious Experience* (Oxford, 1986), 115–16.

initial salvation to mature holiness, is insisted upon by Calvinism. Valdés' writing shares with Calvin's a doctrine of the total depravity of man, although neither of them used the phrase: no value is allowed to the efforts of the human being unaided by the Holy Spirit. Article 10 of the Thirty-Nine Articles was to echo this doctrine faithfully. Good works are dismissed by Valdés in the language of Isaiah 64: 6: 'All our righteousnesses are as filthy rags.'[26] Bishop Bayly, on the other hand, had castigated the Puritan interpretation of this text as 'one of the hinderances which keepe backe a sinner from the Practice of Piety'.[27] In the early seventeenth century the question of what holiness should be was becoming deeply controversial.[28]

The debate about 'good works' occupies far more pages of print in the early modern period than the problem of predestination. The hundreds of popular catechisms published in the late sixteenth and early seventeenth centuries hardly ever mention predestination, although there is a flurry of interest in the early 1620s, the same date as Rous's *The Diseases of the Time*.[29] Only Theodore Beza and Daniel Featley, who both had their own reasons for stressing the doctrine, treat of double predestination at any length. Most catechisms, however, discuss the theology of good works in some detail. Montagu's *A New Gagg for an Old Goose* has five chapters on good works to one on predestination, trying to modify the key Calvinist belief 'that no good works are meritorious'. 'Meritorious' was a term from Catholic theology, used to describe acts that deserve spiritual reward. In the early seventeenth century it became popularized into a negative term for Arminian 'good works'. Henry Burton's anti-Arminian work of 1632, *The Christians Bulwarke Against Satan's Battery*, sneers at the 'meritorious satisfactions' of his opponents.[30] The 1633 catechism

---

[26] For a brief statement of Valdés' attitude to the soteriological function of faith as opposed to good works see Juan de Valdés, *XVII Opuscules*, tr. and ed. J. T. Betts (London, 1882).

[27] Lewis Bayly, *The Practice of Pietie, Directing a Christian how to walke that he may please God. Amplified by the Author*, 28th edn. (London, 1631), 78.

[28] For a longer treatment of this subject, see Hodgkins, *Authority, Church, and Society in George Herbert*, 12–16.

[29] See I. Green, '"For Children in Yeeres and Children in Understanding": The Emergence of the English Catechism under Elizabeth and the Early Stuarts', JEH 37 (1986), 404 n.

[30] Henry Burton, *The Christians Bulwarke, Against Satans Battery. Or, The Doctrine of Justification* (London, 1632), sig. A1ᵛ.

Grounds of Christian Religion makes it clear that good works are not to be regarded 'as meritorious causes of salvation, but only as fruits of faith, and duties of love'.[31] In the 1641 pamphlet *The Arminian Nunnery*, the charitable works of the Ferrar family at Little Gidding, described as 'meritorious', are assumed to be one criterion for condemnation.[32] Even an extremely brief catechism, addressed to 'the symple sort', taught that these works of traditional piety, 'giving of almes, visiting the sicke, buylding of schooles, and houses for the poore', were no longer to be valued.[33] The debate over 'good works' between Arminians and Calvinists was essentially over causation. Calvinists saw the Arminian doctrine of free will, whereby the human being had the power to will his own good works, as impinging on God's sovereignty.[34] This applied not only to salvation, but to sanctification, the living of a holy life. The doctrine of the perseverance of the saints was discussed at Dort because it was the ultimate expression of Calvinist belief in the divine, efficacious causation of 'good works' in the believer. Hence William Prynne's *The Perpetuitie of a Regenerate Mans Estate*, published in 1626 to combat what he sees as a rising tide of Pelagianism, Popery, and Arminianism, argues fiercely for the triumph of the power of God in the believer, assuring a lifetime of holiness for Christians who are 'so over-ruled and mastered by the spirit, that they cannot fulfill the lusts of the flesh and doe the evill that they would'.[35]

---

[31] H. B., *Grounds of Christian Religion Laid downe briefly and plainely by way of Question and Answer* (London, 1633), 12.

[32] The pamphlet *The Arminian Nunnery* and Edward Lenton's letter on which it is based have been conveniently reprinted by the present Little Gidding community (see n. 15). 'Meritorious' is a word inserted by the pamphleteers to describe the Ferrar family's charitable works, which Edward Lenton was unreservedly impressed by in 1634. Lenton's letter expresses reservation about their treatment of 'things indifferent'—genuflection, ceremonies, using the sign of the Cross—but does not question their orthodoxy. The later pamphleteers discerned a belief in Arminian doctrine in this account of their practices. See 'Letter from Edward Lenton to Sir Thomas Hetley', 10, and *The Arminian Nunnery*, 7.

[33] *A breefe Catechisme so necessarie and easie to be learned even of the symple sort, that whosever can not or will not attayne to the same, is not to be counted a good Christian, much lesse to be admitted to the Supper of the Lorde* (London, 1576), sig. A7ʳ.

[34] Muller, *Christ and The Decree*, 171. Norton, *The Orthodox Evangelist*, 125, concedes that Arminians 'yeild a concurrence of the Spirit to be necessary to each act of obedience'. The problem is that it is the believer who initiates the good work: 'they make it subsequent, not antecedent' to the human act of willing.

[35] Prynne, William, *The Perpetuitie of a Regenerate Mans Estate* (London, 1626), 94.

Herbert considered Valdés to be an expert in the implementation of God's sovereignty on human beings: he is commended for 'observation of Gods Kingdome within us, and the working thereof, of which he was a very diligent observer'. Valdés' extraordinary circle in Naples, which included the Capuchin Bernadino Ochino, and the poets Marcantonio Flaminio and Vittoria Colonna, was nicknamed by him 'The Kingdom of God'. Valdés doctrine of good works is described by Herbert in explicitly Calvinist terms: salvation is 'in the acceptation of Christs righteousnesse'. Herbert identifies this passive attitude to righteousness as a 'great stumbling-block' to 'the Adversaries'.[36] The biblical context for Herbert's choice of word is the doctrine of righteousness through faith, which is seen as profoundly anti-rational, and for which the sign is death on a cross:

For the Jews require a sign, and the Greeks seek after wisdom: But we preach Christ crucified, unto the Jews a stumbling block, and unto the Greeks foolishness.[37]

The disruptive sign which is the Cross and the anti-rational doctrine of Christian righteousness are linked by the mechanism of mortification, which Herbert approvingly notes as central to Valdés' treatise.[38] In approving the publication of *The Hundred and Ten Considerations*, Herbert is taking up an anti-Arminian position, and clearly intended this treatise to be a Calvinist intervention in the debate.

Mortification and 'Motions'

Like that of Savonarola, and François de Sales, Valdés' spirituality aspires towards the closest possible unity between God and the believer, which is possibly the reason why the author of 'Clasping of Hands' and 'The Search' was attracted to all three writers. Savonarola approaches the problem via the medieval causal chain, characterized by the movement of one agency upon another. Valdés' writing shows traces of the same concepts and vocabulary, employed to rather different ends. Both writers begin with the assumption that God, the First Cause, moves everything by his will. Valdés distinguishes two wills in God, the Immediate

---

[36] Herbert, *Works*, 305.   [37] 1 Cor. 1: 22–3. See also Rom. 9: 32.
[38] Herbert, *Works*, 305.

and the Mediate. The Mediate is God's general will for the universe: the Immediate is God's particular will for the redeemed.[39] Like Savonarola, Valdés envisages the collapse of the causal chain for the believer, so that he becomes subject to the Immediate Will of God, as man was before the Fall, and as Christ was. This essentially Calvinist concept of causation differs in some respects from the Thomist theology of Savonarola. Whilst Savonarola assumes a divine principle implanted in the believer as the source of motion towards God, Valdés does not. Calvin rejects this secondary cause of piety in believers because it implies power-sharing:

they part the government between God and man, that God by his power inspireth into man a motion whereby he may worke according to the nature planted in him.[40]

In place of this one 'motion', Calvin posits a continuous series of divine motions, by which the individual Christian is directed in God's will:

God poureth in singular motions, according to the calling of every man....the wittes of men are in the hand of God to rule them at every moment.[41]

Calvin does not want to allow the believer any kind of autonomy: there is no 'mutuall meeting together by ye motion of both God & man'.[42] This is also the absolutist vision of *The Hundred and Ten Considerations*:

From this divine union it proceeds, that a man altogether, and in all things remits himselfe to the will of God, dispoyling himselfe of his own proper will, and so brings himselfe to will that which God wills, and in that manner which God wills, to love that which God loves, and in that manner which God loves it, and consequently not to will that which God wills not, and not to love that which God loves not... and he shall understand, that he so far stands united with God as far as he stands thus remitted, and thus reduced.[43]

Despite the supreme power of the Holy Spirit, the hindrance to his work is the conflict between God's will and man's will. Man's will has to be 'mortified'—'put to death'—in order that God's will

---

[39] Valdés, *110 Considerations*, 97.
[40] Calvin, *Institution* I. xvi. 4, p. 71.
[41] Ibid. II. ii. 17, p. 101.
[42] Ibid. II. iii. 11, p. 113.
[43] Valdés, *110 Considerations*, 186.

may prevail. This process is described over and over again in the many popular catechisms of the period.[44]

The poems of *The Temple* were reportedly described by their author as 'a picture of the many spiritual Conflicts that have past betwixt God and my Soul, before I could subject mine to the will of Jesus my Master'.[45] It is not surprising, then, that so many poems in *The Temple* seem to chart the progress of 'reduction' of Herbert's will to God's. In 'H. Baptisme (ii)' the 'reduction' is figured in the very layout of the original manuscript. 'Let me be soft and supple to thy will' he prays: and the layout of the poem describes a funnelling into the straight and narrow way which is the will of God. Baptism, with its imagery of death and resurrection, remains a continuing experience for the believer. St Paul, in chapters 6, 7, and 8 of Romans, expounds the process by which the believer 'dies' with Christ at baptism.[46] The sinful human nature which was the inheritance of the Fall is put to death, and a kind of resurrection happens, by which the Holy Spirit gives a new, godly life to the believer.

When we were in the flesh, the motions of sins, which were by the law, did work in our members to bring forth fruit unto death. But now we are delivered from the law, that being dead wherein we were held; that we should serve in newness of spirit.[47]

The only way out for the believer is his own death, the death of the 'natural' man with his own desires and will. Paul's doctrine of a death to self and a life in Christ for every Christian is already radical enough: but Valdés is prepared to make explicit the assumptions contained within it. The opposition throughout these chapters of 'flesh' and 'spirit' is one that Valdés seizes on, in his commentary on Romans, to develop his own version of the concept of mortification that is contained in Romans 8: 13: 'For if

---

[44] See for example, *A Catechisme or Briefe Instruction in the Principles and Grounds of the true Christian Religion* (London, 1617); William Gouge, *A short Catechisme, wherein are briefly handled the fundamentall principles of Christian Religion. Needfull to be knowne by all Christians before they be admitted to the Lords Table.* This went into 7 editions by 1635. Most conclusive of all, Stephen Egerton's *A Briefe Methode of Catechising*, which went into 43 editions by 1645, in reducing his catechism even further to four points only, made this his third point: 'whosoever doth truly beleeve in Christ Jesus, is a new creature, daily dying to sinne, and rising againe to righteousnes and holines': *A Briefe Methode of Catechising* (London, 1615), 27.

[45] Isaak Walton, *The Life of Mr. George Herbert* (London, 1670), 109.

[46] Rom. 6: 3.

[47] Rom. 7: 6–7.

ye live after the flesh, ye shall die: but if ye through the Spirit do mortify the deeds of the body, ye shall live.' Valdés makes this exchange of life in the flesh for divine spirit the distinctive mark of the Christian, and it is one that has to be deeply felt:

they, who do not inwardly feel the effect of Christ's death, and the effect of Christ's resurrection and life, although they call Christ LORD, do not call Him as do Christians, nor do they call Him by the Holy Spirit, but by their own spirit: not by faith, but by opinion: not by experience, but by lore.[48]

The contrasting of 'faith' with 'opinion', and 'experience' with 'lore' (human knowledge), is a set of oppositions familiar to the reader of *The Hundred and Ten Considerations*. True faith is super-natural and experimental, and it involves the extermination of human impulses so that the motions of the Holy Spirit can take their place. Consistently in his commentary on Romans Valdés calls for the extinction of *los afectos i apetitos de la carne* (the passions and appetites of the flesh) so that the true Christian will be able to feel *los movimientos i las inspirationes del Spiritu* (the motions and inspirations of the Spirit). He concludes, in the note on Romans 12: 1, that the replacement of the human motions by spiritual ones is the definitive experience of the Christian life.

The 'mortification of the flesh', with its project of the imitation of Christ, was not a new doctrine. It was a key feature of tradi-tional piety, and was construed as continual self-denial, as ex-emplified in Herbert's 'The Thanksgiving'. This poem is a demonstration of how not to practise mortification in a Reformed theology. It is described by Ilona Bell as a demonstration of the futility of the *imitatio Christi* of the Ignation exercises.[49] The poem is concerned with traditional 'good works'—building a hospital, giving to the poor, renouncing the world, 'using' the gifts of the creation in true Augustinian fashion, fulfilling the role of Chris-tian poet and acknowledging God as the source of all talent.[50] However, the syntax, with its repetition of 'I will', should have given the clue that the poem ironizes an Arminian celebration of the free will of the poet rather than a reduction to the will of God.

[48] Valdés, *Epistle to the Romans*, 262.

[49] Bell, 'Herbert's Valdésian Vision', 316–17.

[50] As Richard Strier notes, 'nowhere else in Herbert is there this confidence in the adequacy of art to God's nature': R. Strier, *Love Known: Theology and Experience in George Herbert's Poetry* (Chicago, 1983), 52 n.

It is only when faced with the Cross of Christ, that symbol of mortification, that the verbose poet shudders to a halt, and the potential submission of his self-will is figured by the silencing of the confident rhetoric. 'The Reprisall', which is clearly connected with the previous poem by its position opposite it in the W manuscript, seems to begin again after a pause for thought, and the nature of the conflict becomes clearer. The skipping rhythm and cheerful rhyming couplets give way to a more reflective tone and pace as the poet acknowledges there is nothing he can do to repay Christ for what He suffered on the Cross. In 'The Reprisall' the true implications of human depravity are considered. Since Christ's death is the cause of every good act the believer can do, there is nothing the believer can give to Christ. However, the very fact that the poem is called 'The Reprisall' seems to indicate that in the believer's mind there is still a battle going on, the same one described in the poem from the W manuscript, 'Love':

> Thou art too hard for me in Love:
> There is no dealing with thee in that Art:
> That is thy Master-peece I see.
> When I contrive & plott to prove
> Something that may be conquest on my part,
> Thou still, O Lord, outstrippest mee.

At the end of 'The Reprisall' the believer not only recognizes the futility of the competition, but realizes that the attempt to outdo God in love and piety is actually a manifestation of the sinful human will which cannot accept its own limitations. However, there is still something that the believer thinks he can do for God: he is going to change sides and fight against himself, his own sinful will. This, presumably, is the 'Reprisall' of the title, but it seems to be against God and against himself at the same time, and apart from the problem of self-division, Herbert seems to have forgotten that the battle is supposed to be over. All God actually wants is the 'resigning' advocated in 'Dialogue': the 'dispoyling himself of his own proper will' described by Valdés.

It is such 'reduction' to God's will, which seems to imply the annihilation of the believer's identity, that Stanley Fish observes in Herbert's poetry. However, Fish does not seem to understand the double dynamic of mortification, which involves resurrection as well as death. 'Aaron' is a poem which typographically figures this dual process of mortification and vivification. It is also a commentary on less Reformed ideas of holiness, which were regaining currency at the time Herbert was writing this poem. Laud's catchphrase, 'the beauty of holiness', was associated with Arminian theology which, as we have seen, stressed the necessity of good works for salvation. Linked with this emphasis was a concern for other 'externals': the order and decoration of the church building, the setting apart of the sacred altar, the wearing of vestments, and the strict following of the liturgy. The new Church hierarchy was attempting to enforce all these measures. 'Aaron' starts with a description of the archetypal priest, but even in the first stanza the clothing is described in terms of its spiritual function, rather than in a Laudian celebration of vestments:

> Holinesse on the head,
> Light and perfections on the breast,
> Harmonious bells below, raising the dead
> To leade them unto life and rest:
> Thus are true Aarons drest.

In the second stanza the poet laments his own inadequacy in comparison: he is a 'poore priest'. However, as the details of Aaron's clothing in Exodus 28 make clear, Aaron's holiness is merely external and symbolic. The priesthood of Christ is far superior, and Herbert can be part of that order by the process of mortification—death and resurrection—described in stanza four. In Christ he is 'new drest': and the results are shown in the final stanza.

> So holy in my head,
> Perfect and light in my deare breast,
> My doctrine tun'd by Christ, (who is not dead,
> But lives in me while I do rest)
> Come people; Aaron's drest.

The conclusion from the poem is inescapable: true holiness is located in the head and the heart. This means that it is an attitude rather than a set of actions. The correct attitude is one of 'rest'— inaction, the 'resigning' of 'Dialogue'. The 'rest of God' is a phrase which resonates throughout Herbert's work. Its biblical context is in Hebrews, where the people of God are promised an end from their labours, just as God rested on the Sabbath. Richard Baxter, who sympathized deeply with Herbert's piety, describes it in *The Saints Everlasting Rest* as 'the end and perfection of motion'.[51] However, there is an awesome price to be paid for this rest: it is the rest of death. If not the peace of physical death, which Herbert describes at the end of his poem 'Death', it is the peace of mortification, dying to yourself, the end of human activity: 'he that is entered into his rest, he also hath ceased from his own works.'[52] This of course is the very best preparation for death itself. According to Walton, Herbert's practice at this stood him in good stead on his deathbed:

I praise God I am prepared for [death]; and I praise him that I am not to learn patience now I stand in such need of it; and that I have practised mortification, and endeavoured to die daily, that I might not die eternally.[53]

This piety practises self-extinction in preparation for physical death, but it does not face the problem of what legitimate human agency might be. The last stanza of 'Aaron' leaves the reader in no doubt as to Herbert's status before God, but it is not clear whether God's new kind of holy priest is actually performing any holy actions. What is clear is that actions are no longer Herbert's responsibility: he is resting, Christ is the one in charge. Ultimately, holiness is conferred independently of any holy actions, just as justification by faith does not depend on works. This is high-lighted by the metaphor of dress, picking up the biblical image for the 'clothing' of the believer in Christ.[54] Dress is a temporary, if effective covering: God sees only the actions of Christ, but it is not absolutely clear what other people in this world can see. The essentially cosmetic nature of this enterprise is almost literally underlined by the sequence of typographical changes in the B manuscript. The last word of each line is 'dressed' in a way that reflects the death and resurrection process: the progression is from highlighted capitals—letters physically larger than the others—to

---

[51] Richard Baxter, *The Saints Everlasting Rest*, 2nd edn. (London, 1651), 6. Helen Wilcox notes that this particular work 'is full of remembrances of Herbert's verse': H. Wilcox, 'Something Understood: The Reputation and Influence of George Herbert to 1715' (Univ. of Oxford D.Phil. thesis, 1984), 219.

[52] Heb. 4: 10.

[53] Walton, *Life of Herbert*, 112.

[54] Eph. 4: 22–4: 'Put off concerning the former conversation the old man, which is corrupt according to the deceitful lusts; And be renewed in the spirit of your mind; And . . . put on the new man, which after God is created in righteousness and true holiness.'

unhighlighted capitals, through to lower-case letters, as the trappings of the Old Testament priesthood are removed. The process is reversed in the final stanzas as the priest is reclothed in Christ.

Effective, Visible Holiness

Predictably, it is in his discussion of Christian liberty that Valdés moves closest to an Antinomian position:

Christian liberty consisteth in this, that a Christian shall not bee chastized for his evill living, nor shall be rewarded for his well living...being governed by the holy spirit, on the one side they finde, and know themselves to be free, and exempted from the law...on the other side they finde, and know themselves obliged to be like unto Christ in their life, and manners.

George Herbert admits that this discourse 'may seeme strange', but after an investigation decides that it can stand, because of his great respect for the doctrine of grace through faith: 'all the point lies in believing or not believing.'[55] Thus cogently summarized by Herbert, this doctrine leaves very little place for good works. From the earliest years of the seventeenth century through to the Westminster Assembly of the 1640s it was the concern of theologians to correct this emphasis without lapsing into Pelagianism, or falling into Antinomianism. Antinomianism is defined by Gertrude Huehns as a result of regarding God as the universal immediate Cause, and this is clearly one possible extreme of Calvinist theology. The question of second causes, which includes human agency, shows the careful reasoning of Reformed theologians at full stretch. Their Calvinist inheritance dictates that God has to be sovereign First Cause of every good act, yet they are well aware of the dangers of Antinomianism and spiritualism. John Norton was typical in attacking Antinomians who 'deny the Efficiency of the second cause': a place for human agency is essential.[56] However, since the will of God had to prevail in all circumstances, theologians found it difficult to give the second cause, the human being, any real integrity. William Ames suggested that although the First Cause of an action was God, and the final result always the fulfilment of God's will, there was not in fact any compulsion on the intervening secondary causes to carry it out. This appears to allow a kind of agency to human beings in

[55] Herbert, *Works*, 311.   [56] Norton, *The Orthodox Evangelist*, 111.

doing good works, and there would be reward for good works accordingly.[57] John Norton argued that the Spirit of God only influenced the human being to do what he would have done had God not willed it in the first place:

> the Will placed under the determining Motion of God, inclineth it self freely to the Act, and to that only, whereunto it would have inclined it self, if (upon a supposition of impossibility) there were no decree.[58]

This was more or less the compromise adopted by the Westminster Assembly in 1643:

> although, in relation to the foreknowledge and decree of God, the first cause, all things come to pass immutably and infallibly: yet, by the same providence, he ordereth them to fall out according to the nature of second causes.

These sophisticated arguments appear to weaken the believer's dependence on God, but the injunction of all theological treatises is still to mortify the human will in order that God's will may be worked out in the life of the Christian, a process that, as we have seen, reduces as far as possible the role of the secondary cause in bringing about a good work. The spectre of fanaticism, whereby a believer elides his own identity with that of God as 'frantic Hackett' did in 1591, is technically avoided. The logic of this position, however, is not easily grasped. More assimilable are the broad strokes with which Calvin made his break with Catholic theology: the vivid language of mortification and vivification, and divine 'motions'. Hacket's followers had no access to the learned analyses, and could not have made the subtle distinctions. Even the willing Philagathus in *The Plaine Mans Path-way to Heaven* has problems understanding why the 'new birth' does not eradicate old human impulses: 'This seemeth verie obscure' he says to his teacher Theologus, giving him two more pages to try to explain.[59] Calvinist theology had created a climate in which radical religion, which offered a more streamlined version of its doctrines, could take hold. Gertrude Huehns's characterization of Antinomian belief includes 'instantaneous obedience to the promptings of

---

[57] William Ames, *The Marrow of sacred Divinity, drawne out of the holy Scriptures, and the Interpreters therof, and brought into Method* (London, 1642), 34, 146.

[58] Norton, *The Orthodox Evangelist*, 115.

[59] Arthur Dent, *The Plaine Mans Path-way to Heaven, wherein every man may clearly see whether he shall be saved or damned*, 13th imp. (London, 1611), 14–15.

the holy Spirit'.[60] Yet the injunction to obey the motions of the
Holy Spirit is explicit in most popular catechisms, and had been
part of popular Protestant spirituality since Cranmer had written
the new Collect for the First Sunday of Lent into the 1549 Prayer
Book: 'Give us grace ... that, our flesh being subdued to the Spirit,
we may ever obey thy godly motions in righteousness and
true holiness.' Henry Arthington in 1592 describes with bitter
bewilderment his 'seduction' by Hacket, particularly an episode
in which the two of them were praying for the Queen:

Before we departed, I felt my selfe verie hot within, which I verelie then
thought had beene an extraordinarie motion of the holie-ghost, (as
Christs Disciples hadde going to *Emaus*;) which the Lord had sent
downe as a blessing of his love upon our exercise, so I departed a very
glad man. The next night following as I laie in my bed, I found my selfe
moved to pen a curssed *Prophesie* against the citty of *London*.[61]

Although this text apparently contains Arthington's 'unfained
repentance' its predominant tone is self-justifying: the careful
Scriptural reference for the 'extraordinarie motion', the context
of loyal prayer, and his own ingenuous responses are recorded in
excuse of his support for Hacket. The subtext is that any orthodox
believer would have interpreted the situation as he did. The only
alternative explanation for his own lack of agency as reported
here is that the 'motion' was from Satan. The prophecy against
London is 'curssed', explains Arthington, because he now believes
himself to have been demon-possessed. Geoffrey Nuttall believes
that the logical conclusion of the Puritan doctrine of the Holy
Spirit is radical Quaker spiritualism, which depended on 'extraordinarie' motions of this kind.[62] Nigel Smith points out that the
poems of George Herbert were used in defence of Antinomianism
by Henry Pinnell, particularly the poem 'Submission', which
stresses the disabling of the believer and the pre-eminence of
God's power in good works, and the poem 'Conscience', which
silences an inner, Arminian-sounding voice demanding traditional

---

[60] G. Huehns, *Antinomianism in English History with Special Reference to the Period 1640–1660*
(London, 1951), 87.
[61] Henrie Arthington, *The Seduction of Arthington by Hacket especiallie, with some tokens of his
unfained repentance and Submission* (London, 1592), 15.
[62] G. F. Nuttall, *The Holy Spirit in Puritan Faith and Experience*, new edn. (Chicago,
1992), 14.

piety.[63] George Herbert found so much in Valdés' treatise that was congenial to his Reformed spirituality that he was prepared to overlook Antinomian excesses in *The Hundred and Ten Considerations*. Consideration 46, which uses Antinomian imagery for the spiritual Sun which is to be the believer's only guide, is translated by Herbert into moderate Calvinist terms:

> he meaneth (I suppose) that a man presume not to merit... by any acts or exercises of Religion; but that he ought to pray God affectionately and fervently to send him the light of his spirit... hee in the meane while applying himselfe to the duties of true Piety, and syncere Religion, such are Prayer, Fasting, Alms-deedes, & c.[64]

Needless to say, the final sentence is wishful thinking on Herbert's part. Nowhere in *The Hundred and Ten Considerations* are such 'duties of true Piety' recommended.

There are places where Herbert draws the line, however, and he comments on certain Considerations which smack of heresy. Juan de Valdés believes that since God is the immediate cause of every good action, external rules are unnecessary, and even unhelpful, to the Christian, who is regulated by the Spirit of God; there is no need to give him rules for the exercise of charity, for he has within himself the true and certain rule, which is the Holy Spirit.[65]

The sign of true mortification ought to be overwhelming success, as God Himself is living the Christian life through the believer. Of course, this means that the Christian does not have to avoid sin, since he will be divinely enabled to resist it:

> they who *mortifie themselves* in the occasion of erring doe miserably loose themselves: For being deceived by humane wisdome they doe alwaies goe avoiding the occasions, which incite them to erre: And they who are *mortified*, in the occasions of erring, that offer themselves unto them, are refined as gold in the fire, for being helped by the holy spirit in the proper occasions they are mortified, not avoiding any of them.[66]

At this point the pious and practical Herbert, somewhat shocked by this presumption, tries to rewrite Valdés' 'occasions of erring' as 'ordinary and necessary duties'. However, there is

---

[63] N. Smith, 'George Herbert in Defence of Antinomianism', *Notes and Queries*, 31 (1984), 334–5.

[64] Herbert, *Works*, 312.

[65] Valdés, *Epistle to the Romans*, 242.

[66] Herbert, *Works*, 314.

every evidence from the rest of the *Considerations* that Valdés does have this much confidence in the work of God in the truly mortified believer. He insists that the agent in all authentic Christian activities—thought, speech, and action—is not the human being but the Holy Spirit:[67]

S. *Paul* doth not say; *That the holy Spirit teacheth us to pray*, but that he *prayes by* us, and that he *prayes in us.*

The inevitable implication of Valdés' system is that the mortified believer shares the divine nature, rather than the human. 'The Sonnes of God' are continually contrasted with the 'Sonnes of Adam'. Everything human—human wisdom, reason, discourse—is consistently anathematized in the *Considerations* as separating man from God. On the other hand, if the believer is able to die to himself and live completely in the strength of the Holy Spirit, he will partake of divine knowledge, wisdom, and discourse, which are completely alien to the human being. 'None understand it,' says Valdés on Christ's teaching about knowing God, 'but they that leave to be men, that is, they which leave the image of *Adam*, and take the image of Christ.'[68] There is considerable benefit to the believer in this trade-off: divine attributes have the advantage of being infallible, and all-powerful. It is inevitable, given Valdés' longing that God should be the efficient cause of the believer's every action, that he will finally collapse the identities of believer and Holy Spirit. The process of dehumanizing involves the killing of the *afectos i apetitos* of the flesh (which had figured so largely in the commentary on Romans):

when he shall know in himselfe any affection, or any appetite which belongs to a man, that lives to the world, straight way he will labour to kill it, saying, this belongs not, nor appertains to me, who am *dead to the world.*[69]

This grammar of human agency is not really acceptable to Valdés because it sounds as if the cause of the action is the believer's own will. In Consideration 56 he remembers to correct this rather active rhetoric:

I shall say rather better, that doing after this manner the Holy Spirit is that which mortifieth him.

---

[67] Valdés, *110 Considerations*, 117.   [68] Ibid. 3.   [69] Ibid. 46.

In this way Valdés also rewrites the instructions for holiness in Scripture, which, he says crossly, give some 'molestation' to Christian believers.[70] Consideration 18 indicates that the exhortations to holiness are not intended to be carried out by the believer himself: they are to form the basis of a prayer to God to carry them out within him, on his behalf but without his aid.[71] This is a modification, or at least an explanation, of the rhetoric of Scripture: for 'the believer' as agent of a spiritual action, the Christian will read 'the Holy Spirit within the believer'. Presumably Valdés expected his readers to make a similar adjustment to the rhetoric of *The Hundred and Ten Considerations*.

George Herbert, often regarded as a model of orthodox Church of England doctrine and practice, was not unaware of Valdés' excesses, yet he still recommended publication in the strongest terms—as a duty from God. In 1632, however, Antinomian sects were not perceived as so great a threat to orthodoxy as an Arminian hierarchy, as the anxious correspondence between Herbert's own bishop and the Puritan master of Sidney Sussex College makes clear.[72] Because the Arminian position on holiness is at the other extreme to the Antinomian, Juan de Valdés' treatise could be used as part of the traditional Calvinist answer to an Arminian threat. Valdés' *Considerations* are as ruthlessly uncompromising as Calvin's *Institutes*. For Calvin, the human will is ruled either by God or Satan:

> beinge bewitched with the deceites of Satan, it of necessity yeeldeth it selfe obedient to every leading of him. For whom the Lord vouchsafeth not to rule with his spirite, them by iust iudgement he sendeth away to be moved of Satan.[73]

Heiko A. Oberman states that there are no real second causes in Calvin's thought, only metaphorical ones. The human agent disappears under pressure from the opposed spiritual entities competing for control. Thus Paul Bayne dramatically formulates

---

[70] Valdés, *110 Considerations*, 263.

[71] He does concede, at the end of Consideration 19, that there are some outward and physical actions a believer can do to prepare himself for the coming of the Spirit. This somewhat clashes with his insistence elsewhere that everything done without the Spirit is hateful to God.

[72] See letters to Samuel Ward from John Davenant, Bodleian MS Tanner 72, Fos. 135, 310, 312.

[73] Calvin, *Institution*, II. iv. 1, pp. 115–16.

the believer's plight in terms reminiscent of the Hercules myth, which, of course, was also used for Christ:

> when God giveth us a good motion and purpose, the divell doth watch it, as hee did the Infant, that he may kil it in the cradle, yea, smother it in the womb where it was conceived.[74]

Since the believer has no strength of his own, the solution Bayne offers is simply 'dying to our owne thoughts, words and deeds dayly'. With the removal of the human impulses, effective divine motions can have free rein against the work of Satan.

Reformed theologians after Calvin were faced with the task of reinventing human agency, but the habit of thinking in dichotomies was already deeply entrenched. In Pauline thought, which dominated Reformation theology, the human psyche was radically split into the 'old man' dominated by Satan and the 'new man' born of God. Devout Protestants, in innumerable catechisms and sermons, were encouraged to organize their experience in such oppositional categories, and see the transition from one state to another in dramatic terms. Thus Valdés comments on the Pauline doctrine of baptism:

> the Christian becomes, as soon as he believes, a member of Christ, that he really actually dies with Christ, for that God in his estimation holds him to be dead.[75]

Reformed theologians want to give such biblical concepts a literal reading, no matter how startling the result, or how remote it is from human experience. Thus Perkins, trying to distinguish between true and false Christians, claims that vivification, the second half of the death–resurrection dynamic, is the process 'by which *inherent righteousnes* is reallie put into them'.[76] The insistent vocabulary of literalness—'reallie', 'actually'—reveals the strain of holding together readings which are at the same time literal and spiritual. But the polarities thus opposed—death–resurrection, old man–new man, flesh–spirit—are the stuff of which the Reformation was made. Valdés' treatise perpetuates the dualism in vivid terms.

[74] Paul Bayne, *Holy Soliloquies, of A Holy Helper in God's building*, 2nd edn. (London, 1618), 18.

[75] Valdés, *Epistle to the Romans*, 115.

[76] William Perkins, *A Treatise, tending unto a Declaration, whether a man be in the estate of damnation, or in the estate of grace* (London, 1592), 32.

The Signs of a True Christian

Like many Calvinists in England, whose continuing project was the purification of the Church, Valdés is obsessed with the necessity to distinguish between true and false Christians.[77] Valdés would like to find clear evidence of regeneration in the life of true Christians: this is the logical outcome of his scheme for mortification and sanctification. Consideration 21, for example, makes the unexceptional statement that 'to live chast, and pure, and modest, is a sign of mortification'. This congruity of internal and external signs is what Savonarola demanded of Christian *simplicitas*. The lack of evidence for holiness in so many Christian lives, however, is a problem, as is Valdés' belief that it is easy to counterfeit the signs of a Christian. Even his Christian alphabet for children begins 'I know from experience that the human mind very readily conforms to false religion... and is wrought with great difficulty to conform to true religion.'[78] Such a scepticism was shown by English spiritual writing such as Arthur Dent's hugely popular *The Plaine Mans Path-way to Heaven* whose title promises *wherein every man may cleerly see whether he shall be saved or damned.* Hypocrisy is a huge problem, and Dent offers only eight positive signs of a Christian, to seventeen counter-indications: it is easier to identify the damned than the saved.[79] Over twenty of *The Hundred and Ten Considerations* are directly concerned with the signs and counter-signs of a true Christian, while many others are written in an attempt to distinguish between true and false piety, inspired and uninspired prayer, God's wisdom and natural wisdom. The difficulty of distinguishing between almost identical spiritual phenomena is mirrored in William Perkins's work, *A Treatise tending unto a Declaration, whether a man be in the estate of damnation, or in the estate of grace.* Even 'a meere natural man', who is, of course, damned, may be capable of such holy-sounding activities as preaching, effective prayer, and love of God.[80]

Valdés does not contemplate the full horror of Perkins's 'temporary grace', whereby 'a man may goe in the profession of the Gospell, and yet be a wicked man and a Reprobate', yet the same

[77] See Hodgkins, *Authority, Church, and Society in George Herbert*, 14–15.

[78] Juan de Valdés, *Two Catechisms*, tr. W. B. Jones and C. D. Jones, ed. J. Nieto and introd. (Lawrence, Kan., 1981), 179.

[79] Dent, *The Plaine Mans Path-way to Heaven* 13th edn. (London, 1611), 30–2.

[80] Perkins, *A Treatise, tending unto a Declaration*, 1–12.

longing for exact categories and clear distinctions drives both writers to conclude that the most accurate sign of a true Christian is mortification. As we have seen, mortification is the key process by which a 'son of Adam' may become a 'son of God'. All Reformed theologians, including Valdés, Perkins, and Herbert, would have agreed with this. But the invisible process of mortification cannot function as a sign. Like Perkins, Valdés is reluctant to enter into a discussion of the external signs of mortification. He sees very little point in the practical instructions of chapter 12 of Romans 'because that in all this, being outward, there may be feigning'. Furthermore, just as there is a counterfeit for every other godly activity, so, it seems, there is a counterfeit of genuine mortification. Valdés graphically describes those who 'procure to mortifie themselves with their own proper industry' as men who have had their heads cut off with a rusty saw—instead of the sharp sword of the Spirit by which God performs His executions. Such a messy and ineffective mortification is demonstrated by Herbert in 'The Reprisall'.

Even mortification, the defining experience of a Christian life, cannot accurately signify holiness. William Ames identifies the problem. Sanctification 'doth not consist in ralation and respect, but in reall effecting: therefore it admits divers degrees, of beginning, progress, and perfection'.[81] Ironically, it is because sanctification is a 'reall change of state' involving a process that it cannot function as a sign. Valdés, along with orthodox Reformed theologians, has to admit that mortification is 'an imperfect death' and vivification merely 'an imperfect resurrection'. Despite his insistence on 'real' vivification, Perkins elsewhere admits that even in the sanctified,

the flesh and the spirit are mixt together... If any replie, that good works are the works of Gods spirit, & for that cause perfectly righteous I answer, it is true indeed, they come from the holy Ghost that cannot sinne, but not onely and immediately. For they come also from the corrupt minde and will of man.[82]

Having described the dual process of mortification and vivification, William Ames has to admit that 'this sanctification is imperfect whilst we live here as infants . . . unlesse in the dreames of some

---

[81] Ames, *Marrow of Divinity*, 140.
[82] William Perkins, *Two Treatises* (London, 1611), 148.

fanatick persons'.[83] The spiritual success of divine causality in the believer is not overwhelming, because there is always the trace of the human agent to interfere with the causal chain and hinder the Immediate Will of God. In Consideration 106 one can discern Valdés' lament for clear-cut systems, and the elusive dream of divine efficiency as a substitute for human frailty:

the felicity would be much greater... that *the knowledge of good and evill* were totally extinct, and dead, and the spirituall light were totally kindled and alive. But I understand that the flesh passible and mortall is not a subject habilitated for so great felicity.

Mortification is not absolutely effective: the exchange of divine attributes for human is not complete.

Herbert's poem 'The Altar' should perhaps triumphantly enact the purifying process of mortification of poetic gift looked forward to so hopefully in Herbert's poem 'Love (ii)': 'then shall our brain | All our invention on thine Altar lay.' On the most superficial level this poem does follow the mortification–vivification pattern, where all agency is God's. The 'altar', which is present visually before the poem is read, is represented in the first line as 'broken', a classic operation of God's Spirit in mortification. The presence of 'tears', the sign of true repentance, confirms the godly quality of the work. The fact that the altar on the page is clearly not 'broken' might point to God's intervening grace, but when Herbert seems to claim just such a divine inspiration in the third and fourth line, the effect is disruptive:

> Whose parts are as thy hand did frame;
> No workmans tool hath touched the same.

The 'shape' poem is perhaps the most obvious manifestation of workmanship in poetry, and a further problem for Herbert's seventeenth-century readers would have been that it is an imitation of a poem in the *Greek Anthology*, a popular textbook for schoolboys. An alternative interpretation has to be found, and the next lines make the riddle clear.

> A HEART alone
> Is such a stone,
> As nothing but
> Thy pow'r doth cut.

---

[83] Ames, *Marrow of Divinity*, 145.

The inner space of the heart is reserved for God alone in a way that even the sacred altar, like any other writing surface, is not. All external phenomena including religious furniture and religious writing are subject to human influence and corruption. The point is made by the fact that the 'altar' is a classical one: altars can be built to strange gods. The poem 'The Altar' is finally represented as a thorough mixture of inner godly emotion and outer poetic frame:

> Wherefore each part
> Of my hard heart
> Meets in this frame
> To praise thy Name.

The resulting 'good work', words and intentions, is a mixture of flesh and spirit in the way that Perkins describes, and it will need the grace of sanctification before God will own it as a work of His. This will involve 'dying to' the poem:

> O let thy blessed SACRIFICE be mine,
> And sanctifie this ALTAR to be thine.

Ironically, the shifting reasoning of the godly heart is in opposition to the solidity of the poetic 'frame' in which it expresses itself. The perfect pagan altar on the page is a monument not to godly vivification but to human poetic skill. This predicament is enacted to some extent in all the poems of *The Temple*.

The admission that mortification is not complete in the believer confirms the failure of mortification to function as a sign, because the process of mortification itself is infinitely deferred. Worse, the mechanics of mortification, by which all human functions are gradually exterminated, mean that signification is disrupted, at least temporarily. Valdés explains in Consideration 45 that the Christian has to feel all the sins and weaknesses of the human state before he can put them to death. Thus, in the initial phase of mortification, the sons of God can appear less virtuous than sons of Adam, and the elect can feel more doubt about their salvation than the damned. English spiritual writers also observed the phenomenon whereby the outward signs in a believer's life might not match his inward spiritual state. Arthur Dent spends some time attempting to explain why 'some which are not regenerate, doe in some things excell the children of God'. Perkins seeks to reassure those who are worried about their inability to refrain from sexual sin in a classic illustration of the text 'the spirit is willing, but the flesh is weak':

> God will approve of thee for his owne worke which hee hath wrought in thee, and not reiect thee for thine. There is one manner of sinning in the godly, and another in the ungodly.[84]

Without access to God's perspective, however, one might assume that the sin itself would look identical. Such a disruption of sign and signified was envisaged by Calvin, in a discussion of whether the saved are actually holy:

> they are not, in respect of themselves, yet with thee they are, according to that saying of Paule, not of the workes of righteousness, but of him that calleth.[85]

Of course, such double-think is required for an understanding of the Reformed doctrine of justification, and many catechisms carefully emphasized the distinction between actual righteousness and imputed righteousness. But Reformed theologians working in the early seventeenth century were concerned to reinvent piety as a concept in Reformation theology. To do so, they needed to unite those entities, man's good works and God's righteousness, which had so thoroughly been separated in the technical process of justification, in the 'real' process of sanctification. However, the oppositions had been very firmly set up. Natural wisdom had been thoroughly discredited by the concept of spiritual wisdom; human strength was seen to exclude divine strength; carnal righteousness was the enemy of godly righteousness. All these disjunctions had the power to disrupt any Christian system of signification: worst of all, the inward–outward dichotomy was always going to be fatal to any attempt to make the signs of a Christian accurate and consistent. Thus a 1576 catechism rejects the extremely visible good works of building schools and almshouses in favour of 'the pure worshipping of God . . . trusting and depending of his good providence . . . hearing of his holy worde', works which may be 'much more excellent' but are certainly much harder to discern.[86] Such a rejection of the traditional

---

[84] Perkins, *A Treatise, tending unto a Declaration*, 38.
[85] Calvin, *Institution* III. ii. 25, p. 229.
[86] *A breefe Catechisme*, sig. A7^r.

and obvious good works of piety is enacted in Herbert's 'The Thanksgiving'.

The fundamental disruption of sign and signified, however, is contained within Puritan doctrine on human reason. Francis Rous in 1622 triumphantly proclaimed the superiority of the divine to the philosopher:

Divinitie commendeth goodnesse because it is good, but then it goes farther and iudgeth it to bee good, because it is conformable to the highest Rule of goodness; and so it teacheth the practiser to make God the Rule & Square of Vertue. It resteth not in thee that goodness is supposed to be goodnesse, but it fetcheth the practice of goodnesse from God.[87]

The distance between human and divine conceptions of goodness opened up here is unbridgeable except by divine revelation. God alone is the standard by which goodness is to be judged, and His standards are not our standards. This of course is why the thirteenth of the Thirty-Nine Articles declares that good works done before salvation 'have the nature of sin'. For Alexander Nowell, dean of St Paul's, whose catechism went into fifty-six editions between 1570 and 1645, this pessimism extends to 'the dutiefull works of godlinesse', which are 'in dede acceptable to God, yet not by their own deserving'.[88] This 'technical' holiness is called 'condign' by the theologians: good works which actually reach God's standard are 'congruous'. For the Calvinist who considers God's righteousness as of a different order to human good works, even sanctification is a technical rather than an actual process. Henry Burton rejects all *ex congruo* righteousness in a treatise clearly directed against Arminians.[89] John Ball's catechism, which went into thirty-three editions by 1645, noted problems with the epithet 'good', but was still prepared to use it:

A man by nature may doe an act that is good for the substance thereof, Dan. 4, 27 or 24. Rom. 2, 15. but never that which is truely and spiritually good . . . the good acts hee doth, proceede, not from a good roote, *viz.* faith and the spirit of sanctification, 2 Tim. 1, 5. neither is it

---

[87] Rous, *The Diseases of the Time*, 25.

[88] Alexander Nowell, *A Catechism, or first Instruction and Learning of Christian Religion* (London, 1570), 51.

[89] Burton, *The Christians Bulwarke*, 15.

done in a right manner, Iam. 4, 3. nor to a lawfull end, *viz.* the glory of God... all of which are required to the being of a good act.[90]

It is the unseen source of the works which is crucial, in the will of God and the prompting of the Holy Spirit. Edward Dering, whose catechism went into forty editions between 1572 and 1634, could imagine two kinds of 'good' works, one 'good in the sight of God', and one 'abhominable':

Q. *What workes callest thou good works?*
A. Our workes can never be acceptable & good in the sight of God, unlesse in doing them wee keepe these two thinges, first, that they be framed according to the rule of Gods lawes & commaundements and not after our one devises. Secondlye, that they proceede from an hart purged by faith. If either of these two pointes be lacking our works are abhominable in the eyes of God, although they appeare never so glorious in the sight of men.[91]

Neither of these definitions of 'good' is useful to human signification, because they belong to a divine and explicitly different system. To complete the disruption of human signification, abominable deeds done by a Christian may in some cases be acceptable to God. At the outset of the English Reformation, William Tyndale stated that 'To steale, robbe, and murder, are no holy workes before wordly peple, but unto them that have their trust in God, they are holy when God commaundeth them'.[92] Many years, many disasters, and many equivocations later, the careful William Ames can imagine circumstances in which acts that 'have an evill sound', such as killing a man, 'are sometimes made good'.[93] The assumed divinity of inner motions, linked with a cultural construct of 'the glory of God', is responsible for deeds notorious in Renaissance literature, such as Hamlet sending Rosencrantz and Guildenstern to their deaths, or Samson pulling down the roof on Philistine Gaza. Both these acts fulfil the Reformation criteria for 'good works', which spring from faith and an inner impulse to act, and accomplish what within the terms of the text is the 'glory of

[90] John Ball, *A Short Treatise Contayning all the Principall Grounds of Christian Religion By way of Questions and Answers, very profitable for all men, but especially for Housholders*, 10th edn. (London, 1635), 71.
[91] Edward Dering, *A bryefe and necessary Catechisme or Instruction* (London, 1577), sig. Ciiiir.
[92] William Tyndale, *The Whole Workes of W. Tyndall, Iohn Frith, and Doct. Barnes*, 2 vols. (London, 1573), i. 6.
[93] Ames, *The Marrow of Divinity*, 239.

God': justice for the guilty in *Hamlet*, defeat of the godless Philistines in *Samson Agonistes*. This is the reasoning behind the astonishing claims of Valdés' sixty-second Consideration, which, citing, like Tyndale, the Abraham and Isaac story, asserts that the saints cannot be judged for their actions, even criminal actions such as killing. Herbert reacts here with a comment that is inexplicable outside the context of the development of Reformed theology. He is prepared to allow for the possibility that God could inspire a believer to kill. However, he insists on some sign that is outward and assessable by others: 'otherwise any Malefactor may pretend motions, which is unsufferable in a Common-wealth.'[94]

Charles Lloyd Cohen has investigated the fascination for the Reformers of the 'mechanics' of salvation, which he identifies as the motions of the Spirit.[95] In a sense, the experience of motions is the quintessential Protestant experience, giving rise to assurance in the way Perkins describes above. Given the obedience of the Christian subject it can ensure perseverance, and guarantee a range of experiences from correct interpretation of Scripture to spiritual help in life choices. Spiritual motions had been conceptualized by Calvin as the means by which God's Decree was carried out in the world, and although later theologians such as Perkins and Ames tried to qualify the effectiveness and impact of such 'motions' it is not surprising that in popular spirituality the word came to denote an extraordinary, unmediated method of communication with God. The appeal of the concept is demonstrated by the ubiquity of the word in pre-Civil War catechisms and spiritual treatises. It is impossible, it seems, to discuss prayer or holiness in the early seventeenth century without mention of spiritual 'motions'. Even Lewis Bayly, in his *Practise of Pietie*, a text to which the Reformation mechanism of mortification and doctrine of good works is alien, suggests to Prince Charles that 'some good motion' may prompt people to read his book.[96] Perhaps the greatest testimony to the hold which the spirituality of 'motions' had over the English public is that the carefully judged *Eikon Basilike* felt the need to engage with it in 1649, defending 'Set and prescribed Forms' of worship and prayer as being in accordance with the motions of

---

[94] Herbert, *Works*, 316.   [95] See Cohen, *God's Caress*, 75, 109–10.
[96] Bayly, *Practise of Piety*, sig. A3ᵛ.

the Holy Spirit.[97] The impact of the passive spirituality associated with spiritual motions can be seen in the various reactions against it. Elnathan Parr in his treatise on prayer laments that 'some thinke that we must never pray, but upon the sudden and extra-ordinary instinct & motion of the Spirit. This is a fancie'.[98] Samuel Ward and William Bedell conducted an intense corre-spondence about the problem in 1627, Bedell finally concluding

I doubt not but often new impulses are given, to avoide sinne, or put on the faithful to a higher degree of any gracious habite: and it is our duty to pray for these, & if it be the will of god that we may not be tempted, or at least heare that voice *Here is the way*, when we are ready to turne to the right hand or left.

However, Bedell resists the conclusion that without a new motion 'we *can do* nothing'.[99] Likewise, George Herbert reacts strongly to Valdés' forty-ninth Consideration, which argues that Christians should remain inactive 'when they doe not perceive any motion, understanding it, that God would have them to remain quiet'. Herbert qualifies this assertion with some vigour:

in indifferent things there is roome for motions and expecting of them; but in things good, as to relieve my Neighbour, God hath already revealed his Will about it. Therefore we ought to proceed, except there be a restraining motion.[100]

In this attempt to restore human agency Herbert was anticipating the Westminster Confession, which acknowledged that 'there is required an actual influence of the . . . holy Spirit' to do good works but warned that Christians 'are not hereupon to grow negligent, as if they were not bound to perform any duty, unless, upon a special motion of the Spirit'.[101]

Although all religious writing emphasizes their importance, spiritual 'motions' by their very nature are inward and invisible. Such a spirituality requires intense self-scrutiny. Herbert lays down the processes involved in discerning such inner impulses in his poem 'The Method'. For the problem of unanswered prayer he advocates a profound self-examination in which his

---

[97] *Eikon Basilike* (London, 1649), 139–45.
[98] Elnathan Parr, *Abba Father* (London, 1618), 31.
[99] William Bedell to Samuel Ward, Bodleian MS Tanner 72, Fos. 243–243ᵛ.
[100] Herbert, *Works*, 313.
[101] *The Confession of Faith and Catechisms Agreed upon by the Assembly of Divines at Westminster* (London, 1650), 32–3.

heart becomes a book that he can read. Within this book there is a record of spiritual motions. One is what Herbert elsewhere calls 'an inviting motion', an impulse to pray, which he has sinfully neglected. Another is, in Herbert's terms, 'a restraining motion':

> *Late when I would have something done,*
> *I had a motion to forbear,*
> *Yet I went on.*

Before God will answer his prayer he has to repent of refusing to obey these motions. Other spiritual writers encourage this kind of self-scrutiny, especially for those seeking assurance of their own election. A perceptible impulse within is the mark of spiritual life. The metaphor chosen to convey this sensation is often that of pregnancy and motherhood:

these holie desires, and prayers, being the motions of the holie Ghost in us, are testimonies of our Faith, although they seeme to us small & weake. As the woman that feeleth the moving of a childe in her wombe, though verie weake, beleeveth and assureth her selfe that shee is with child, and that she goeth with a live childe: so if we have these motions, these holie affections and desires before mentioned, let us not doubt, but that wee have the holie Ghost (who is the author of them) dwelling in us.[102]

Thus, Perkins offers this illustration to those worried about whether they are genuinely elect or the reprobate recipients of 'temporary grace':

A mother carrieth her childe in her armes: if it cry for the dugge, & sucke the same, it is alive: being observed many days togither, if it neither cry nor stirre, it is dead.[103]

The usefulness of the images taken from the experience of motherhood to illustrate a vital but elusive spiritual experience can only be guessed at, especially when selected by male authors.

Not many writers are as optimistic about the discernment of motions as Herbert, who is able to translate these impulses into words which appear to him to be 'written' on his consciousness. The inability to refer to any outward conditions or criteria in judging a person's spiritual state is a real problem for Valdés, in

---

[102] Jean Taffin, *Of The Markes of the Children of God, and of their Comforts in Afflictions*, tr. Anne Locke (Paris, 1609), 27.

[103] William Perkins, *An Exposition of the Symbole or Crede of the Apostles* (Cambridge, 1596), 333.

whose work the discernment of motions becomes all-important. Unfortunately, there is more than one type of 'motions' in spiritual discourse of the period: 'motions' may also be used to refer to psychological phenomena ranging from 'feelings' (equivalent to modern 'emotions') to lusts. Perkins identifies an inward battle, which is fought in terms of good and evil motions. The aim of 'the flesh' is twofold, to 'ingender evill motions and passions', and to 'overwhelme the good motions of the spirit'. The ability of the believer to discern between the two is taken for granted, as it is in the 1633 catechism *A Briefe Catechisticall Exposition of Church Doctrine*, where the content of the Tenth Commandment is starkly summarized:

Q. What is forbidden herein?
A. First motions unto sinne ....
Q. What is commanded?
A. First motions unto god.[104]

Valdés' comment on Romans 13 suggests that it is not that easy to distinguish between the different kind of motions:

I call him a Christian, who is a true member of Christ, showing his Christianity by the mortification of the affections and lusts, which are after the world, and after the flesh, and by the quickening of all the affections and lusts that are after God and the Spirit.[105]

As the English vocabulary indicates, the Spanish vocabulary for the fleshly impulses—*los afectos i los apetitos*—is also used for the spiritual impulses, thus collapsing the distinction between them, despite the necessity to distinguish them as different entities. Valdés' obsession with identifying a true Christian, like Perkins', is finally defeated by his insistence on the discernment of inner impulses which are simply not distinguishable.

Human Signification and Divine Will in The Temple

For both Valdés and Herbert, the reason for all earthly troubles within God's Immediate Will is the mortification of the believer:

from evills he doth sometimes free them, causing that those should not touch them, which should touch them according to ordinary course; At

---

[104] *A Briefe Catechisticall Exposition of Church Doctrine* (London, 1633), 48.
[105] Valdés, *Epistle to the Romans*, 252.

other times depriving them of the feeling of them; and other times
mortifying them therewith.[106]

The helpless dependence on God that this interpretation of the
believer's experience produces is expressed in Herbert's poem
'Josephs coat'. This is a poem deliberately imitative of Petrarch's
lament for a loved one's fickleness. The divine lover is showing the
capacity for an infinite degree of capriciousness in Herbert's
poem. Strangely, the occasion for the lament is what Valdés called
'the depriving of the feeling of [evils]'. Herbert is experiencing joy,
and is able to compose poetry, but is not convinced that his
sorrows are over:

> Sorrow hath chang'd its note: such is his will,
> Who changeth all things, as him pleaseth best.

Rosamund Tuve rightly identifies this poem's theme as 'close to
that of "The Crosse" and "Affliction (iii)" ... the title serves to
indicate a common Christian idea, "Take up My Cross"'.[107]
God's tendency to reverse the believer's experience in the double
movement of mortification is described in the final line. But here
there is no sense of spiritual benefit to the believer—God seems to
be merely 'showing off'.

> I live to shew his power, who once did bring
> My *joyes* to *weep*, and now my *griefs* to *sing*.

Such wilfully capricious behaviour from God may not be enquired
into: curiosity is characteristic of the fallen human being, and something else that has to be mortified, as Consideration 88 declares.
Calvin states the same case even more baldly in his *Institutes*:

---

[106] Valdés, *110 Considerations*, 98. One example is that of physical health. Consideration 3
appears to promise physical health for the believer: he is not to rely on doctors or medicine.
This supernatural health is the result of the Immediate Will of God, implemented by divine
motions. However, because of the process of mortification, the believer will sometimes fall
ill: God is 'mortifying' him for his spiritual health.

[107] R. Tuve, *A Reading of George Herbert* (London, 1951), 178. Tuve's discussion of 'Josephs
coat' shows both the strength and the weakness of her reading in the context of the
symbolism of traditional Christianity. She has identified the connection between Joseph
and Christ, which leads her to the conclusion that the poem is about mortification.
However, an understanding of the dynamic of the Reformed doctrine of mortification,
which is very obvious, would resolve the confusion she expresses about what she calls the
'stronger and deeper' meaning of the poem. Her treatment of 'Aaron' (154–5) is so
concerned to explain what she calls 'traditional symbols' that she misses Herbert's demonstration of the process of mortification.

how great wickedness it is, euen so much as to inquire of the causes of the will of God: sith of all things that are it is the cause, and worthily so ought to be . . . . the will of God is so the highest rule of righteousnesse, that whatsoever he willeth, euen for this that he willeth it, it ought to be taken for righteous. When therefore it is asked, why the Lord did it: it is to be answered, because he willed it.[108]

Since whatever God wills is good, any apparent lack of rationality and of congruence in God's will is clearly part of what mortification means for the believer.

In 'Affliction (i)', in what appears to be an autobiographical account, Herbert laments the inscrutability of God's will at work. The autobiography of the believer for whom human agency has been made irrelevant has a peculiar grammar. Herbert is the object, not the subject, of most of the verbs in 'Affliction (i)'. God enticed him, entangled him, betrayed him, made him ill, took away his life. Unlike most of the poems in *The Temple*, 'Affliction (i)' does not resolve. The poet is left at the dark heart of the chiastic process of mortification: his own strength has been mortified, but the promised strength of the Holy Spirit has not been given.

> Thus doth thy power crosse-bias me, not making
> Thine own gift good, yet me from my wayes taking.

He cannot apostasize, for he has no power to do so: and he cannot 'persevere', since he has not been given grace. Thus he is left in the jaws of a paradox which has been variously explained by Herbert's commentators. This poem describes the mortifying process of God at its most painful, and the final line represents the frustration at being caught between ordinary human rules for living and the supernatural, inscrutable will of God.[109] If nothing he has endured and suffered for God counts as love—and it may not, in the divine economy—then he is not interested in divine

---

[108] Calvin, *Institution* III. xxiii. 2, p. 463.

[109] See Michael Schoenfeldt's discussion of the end of 'Affliction (i)' in *Prayer and Power: George Herbert and Renaissance Courtship* (Chicago, 1991), 77: 'The if-clause posits a human ontology separate from divine will, while the let-clause entails an ontology of total dependence upon God.' Barbara Leah Harman, in 'George Herbert's *Affliction (i)*: The Limits of Representation', *ELH* 44 (1977), 267–85 perfectly articulates the problem: God's will undermines any sense of meaning and sequence in the events of an autobiography. She locates Herbert's devotion in his willingness to go on living in this life-denying situation (274).

assistance for another attempt. He is tired of being played with. The metaphor from the game of bowls, 'crosse-bias', is of course a brilliant reference to the Cross, that sign of Christianity and symbol of mortification.

The characteristic effect of God's mortification in Herbert's poems is extreme disappointment and bewilderment. This is the experience of the traveller in 'The Pilgramage', who has arrived at what he thought was a 'gladsome hill' and found 'a lake of brackish waters'. It is clear that the Cross is his final destination: the pilgrim is warned '*None goes that way | And lives*'. After so many frustrations on his journey the pilgrim sees death as a relief. Yet when Herbert next faces the Cross he is understandably repulsed by it. The life-story in 'The Crosse' is familiar, and the paradoxes even more strongly stated.

> Besides, things sort not to my will,
> Ev'n when my will doth studie thy renown:
> Thou turnest th'edge of all things on me still,
> Taking me up to throw me down.

It is the sheer randomness of God's will that crushes Herbert. He has carried out all the traditional instructions for a holy life. He is even fulfilling a key condition for Reformed 'good works'—he is seeking the glory of God. However, there is another aspect of a good work, according to Reformation theology, and that is the divine source of the motivating impulse: a motion. The repetition of the phrase 'my will' shows that it is a human conception of the will of God that is operating, and a further degree of reduction to God's will is necessary. Herbert's stark vision of what holiness constitutes for a human being is the same as Milton's in *Paradise Regained*, where it is Christ's passive uttering of God's words that finally defeats Satan.[110] The last four words of 'The Crosse' signify Herbert's surrender to God in several ways. The words '*Thy will be done*' are not really his own at all. They are the words of Christ in the Garden of Gethsemane. Herbert has correctly located his own place in salvation history: this is Golgotha. However, he has also correctly judged that the crucifixion to be held is not his own, but Christ's. Taking Christ's response as his own, he identifies himself with Christ's death, just as Romans 6 advocates, in the true experience of mortification.

---

[110] John Milton, *Complete Shorter Poems*, ed. J. Carey, 4th imp. (London, 1981), 517.

The triumphant movement of resurrection in 'The Flower', the poem that immediately follows 'The Crosse', seems to indicate significant progress in the spiritual life of the believer; in Valdés' words, the two poems constitute a 'mortification' and a 'vivification'. However, 'The Flower' also describes the fluctuations in the will of God. The only difference is the mood of the poet: he is experiencing inexplicable joy instead of inexplicable pain.

> These are thy wonders, Lord of power,
> Killing and quickning, bringing down to hell
> And up to heaven in an houre;
> Making a chiming of a passing-bell.

The funeral is over, and even Herbert's poetic gift seems to have been resurrected. Although many critics have noticed that this poem is at the heart of *The Temple*, and in some ways is a turning-point, the words of 'The Flower' should warn against so stable an interpretation. Steady growth is not an option for the Christian. Any apparent success is a snare.

> Many a spring I shoot up fair,
> Offring at heav'n, growing and groning thither:
> Nor doth my flower
> Want a spring-showre,
> My sinnes and I joining together.
>
> But while I grow in a straight line,
> Still upwards bent, as if heav'n were mine own,
> Thy anger comes, and I decline.

In a world which moves at the will of a God like this, no sign is to be trusted. In an apparent attempt to make the discrepancies in God's will less capricious and more meaningful, Valdés finally declares there to be an inverse proportion between inner strength and outer strength: as inner power and virtue grow, the believer looks weaker from the outside.[111] This is a complete reversal of the original logic of Valdésian 'motions', which were originally conceived as successful in the external world. Now the sign system is actually reversed, in what seems to be a deliberate attempt to confuse human beings. It is this kind of thinking that is behind Herbert's description of the work of God in his anti-curiosity poem, 'The Discharge':

---

[111] Valdés, *110 Considerations*, 212.

> He is thy night at noon: he is at night
> Thy noon alone.

This reversal of the significance of events in the real world comes
under Herbert's third category of God's power: spiritual power,
by which outward catastrophe may become inner spiritual advantage, and outward worldly success, inner damnation. Signification,
that most basic of semantic relationships, is disrupted by mortification: it is too much to expect that in the divine rationality the
significance of a sign will always be stable.[112]

Even the poet's language is subject to the disrupting process of
mortification. All the images of growth in 'The Flower' are
favourable, drawn from Scriptural images for holiness which
Herbert employs positively elsewhere. To aim for heaven is
usually a good thing, as it is in 'Coloss. iii. 3': groans are usually
as acceptable to God as they are in 'Sion'. Showers usually represent the grace of God: the 'straight' way is the way to heaven.
The stability of metaphorical signs, however, is too much to hope
for in a world dominated by God's will. Everything God says,
goes. The problem is that human beings have not learned God's
language: 'Thy word is all | If we could spell.' Valdés imagines
the language of God to be silent and instantly communicable, a
language of motions, lost when man sinned:

he lost the spiritual light, and got the naturall light, he lost the divine
science, and got science, and human discourse.[113]

Human language is the result of the Fall, and one of the orders in
God's mediate will that can be disrupted. Thus the signifiers of
human language are not consistently reliable. There are times
when Herbert understands the silent language of God, and is able
to name things in the world correctly, as the poem 'Frailtie' depicts:

> Lord, in my silence how do I despise
> What upon trust

---

[112] Richard Todd argues in *The Opacity of Signs: Acts of Interpretation in George Herbert's 'The Temple'* (New York, 1986) that Herbert eventually learns to 'read' God's language as expressed in Herbert's life events. See p. 66: 'even what initially encourages reproachful conceptualization in terms of "absence" or "unreceptiveness" can be interpreted as a divine signification.' I would agree with this statement as far as it goes. However, I do not think that such an interpretation makes negative situations easier to bear for Herbert: 'absence' remains absence, as I have argued earlier.

[113] Valdés, *110 Considerations*, 230.

Is styled *honour, riches,* or *fair eyes;*
But is *fair dust!*
I surname them *guilded clay,*
Deare earth, fine grasse or *hay.*

In the 'two regiments, the spiritual and the temporall' (Tyndale's phrase) there are two distinct languages.[114] However, this happy state of affairs does not last. 'The Search' describes an ultimate failure of communication—ultimate, because the poet is using what is traditionally the most effective means of communicating with God. The power of wordless emotion was described in detail in Chapter 2, and there are two such classic ejaculatory prayers in 'The Search':

I sent a sigh to seek thee out,
        Deep drawn in pain,
Wing'd like an arrow: but my scout
        Returns in vain.

I tun'd another (having store)
        Into a grone;
Because the search was dumb before:
        But all was one.

The supplicant is bewildered at God's refusal to honour the system of communication which He has validated in Holy Scripture, and this opens the possibility of other radically disruptive divine behaviour. He expresses the fear that God has abandoned human beings altogether, and gone to try His hand at saving another planet. This almost unthinkable heresy becomes a possibility within God's sovereign will for the universe. Even worse, however, is the fear that response to his prayer is simply outside of God's will:

O let not that of any thing;
        Let rather brasse,
Or steel, or mountains be thy ring,
        And I will passe.

The believer's world is entirely contingent upon whatever God wills at any particular time. The natural order, along with human language, may as well not exist for him.

---

[114] Tyndale, *Workes* i. 214.

Of course, the total disruption of human signification is not the norm for Herbert's Christian poetics, although extreme Anti-nomians did eventually embrace such anti-rational discourse.[115] Much of *The Temple* demonstrates a divine *simplicitas*, a profound congruence between sign and signified, as we saw in Chapter 1. Savonarola saw inaccuracy of signification—*duplicitas*—as the result of sinful human intervention, a disruption similar to that produced, in Valdés' terms, by imperfect mortification of the human will. What Savonarola's vision of *simplicitas* cannot accommodate is the possibility of contradiction—the divine Signified's prerogative of representing Himself in ways that undermine human signification. Herbert's acclamation of Valdés' logic of mortification is merely an admission that such disruption is always a possibility within Reformed theology, at least temporarily. There are moments within *The Temple* where such disruption is articulated, usually when a poem confronts the ultimate mystery of God's will. The sign of God's final inscrutability to human intelligence is the 'scandal' that is the Cross. The Cross unites contraries in a way that is anathema to human reasoning. It is, therefore, a hidden and ambiguous sign: in terms of human signi-fication, it does not function at all, or rather, it malfunctions, and becomes a 'stumbling block'. Only faith can interpret the sign of the Cross correctly, as in 1 Corinthians 1: 18, that famous statement of the double significance of the Cross, 'to them that perish fool-ishness; but unto us which are saved it is the power of God'. The Cross has the power instantaneously to reverse the significance of an event in the human sphere. The implications of this disruption for poetry will be explored in the next chapter.

The Hundred and Ten Considerations in Interregnum England

In 1646 *The Hundred and Ten Considerations* was republished, in Puritan Cambridge, with fewer of Herbert's corrective notes: there had been a significant change in the religious climate.[116] Opinion had polarized, and contrasting reactions to this edition were registered. Two years later in his huge volume *A Survey of the*

---

[115] See the writing of, for example, Abiezer Coppe and Jacob Bauthumley in N. Smith, (ed.), *A Collection of Ranter Writings from the 17th Century* (London, 1983).

[116] See D. Ricart, *Juan de Valdés* (Mexico City, 1958), ch. 7 for more detail of the changes to the Cambridge edition, and the quotation from Bacon cited below.

Spiritual Antichrist, Samuel Rutherford denounced Valdés in no uncertain terms, finding in Valdés' work

the grounds and poysonable principles of Familisme, Antinomianisme, Enthusiasme, for he rejecteth the Scriptures, magnifieth Inspirations, vilifieth good works, heighteneth the dead faith, extenuateth sin, &c.[117]

As if to validate this judgement, a work with Familist connections, Roger Bacon's *Christ mighty in Himself and members, revealed in some short expressions by way of Catechisms,* also published in 1646, welcomed the *Considerations* as 'a book happily brought into our English coast'. Roger Bacon was known to be an Antinomian: he had been disowned by the Quaker movement, but maintained a wide acquaintance across a broad spectrum of radical Protestant groups.[118] Bacon's interest in mysticism is shown by his transcription of *The Cloud of Unknowing* and translation of another tract of medieval mysticism. It is more than probable that he eagerly embraced *The Hundred and Ten Considerations* for all the reasons that Rutherford rejected it. The kind of spirituality that could link Roger Bacon with Valdés and George Herbert is illustrated by the final sentences of the catechism *Christ mighty in Himself and members*:

Q. What operation hath these Questions and Answers on you?
A. I have lost myself in love.
Q. What love?
A. The love of God.
Q. How appearing?
A. In Christ.
Q. What do you then?
A. Rest.
Q. And what then?
A. Admire.[119]

The abandonment of self which is mortification and rest leads to the same loving, worshipful peace which is the final achievement of Herbert's poems such as 'The Holdfast' and 'Love (iii)'.

[117] Samuel Rutherford, *A Survey of the Spiritual Antichrist, Opening the Secrets of Familisme and Antinomianisme in the Antichristian Doctrine of John Saltmarsh, and Will. Del, the Present Preachers of the Army now in England, and of Robert Town; Tob. Crisp, H. Denne, Eaton, and others* (London, 1648), 164.

[118] See G. F. Nuttall, 'The Last of James Nayler: Robert Rich and the Church of the First-Born', *The Friends' Quarterly,* 60 (1985), 532.

[119] Quoted in Nuttall, 'The Last of James Nayler', 532.

However, approbation by a sectarian such as Bacon would probably have been more worrying to George Herbert than the condemnation of Samuel Rutherford. Herbert seems to have fore-seen a reading of *The Hundred and Ten Considerations* that would emphasize the mystic, non-verbal elements of the spirituality described there. His warning of the dangers of setting inner revela-tion against the public text of Scripture proved to be prophetic:

As for the Text, *They shall all be taught of God*, it being Scripture cannot be spoken to the disparagement of Scripture . . . Those that have inspira-tions must still use . . . God's Word: if we make another sence of that Text, we shall overthrow all means, save catechizing, and set up Enthu-siasmes.[120]

The Genevan Reformers had criticized the French edition of 1563, *Les cent et dix consyderations divines de Jan Val d'Esso*, for the same fault. The attempt by one Adrien Gorin of Emden to publish a Frisian translation without the corrective notes from the French edition provoked a very strong reaction from Beza.[121] An indictment against Gorin of 1565 from the Calvinist faction in Emden cites as its fifth grievance that he had found fault with Calvin's doctrine and printed a work 'plain de faulse doctrine et de blasphème contre la Saincte Escripture'.[122]

However much Herbert approves of the economy of salvation described in Valdés' treatise, he cannot accept the logical conclu-sion, that no outward 'means' of grace are necessary, including all kinds of verbal activity. He correctly identifies Valdés' tendency to set spirit against word: 'he opposeth the teaching of the spirit to the teaching of the scripture.'[123] The poet and devotee of word-centred Reformation spirituality was suspicious, but not wary enough to deny English readers what he felt to be the inspired truth of *The Hundred and Ten Considerations*. In fact, the implications of such thinking for all kinds of verbal discourse are radical, as we

---

[120] Herbert, *Works*, 310.

[121] Adrien Gorin had ministered in the French-speaking church in London, where his sympathy with the Anabaptists had caused some trouble: he had to leave London for Emden in 1561. J. N. Bakhuizen van den Brink in *Juan de Valdés, réformateur en Espagne et en Italie 1529–1541* (Geneva, 1969), 87, prints a letter from the pastorate of Geneva in which Gorin is reported to have said that he does not see why an English edition of the *Considerations* should not have received official approval when the Italian edition had been received so well in Basle. There is no other evidence of any such projected English edition.

[122] Bakhuizen van den Brink, *Juan de Valdés*, 67.   [123] Herbert, *Works*, 317.

shall see in the next chapter. George Herbert was dead by the time *The Hundred and Ten Considerations* was finally published in 1638. So was Nicholas Ferrar. He did not live to read the accusations of *The Arminian Nunnery* three years later, or to witness the sack of Little Gidding by marauding Parliamentarian troops in 1646, the date of the publication of the second edition of *The Hundred and Ten Considerations*. Even he, however, could not have foreseen just how many 'Enthusiasmes' would have been set up by the time the second edition of *The Hundred and Ten Considerations* was printed. The work which had been intended to nurture the devotional life of the Church of England in fact fostered the reasoning which fragmented it.

5

The Sanctification of Poetry

Herbert succeeded in rescuing *The Hundred and Ten Considerations* for publication, but no amount of his corrective notes could make Valdés' position on the Scripture orthodox. For Valdés, and increasingly for the more extreme sectarians in the seventeenth century, engagement with the written text of the Bible is no longer the characteristic of the true Christian. By this time it was no longer sufficient to give assent to the right doctrines, to quote Scripture in support of belief, or to avoid unorthodox rhetoric (as Melanchthon had believed).[1] The repetition of words in the public domain such as Scripture or the creeds were not seen as particularly useful signs in the endeavour to distinguish the elect from the damned, or as Valdés describes the categories, the 'true Saints' from 'the saints of the world'. Geoffrey Nuttall describes the turning point in the seventeenth century thus:

Hitherto, God's Word in Scripture has been treated as the criterion by which to test faith and experience. Now, the Holy Spirit is introduced as the touchstone by which all else is to be tried, including the Bible itself.[2]

It is important to Valdés that Scripture cannot be understood without the Spirit of God, even (and especially) by the learned: inspiration of the Spirit is essential for intelligent engagement with the sacred text. In emphasizing the precedence of revelation over reason Valdés is both democratizing salvation and at the same time creating an unassailable elite. Not even the basic minimum of intellect is now needed to appropriate the content of salvation: however, salvation is entirely limited to those enlightened by the Holy Spirit. Valdés is at pains to stress that the truly soteriological 'text', which is the inner and non-verbal language of God, is not accessible to any but the true saints: 'they only understand this

---

[1] Philip Melanchthon, *Liber Rhetorices Libri Duo*, tr. and ed. J. M. Lafontaine (Univ. of Michigan Ph. D. diss, 1968), 226.

[2] G. F. Nuttall, *The Holy Spirit in Puritan Faith and Experience*, new edn. (Chicago, 1992), 28.

Language, it being to all others altogether unintelligible'.[3] And if Scripture is unreliable, other kinds of writing are far more dangerous. In *The Hundred and Ten Considerations*, Valdés warns against the dangerous power of all written texts: Scripture is to be handled with care, but the most dangerous activity of all is to 'handle the writings that are written by the humane spirit'. This would seem to include literary texts such as poetry.

Valdés' logic leads to a radical separation of Holy Spirit from human word, and radical Puritanism in England was already developing a similar theory by the time *The Hundred and Ten Considerations* was published. A good example of this thinking about language is found in *Vindiciae Fidei*, the lectures of William Pemble, first published in 1625.[4] William Pemble was not a separatist, and he remained a loyal member of the Church of England throughout his short life as an Oxford divine, but his teaching is as radical as that of Valdés. His Magdalen College tutor, Richard Capel, who was to become a prominent Parliamentarian, published the lectures of his favourite pupil after his death, in the late 1620s and early 1630s. This was a political act in a period when Oxford was still resisting the Arminian influence spreading from the Court, as Capel's combative prefaces make clear. The preface to the 1625 edition, published in Oxford, validates the work in a motif familiar to readers of exemplary biography, including Herbert's own: the book was written when Pemble knew he was dying, and the subsequent discourse, in a resurrection dynamic, is 'full of life and power'.[5] Capel's 'adversary' in this first edition is apparently the Papist, but the preface to the 1627 London edition, which begins, belligerently, 'Books are more necessary to the state than arms', specifies Arminianism as the enemy. In fact, Pemble's work is explicitly anti-Arminian, and his theory of sanctification by divine motions is very similar to Valdés:

concerning the replantation of Holinesse in a Sinfull man, we affirm against Pelagians, Semi-pelagians, Papists, Arminians, or other sectaries,

---

[3] Juan de Valdés, *The Hundred and Ten Considerations of Signior Iohn Valdesso* (Oxford, 1638), 183.

[4] William Pemble (?1592–1623) studied at Magdalen College, Oxford under Richard Capel. In 1618 he was made Divinity Reader of Magdalen Hall, and took holy orders. He was famous for his Calvinist preaching. Capel published many of his works after his death including one on rhetoric: *Enchiridion Oratorium* (Oxford, 1633).

[5] William Pemble, *Vindiciae Fidei, or a Treatise of Justification by Faith* (Oxford, 1625), sig. A4ʳ.

that as the Agent or Efficient of mans Sanctification is simply super-
naturall, *viz.* the Holy Hhost [*sic*], so is his manner of working altogether
Divine beyond the power and without the helpe of any thing in
man.[6]

Pemble is as concerned as Valdés to distinguish between spiritual
and natural motions. However, he is aware of a problem which
Valdés does not make explicit. Rhetoric also produces motions,
which can look very like spiritual ones. Pemble links what he
considers to be an erroneous view of sanctification with what he
describes as a blasphemous assessment of the power of words. He
accuses the Arminians of a serious confusion. They equate saving
motions with rhetorical motions, which he calls this 'new invented
opinion concerning the Excitation of the Affections':

> what is this effectuall power, according to the Arminians, and what doth
> it in all men? It doth, say they, inlighten the understanding, it stires up
> the Sensuall affections (for as touching the Will, it meddles not with that)
> and so gives unto the heart *Sensum verbi*, and by an inward power infused
> doth move and dispose the heart to Beleeve and Convert. Yea, but how
> is all this done? Is it by any proper worke of the Spirit distinct from the
> power of the Word? By no means, say they: It is done by a morall
> perswasion, *per Representationem objectivam.*[7]

Arminian doctrines of salvation and sanctification contain the
same error: a role is being given to human powers and impulses,
which, in the dualistic logic that Calvinists like Pemble follow, are
totally depraved. Pemble realizes that as soon as human impulses
are allowed to have power, rhetoric, which is classically the most
efficient way to produce and manipulate human 'motions', plays a
significant role in both salvation and sanctification.

In William Pemble's work, the dislocation between external
and internal, between human and divine, between Word and
Spirit, is complete. There is no room for human agency, and
therefore no need for human language. Beginning with the pre-
miss that 'The Externall Declaration of God's will' has been made
'by the Preaching of the Word', he traces the effects of this in both
the reprobate and the elect. He takes great pains not only to
separate 'Common and Naturall Illumination' from 'Proper and

---

[6] William Pemble, *Vindiciae Gratiae: A Plea for Grace, More Especially, The Grace of Faith*
(London, 1627), 29.
[7] Ibid. 99.

Spirituall Illumination' as Perkins had done, but also to distinguish between Word and Spirit. The effective preaching of the Gospel has nothing to do with the words used at all:

the Object of this worke of the Holy Ghost is not the Word, as if the Holy Ghost did infuse into it any special Vertue whereby it should worke together with himself, as a partiall Coordinate efficient cause in our Conversion.[8]

For Pemble, conversion and sanctification are not a product of the rational faculty: understanding of the sermon is a mere luxury. The necessary effect is produced supernaturally, by 'the touch or motion of the Will and Affections'. There are, of course, also two categories of Motions, Naturall (which stimulate the passions) and Spirituall (which harness the passions to love good and hate evil). These spiritual 'motions', however, are entirely an effect of the 'touch' of the Holy Spirit: they are wordless.

The Rhetoric of Inspiration

Valdés also describes the performative language of God in terms of silent motions, as we have seen. However, there remains a role in Valdés thinking for inspired human words. It is the one sign of a true Christian which is not undermined in *The Hundred and Ten Considerations*, and it was one which had great significance for spiritualist sects in Interregnum England as well as for George Herbert's poetry. In Consideration 77 Valdés describes the inspired speech of those 'who live after the spirit':

they shew in their words, speaking with more piety, with more faith, with more confidence and with more affection of the things of God, when they speak coldly, and when the force of the spirit moves them to speak of the things of piety, and of faith, and of confidence, and of love, than all the men of the world together, when they set themselves with diligence, and attention to speak thereof.

This is an ideal for inspired speech which completely undercuts rhetorical theory. Quintilian had declared that 'the prime essential for stirring the emotions of others is...first to feel those emotions oneself'.[9] Valdés insists that inspired speakers 'speak

---

[8] William Pemble, *Vindiciae Gratiae: A Plea for Grace, More Especially, The Grace of Faith* (London, 1627), 97.

[9] Quintilian, *Institutio Oratia*, tr. H. E. Butler, 4 vols. (London, 1921), ii. 431.

coldly'. He is concerned to distinguish 'the force of the spirit' from any human element such as emotional force. In this way, the powerful aspects of the speech such as 'confidence' and 'affection', which have been seen as the personal qualities of the speaker, will be entirely attributable to God.[10] Valdés is so pleased with his definition of inspired speech that he extrapolates from it to proclaim the only trustworthy, external sign of a true Christian:

whence it is well gathered, that the signe of what a man hath within him, is to be taken from that which he shewes outwardly, when he stands regardless.

Speech, it seems, is able to mediate mortification directly to the world. 'Stands regardless' is the key phrase here: the believer is employing no human effort at all, yet he is still speaking. Inactivity represents death, as we have seen, and the words spoken 'by the force of the spirit' represent resurrection life.

This theory of inspired speech is developed further in Valdés' commentary on Romans. The inspiration of human speech depends on two conditions: first, the speaker has to be preaching by the express will of God; secondly, he has to be the personal subject of direct inspiration, so that it is God who is speaking, and not the human being:

in order to be the word of God, it is necessary that it should be spoken by the spirit of God, through the mouth of him who announces it.[11]

It is not enough that the preacher repeat the inspired Word of God which is the Scripture. Given the necessity for immediate and fluent inspiration, it is no wonder that Valdés pioneers the promotion of vernacular Spanish. In Valdés' treatise on language, the *Diálogo de las Lenguas* of 1534, the criteria for 'best spoken Spanish' are based on giving clearest expression to the 'concept in your mind', which is presumably planted by the Holy Spirit. There is no room for artifice or invention, because human words have a will of their own, and tend to obscure the expression of the divine will.

[10] This point is developed in his commentary on Romans to exclude the traditionally infallible sign of devotion to God, i.e. tears: he states that emotional expressions such as laughing and weeping are only consonant with Christian piety when the believer does not actually feel such perturbatory emotions: Juan de Valdés, *Juan de Valdés on the Epistle to the Romans*, tr. J. T. Betts (London, 1883), 243.

[11] Ibid. 190.

People . . . don't match words to things (as I said should be done) but rather match things to the words. And thus they don't say what they wanted to say, but what the words they have used want to say.[12]

Words correspond to flesh and should be mortified: subject-matter corresponds to spirit and must be dominant. This applies even more to writing than to speech.

Valdés' own style of rhetoric could be regarded as consonant with an openness to the inspiration of the Holy Spirit.[13] Typically a Consideration will begin on a personal note, describing previous dilemmas and Valdés' own inability to resolve them, or recounting an experience of his own which defies easy explanation, or identifying a paradox in normal Christian experience. This personal rhetoric is a slightly hesitant one, perhaps testifying to the frailty of the human intellect when confronting divine truth. Towards the end of a Consideration his rhetoric tends to become more masterful, particularly in those which describe the positive signs of a Christian. When there is a sense that Valdés has grasped the concept that he is seeking to express, the Consideration culminates in a grateful prayer to Christ, by acknowledgement that all the revelation contained therein is from Him. In this way, many of the Considerations have the movement that might mirror a 'motion', beginning with the human bewilderment of the writer, then following the gradual dawning of inspiration, and finishing in the full flood of Spirit-inspired discourse.[14] In the *Diálogo de las Lenguas* Valdés had affirmed that he had never written so effectively as when he had not known what to say.[15]

---

[12] Juan de Valdés, *Diálogo de las Lenguas*, ed. J. Perry (London, 1927), 158. I am indebted to Pippa Mayfield of Oxford University Press for translations from the *Diálogo*.

[13] The rhetorical analysis in this section is based on the Spanish text of a fragment including 39 of the Considerations, ed. E. Boehmer in *Traditatos* (Bonn, 1880), which Ignacio Tellechea Idigoras in his scholarly edition of *Las Ciento Diez Divinas Consideraciones: Recension inedita del manuscrito de Juan Sanchez (1558)* (Salamanca, 1975) has identified as the only surviving original Spanish version. The Italian edition is very faithful to the Spanish, as Juan Nieto remarks in *Juan de Valdés and the Origins of the Spanish and Italian Reformation* (Geneva, 1970), 3. Nicholas Ferrar's translation is slavishly faithful to the Italian (see D. Ricart, *Juan de Valdés* (Mexico City, 1958), 99) so it is even possible to sense the rhythm of the Spanish prose in the English edition, although the word-play cannot be reproduced (for example, the play on *obrar/orar*).

[14] The magic word *entiendo* ('I understand') usually signals a change in pace and confidence for the rhetoric. Consideration 17 is a good example: various sentences begin, with increasing confidence, *entiendo, mas entiendo, tambien entiendo, a esta resoluzion entiendo*.

[15] Valdés, *Diálogo*, 65.

In his introduction to the *Diálogo* Montesinos confirms the impro-
visatory nature of Valdés' style.[16] Valdés, he affirms, is to be
believed when he says that he is not writing for fame and recognition. He is merely recording his thoughts as quickly and
briefly as possible for the benefit of his friends. He is not concerned with good style but to appeal as directly as possible 'al
animo del lector'. However, Montesinos does not agree that
the result of this 'standing regardless' is effective writing. He
feels that the style suffers in the urge to communicate, to produce
'a prose bristling with gerunds and not short of unfortunate
repetitions, which perhaps are not lacking in catechistical [*sic*]
effectiveness.'[17]

This judgement is consonant with the spirit of mortified discourse. 'Catechetical effectiveness' is all that Valdés is really
interested in: the criticisms of his style, which are, after all,
external, worldly judgements, are the price to be paid for living
after the Spirit. They are the sign of his inner mortification, the
authentic sign of the Cross.

There is much in George Herbert's writing to support this
evaluation. His attitude in 'Jordan (i)' is that no amount of stylistic
criticism will influence him towards rhetorical flourish:

> Nor let them punish me with losse of rime,
> Who plainly say, *My God, My King*.

In 'The Forerunners' Herbert finally accepts the ultimate mortification of his poetic gift, its waning, with the correctly mortified
attitude to human rhetoric:

> Yet if you go, I passe not; take your way;
> For, *Thou art still my God*, is all that ye
> Perhaps with more embellishment can say.

However, the exquisite poems of *The Temple* are very different
from *The Hundred and Ten Considerations*, although as we have seen,
Herbert's poetry may also mimic a 'motion'. The careful deploy-
ment of various rhetorical techniques to simulate the effect of
direct inspiration might well have been seen by Valdés as the
worst manifestation of human wisdom, in 'pretending piety'. Yet

---

[16] Juan de Valdés, *Diálogo de las lenguas*, ed. J. F. Montesinos (Madrid, 1928), pp. xliii–xliv.
[17] See Nieto, *Juan de Valdés*, 186.

Herbert was particularly impressed by Valdés' description of mortification, and this chapter will suggest ways in which this dynamic can enter poetic composition.

The Mortification of Poetry

There is nothing in *The Hundred and Ten Considerations* to encourage the would-be Christian poet. Although language is seen as a signifier of divinity in the mortified believer, inspired speech demands the passivity of 'standing regardlesse' and allowing the divine motions to express themselves.[18] Such a severe aesthetic was shared by William Pemble, who insisted that truth is 'most beautifull when naked': this would seem to allow no role for the Christian poet.[19] Valdés himself warned that it is dangerous 'to handle the writings that are written by the humane spirit'.[20] However, Valdés was not entirely hostile to Christian poetry. In the *Diálogo de las Lenguas* he mentions the work of Juan del Encina as worth reading. Juan del Encina's poetics of 1496 argues for the dignity and antiquity of poetry, quoting the familiar names of the Old Testament poets as evidence that sacred poetry is possible, and citing the *De Musica* as evidence that St Augustine was a poet.[21] Even Valdés clearly sees the production of a Christian poetry as a possibility. His circle in Naples included several poets, including Marcantonio Flaminio and Vittoria Colonna. Ralph Knevet, writing in the 1640s about sacred poetry and poets, thought Vittoria Colonna the only Italian poet to compare with Herbert, excluding Dante and Petrarch, who were simply not holy enough. Only Herbert and Vittoria Colonna had managed to overcome the inherently self-publicizing nature of poetry to produce 'that divine Poesye, which immediately aymes at the

---

[18] Patrick Grant, in *The Transformations of the Word: Studies in Donne, Herbert, Vaughan and Traherne* (Montreal, 1974), 123 claims to find 'an acknowledgement of the pedagogical usefulness of rhetorical indirection' in *The Hundred and Ten Considerations*. Unless he means the anecdote and simile with which *The Hundred and Ten Considerations* is illustrated, I can find no evidence of this. Anecdote and simile, I would argue, would not be seen as a verbal effect at all, but part of the essential message: this aspect of poetry was the reason why Savonarola could class poetry as philosophy.

[19] Pemble, *Vindiciae Gratiae*, preface (paginated separately), 23. See R. Fraser, *The War Against Poetry* (Princeton, 1970), 23–6 for the 'delight in essence' characteristic of the period.

[20] Valdés, *110 Considerations*, 71.

[21] E. R. Curtius, *European Literature and the Latin Middle Ages*, tr. W. R. Trask (London, 1953), 549.

glory of the Almighty'.[22] This chapter will explore how the severe aesthetic embraced by Valdés, and, as we have seen, endorsed by Herbert, produces a poetry which in seventeenth-century England signified holiness.

There are various places in *The Temple* where Herbert seems to be employing a Valdésian critique of language, and as in Valdés' work, a correct attitude to language is linked with the mortification of the self. Stanley Fish identifies the self with the language of poetry, and thus sees Herbert's poems as 'self-consuming artifacts' which chart the extinction of the poet.[23] Barbara Leah Harman identifies many poems in *The Temple* which 'collapse' or 'reverse', again signifying a Valdésian recognition that 'to figure at all is to act where there is no sanction to act, to participate in a decision where participation has already been pre-empted and is therefore unnecessary'. She describes the 'discomfort' this movement produces in a modern reader, and suggests that critics' polarized responses have been inadequate: either, like Fish, they 'stress... a poem's final collapse at the expense of what precedes it', or, like Martz, they 'divert... attention from collapse in order to credit what precedes it'.[24] An understanding of Valdésian mortification helps to explain these differences in judgements of Herbert's poetry. As I shall argue, both the 'collapse' and the rhetoric that precedes it are equally important in a mortified poetry.

All of the potential areas for controversy are present in 'The Quip', which appears to describe the optimum relationship between human and divine speaker in Valdés' system of mortification. The situation is designed—by the will of more than one agent—to test the believer's mortification to the limit.

> The merrie world did on a day
> With his train-bands and mates agree
> To meet together, where I lay,
> And all in sport to geere at me.

As usual, sinful humanity is expending its energy in talking, and in turn is provoking the believer to the talk which would be sin. The

---

[22] From Ralph Knevet, *A Gallery to the Temple*, written in the 1640s, not published until 1766: quoted in *George Herbert: The Critical Heritage*, ed. C. A. Patrides (London, 1983), 64–5.

[23] See S. E. Fish, *Self-Consuming Artifacts: The Experience of Seventeenth-Century Literature* (Berkeley, 1972), 156–223.

[24] B. L. Harman, 'George Herbert's *Affliction (i)*: The Limits of Representation', *ELH* 44 (1977), 267.

structure of the poem follows that of Christ's temptations in the wilderness. Each stanza vocalizes a particular temptation in the first three lines. It is tempting to see these four characters as personifying the wordly gifts which were most attractive to Herbert: Beautie, Money, Glorie, Wit, and Conversation. The first two speakers demand an answer to their questions, and the fourth line of the stanza, by the laws of conversation, should contain Herbert's answer. However, the words of line 4 of each stanza do not answer any of the questions. They are addressed to God, and take the form of a prayer. Just as Christ answered the temptations of the Devil with the words 'it is written', and quoted from Scripture, Herbert answers the tempters with the inspired word of God from Psalm 38, thus renouncing the responsibility for speech: '*But thou shalt answer, Lord, for me.*' The Christlike scenario of mortification is created: the human speaker is silent, and 'stands regardlesse', while God speaks for him. In fact, the repetition of the lines like a refrain, or a mantra, does have the uncanny effect of silence. The tempters do not achieve their goal of provoking him to speech. There is another, greater design at work: God has already anticipated this situation and prepared for it, with the 'quip' of the title. The utterance is not, in human terms, at all witty, consisting as it does of three simple words. The significance of these words is so great, however, that the believer is confident they will have the desired effect on his tormentors. It is an owning of the believer by God, rather like the words spoken by God over His Son at baptism. The effect is rather like Christ's powerful silence in answer to Satan's third temptation at the climax of *Paradise Regained*:

> To whom thus Jesus: Also it is written
> Tempt not the Lord thy God, he said and stood.
> But Satan smitten with amazement fell.[25]

Such a silence, in which God is able to speak His word, is the answer to Herbert's prayer in the sermon: 'Oh my Master, on whose errand I come, let me hold my peace, and doe thou speak thy selfe.'[26]

---

[25] John Milton, *Complete Shorter Poems*, ed. J. Carey, 4th imp. (London, 1981), 517.
[26] George Herbert, *The Works of George Herbert*, ed. F. E. Hutchinson (Oxford, 1945), 233.

However, even silence has been colonized for rhetoric, theorized by Puttenham in *The Arte of English Poesie* as the figure of silence: aposiopesis.[27] As always, Herbert is in the paradoxical position of having to use words to create the effect of silence. The divine 'quip' is not actually spoken by the end of the poem, even though this scenario was in the past. Justice is deferred, and the believer has to supply the words God will say, and the effect they will have on his tempters. A. D. Nuttall calls this presumption 'bumptious', but actually the poet has no other choice. The answer is not addressed to the tormentors, and is apparently addressed to God: but the real audience at this point is the reader. The poet has to resolve the sense of expectation he has created, and has to supply the moral of the message about mortification. To do this, he has either to represent God actually speaking, which is fraught with dangers, or tell the reader what God is going to say.

This poem illustrates the difficulty of writing poetry within the scheme of mortification. In some ways it is a brilliant success: the quiet refrain of the final lines is very effective in signifying the appropriate degree of humility and resignation. However, the recurrent refrain has created a rhetorical sense of expectation, and the readers—as opposed to the tormentors, or God—need an answer to make the rhetorical scheme of the poem complete. Herbert has no choice but to supply the answer which is the reward of his mortification as a speaker within the poem. Yet the fabrication of such an answer would seem to be inconsistent with his mortification as a poet. The artifice of representation makes it unlikely that the re-creation of mortification by rhetorical means could accurately signify inner mortification. This chapter traces some of Herbert's strategies in his attempt to represent the mortification of his poetry, and some of the problems he encounters.

Correctio *and Mortification*

Richard Strier observes that 'Herbert's use of *correctio* . . . is deeply significant theologically'.[28] The reason for this is that *correctio* is the

---

[27] See George Puttenham, *The Art of English Poesie*, ed. G. D. Willcock and A. Walker (Cambridge, 1936), 166–7. Puttenham's 'silence' is also relative: all his examples constitute interruptions of the discourse.

[28] R. Strier, *Love Known: Theology and Experience in George Herbert's Poetry* (Chicago, 1983), 11.

easiest rhetorical method of signifying mortification: the first statement of the human author is curtailed by a correcting motion, whose origin is divine. As Ernest B. Gilman notes, 'Herbert is...attentive to the divine voice and faithfully resolved to submit his language for pruning and paring at the hands of a higher artist.'[29] In 'Giddinesse', the speaker describes the plight of mankind, and his final prayer, which begins conventionally, ends radically:

> Lord, mend or rather make us: one creation
> > Will not suffice our turn:
> Except thou make us dayly, we shall spurn
> > Our own salvation.

This is the Valdésian system at work. It is not enough that the believer 'die daily', which could be used to describe traditional mortification of the flesh: he needs a continual re-creation, in the process of 'vivification' conceived by Valdés. The *correctio* of the poem simulates the divine process at work. The correction at the end of 'Clasping of Hands' is also radical in import. Again, whereas the first utterance is typical of traditional piety, the second asserts the absolute unity with God described by Valdés.

> O be mine still, still make me thine,
> Or rather make no *Thine* & *Mine*.

In quoting these lines I have used the punctuation and typography of the B manuscript, partly because I see no reason for the excessive use of exclamation marks in the 1633 edition, and partly because the words 'Thine' and 'Mine' are distinguished from the rest of the poem in the B manuscript. In both manuscripts the distinguishing of words by italics or larger lettering is a signifier of divinity. Words spoken by God are distinguished in this way, and in 'Clasping of Hands' I take the convention to indicate that the correction is, indeed, God's view of the situation. Both God and Man are incorporated into a new entity: the sanctified believer, who has abandoned the image of Adam, and taken on the image of Christ.

Herbert is conscious of the implications for authorship of the dynamic of mortification, and this awareness shows in the very

---

[29] E. B. Gilman, *Iconoclasm and Poetry in the English Reformation: Down Went Dagon* (Chicago, 1986), 54.

first poem of *The Temple*. In 'The Dedication' of Herbert's poems there is a glaring omission of what would seem to be a basic constituent of all dedications: the first-person subject pronoun.

> Lord, *my first fruits present themselves to thee:*
> *Yet not mine neither: for from thee they came.*

Even the first statement, where the only reference to the author is in the possessive first-person pronoun, does not represent a sufficiently mortified attitude to authorship, and the pronoun, like the self, has to be eradicated. A. D. Nuttall comments, 'already the theology is utterly radical . . . even something as apparently simple as a humble dedication cuts itself to pieces before our eyes.'[30] Herbert had been chary of presuming to offer his poems, preferring them to offer themselves, whatever that might mean: in the new formulation, God, their author, is offering them back to Himself, whatever that might mean. In 'Perseverance', a poem also about authorship, there is an even stronger sense of a divine motion substituted for a human motion: the poems are written

> as for the present I did move,
> Or rather as thou movedst mee.

However, these poems expose the duplicity of the rhetorical device of *correctio*, which pretends to duplicate human speech. In writing, though not in speech, there is never a need for a written correction: the appropriate technique for the correcting of a mistake is complete erasure, not *correctio*. The material nature of the verbal signifier militates against the spiritual purpose for which it is employed. In Herbert's poems, the incorrect first statement is allowed to stand, *sous erasure*, as it were. Thus the denial of individual human authorship actually has the effect of positing a joint project between the human author and God. The device which was meant to signify the suppression of human authorship actually has the effect of asserting it.

Joint Authorship for The Temple?

The most extensive use of this technique of *correctio* is in 'The Holdfast', which sets out the Christian speaker's road to the

---

[30] A. D. Nuttall, *Overheard by God: Fiction and Prayer in Herbert, Milton, Dante and St. John* (London, 1980), 32.

Cross. It describes a series of word-acts which the poet performs in the hope of achieving favour with God. The first sounds like a summary of 'The Thanksgiving' and 'The Reprisall': the believer is in battle mode, determined to do something towards his own sanctification.

> I threatened to observe the strict decree
> Of my deare God with all my power & might.

The reader of *The Temple* has been alerted to the spuriousness of such self-effort since the first poems in *The Church*, but there are further lessons to be learnt. Not only are speech acts of promising, trusting, and confessing futile in God's terms: the very description of spiritual truth is also illegitimate.

> Then I confesse that he my succour is:
> But to have nought is ours, not to confesse
> That we have nought. I stood amaz'd at this.

One by one all human statements are invalidated by a mysterious Other who overturns the logic of the human discourse. The confusion this produces in the believer was echoed by Thomas Savage, a condemned murderer who was converted by the combined efforts of several Presbyterian ministers, but could not understand why his repentant confession had to be accounted as of no spiritual value.[31] If the declaration of the truth, which was the function of discourse in Savonarola's vision of *simplicitas*, is not legitimate, the only option for the human being is silence. The friend with whose words the poem ends is probably divine: and what He expresses is that everything human lost in Adam (including human speech) is kept in Christ. This is exactly the transaction described by Valdés. It seems that silence, the death of human language, is the first step, and indeed the poem finishes with the words of a 'friend' who says that the poet has to surrender to God the right to speak at all. There is a resource for the would-be user of effective language, and that is to be found in Christ's supremely effective words: 'all things were more ours by being his.' This is the trade-off for the cessation of human speech. However, it is

---

[31] See P. Lake, 'Popular Form, Puritan Content? Two Puritan Appropriations of the Murder Pamphlet from Mid-Seventeenth-Century London', in A. Fletcher and P. Roberts (eds.), *Religion, Culture and Society in Early Modern Britain: Essays in Honour of Patrick Collinson* (Cambridge, 1994), 320.

hard to understand what that could possibly mean in regard to discourse, unless it means that the poet's words are now God's. Of the final couplet of the poet Richard Strier comments that 'it is impossible to assign these lines. They either continue to report what the "friend" expressed or represent the speaker's conclusion in the present. The voices merge.'[32] These two lines are designed to represent an absolute conflation of human rhetoric and divine voice, and this is the logical outcome of the application of Valdés' system of mortification: dying to human rhetoric should mean that the divine language comes in to take its place.

There is one complete poem that describes 'vivification' as Valdés conceives it, and that poem is 'Faith'. It describes a series of divine acts performed by a human being, by faith. These include the ability to make real anything that the Christian chooses to imagine, from food to medicine to learning. The benefit of the divine power of faith is that it creates a level playing field: no one has an advantage, whether he be rich or wise or strong. Believers with these strengths have to be mortified, because they lead to human pride:

> Thou dost make proud knowledge bend & crouch,
> While grace fills up uneven nature.

The inclusion of items apparently unessential to the Christian life, such as learning or money, shows that this dynamic is not limited to 'all that bears on salvation or damnation', as Richard Strier believes.[33] 'All things' are brought to the believer by faith. The logical conclusion of this doctrine for poetry is that if Herbert is prepared to mortify his rhetorical skills, and imagine superlative poetry, God will supply it. The omission of poetry, however, in a poetic representation of faith is a glaring one.

Divine language is easier to envisage in theory than in practice. It is relatively easy to represent the mortification of human language, but there are only the barest traces of a vivification, which is much harder to represent, in Herbert's poetry. As Herbert comments in his notes on *The Hundred and Ten Considerations*, 'restraining motions are much more frequent . . . then inviting motions'.[34] Perhaps wisely, Herbert does not show off his new 'divine' voice: 'The Holdfast' finishes at the point where the

---

[32] Strier, *Love Known*, 72. [33] Ibid. 65. [34] Herbert, *Works*, 313.

exchange has been explained. Other poems in which God has a speaking part—'Jordan (i)' and 'Jordan (ii)', 'The Collar', 'Redemption', and 'A true Hymne'—also finish just as the divine voice has started. This reticence on the part of the Almighty could be accounted for by the fact that, as in 'The Quip', God does not need to speak 'at large'. His words are supremely performative. However, it is far more likely that the human author of the poems is embarrassed at having to invent words for the Word. God often speaks only one word, and never more than two or three lines. Tessa Watt notes that in the seventeenth century the attitude to textually created voices for God actually hardened: godly ballads based on secular love songs which contained a dialogue between the Christian and God did not, on the whole, survive into seventeenth-century popular stock.[35] The single example which did survive is important for Herbert's poetry, as we shall see. It is not surprising that even the small number of words attributed to God in Herbert's poetry has attracted much modern critical comment. A. D. Nuttall rehearses all the ethical problems involved, finally proclaiming that 'the "joint-authorship" account is simply incredible'.[36] William Pahlka, on the other hand, insists on a divine co-author: 'God is the efficient cause of the poetry as well as the formal and the final cause.'[37] The difference between these viewpoints is that Nuttall resists the Calvinist and Valdésian account of sanctification, and Pahlka appears to embrace it, declaring that 'the proper means to poetry is for the poet to surrender all claim to be its efficient cause'. Nuttall's conclusion is the more common one, but Pahlka's argument merits consideration simply because, without referring to Valdés explicitly, he has correctly identified the clash of divine and human wills in Herbert's poetry, and suggested a poetic dimension for the voice of God.

Pahlka's argument for the presence of God in Herbert's poems hinges on the belief that the poetic impulse is always sinful and self-glorifying. This is a viewpoint current in the English Reformation, as we have seen, and something that Herbert is all too aware of. Pahlka seems to envisage God intervening with a

---

[35] T. Watt, *Cheap Print and Popular Piety, 1550–1640* (Cambridge, 1991), 105.
[36] Nuttall, *Overheard by God*, 8.
[37] W. H. Pahlka, *Saint Augustine's Meter and George Herbert's Will* (Kent, Oh., 1987), 101–2.

corrective 'motion' that sanctifies the poetry, and stamps it as God's own. Quoting St Augustine's *De Musica*, Pahlka identifies metre, the source of physical movement in verse, as the signifier of divinity. It functions as a mediator between God and man, harmonizing the poet's sinful impulses and the sovereign movement of God's will:

Random, wayward motions, erroneous though they may be, are incorporated in an imitation, an artistic whole that mediates between the sadly defective expressions of the human will and the perfections of divine will.[38]

St Augustine teaches that the profoundly rational 'numbers' of metre are actually a divine institution employed to lift language out of its fallen condition. Pahlka's argument that the harmony of metre brings divine order to the dissonances of human motivation is persuasive, and his analysis of metre in George Herbert's poems masterly. It could well be argued that the profound rhythms of metre correspond to the unconscious moving of God in the soul, and Pahlka understands seventeenth-century thinking about motions:

A heart that is 'moved' is not merely in a state of aroused emotion: it is a heart whose motions are supplied by God, a heart that in turn supplies these motions to its words.[39]

The link with music gives Pahlka's thesis some credence, as Herbert acknowledges the divine power of music in several poems, including 'Church-musick', where he experiences a kind of unconscious, bodiless movement:

> Now I in you without a body move,
> Rising and falling with your wings.

The result is an ecstatic union in which Herbert, in a 1630s colloquialism, is able to pity the circumstances of kings.[40] This seems to be the experience requested in 'Easter-wings', where both rhythm and layout figure death and resurrection. Herbert asks to be incorporated into the wings of God, to further his

---

[38] Ibid. 177.
[39] Ibid. 186.
[40] See Bodleian MS Tanner 67, fo. 32, letter amongst the correspondence of Samuel Ward, to Arthur from G. S.: 'wanting Thee, I want that, w[ch] enjoyed hath often made me cry out in the height of my contentment, Alas poore kinges!'

sanctification and his song. In 'Aaron', which also typographically figures mortification, Christ is the music which both strikes the 'old man' dead and resurrects the holy priest. 'Providence' describes exactly the activity that Pahlka is claiming for the poet God, with music as the metaphor for God's will:

> For either thy command or thy permission
> Lay hands on all: they are thy right and left....
> Nothing escapes them both; all must appeare,
> And be dispo'd, and dress'd, and tun'd by thee,
> Who sweetly temper'st all. If we could heare
> Thy skill and art, what musick would it be!

Gene Veith points out that this poem shows Herbert glorying in the exceptions to the natural order, as well as the created order itself, because God's design is complex and unifying enough to incorporate them. This long poem manages to incorporate many diverse elements of creation into its rather simple metre and form, and Herbert seems to be aware of the relationship between his role as poet and the harmonizing power of God.[41] In the final stanzas he plays on his role as 'Secretarie of thy praise' to claim that in including the way each creature glorifies God, this particular poem praises God more than any other he has written. The activity of God in his 'sustaining' and 'governing' power (Valdés' Mediate and Immediate Will) is described in orthodox Calvinist terms:

> Who dost so strongly and so sweetly move,
> While all things have their will, yet none but thine.

God's will is able to overarch and incorporate the free will of all his creatures. There is an analogy with the poet's activity, controlling all his characters and speakers from the outside, crafting the description of the real world according to artistic form.

This broad conception of the will of God may help to explain Herbert's ordering of *The Temple*, with its well-discussed alternation of poems of joy and poems of desolation. Gene Veith correctly identifies this as analogous to the process of sanctification:

---

[41] Michael McCanles noticed that the regularity of the poem's form is played against enjambment and continual shifts of caesura: M. McCanles, *Dialectical Criticism and Renaissance Literature* (Berkeley, 1975), quoted in G. E. Veith Jr., *Reformation Spirituality: The Religion of George Herbert* (Lewisburg, Pa., 1985), 86.

'so many deaths', as Herbert puts it in 'The Flower', and as many 'vivifications'—Valdés' term.[42] There is also a sense in which, like each section of *The Hundred and Ten Considerations*, each poem in *The Temple* begins from a different standpoint and follows its own logic to its inevitable end.[43] The poet's design, like God's, was broad enough to be able to imagine and plan for all kinds of diverse experience.

However, the evidence of Herbert's careful restructuring of *The Temple* right up to his death belies the idea of a surrender of the poetic activity to God, and militates against a theory such as Valdés' which allows no active interference with the original motions.[44] The best example of Pahlka's theory is 'The Collar', where the underlying metre is reasserted at the end of a disrupted poem to show that God really was in control: but we have already seen in Chapter 3 how the effect of God's take-over is carefully constructed by Herbert using grammatical and rhetorical means, as well as metre. In the end, even Pahlka admits that it is Herbert who deliberately employs organizing schemes such as metre and rhyme, not God. In what seems to be a complete reversal of Pahlka's thesis, his book concludes that in all the cases where God appears to be speaking, Herbert is in fact constructing an ideal for true art. Nuttall agrees with Pahlka that Herbert makes gestures towards a Calvinist-Valdésian scheme of mortification in this poetry, but concludes that by playing on his readers' familiarity with Reformed theology in this way, Herbert is deliberately establishing 'a kind of moral credit'.[45]

Rhetoric as a Human Medium

Herbert cannot in the end subscribe to a spiritual poetics that identifies divine *res* in any aspect of human *verba*. Quintilian draws attention to the duplicity involved in the technique of prosopopoeia, which allows the rhetorician to 'pretend that we have before our eyes the images of things, persons or utterances'.

---

[42] Veith, *Reformation Spirituality*, 134.

[43] William Pahlka charts some of the contradictions produced by this method of working: the difference between 'Content' and 'The Quidditie', 'The Dawning' and 'Businesse', 'Joseph's coat' and 'The Pulley'. See *Saint Augustine's Meter and George Herbert's Will*, 189.

[44] George Herbert, *The Bodleian MS of George Herbert's Poems: A Facsimile of Tanner 307*, ed. with intro. by A. M. Charles and M. A. Di Cesare (Delmar, NY, 1984), xvii.

[45] Nuttall, *Overheard by God*, 9.

There is a particular rhetorical risk involved in giving the gods a voice. Quintilian celebrates the power of such dramatic representations but also warns against the main disadvantage: 'either they will move our hearers with exceptional force because they are beyond the truth, or they will be regarded as empty nothings because they are not the truth.'[46] The reader either accepts that the poet's art is giving some kind of representation to the voice of God, which cannot be represented in any other way, or he questions the possibility of such representation. In human writing there is no escape from rhetorical considerations, even for the words of God. Faced with the alternative of complete silence, Savonarola, Valdés, and Herbert all prefer to represent the voice of God, for pedagogical purposes. Herbert's poetry cannot directly represent the absolute word of God: instead, it tries to figure what the result of the word of God on human discourse might be. Thus he creates a voice in *The Temple* which signifies the divine, and opposes the other voices, which are characterized as distinctively human and sinful.

In 'Jordan (ii)' Herbert insists on a separation between spiritual truth and poetic expression, much as Savonarola did, prioritizing the kernel of the divine message over the human words which are its shell. As we have seen, the fact that poetry was concerned with words, the worthless husk of truth, had been one of the main arguments against it in the English Reformation.[47] Herbert diverts attention from the rhetoric of 'Jordan (ii)' by apparently rejecting poetry for truth. There is a hint in *The Country Parson* of what Herbert meant by a spiritual message 'readie penn'd': the chapter entitled 'The Parson's Library' describes an inner, experiential *copia* of material for sermons, to be preferred to a perusal of written texts. 'The Parson, having studied, and mastered all his lusts and Affections within ... hath ever so many sermons ready penn'd, as he hath victories.'[48] The divine subject-matter is that which is already written on the poet's heart, that victorious spiritual experience which in 'Easter-wings' allows the poet to give voice, and is a result of an overwhelming divine act within

---

[46] Quintilian, *Institutio Oratoria*, tr. H. E. Butler, 4 vols. (London, 1921), iii. 393.

[47] See Fraser, *The War Against Poetry*, ch. 1. This husk–kernel image for the letter–spirit dualism is common in the 17th century, in both mainstream Puritan and radical discourse: see N. Smith, *Perfection Proclaimed* (Oxford, 1989), 234.

[48] Herbert, *Works*, 278.

him. Because, like Valdés, Herbert gives priority to inner over outer, he tries to create in his poems a sense of inner space in which the authorizing experience that gives rise to the poetry has its origin. The *locus* for Herbert's poems and ejaculations is established on the title-page: they are spoken 'within the Temple', which in Protestant terminology is the human heart. However, the seat of authentic selfhood in Herbert's poetry is in hidden rooms behind walls behind outer defences, as in 'The H. Communion', or in tills within boxes within chests within closets in 'Confession'.[49] Not only is this self hidden away, it is also slippery and evasive. At its very best, it is 'stone', hard and unresponsive to God, as in 'Sepulchre' and in the vast ruined quarry which is the interiority of 'The Sinner': but at least that substance is fixed enough to be written on. The existence of a stable surface makes possible a divine writing represented as being at a place central to the poet's being. In 'Good Friday' the heart where the divine writing is to take place is imagined as located in a separate space from that where the voice of the poem is heard. The assumption of the poems that deal with 'writing on the heart' is that such writing will be authoritative and unite the fragmented consciousness of the poet, as in Jeremiah 31: 33: 'I will put my law in their inward parts, and write it in their hearts; and will be their God, and they shall be my people.' However, such uniting of the poet's voice and God's is usually only potential: his poetry tends to chart the perceived dissonance between the two voices. Herbert is only too aware of the ultimately superficial nature of his rhetorical strategies in describing a truth which is both internal and transcendent. All he can do is to try to represent the dynamic of mortification, and it is easier to represent the mortifying than the vivifying cycle.

Herbert shows relative value in his poetry by representing unsanctified human discourse, and then correcting it. Thus he needs to create a separate, authoritative voice for God, because it is that voice which is used as the signifier of truth and ultimate sincerity throughout his poetry. It is that voice which is always clearly heard above the babble of the merely human voices, even the most sincere, and is able to modify, or even silence them. The

---

[49] 'Till', according to the *OED*, which cites this reference, is 'a small box, casket, or closed compartment, contained within or forming part of a larger box, chest, or cabinet'.

style of the final two lines of 'The Holdfast', which Strier describes as 'a hymnlike, impersonal couplet', is rather typical of the sententious voice which speaks when the individual voice has been silenced. Herbert, along with other famous Renaissance figures such as Erasmus and Bacon, is an obsessive collector of just such impersonal, authoritative utterances, and his use of them in the poetry is to create a powerful voice which can silence the often rebellious tones of the individual. The mysterious, anonymous character of proverbial discourse functions well as a figure for the voice of God: in fact, for a Renaissance readership, it is one way that the voice of God can authentically be heard in human discourse. The sententious tone gains authority from its very impersonality: rather than being an individualistic voice, it is the voice of the Church as a whole, and therefore more likely to be God's. The balanced rhetoric and regular metre convey authority at a subconscious level. Herbert uses such impersonal, proverbial utterances to strengthen the authority of the appeals to the soul at the end of 'Vanitie (ii)', 'The Size', and 'Businesse'. Sometimes the previous speaker in the poems submits to the authoritative voice as one might submit to God, and it seems fitting that he does so. At the end of 'Assurance', which has mimicked both a demonic motion and a human motion, the divine motion is figured in such authoritative utterances with a biblical resonance. Even more daring, perhaps, is the strategy spotted in 'Jordan (ii)' by Coburn Freer. Underlining the content of the poem, which is about the baptism of poetry and the mortification of secular rhetoric, is what he calls 'an hourglass plot':

lavish and ersatz-graceful ideas are set forth in a plain style and then are contrasted with plain ideas stated in a genuinely graceful style.[50]

A better word for 'hourglass' would be 'chiasmus': what Freer is describing is the figure of the Cross. However, this use of elaborate rhetoric to simulate the mortification of rhetoric represents the kind of paradoxical manœuvre which a Christian poet must perform.

Herbert allows human speakers to annex the authority of a rhetorically created 'divine' speech. In 'Conscience' the problem

---

[50] C. Freer, *Music for a King: George Herbert's Style and the Metrical Psalms* (London, 1980), 233.

is a Valdésian one. The believer's sinful humanity is manifesting itself in busy activity, the activity characteristic of sin in *The Temple*: it is talking too much. Traditionally, the conscience was seen as God's messenger in human beings. However, the radical doctrine of justification by faith makes the conscience redundant. In Valdés' vision it is not simply redundant, but sinful, because its motions interfere with God's. Herbert's poem articulates this message. The 'pratler' has to be silenced—put to death—and the means is, of course, the Cross of Christ.[51] The conversational rhythms of the poem, which do give the impression, by the final stanza, that Conscience is still arguing, are abruptly halted by the sententious final couplet, which proclaims the power of the Cross as an offensive weapon.

> The bloudie crosse of my deare Lord
> Is both my physick and my sword.

'The Priesthood' is also an example of Herbert apparently talking to himself. The problem this time is that he would like to become one of the 'blest order', but is aware of his own unworthiness. He formulates the choice in this way: 'exchanging my lay-sword | For that of th'holy Word.' Since 'the sword of the spirit . . . is the word of God' this choice could be reformulated as that between secular and sacred rhetoric: and sacred rhetoric is greatly to be desired because it is so powerful, as the first stanza powerfully claims. Herbert is not stupid enough to presume to the status of priest, but is aware that a sense of unworthiness is the greatest qualification for it, and the poem concludes with Herbert in the correct attitude:

> since God doth often vessels make
> Of lowly matter for high uses meet,
> I throw me at his feet.

> There will I lie, until my Maker seek
> For some mean stuffe whereon to show his skill.

As if to mirror Herbert's physical position, the rhetoric comes to a halt here: the last few lines of the poem are sententious and impersonal in the way we have come to expect of divine language.

---

[51] Calvin's teaching on the conscience is rather similar to Valdés'. In the *Institutes*, he follows a discussion of the essential role of mortification in Christian liberty with this statement: 'the knowledge of this liberty also is very necessary for us, for if it shall be absent, there shall be no quiet to our consciences': John Calvin, *The Institution of the Christian Religion*, tr. Thomas Norton (London, 1578), III. xix. 6, p. 344.

Most distinctly divided of the discourses of *The Temple* is that of self-examination in 'The Method', where the possibility is envisaged of a divine writing which can be, at least initially, ignored. This time the model of interiority is a book, the pages of which will need to be turned. There is little sense of inner depth here: the impression is of a reader, book in hand, musing to himself over the contents. God's instructions are plainly written there, but the poet has ignored them. Not even the divine writing, it seems, is necessarily performative. However, God has a sanction which can operate to draw attention to the disharmony in the poet's consciousness, by disrupting the poet's sense of harmony with God. The last words of the poem, which are God's words in an imagined future, signify the reuniting of consciousness, and the consequent pleasure for the (potentially) healed self. The poem assumes the conventional meditative trope of the soul as a book: it attempts to make God's writing special by announcing it with rhetorical questions, and marking it off from the rest of the page in italics. However, the 'divine' discourse cannot be finally separated from the human language of the rest of the poem: the fact that Herbert has to distinguish it with fairly crude techniques shows that by itself it is not distinctive. However true Herbert may have been to an inspiring divine impulse, however precisely he may chart the movement of the divine Spirit, all he has to work with, and all there is for his readers to deal with, is the rhetorical and typographical surface which is human discourse. As we have seen, this is a real problem in attempting to represent the mortification of language, where the representation of silence requires the permanent inscription of words. Writing cannot reproduce a linear chronology, and in a poem the noisy words continue to exist beyond the temporary silence which is the spatial end of the graphic representation.[52]

God's Rhetoric in The Temple

Herbert's problem with writing poetry is that rhetorical effort can never articulate the divine principle: indeed, it fundamentally obscures the divine message by articulating itself, an activity

---

[52] As Stanley Fish notes, 'Herbert's speakers can fall silent...but the poem would seem to be irreducibly there': *Self-Consuming Artifacts*, 189.

described by both Herbert and Savonarola as expressing the sinful human self, the 'flesh'. Thus they are prepared to make compromises with the rigours of pure theory. Some rhetorical techniques are better than others: simple rhetoric is less self-conscious, and therefore more godly. Herbert's part-solution to his problem is to maintain a relative simplicity compared with other Renaissance poetry. Thus he deals with relatives: relative simplicity, relative silence. Simplicity replaces complexity in Herbert's poems, in a dynamic that simulates mortification: Nicholas Ferrar described Herbert's poetic style as 'naked simplicitie'. This is a relative nakedness, however, which for Herbert consists in homely comparisons, simple vocabulary, and bare stanza forms. Coburn Freer suggests that many of Herbert's poems would remind his audience of the Sternhold and Hopkins Psalms, ridiculed by contemporary poets as 'Geneva jigs'. English Psalm translators 'eschew grace in translation as worldly wisdom well avoided' and Herbert, imitating their 'countrey-aires' in poems like 'Complaining', is sharing in this mortification of a poetic gift.[53] Another gesture in the direction of deliberate rusticity is in the similarity of some poems in *The Temple* to popular ballads. 'Love (iii)', for example, although infinitely more subtle in style and form, might well have reminded seventeenth-century readers of the popular ballad 'A Christian conference betweene Christ and a sinner', which according to Tessa Watt was the only dialogue between Christ and the believer to survive into seventeenth-century ballad stock.[54] As in Herbert's poem, the believer is so conscious of his sin—'My carcasse is filthy, and nothing but clay'—that he resists all the arguments employed by Christ. These cover ground familiar to readers of 'Love (iii)': reassurance about forgiveness of sins, assertion that Christ has suffered the penalty. Each of Christ's utterances end with the invitation 'I that redeemed thee bids thee come to me'. As with 'Love (iii)' the believer's scruples are finally overcome in the last verse.[55]

However, neither *correctio* nor deliberate simplicity are Herbert's favoured way of simulating mortification. The method he chooses is daring: it involves the rhetorically created sense of an

---

[53] Freer, *Music for a King*, 20–3, 159–60.   [54] Watt, *Cheap Print*, 105.
[55] W. Chappell and J. Woodfall Elsworth (eds.), *The Roxburghe Ballads*, 8 vols. (London, 1871–97), iii. 164–7.

entirely separate voice for God. In many poems the words of God come as audible voices from a separate identity—a 'friend'. These scenes appear to take place in a setting external to the poet, again creating a sense of materiality for the divine voice. Although most of Herbert's poems represent a personal and emotional engagement with God, they do not read as private meditations: their nature as inner dialogue is not often made explicit, and sometimes the rhetorical strategies are those of audible, public dialogue. 'Dialogue' sees God entering into a language game started by the poet. The echo poem which is 'Heaven' also suggests an audible voice. The dramatizations of spiritual experience such as 'Redemption' and 'Christmas' are very different from Counter-Reformation meditation, which takes place firmly within the Christian's consciousness and has nothing like the imaginative power that takes the mysteries off the sacred page and re-creates them in Jacobean England. It is impossible to locate the exact space in which some of the dialogues take place. There has been some controversy, for example, over the setting for 'Love (iii)': is it heaven, or Holy Communion, or simply the experience of mystical marriage within the believer's consciousness? Such dialogue, which gives the impression of being physically audible, has the rhetorical advantage of allowing the reader to find a place at the scene of the conversation. As we have seen in Chapter 3, God often ends up talking to him.

This textually created voice for God is the touchstone by which Herbert intends the reader to judge the various discourses which emerge. In line with Herbert's idea that 'restraining motions are much more frequent...than inviting motions' God usually intervenes at the end of a poem with a short utterance that passes judgement on the previous lines. Thus the words of God at the end of 'The Collar' instantly bring the errant discourse into line. 'Love Unknown' apparently starts a conversation with the reader, but a third person, who seems as real as the reader, enters the poem to reinterpret the narrative. However, both voices are, of course, rhetorically created: Herbert may try to signal the special nature of the divine discourse by rhetorical and graphical distinction, but he cannot actually get God to speak. In the end, poems like 'The Holdfast', 'Jordan (ii)', or 'Deniall' merely provide a rhetorical model for a spiritual truth. They figure an openness to an extra-rhetorical, spiritual influence that can correct the statements, change the direction of the rhetoric, or complete a poem. Coburn Freer formulates this poetic tendency in the Biblical terms which signify mortification: 'as one finds oneself by losing one's self, so the poem may complete itself by what may at first seem to be a loss of control.'[56] The loss of control, however, is merely a simulation: the 'divine' intervention is completely implicated in the rhetorical strategy of the poem. As Barbara Leah Harman concludes in her study of 'Affliction (i)', the ending to a particular poem is deliberately suppressed at its start in order to permit 'the feeling of free movement'.[57] This illusion of freedom is important if the voice of the unregenerate human being is to be fully heard. However, the poet has already predestined the collapse of the unregenerate voice. The careful control of form and tone in 'The Holdfast' and 'The Thanksgiving' allows for no false starts such as are suggested by the subject-matter of these poems, which is the misguided reasoning of the human heart. In any case, a false start is impossible to represent in written discourse, because it can simply be erased. Despite the rhetorically created sense of the speaking voice in Herbert's poetry, which gives a sense of movement and change within a poem, the permanent, physical space of the poem militates against the temporal space in the reader's consciousness within which Herbert attempts to work. However powerful the sense of God speaking at the end of the poem, it cannot erase the sinful human words at the beginning. Yet it is the apparent openness to correction by the divine voice which is important to Herbert's seventeenth-century readership.

Silent Motions

As we have seen, there is a way of regarding inspiration in the seventeenth century that does not involve the actual words at all. Juan de Valdés, like William Pemble, asserted that the soteriological function is not located in words, even the divine words of Scripture, but in the Spirit that motivates the discourse. Valdés allowed for the possibility of a spontaneously inspired speech that would carry divine signification, but that is hardly a description of the careful lyrics of *The Temple*. However, William Pemble

---

[56] Freer, *Music for a King*, 49.
[57] B. L. Harman, 'George Herbert's *Affliction (i)*: The Limits of Representation', *ELH* 44 (1977), 269.

dislocated Spirit and Word to the extent that no human words could ever represent the Word of God. The power of any discourse is located entirely in the 'vertue of the Spirit', which may or may not operate in the heart of the reader, depending on the will of God:

> where the vertue of the Spirit is wanting, as it is in most, there the Word hath no other vertue, than to bee as a faire Mappe presented to the eye, wherein are described many matters of excellent knowledge, which the unregenerate may gaze upon, in a kind of shallow heartlesse specula-tion, which will differ as much from good knowledge, as the knowledge of a Countrie by the Mappe and by the eye in travelling it.[58]

The logical conclusion of the theology of Pemble and Valdés is that effective spiritual communication is a silent accompaniment to human words: it depends on the spiritual receptiveness of the reader to a 'motion' from God. In one sense this makes the poetry of *The Temple* a redundant 'faire Mappe': in another, it relieves Herbert of responsibility. Because God has to provide the spiritual power for any human words, even the words of Scripture, the role of the human author is not crucial. In the logic of mortification God could undermine the meaning and power of Herbert's poetry for reasons of His own to do, perhaps, with the spiritual state of each reader. Taking this argument to its logical conclu-sion, Herbert might as well have followed Valdés' strategy of verbal abandonment, and have produced spontaneous, inspired writing. This was an option followed by other seventeenth-century radical Christians.[59]

Instead, Herbert takes another option. As if to assist in his own mortification, he actually draws attention to the rhetorical strat-egies in his poems. The poet who was disingenuous enough to confess his strategy to God in 'Gratefulnesse', 'See how thy beggar works on thee | By art', is not prepared to deceive the reader, either. As Richard Strier remarks, 'Deniall' is carefully written to make clear that the corrected rhyme must figure God's interven-tion, rather than constitute it. 'The poet is asking that God do something to him analogous to what he has done in the poem— but not identical with it.'[60] The reverse strategy, in 'Home', draws attention to itself and its artificiality. When God speaks, Herbert not only makes clear that he is representing the two voices on the

---

[58] Pemble, *Vindiciae Gratiae*, 98–9.
[59] Smith, *Perfection Proclaimed*, 25.   [60] Strier, *Love Known*, 190.

same page, but that he experiences the two voices as part of the same consciousness. The words spoken by the divine voice are given as much rhetorical authority as Herbert can muster: yet he himself casts doubt on the audible nature of the voice in the reader's world. 'While I bustled, I might heare a friend | Whisper'. 'Mee thoughts I heard one calling.'[61] The voice is audible only to Herbert, and even then he is not sure that he has heard it with his physical ears. Thus the apparently outward and audible voice becomes an inward voice in Herbert's consciousness: and within the poem, it becomes just another example of prosopopoeia, which gives the reader the choice as formulated by Quintilian, to accept the human words as a representation of God's voice, or reject them.

Reading the Codes of Mortification

Herbert enacted his own rejection of 'wit' in poems like 'The Posie':

> Invention rest,
> Comparisons go play, wit use thy will.

He was clearly aware of the necessity to mortify his own poetic gift, in the process of baptism described in 'The Forerunners'. Two poems entitled 'Jordan', the biblical river of baptism, highlight its importance: baptism is not merely cleansing, but the simulated death and resurrection of mortification. In composing a 'posie', that conventional vehicle for a poet's most ostentatious wit, Herbert's final choice—*Less than the least of all God's mercies*—is a post-baptismal utterance from Genesis 32. The story of Jacob's crossing of the brook Jabbok, which incidentally is a tributary of Jordan, has been read by Roland Barthes as a narrative about the production of language.[62] For Herbert's Reformation spirituality, however, the significance of the story was as an epiphany of Christ, and the wrestle with the angel as the kind of 'death' experience—mortification—of which baptism is a symbol. The result of the struggle is that Jacob is lamed, and limps, in fact, for the rest of his life: his stick is a type of the Christian's dependence

---

[61] Herbert, *Works*, 103, 154.
[62] R. Barthes, *Image Music Text*, tr. S. Heath (New York, 1977), 125–41.

on the Holy Spirit, which the death of the old self in baptism necessitates. The self-effacing utterance of chapter 32, *I am not worthy of the least of all thy mercies*, becomes the self-erasing 'Posie', *Less than the least of all God's mercies*, which ends Herbert's poem.

Charles Wesley, who read Herbert's poetry avidly, wrote a version of Genesis 32 in which the disablement which is baptism is celebrated as a resurrection of divine strength:

> Lame as I am, I take the Prey
> Hell, Earth and Sin with Ease oercome
> I leap for Joy, pursue my Way,
> And as a bounding Hart fly home.[63]

In the Jacobean period the story was interpreted in a similar way. Samuel Ward reads it as a type of mortification:

Die to thy selfe, renounce the broken Reed of thine owne Free-will which hath so often deceived thee: and put all thy trust in the grace of Christ, and it will crucifie the old man, and give him his *hoc habet*, his deaths wound, pierce his sides, and breake his knees in pieces.... Leave tugging and struggling with thy sinne, and fall with *Jacob* to wrestle with Christ for a blessing, and though thy selfe goe limping away, yet shalt thou be a Prince with God.[64]

Applied to poetic composition, the dynamic of mortification should mean that even a deliberately 'maimed' poem, such as 'The Posie', can be successful. However, both seventeenth-century and twentieth-century readers have disagreed as to whether Herbert's lyrics represent rhetorical, or spiritual, success. Richard Strier thinks that Herbert has deliberately marred the poem 'Home'. The rhyme scheme is disrupted in the final stanza in order to stress the strength of the poet's longing:

> And ev'n my verse, when by the ryme and reason
> The words is, *Stay*, sayes ever, *Come*.

The final word does not rhyme within the stanza: it actually does rhyme with the title, 'Home'. However, there is no lingering echo of the title left by the end of the final stanza, and the poet cannot exploit any residual sound-effect in this way. Herbert has been

[63] Charles Wesley, 'Wrestling Jacob', in *Representative Verse of Charles Wesley*, ed. F. Baker (London, 1962), 39.

[64] Samuel Ward, *A Collection of Such Sermons as have been Written and Published* (London, 1636), 93.

called upon to make the sacrifice of the outer harmony of rhyme for the inner 'rhyme' of words and heart, as he declared he would do in 'A true Hymne'. As Strier says, 'he associates rhyme with reason and rejects both'.[65] This of course is a very Valdésian conclusion. Strier declares both 'Home' and 'Grief' to be poetic failures.[66] Perhaps the most likely poem to show this kind of mortified style is 'Discipline', which charts a failure of poetic facility as well as spiritual suffering:

> Though I fail, I weep:
> Though I halt in pace,
> > Yet I creep
> To the throne of grace.

It is not only Herbert's soul which is limping, but his verse. This monosyllabic, lurching poem represents a subversion of eloquent, harmonious Renaissance poetics. However, the consonance between spiritual emotion and poetic form is not necessarily poetic failure. Herbert is not the first to represent spiritual grief by spare stanzas and ugly metrical effects: Sidney's version of Psalm 13 employs exactly the same strategy.

> Behold me, Lord, let to thy hearing creep
> My crying.[67]

Herbert's poems often display such a satisfying consonance between spirituality and poetic form. In 'Submission' a voluntary blindness in spiritual things, and a willing renunciation of claims to wisdom, is mirrored in the adoption of the ballad form, one of the simplest poetic forms in English. The title is inevitably reminiscent of St Augustine's humblest rhetorical mode, *submissus*, which he recommends as the most suitable mode for teaching. As such it is a rhetorical strategy, and the adoption of even this most simple style is defined by Cicero as 'eloquence', as long as the subject-matter is appropriately humble.[68] As Thomas Watson engagingly states in the prefatory letter to *A Passionate Centurie of Love*:

---

[65] Strier, *Love Known*, 196.

[66] See my discussion of the poem 'Grief' in 'Sacred Singer/Profane Poet: Herbert's Split Poetic Persona', in H. Wilcox and R. Todd (eds.), *George Herbert: Sacred and Profane* (Amsterdam, 1995), 23–32.

[67] Mary Sidney and Sir Philip Sidney, *The Sidney Psalms*, ed. R. E. Pritchard (Manchester, 1992), 30.

[68] St Augustine, *On Christian Doctrine*, tr. D. W. Robertson Jr. (New York, 1958), 143.

it is nothing *Praeter decorum* for a maiemed man to halt in his pase, where his wound enforceth him, or for a Poete to falter in his poeme, when his manner requireth it.[69]

Coburn Freer argues that 'Submission' shares the clumsy form of the Sternhold and Hopkins Psalter, and that the poet has deliberately 'blinded' himself: 'the only way for a poet to lose his eyes is to lose his ears.'[70] But a critic who can equate the simplicity of this ballad form with the awkwardness of a Sternhold and Hopkins Psalm has his own hearing problem. Herbert's poems of divine absence, grief, and authorial frustration are as rhetorically effective as those of spiritual joy, and just as self-consciously constructed. Herbert, like Savonarola, is careful to maintain decorum. In a poem about spiritual failure he uses an appropriate style which is not poetic *aporia*, but plenitude.

The relationship between spiritual and rhetorical success as Herbert describes it is unstable, and many critics have argued over it.[71] In a Valdésian critique of language, this is to be expected. Signification was one of the systems seen to be disrupted in *The Hundred and Ten Considerations*. The sign of mortification could be success or failure, depending on the stage of the mortifying process. Whatever is in the will of God is good, despite its ontological status. Thus a 'good' poem in God's eyes may well not be rhetorically successful: and human rhetoric may by God's grace have divine authority. Herbert hints as much in his deepest wrestling with God's will, 'The Crosse'. He seems to be asking, not that his poems should be good, but that God will reckon them to be good: 'What I would do for thee, if once my grones | Could be allow'd for harmonie.' If God accepts the poems, they will have spiritual power, not rhetorical power, the spiritual power that changes the significance of an event in the real world. God will intervene in the reading process to the effect that the supernatural motions that accompany the words can make them mean anything God wills them to be. The magic of 'The Elixir' will work to transform the poems as 'God doth touch and own' the human rhetoric.

---

[69] Thomas Watson, *Works*, ed. E. Arber (London, 1870), 21.

[70] Freer, *Music for a King*, 192–3.

[71] See Strier, *Love Known*, 190–5, where he quarrels with those critics who equate poetic and spiritual success in Herbert's poems.

Paradoxically, to a readership that understood the dynamic of mortification, the explicit acknowledgement of the flawed authorship of the poems confirmed their status as inspired lyrics. Barnabas Oley had no doubts that the poems of *The Temple*, which he calls 'these poems propheticall', were 'distilled from above': and at least one factor in this judgement seems to have been Herbert's description of his difficulty in composing the poems. Far from being aided by God, Herbert reports the experience of being deliberately disabled by Him: 'God has broken into my Study and taken off my Chariot wheels, I have nothing worthy of God.' This obscure adoption of the Biblical text in which the fate of the Egyptian armies is described makes perfect sense to Oley, who interprets it as the first stage in Herbert's mortification as a poet. As a reader, he is able to report the triumphant vivification of the lyrics of *The Temple*, but this spiritual resurrection seems to depend on Herbert's acknowledgement of mortification: 'and even this lowliness in his own eyes, doth more advance their worth.'[72] The supernatural dynamic of mortification may mean that despite, and perhaps because of, Herbert's admission of his own flawed authorship, God could intervene to make the poems His own. There is evidence that seventeenth-century readers picked up the codes of mortification implanted in the poems. A eulogist for Christopher Harvey, John Legate, was clearly referring to the process of mortification when he prescribed that anyone who follows Herbert's example must 'baptize his Quill' in 'his Saviours sides'.[73] All readers are convinced that the result of Herbert's rigour was a divinely inspired poetry: 'Divine Herbert' is a common epithet in seventeenth-century reactions to *The Temple*. However, as C. A. Patrides notes, Anglicans and Nonconformists differed in their evaluation of the poetry as rhetoric. John Legate, the Royalist, clearly thought that the mortification of Herbert's poetic gift had led to vivification, even in terms of poetic style: he recommends such a sacrifice to those who would be 'as elegant as he', and describes the blood of Christ as

---

[72] Barnabas Oley (ed.), *Herberts Remains, Or, Sundry Pieces of that Sweet Singer of the Temple, Mr. G. H., sometime Orator of the University of Cambridge, Now exposed to Public Light* (London, 1652), sig. c6ʳ.

[73] Poem postfixed to Christopher Harvey's *The Synagogue*, 2nd rev. edn. (London, 1647), sig. C8-C8ᵛ.

A Jordan fit t'instill
A Saint-like stile, backt with an Angels skill.

Richard Baxter, however, dismissed Herbert's poetic achievements, rating him below poets such as Abraham Cowley, and reading him entirely for his spiritual value.

I know that *Cooly* and others far excel Herbert in Wit and accurate composure. But... Herbert speaketh to God like one who really believeth a God, and whose business in the world is most *with God*. Heart-work and Heaven-work make up his book.[74]

Patrides traces this difference between Anglican and Nonconformist responses to Herbert's poems during the seventeenth century. He offers as part of his evidence for the fact that Nonconformists 'remained aloof from his poetry as poetry' the lack of imitators of Herbert from that shade of political opinion, although many quote him, particularly in sermons. It is certainly true that Anglicans such as Cardell Goodman, Christopher Harvey, and Henry Vaughan seem to have found in Herbert an authorized sacred style as well as divinely inspired content.[75] It is important to remember, however, the relative prolixity of Anglican poetry in the mid-seventeenth century compared with that of Nonconformists, who were still suspicious of elaborate rhetoric.

The discourse of mortification was part of Herbert's readership's Reformation heritage, for the codes and significance of the doctrine were firmly in place for all mid-seventeenth-century readers. All they needed was a sign that the double dynamic of mortification was about to operate. The authentic mark of the Cross is a deliberate disablement by God, such as Jacob's lameness in Wesley's reworking of Genesis 32, and Herbert gives his readers plenty of evidence for this. The triggers for the dynamic of mortification are the divinely induced blindness of the poet in 'Submission', which requires God to 'lend [him] a hand'; the divine torture of 'The Temper (i)', which puts 'the poore debter' on the rack; the actions of God as reported in 'The Crosse', which reduce the poet to 'a weak disabled thing'. Sometimes, as in 'The Flower', the poet can read divine vivification into his experience

---

[74] Quoted in H. Wilcox, 'Something Understood: The Reputation and Influence of George Herbert to 1715' (Univ. of Oxford D.Phil. thesis, 1984), 219.
[75] Patrides, *George Herbert: The Critical Heritage*, 10.

as well as mortification. Usually, however, it is left to the spiritually alert reader to recognize spiritual health in the description of physical, emotional, or intellectual crippling: and the obvious place to find that spiritual life is in the very quality of the poems. Thus, the Christian readership of the seventeenth century read the lyrics of *The Temple* as divinely inspired, marked by the sign of the Cross as God's own. In this sense, Nuttall is right that Herbert is deliberately establishing 'a kind of moral credit' by his insistent use of the codes of mortification.[76]

Interpreting a Life: Exemplary Biography

If the seventeenth-century readership had any difficulty reading Herbert's poetry in this way, help was at hand. The biographies of Herbert which accompanied his poems from the first edition onwards, and which, as Helen Wilcox has shown, played an important part in his reception as spiritual poet, clarified the coded message of the text with extra-textual confirmation. Spiritual diaries and exemplary biography of mid-seventeenth-century Puritans display a common structuring principle, in what David Leverenz has called a 'relatively inflexible application of God's pattern'.[77] A life which conforms to a Puritan idea of godliness should show a recurring cycle of mortification and vivification, a self-emptying process that moves towards complete dependence on God. Thus diaries and biography focus on crises, as God's mechanism for disabling the 'old Adam'. John Winthrop, Governor of Massachusetts, records a series of crises in his spiritual diary, beginning with his recognition, while reading Perkins, that his spiritual experience could be explained in terms of temporary grace, rather than genuine election. Looking back in 1637 on 'som affliction' of 1619, he construes it in terms of God's gracious intervention: the severe but unspecified experience 'laid me lower in myne owne eyes then as at any time before, and shewed mee the emptiness of all my guifts and parts, left mee neither power nor will, so as I became as a weaned child.'[78] This

---

[76] Nuttall, *Overheard by God*, 9.

[77] D. Leverenz, *The Language of Puritan Feeling: An Exploration in Literature, Psychology and Social History* (New Brunswick, NJ, 1980), 6.

[78] A. B., Forbes *et al.* (eds.), *Winthrop Papers*, 5 vols. (Boston, 1929–47), iii. 342–3, quoted in C. L. Cohen, *God's Caress: The Psychology of Puritan Religious Experience* (Oxford, 1986), 259.

disablement is a highly desirable, even necessary event in the life of a Christian, since it signifies a greater dependence on God's strength thereafter, and thus a higher degree of holiness. Thomas Shepherd's *Confessions*, collected in the late 1630s and early 1640s in Cambridge, Massachusetts, are a record of 'part of the procedure by which New England saints distinguished a church—a covenanted company of truly professing believers bound together in "worship" and "mutual edification"—from the rest of the congregation'.[79] The criterion for acceptance into such an *ecclesia* was a genuine experience of grace—unmerited favour from God. Thus, many of the fifty-one confessions show the pattern of disablement and subsequent divine enabling. For one William Hamlet the crisis came when he was shot in the hand, and despaired of life. Shepherd comments 'the demise of carnal self-esteem ushered in a renewed life of faith . . . relinquishing his pride, he gave himself over to Gods potency'. The last sentence of Hamlet's biography, apparently recording his own words, articulates a correctly mortified humility: 'I desire to walk under the feet of God and His people and all men, being more vile than any.'[80] This sentiment has a familiar ring. A similar statement of Herbert's, expressing his superlative unworthiness, is used by Ferrar to conclude his biographical introduction to *The Temple*: 'less then the least of Gods mercies.' For Ferrar, and for Shepherd presenting the life of William Hamlet, these words clearly signify the opposite of what they appear to say. Herbert and Hamlet are exemplary saints because they are so aware that they are sinners. Their supposed statements are to be read not as irony, but as signifiers of mortification. The self-consciousness of this strategy is shown in the biographers' sense that they have to equal their subjects' mortified utterances. Barnabas Oley, in writing biographies of George Herbert, Nicholas Ferrar, and Thomas Jackson, is careful to record not only their disablement but his own: 'God, by convincing me of disability, hath taken away any hopes and desires of publishing any work of mine own.' And he is surely straining for the highest (or lowest) degree of mortification when

[79] Cohen, *God's Caress*, 140.

[80] For Hamlet's autobiography, see G. Selement and B. C. Woolley (eds.), 'Thomas Shepherd's "Confessions"', in *Publications of the Colonial Society of Massachusetts*, 58 (1981), 125–8; treated in Cohen, *God's Caress*, 236–9.

he professes himself 'unworthy to *carry out the Dung of Gods Sacrifices*'.[81]

The deathbed scene is a particular focus for exemplary biography: one-tenth of Walton's *Life* is taken up with Herbert's death. One of the reasons for this is that the deathbed is the site of the long-deferred revelation of the elect. Only at the point of death can it be ascertained that the Christian has received saving grace, rather than temporary grace: it is the end of the story. Attempts to distinguish between the elect and the reprobate are dogged, as we have seen, by the unstable signification of mortification, and the only certainty is that God will not allow his elect finally to fall. Physical death is, of course, the ultimate form of mortification, and the renunciation of the last vestiges of merely human strength. Tyndale had spelt out the significance of the deathbed experience in revealing the true spiritual state of the dying:

I have knowen as holy men as might be, as the world counteth holyness, which at the hour of death had no trust in God at all. . . . I have knowen other which were despised, as men that cared not for their divine service, which at death have fallen so flat upon the bloud of Christ as is possible and have preached unto others mightily.[82]

Hence the interest in condemned men shown by Presbyterian divines who flocked to the cells to record deathbed confessions and last-minute conversions. Peter Lake suggests that 'the sheer arbitrariness of God's intervention to save the seemingly damned and damnable young sinners' was a useful tool against Arminianism.[83] However, predestination was less at issue here than the Calvinist doctrine of good works. The incapacity of these hardened criminals for meritorious 'good works' was assumed proven: thus it was by the power of the Holy Spirit alone that they produced Calvinist 'good works'—praise, prayer, and preaching—in the days before their execution. In the context of the deathbed, Tyndale rehearses the conditions for election:

so long as thou findest any consent in thyne hart unto the law of God, that it is righteous and good, and also displeasure that thou canst not fulfil it, dispayre not, neither doubt, but that Gods spirit is in thee, and

---

[81] Oley, *Herbert's Remains*, sig. c8ᵛ.

[82] William Tyndale, *The Whole Workes of W. Tyndall, Iohn Frith, and Doct. Barnes*, 2 vols. (London, 1573), i. 306.

[83] Lake, 'Popular Form, Puritan Content?', 313–34.

that thou art chosen for Christes sake, to the inheritance of eternall lyfe.[84]

Since powerlessness is essential for salvation, successful church-men, including Herbert, might be more disadvantaged than con-demned criminals. Samuel Clarke felt the need to show that his eminent divines had 'fallen as flat uppon the bloud of Christ as is possible' on their deathbeds. This is how the last words of Arch-bishop Ussher are represented:

Lord in special forgive my sins of Omission and yet he was a person never known to omit an hour, yet did he die with this humble expression *Lord forgive my sins of Omission*. A speech that may give us all matter of solemn meditation, and imitation.[85]

The perceived worth of this statement is in its inaccuracy: such an underestimation of the believer's deserts is to be recommended. The function of these utterances is to signify not mere humility, but the total dependence of the human being on Christ. The gap between the Christian's self-deprecation and his actual achieve-ment in the world is the measure of how far he is mortified: how far he is aware that it is God who is working within him. Exactly the same gap in Herbert's estimation of his poetry is recorded by Oley, introducing *The Country Parson* to the reading public:

He had small esteem of this Book, and but very little of his Poems. Though God had magnified him with extraordinary Gifts, yet said he 'God has broken into my Study and taken off my Chariot wheels, I have nothing worthy of God.'

Writers of biography also found it necessary to hint at post-mortem resurrection. The foretaste of heaven that many of their dying subjects received was proof that their mortification was complete. William Gouge was one of many who 'seemed to be in Heaven, even while he was upon the earth'.[86] Nicholas Ferrar's preface to the first edition of *The Temple* is meant to validate Herbert's poetry, rather than his life, but it follows the same strategies. He faithfully quotes Herbert's words of resignation and sacrifice at the mention of his good works, 'it is a good work, if it be sprinkled with the bloud of Christ'.[87] Although

---

[84] Tyndale, *Workes* i. 62.
[85] Samuel Clarke, *A Collection of the Lives of Ten Eminent Divines* (London, 1662), 242.
[86] Ibid. 124.   [87] Herbert, *Works*, 4.

specifically referring to the rebuilding of Leighton Bromswold Church, this is obviously meant to characterize Herbert's general attitude, 'dying to' his good works and leaving it to Christ to sanctify them if He saw fit. The story of Herbert's willingness to burn his poems, carefully reported by Walton, is also important in maintaining the mythology. Like Abraham about to sacrifice his dearest son, Herbert would be seen as utterly mortified and resigned to God's will: he did not need to actually throw the manuscript onto the flames. And like Isaac, the poetry would be considered as saved from the flames and given its life by God. This kind of 'martyrdom of the book' was built into Herbert's deathbed scene as narrated by Barnabas Oley, although the book in question was not *The Temple* but *The Book of Common Prayer*. Oley makes a direct comparison between Herbert dying with the words of the liturgy on his lips and the Marian martyrdom of John Hullier, Vicar of Brabam, who held the Prayer Book as he was burned at the stake. 'The very Book it selfe suffered Martyrdome' comments Oley, clearly exploiting the cycle of death and resurrection to vindicate *The Book of Common Prayer* for a hostile age.[88] The power of Herbert's exemplary life and attitudes as narrated by Ferrar and Oley is shown by the way in which his closest seventeenth-century imitator followed him in constructing himself as a sacred poet. Henry Vaughan, who adopted the subtitle of *The Temple* for his volume *Silex Scintillans* and expressed his devotion to Herbert in the preface, was careful to record experiences both of mortification and disablement. The Latin emblem 'Of himself' finishes 'How wonderful is your might! By dying I live again, and amidst the wreck of my worldly resources, I am now more rich.' The final words of the preface, along with conventional expressions of humility, assert that the volume was almost 'fatherless' as he was near death when he finished it: the readers are clearly expected to assume that the poems are indeed 'Fathered', by a divine rather than a human author.[89]

[88] Oley, *Herberts Remains*, sigs. C3^v-C4^r.

[89] A. Rudrum (ed.), *Henry Vaughan: The Complete Poems*, rev. edn. (London, 1983), 138, 143. Arthur Marotti has traced a similar authorizing example for the secular lyric in the poetry of Philip Sidney, which was presented in the context of the hagiography of its Protestant martyr-poet. See A. Marotti, *Manuscript, Print, and the English Renaissance Lyric* (Ithaca, NY, 1995), 233.

Paradoxically, the tracing of mortification in the lives of their subjects authorizes the writers of exemplary biography to bestow praise. Within the framework of the Christian's mortification it is not human ability that is being glorified, but God's divine power. Barnabas Oley's biography is constructed around Herbert's renunciation of worldly praise and critical acclaim. He carefully reports the opinion of some (obviously unmortified) observers that Herbert had 'lost himself in an humble way'. The Christian reader would interpret this utterance in the light of Jesus' oft-repeated words, 'he that loseth his life for my sake shall find it'.[90] For Barnabas Oley, and for his Christian readers, the worth of the poetry is guaranteed by this kind of sacrifice. Walton posits a crisis of vocation for Herbert out of the competing claims of worldly glory and the service of God: the resulting self-sacrifice is the beginning of 'an almost incredible story, of the great sanctity of the short remainder of his holy life'.[91] Walton's construction of an experience of mortification allows him to proceed with the risky strategy of an 'almost incredible' degree of sanctification. It is perhaps no surprise that this long section of the biography represents Herbert as Walton's ideal priest, justifying every detail of Prayer Book ceremonies with a fanaticism calculated to vindicate the post-Restoration Church, if not characteristic of *The Temple* or *The Country Parson*. David Novarr christens this part of the book 'Isaak Walton's "The Compleat Parson, or, the Religious Man's Occupation"'.[92]

The literary form of exemplary biography, with its emphasis on crisis and the recurring pattern of mortification–vivification, legitimizes the glorification of human behaviour, and thus becomes available for political polemic. Oley and Walton use a particular construction of George Herbert's life for Royalist purposes, whilst Samuel Clarke's volume is intended to vindicate the great Puritan figures of the Interregnum. David Lloyd's emphatically Royalist *Memoires* actually uses Herbert's poetry to structure some of his exemplary Lives.[93] Such representations depend on a kind of

---

[90] Matt. 10: 39, Mark 8: 36, Luke 9: 24.
[91] Walton, *Life of Herbert*, 60.
[92] D. Novarr, *The Making of Walton's* Lives (Ithaca, NY 1958), 322.
[93] David Lloyd, *Memoires of the Lives, Actions, Sufferings & Deaths of those Noble, Reverend and Excellent Personages that suffered Death, Sequestration, Decimation for the Protestant Religion, and the great Principle thereof, Allegiance to their Sovereign, in our late Intestine Wars 1637–1660* (London, 1668), 540, 541, 545.

symbolic economy: the biographical construction of 'mortification' produces a vivification of the text, in that the author's
polemic is authenticated. Jessica Martin posits an even closer
relationship between the textual construction that is biography
and the life of its subject:

> the exemplarity of ecclesiastical narrative should not be seen as by any
> means exclusive to its narrators, but that its subjects should also be
> acknowledged as 'authors' of a kind, shaping the conduct of their lives
> with a regard for the eventual patterning of that conduct into a written
> form, so that lives are lived in order to become Lives.[94]

There is a twentieth-century scepticism implicit here about the
relationship between life and text which is not characteristic of
late Reformation England. Walton expresses a wish that his subjects had 'writ their own lives', and almost makes Herbert a co-
author with him, taking many of his observations from Herbert's
own writing, as David Novarr has shown.[95] Thus Walton has
Herbert say 'I will be sure to live well, because the virtuous life
of a clergyman is the most powerful eloquence to persuade all that
see it to reverence and love'. This sense of life as persuasive text is
taken from Chapter 33 of *The Country Parson*, entitled 'The Parson's Library'. The 'library' is startlingly identified in the first
sentence with the parson's own holy life. Herbert's experience of
temptations overcome is described as 'sermons ready penn'd', a
description that confirms the closeness of experience and textual-
ity suggested by the poems of *The Temple*. Herbert experiences his
life as already written in the patterns of Scriptural story, as 'The
Bunch of Grapes' makes clear, a poem which is itself about the
circle of mortification and vivification. Walton uses as his source-
material for the central structuring experience of renunciation in
his *Life of Herbert* the poem 'The Pearl', in which Herbert has
applied Christ's teaching on mortification to a textual construction of his own life. And of course the Life which serves as the
pattern for all lives, that of Christ, is the recorded story that
Herbert has to copy: it is Christ's cross that he encounters, and
Christ's recorded response that he echoes. Reformation Christians have been taught to fashion their lives according to the book,

[94] J. Martin, 'Isaak Walton and his Precursors: A Literary Study of the Emergence of
the Ecclesiastical *Life*' (Univ. of Cambridge Ph.D. thesis, 1993), 209.
[95] Novarr, *Walton's Lives*, 333–6.

as Stephen Greenblatt's study of the life of James Bainham, executed in 1531, asserts:

one should not, in principle, be able to say where the book stops and identity begins. This absorption of the book at once provides a way of being in the world and shapes the reader's inner life.[96]

A consequence of this profound sense of life as a copy-text is that all Christian biography, and autobiography, follows a familiar structure. Essentially, there is only one story to tell—the story of Christ living His life in believers—and the characteristic motif of a Christ-filled life is death and resurrection.

'To turn his double pains to double praise.'

It is not easy for the Christian to live with the 'double motion' of 'Coloss. 3.3.', or the simultaneous living and dying of 'Mans medley'. At its best, the sanctified life is at the same time self-motivated and divinely willed. Valdés uses the image of writing to express what became the Reformed view of the relative responsibilities:

such a person contents himselfe seeing a letter made with his hand, although not with his industry, attributing the industry to him that guided his hand, and attributing to himselfe the errours that are in the letter.[97]

Although it is the human being who physically performs the writing, all positive effort is attributed to God. This lack of industry is what Valdés elsewhere called 'standing regardlesse', and what Herbert described as 'resting', the experience of prostration described in 'The Priesthood':

> I throw me at his feet . . .
> There will I lie, untill my Maker seek
> For some mean stuffe whereon to show his skill.

Marcantonio Flaminio, the most famous poet in the Valdés circle, and a model for English poets such as Joseph Hall, seems to have annexed this passivity for his own poetics, insisting throughout his career on his inability to write to order, as if his poetic gift were at

---

[96] S. Greenblatt, *Renaissance Self-Fashioning: From More to Shakespeare* (Chicago, 1980), 84.

[97] Valdés, *110 Considerations*, 154. Pemble also uses the metaphor of dual authorship in writing. See *Vindiciae Gratiae*, 32: 'We indeed move our hands to write, but like raw schollers we shall draw mishapen characters, unlesse our heavenly Master guide our hand.'

the disposal of another, more sovereign will.[98] In spite of the writer's lack of control, however, he is still mysteriously to blame for the mistakes in his writing. God has all the power and the human being has all the responsibility, as in the Calvinist (and Valdésian) doctrine of salvation. William Ames, in his magisterial work of Reformed theology, formulated the same idea in rather more technical terms, but without balking at the apparent paradox:

He worketh all in all things, because the Efficiency of all and every thing, depends upon the first cause, not only as touching its substance, but also, as touching all reall circumstances. . . . whatsoever hath any perfection *in genere moris*, in matter of manners, is accounted among the workes of God: but not imperfection or defects.[99]

Thus Herbert takes extraordinary care in poetic composition, as we have shown. He works 'as if' he were the efficient cause of the writing: 'as if' the normal processes of persuasive rhetoric will function and the reader be helped towards a relationship with God. He can do no other: that is the only way to write poetry. Rhetoric is the quintessential human activity, rather than a signifier of the divine. However, Stanley Fish's assessment of Reformation piety and poetics is correct: 'One must do the best that one can while at the same time believing that, unaided, one can do nothing.'[100] Herbert complains about this 'double' trouble in 'Mans medley', and in 'Affliction (i)'. It is the reason why on his deathbed he could not accept praise of his own good works, whether his charitable deeds or the poems of *The Temple*: he was not able to judge whether the dynamic of mortification had operated. Thus to the praise of his 'good works' he replied with another way of formulating the process of mortification: 'it is a good work, if it be sprinkled with the bloud of Christ.'[101]

In Consideration 30 Valdés stages a dialogue with God very much like those of Herbert's lyrics, except that Valdés' God is more forthcoming. Valdés is complaining about the difficulties for the human being caught between divine perfection and human imperfection, and asking to know why God does not finish the job of sanctifying the believer in one glorious gift of the Holy Spirit.

[98] C. Maddison, *Marcantonio Flaminio: Poet, Humanist and Reformer* (London, 1965), 113.
[99] Ames, *Marrow of Divinity*, 22.
[100] S. E. Fish, *The Living Temple: George Herbert and Catechising* (Berkeley, 1978), 160.
[101] Nicholas Ferrar, in the preface to *The Temple*: Herbert, *Works*, 4.

I will, that the spirituall persons labouring, and traveling themselves should submit themselves to believe and to love, and that they should so get iustification, and the holy Spirit; and I will, that they attribute all to me.[102]

This is exactly Herbert's strategy. He works hard to develop a poetry of submission and love, against all precedent: yet he disowns the achievement, attributing anything positive to God Himself. Herbert makes poetry that is both human rhetoric and sacred praise out of his dilemma, thus fulfilling his wish in 'Mans medley':

> Happie is he, whose heart
> Hath found the art
> To turn his double pains to double praise.

Herbert's contemporary readership knew how to read a discourse which resolutely faces the human reader whilst at the same time it gestures towards the divine. They read the poems not only for their verbal rhetoric, but for the traces of divine 'motions', both inviting and restraining ones. As we have seen throughout this study, the awareness of 'motions', with their double force, is what characterizes Herbert's poetry. In its twin movements of empowering and disablement the seventeenth-century reader recognized the characteristic motions of God.

---

[102] Valdés, *110 Considerations*, 71.

CONCLUSION
Poetry, Signification, and Silence

Eventually, all voices in a written dialogic discourse collapse into one rhetorical and typographical surface. Herbert is all too aware that no external voice actually intrudes into his poetry: at least, if it does, it speaks in his own familiar accents. However, he is so committed to the possibility of representation and communication that he is willing to take any risks involved in representing the divine Word in human words. Chapter 7 of *The Country Parson*, 'The Parson Preaching', silently acknowledges that all the Christian orator has is human language. In the Reformation it was nominalist philosophy that brought this awareness to the fore, as Stephen Ozment suggests:

In the final analysis, words are the connecting link between the mind and reality and between the soul and God. Man must come to grips with the world around him through 'signs voluntarily instituted'; and he must work out his salvation on the basis of 'laws voluntarily and contingently established' by God. In the final analysis, all he has is willed verbal relations.[1]

'Willed verbal relations' is a perfect description of Herbert's spirituality. He proceeds 'as if' it is the rhetoric that creates the link between God and man: he has no other option. Words are the medium by which God carries on a relationship with human beings, and in a universe where all things are dictated by God's will, that relationship is crucial for the believer's survival.

Written Scripture demands from human beings a stream of loving discourse that includes prayer and song, however problematic this may be in theory or practice: as Herbert affirms in a poem that shows full awareness of the difficulties of composition, 'The Altar':

> if I chance to hold my peace,
> These stones to praise thee may not cease.

[1] S. Ozment, 'Mysticism, Nominalism and Dissent', in W. Trinkaus and H. Oberman (eds.), *The Pursuit of Holiness* (Leiden, 1974), 80.

In fact, the anxieties that many critical works, including this one, meticulously chart represent only a fraction of Herbert's poetic output. Most of the time he writes as if he were as optimistic about the use of human rhetoric as St François de Sales. Poems such as 'Mattens', 'Even-song', 'Constancie', and 'Sunday' do not falter in their assumption that poetic form is perfectly suitable for divine subject-matter. In this apparent inconsistency, however, Herbert is not alone amongst Reformed writers. William Pemble was extremely rigorous in his stance against sacred rhetoric in his 1627 volume *Vindiciae Gratiae*:

> most unhandsomely doth this Rhetorick suite with such as plead God's cause before mortall men, who if they will acknowledge their allea-geance must yeeld attention upon a Sic dicit Dominus, without further art.[2]

Yet the very same William Pemble wrote an *Enchiridion Oratorium*, a handbook for orators, because of the parlous state of ordinary language. Rhetoric has the ability to heal, and to recover the truth from its diseased state. This is close to Cicero's formulation of the need for rhetoric to do a public relations job on reality:

> there can be no doubt that reality beats imitation in everything, and if reality unaided were sufficiently effective in presentation, we should have no need at all for art. But because emotion, which mostly has to be displayed or counterfeited by action, is often so confused as to be obscured and almost smothered out of sight, we have to dispel the things that obscure it and take up its prominent and striking points.[3]

This is a role for rhetoric compatible with the most severe concern for truth: rhetoric is able to salvage the truth from the distracting mess that is reality. As Anne Southwell writes in around 1616, defending poetry against the familiar charge that it is fiction:

> Nor marres it truth, but gives wittes fire more fuel
> And from an Ingott formes a curious Jewell.[4]

Of course, there is a precedent for the successful use of rhetoric to convey divine truth. Not only, as Donne observed, was God

---

[2] William Pemble, *Vindiciae Gratiae, er, a Plea For Grace* (London, 1627), 17.
[3] Cicero, *De oratore*, tr. E. W. Sutton (London, 1952), 215.
[4] Anne Southwell, Folger MS V. b. 198, fo. 161.

'content to take a *body*': he was content to incarnate his divine Word in human poetry. It is possibly the example of the Bible that gives Herbert his greatest inspiration. Certainly, the reading of the Scriptures is for Herbert a place where the power of rhetoric and the power of Spirit meet, and the result is almost literally explosive. We have seen how a 'motion' from God came in the form of a falling star, in 'Artillerie': the spiritual and rhetorical motions of Scripture have a far more penetrative effect. The experience is most vividly described in the Latin poem on the Bible, 'In S. Scripturas'. The internal movement produced by the reading of Scripture is so violent that Herbert asks whether he has swallowed a falling star. He then goes on to chart its progress through his innermost psyche, in architectural terms:

> Most Holy Writ, it's you who've traveled through
> All the dark nooks and hidden pleats
> Of the heart, the alleys and the curves
> Of flying passion. Ah, how wise and skilled you are
> To slip through these paths, windings, knots.[5]

It is the power of the Holy Spirit which makes this rhetoric so effective: the poem concludes 'the spirit that built the building knows it best'. Stars and effective discourse are closely connected in Herbert's poetry. The Scripture is described as 'a book of starres'. In 'The Storm' the stars are seen as being able to prevail with God: Herbert imagines a repentant conscience having the same force. In 'The Starre' the poet envisages stars as beings which are able to praise God worthily: he asks to be purified within by their workings and take his place in the heavenly praise. The secret of the link between stars and effective rhetoric seems to be in the 'trinitie' of 'light, motion and heat' which makes up a star. All three words are appropriate for the sort of rhetoric Herbert longs for: light, to bring wisdom: motion, to be effective: heat, to kindle love.

However, although stars which fall from heaven, motions from God, are always effective, would-be stars who take aim from earth do not always reach their objective. 'The Answer' seems to describe Herbert's own career in oratory. He describes his ambition

---

[5] George Herbert, *The Works of George Herbert*, ed. F. E. Hutchinson (Oxford, 1945), 411; *The Latin Poetry of George Herbert: A Bilingual Edition*, tr. M. McCloskey and P. R. Murphy (Athens, Oh., 1965), 85.

as a 'young exhalation' which 'means the sky': however, the magic formula of light, motion, and heat gradually deserts him.

> But cooling by the way, grows pursie and slow,
> And setling to a cloud, doth live and die
> In that dark state of tears.

The poem is an enigmatic one, which ends with a riddle. It seems that Herbert's career only looks like a failure from the outside: it is the false estimation of contemporaries such as those Barnabas Oley spoke to whom he would like to answer.[6] However, the answer is not forthcoming.

> To all, that so
> Show me, and set me, I have one reply,
> Which they that know the rest, know more then I.

This conundrum can perhaps be solved by looking at other poems in *The Temple*. The only other poem in which Herbert has deferred his answer to mocking onlookers who think his career has foundered is 'The Quip'. In that poem it is God who is to supply the answer, which is very simple. To belong to God is worth more than any of the earthly distinctions offered by 'the merrie world'. Here, the answer is known only by those 'that know the rest'. The word 'rest' is played on in other poems in *The Temple*, such as 'The Pulley'. Here, as there, it has the sense of 'everything else': it seems that there are some who know the full story, and not just the pathetic history recounted in this poem. But there is the other significance of 'rest', with more profound implications for the Christian poet. As we have seen, the 'rest' is the result of mortification. It is possible that God will allow the words, the works, the rhetorical career, to fail, in order to pursue His own mysterious purposes. The poet does not have an answer to the apparent disjunction between expectation and performance in his career. All he knows is that there is a reason, and that those who are also following the way of the Cross will understand. Finally he has to accept the inadequacy or failure of signification as in 'The Forerunners', which also takes the form of an ageing poet meditating upon possible failure.

---

[6] 'I have heard sober men censure him as a man that did not manage his brave parts to his best advantage and preferment, but lost himself *in an humble way*': Barnabas Oley (ed.), *Herberts Remains, Or, Sundry Pieces of that Sweet Singer of the Temple Mr. G. H.* (London, 1652), sig. b7ʳ.

> Go birds of spring: let winter have his fee;
> Let a bleak paleness chalk the doore,
> So all within be livelier than before.

The writing that means death is not the whole truth for the Christian poet whose rhetorical powers are failing. However, the poem 'The Answer' does 'die', in that it goes silent at the point when words are expected in the logic of the argument. In fact, the answer of the title is silence itself.[7] Silence, as Henry King said, is 'a kind of death', particularly to a poet.[8]

In spiritual terms, the Temple is never built. Never is Herbert allowed to feel he has achieved anything in terms of personal holiness, or consistent relationship with God.[9] However, the process of continual mortification militates against any permanent steps forward: 'in this regard progress is properly the recognition of our lack of progress.'[10] By the end of *The Temple*, Herbert is no further forward than he was at the beginning: in the final lyric he has still to learn to be quiet, and to rest. *The Temple* ends with a moment of silence that leads to the life-giving activity of eating: but unless the banquet being described is the heavenly one, that moment is only a temporary respite.

Strangely, it seems that the only constructive enterprise going on throughout *The Temple* is a verbal one. The poet remains trapped in the vicious circle described graphically in 'Sinnes round', which deals with the futility of human attempts at construction. Poetic discourse is deeply implicated in this activity, as Ernest B. Gilman shows: 'its "perfected...draughts" are not in the end completed drawings for a stable structure, but, in a parody of poetic inspiration, the hot winds that will fan the fire

---

[7] Louis Martz thinks that 'he, and we, know the answer: it has already been given in "The Quip"': *The Poetry of Meditation: A Study in English Religious Literature of the Seventeenth Century* (New Haven, 1962), 312. If this is so, the answer is still the poet's silence.

[8] Henry King, 'Silence: A Sonnet', in *The New Oxford Book of Seventeenth-Century Verse*, ed. A. Fowler (Oxford, 1992), 292.

[9] A. D. Weiner, in *Sir Philip Sidney and the Poetics of Protestantism* (Minneapolis, 1978), 15–16 describes this pattern and suggests that holiness for the Protestant consists in this continual failure and repentance. Ilona Bell, in 'Herbert's Valdésian Vision', *ELR* 17 (1987), 303–28 rightly perceives a link between the structure of *The Hundred and Ten Considerations* and that of *The Temple* but wrongly finds spiritual progress in both discourses. This is, I think, to ignore the presence of dark poems such as 'Discipline' towards the very end of *The Temple*.

[10] W. Niesel, *The Theology of Calvin*, tr. H. Knight (Philadelphia, 1956), 129. Quoted in G. E. Veith Jr., *Reformation Spirituality: The Religion of George Herbert* (Lewisburg, Pa., 1985), 134.

of his words.'[11] The words become the fiery, destructive exhalations of a volcano. The explicit comparison is with the tower of Babel, and the language of the poet must suffer the same fate as that of the builders of the tower, to be confounded: the poem is condemned to repeat itself endlessly, building and rebuilding a verbal structure three stanzas and 'three stories' high which is brought to nothing by the end of the poem. All that remains is the verbal structure which charts this process.

Not all Herbert's poetry is this kind of 'self-consuming artefact', but when he is able to construct a successful poem, such as 'The Flower', the success is only temporary. His situation as represented in these poems is identical to Adam's in *Paradise Lost*. After the Fall Adam is able to make a repentant and therefore righteous speech to God, acceptable to the Son at any rate. However, Milton has already explained that this speech is actually the product of 'prevenient grace', 'implanted' in Adam by God.[12] God patiently explains to Christ and the rest of the heavenly company (just in case they should feel that Adam is hard done by):

> He sorrows now, repents, and prays contrite,
> My motions now, longer than they move,
> His heart I know, how variable and vain
> Self-left.[13]

This would seem like a no-win situation for Adam: his sin is his own responsibility, his righteous acts are to God's credit. This double bind is the reason why no spiritual progress occurs in *The Temple*. As soon as the motions of God cease, the Christian, 'self-left', lapses into failure again, a frustration which is expressed in 'The Temper (ii)' and 'The Glimpse'. This is the Valdésian vision, which makes moment-by-moment self-scrutiny essential: such severity of self-criticism is the norm in *The Temple*.

Milton claims that his sacred poetry is the product of divine inspiration. In his scheme for poetic composition, which collapses human rhetoric and divine motions, that is the only authorship model possible. However, Herbert does not make such claims for the poetry of *The Temple*. Although the consistent message of the

---

[11] E. B. Gilman, *Iconoclasm and Poetry in the English Reformation: Down Went Dagon* (Chicago, 1986), 56–9.

[12] John Milton, *Paradise Lost*, ed. A. Fowler (Harlow, 1971), 563.

[13] Ibid. 568–9.

poetry is that no human action is worthy of God, the human rhetoric in which the message is couched is allowed to stand. There are a few half-hearted gestures in the direction of the possibility of inspiration, as we have seen. There are also more imaginatively realized motions in the opposite direction: that the entire poetic enterprise is invalid and that the better option is inarticulate gasps, plain-style prose, or silence. On the whole, however, Herbert operates as if his human rhetoric is sanctioned, and indeed, uses rhetorical strategies which give the impression of validating the poetry.

We have looked at those poems which posit two separate discourses within Herbert's poetry, one human and fallible, one authoritative and possibly divine. The intention seems to be that the latter should validate the former: if Herbert is open to God's correction in his poetry, the poems which experience no such correction must be divinely sanctioned. Of course, Herbert is only too aware that this in itself is a rhetorical strategy. Paradoxically, what the so-called 'corrections' do achieve is a highlighting of the anxiety about poetic authorship that permeates *The Temple*. If we are to believe Isaak Walton's anecdote about Herbert's deathbed speech, his anxiety is focused on the well-being of his prospective readership. 'Obedience' discusses one kind of reading which is the best possible response to the poetry as far as its author is concerned. It begins with an admission of the doubtful status of writing in God's eyes, and of the inadequacy of 'this poore paper' in particular. Herbert insists in stanza two that this poem is entirely functional, deeply sincere and without unnecessary rhetoric:

> my heart doth bleed
> As many lines, as there doth need
> To passe it self and all it hath to thee.

By the end of the poem, however, Herbert has dared to express his deepest ambition as a sacred poet:

> How happie were my part,
> If some kind man would thrust his heart
> Into these lines!

Herbert represents the reader's optimum response as a condescending but whole-hearted endorsement: the physical motion of 'thrust' implies the spiritual motion that caused it. This extra-rhetorical criterion would ultimately validate his lines, so much so that they would be permanently written in heaven, a distinction that is 'farre above their desert' as human words.

By drawing attention to the impossibility of a self-validating discourse, Herbert in fact puts responsibility onto the reader: it is the reader's response to the poetry which will validate it as spiritual discourse. Thus Herbert supplies the careful reader of *The Temple* with the rationale which could utterly undermine it. In the end, however, Herbert seems to have been afraid to trust his prospective readers with the discernment to judge his poetry correctly, for fear of harming them in some way. Instead, he put it through the ultimate, extra-rhetorical test. Having entrusted the carefully revised version of *The Temple* to Nicholas Ferrar he gave his friend the choice whether to publish the volume, making the criterion for publishing the possible benefit to readers. Herbert apparently posited the alternative to publication as destruction by fire, which seems to have been Nicholas Ferrar's favoured treatment for unedifying poetry: he burned all his secular books just before his death. In this way, Herbert was submitting to his friend's spiritual judgement, to a guiding 'motion' from God acting in Ferrar. Fortunately, Ferrar seems to have felt a 'restraining motion' about burning the manuscript, and an 'inviting motion' about publishing it: thus the poems survived the ordeal of their author's spiritual mortification and physical death.

A Model for a Mortified Poet

Herbert is only too aware of the dilemmas and contradictions embodied in the various models of Christian authorship available to him. Spiritual authorship in *The Hundred and Ten Considerations* seems to require a kind of 'automatic writing': in Savonarola's works it demands a faith in the ability of human words to represent the divine. Herbert is too literary a man to consider the first, and too humble a man to believe the second. Instead, he takes up a position absolutely in the middle of the continuum which identifies God's purposes and human rhetoric at the one end, and at the other makes words of any sort unnecessary. Janus-like, his poetry is open to both extremes. Most of the time he operates as if rhetorical and spiritual motion can be identified, even, as we have seen, to the extent of mimicking divine motion in his poetry: he is daring enough to use the deepest spiritual operation of Calvinist theology as a trope. Lest this simulation should be seen as duplicitous there are constant protestations of sincerity and constant references to the glory of God, which according to the gospel of John are an authentic sign of sincerity: 'He that speaketh of himself seeketh his own glory: but he that seeketh his glory that sent him, the same is true, and no unrighteousness is in him.'[14] However, for a non-Arminian Protestant, the only way to validate any 'good work', including a poem, is, as Herbert reportedly declared on his deathbed, to sprinkle it with the blood of Christ: to make it undergo a baptism of death to the self-serving purposes of human authorship. In literary terms, this means that his poems are always apparently open to being altered, or curtailed, by a divine editor. However, the very fact that Herbert represents the original writing as well as the divine correction again reduces it to an authorizing sign not by the divine, but by the human author. In the end, the work has to be subjected to a non-literary test. If it is godly, it will bring its readers closer to God. It seems that Herbert subjected his volume to the spiritual judgement of Nicholas Ferrar, and thus to the possibility of a 'restraining motion' from God when Ferrar considered publishing it. The alternative to publication is the burning of the poetry, which is the reduction of the poet to complete silence. This experience of absolute mortification of the poetic gift must always remain an option.

The particular dilemma of the Reformation poet is horrifyingly encapsulated in a poem that was left out of *The Temple*, possibly because it would make too much disturbance there. The title of the poem explicitly refers to one of the key doctrines of Calvinism, and one that was discussed at Dort, the perseverance of the saints. 'Perseverance' is a poem about authorship that demands to be read in a particular theological context. It is about 'motion': the motion towards authorship by the author, and the movement of the author by God which is inspiration. But it is also about that other type of motion, from the Catechism which prefaced the Geneva Bible, the saving motion which is meant to guarantee the perseverance of the saints. The position of 'Perseverance' in

---

[14] John 7: 18.

the Williams manuscript is interesting: it is placed two poems after 'Invention', that poem of poetic anxiety that became 'Jordan (ii)', and subsequent to 'Perfection', which in the final version of *The Temple* became 'The Elixir'. 'The Elixir' offers an easy solution to Herbert's problem of spiritual authorship, a baptism of human effort into something 'which God doth touch and own' simply through doing everything for God's sake. In the B manuscript it is then followed by 'A Wreath', which replaces 'Perseverance' in the sequence just before Herbert's meditation on the last four things: 'Death', 'Dooms-day', 'Judgement', and 'Heaven'. 'A Wreath', like 'Perseverance', deals with authorship, but in the relatively simple terms of avoiding deceit and adhering to simplicity. Although the poem itself is not simplistic—it is particularly complex and subtle—it is far more positive than 'Perseverance'. All in all, the original sequence in the W manuscript represents Christian authorship in far more problematic terms. 'Perfection' envisages real difficulties finding 'works' which avoid error, and please God. By the end of the poem no real solution has been posed except rigid self-scrutiny and honesty:

> Happy are they that dare
> Lett in the Light to all their actions
> And show them as they are.

'Perseverance' is just such a ruthlessly honest poem. Every authorship theory represented in the devotional treatises we have considered is represented here. First of all, poetry is described as a dish prepared for God's pleasure by the author, given warmth and savour by the emotion in his heart, very much after the manner of acceptable Christian discourse posited by St François de Sales. However, the poet immediately corrects his proposition: he himself is not the originator of his poems.

> My God, the poore expressions of my Love
> Which warme these lines & serve them vp to thee
> Are so, as for the present I did moue,
> Or rather as thou mouedst mee.

This soothing identification of the impulse towards authorship and the authorizing impulse is utterly disrupted in the rest of the poem. The possibility is raised that the words he has written may well help another: as we have seen, in Walton's account of the serene deathbed discourse, this criterion was regarded as the genuine sign of spiritual authorship.

Not so in this dark poem. There is no genuine chain of causality here. The poems can be at the same time another's salvation and his own damnation. Ullrich Langer locates the increased authorial freedom of the Renaissance in the late scholastic, nominalist philosophy which undermined the hierarchical and mediated view of causality. God could intervene at any point in the causal chain: therefore in one sense God was the immediate cause of everything. As Ullrich Langer concludes, 'God causes everything, but one may also say that he causes nothing, from the point of view of the reasoning creature.'[15] Langer's thesis is that such a paradigm shift made possible the increased authority of the author in the Renaissance period: the author was now free to create alongside God. However, it is possible to argue the reverse. If God is the immediate cause of everything, He can intervene at any stage in the authorial process, rather than being relegated to one end of the chain as in scholastic philosophy. This would actually reduce the authority of the author over his own creation. Because God can interfere at any point in the literary process, as nominalist philosophy posited, He could inspire a godly reading of poetry, even if it sprang from an essentially self-aggrandizing and therefore sinful impulse. This would represent the grace of God intervening to bring good out of evil, as Herbert described in the original version of 'Perfection':

> And when the Divel shakes ye tree
> Thou saist, this fruit is mine.

Thus, the perceived beneficial effect of a poem is not a trustworthy sign of its godly authorship. The image for Herbert's own poetry here is a startlingly destructive one, that of a faulty gun: 'As a burst fouling-peece doth saue the birds | But kill the man.' The poem, it seems, is beneficial to its intended readers—its prey, if you like—only in so far as it does not fulfil the intentions of the author. It must destroy both itself and the poet.

So the corrective to Herbert's view of his own authorship—that God moved him to it—becomes deeply problematic. How can

---

[15] U. Langer, *Divine and Poetic Freedom in the Renaissance: Nominalist Theology and Literature in France and Italy* (Princeton, 1990), 91.

something which is originally inspired by God become the agent of the author's destruction? Where was the godly chain of causation disrupted? The answer is in line 3, in the passage of time. There is a time difference between the writing of the poem and the reading of the poem, and even in that gap sin and self can operate. Of course, the words of the poem will not change over time: but maybe the spiritual virtue of literature is actually not in the words at all, as Valdés suggested, but in the way God uses them. In the end there is no way to guarantee the godliness of writing: not the holiness of the author, nor the sense of inspiration at the start of the process, nor even the beneficial effect to the reader at the end. The human language which connects intention to effect is irremediably corrupt: the chain of signification has been disrupted for ever.

In stanza three this dilemma of authorship becomes a symbol of the wider problem for a Calvinist: how to be assured of his salvation. It appears that the subtle insinuations of sin into the process of authorship, of which Herbert is all too conscious, have the effect of alerting him to the possibility of similar disruption in his spiritual life, a disruption which may have fatal consequences for him. 'The Answer' has already raised the spectre of possible reprobation. The image of the meteor which dominates that poem is used in seventeenth-century Calvinism for that most cruelly deceptive of spiritual phenomena, temporary grace. Samuel Ward posits this distinction between truly spiritual Christians and their counterfeits:

such as proove falling starres, never were ought but meteors; the other never lose light and motion: spirituall motions may be violent and perpetuall.[16]

Herbert had noted the violence of these motions, the genuine stars, in his poem 'The Storm'. However, the key word in this formulation is 'perpetuall'. A genuine calling will show itself in the ability to endure and it is just this ability which is in doubt in 'Perseverance'. There is no solution to the problem posed in this poem, merely a statement of all there is left for the Christian author to do. There are only two 'motions' left to him, one verbal,

[16] Samuel Ward, *A Collection of such sermons as have been written and published* (London, 1636), 269.

279

one non-verbal. He will continue to exhaust all the resources of human discourse: he will trust in the promises of God and use that most powerful rhetorical tactic, 'crying without cease'. The other activity, represented in vividly physical terms, is the equivalent of a non-verbal motion. There is a desperate act of will represented here, as of someone clinging to the edge of a precipice by his fingertips.

> Onely my soule hangs on thy promises
> With face and hands clinging unto thy breast.

The content of the final cry is significant: Christ represents for the believer both physical and spiritual security. Physical security is in Christ as rock: spiritual security is in Christ as 'rest'. The 'rest' of God, when the believer ceases from his own works and words, represents the ultimate security for the Christian poet. It may mean falling silent, or even dying. It is no coincidence that in the Williams manuscript the 'rest' is the last word uttered before physical death, which is confronted in the following poem. However, as Baxter notes, 'rest' is promised 'only to persevering Believers': and perseverance in this poem is problematic.[17] Silence was the intended fate of this poem. Herbert's revisionary 'motions' did not allow utterance to such a dark vision. For the Christian poet the rest may, literally, be silence.

[17] Richard Baxter, *The Saints Everlasting Rest*, 2nd edn. (London, 1651), 4.

SELECT BIBLIOGRAPHY

Manuscript Sources

Bodleian MS Tanner 67.
Bodleian MS Tanner 72.
Bodleian MS Tanner 307.
Bodleian MS Tanner 456.
British Library MS Lansdowne 740.
Folger MS V. a. 162.
Folger MS V. b. 198.

Primary Sources

AMES, WILLIAM, *The Marrow of sacred Divinity, drawne out of the holy Scriptures, and the Interpreters therof, and brought into Method* (London, 1642).

ARTHINGTON, HENRIE, *The Seduction of Arthington by Hacket especiallie, with some tokens of his unfained repentance and Submission* (London, 1592).

AUGUSTINE, *St. Augustine's Prayers*, tr. Henry Denham (London, 1581).

—— *On Christian Doctrine*, tr. D. W. Robertson Jr. (New York, 1958).

B., H., *Grounds of Christian Religion Laid downe briefly and plainely by way of Question and Answer* (London, 1633).

BALINGHEM, ANTONIO DE, SJ, *Pia Mentis in Deum Libratio Per Breves Orationes Et Ardentes Ad Eum Aspirationes* (Antwerp, 1624).

BALL, JOHN, *A Short Treatise Contayning all the Principall Grounds of Christian Religion By way of Questions and Answers, very profitable for all men, but especially for Householders*, 10th edn. (London, 1635).

DU BARTAS, G., *L'Uranie ou Muse Céleste de G. de Saluste, Seigneur du Bartas* (London, 1589).

BAXTER, RICHARD, *The Saints Everlasting Rest*, 2nd edn. (London, 1651).

BAYLY, LEWIS, *The Practice of Pietie: directing a Christian howe to walke that he may blesse God*, 28th edn. (London, 1631).

BAYNE, PAUL, *Holy Soliloquies, of A Holy Helper in God's building*, 2nd edn. (London, 1618).

BENEDETTO OF MANTUA, *The Benefite that Christians receive by Jesus Christ Crucifyed*, tr. A. G. [prob. Arthur Golding] (London, 1573).

—— *The Benefite that Christians receyue by Iesus Christ crucified, translated from the French by A. G.* [prob. Arthur Golding] (London, 1575).

BEZA, THEODORE, *Poemata*, ed. George Buchanan (Paris, 1576).

BILLINGSLEY, NICHOLAS, *A Treasure of Divine Raptures: Serious Observations, Pious Ejaculations and Select Epigrams* (London, 1667).

BILLIUS, JACOBUS, *Anthologia sacra* (Paris, 1575).

BLOSIUS, *Institutio Spiritualis*, in *Omnia Opera* (Antwerp, 1632).

—— *The Manual of the Spiritual Life* (London, 1871).

BONA, IOANNIS, *Opera Omnia* (Antwerp, 1777).

A breefe Catechisme so necessarie and easie to be learned even of the symple sort, that whosever can not or will not attayne to the same, is not to be counted a good Christian, much lesse to be admitted to the Supper of the Lorde (London, 1576).

BURTON, HENRY, *The Christians Bulwarke, Against Satans Battery. Or, The Doctrine of Justification* (London, 1632).

CALVIN, JOHN, *The Institution of the Christian Religion*, tr. Thomas Norton (London, 1578).

Carmina Quinque Illustrium Poetarum: Petrus Bembus, Andreas Naugerius, Balthassar Castilioni, John Coltas, Marcantonio Flaminio (Venice, 1548).

A Catechisme or Briefe Instruction in the Principles and Grounds of the true Christian Religion (London, 1617).

CICERO, *De oratore*, tr. E. W. Sutton (London, 1952).

The Cloud of Unknowing, ed. P. Hodgson, Early English Text Society (Oxford, 1957).

The Confession of Faith and Catechisms Agreed upon by the Assembly of Divines at Westminster (London, 1650).

COSIN, JOHN, *A Collection of Private Devotions or The Houres of Prayer* (London, 1627).

DENT, ARTHUR, *The Plaine Mans Path-way to Heaven, wherin every man may cleerly see whether he shall be saved or damned*, 13th imp. (London, 1611).

DERING, EDWARD, *A bryefe and necessary Catechisme or Instruction* (London, 1577).

DUPLESSIS-MORNAY, PHILIPPE, *Philip Mornay, Lord of Plessis, his Teares for the death of his Sonne. Vnto his wife Charlotte Baliste. Englished by Iohn Healey* (London, 1609).

EGERTON, STEPHEN, *A Briefe Methode of Catechising* (London, 1615).

ESTELLA, DIEGO DE, *Livre de la vanité du monde*, tr. G. Chappuys (Paris, 1587).

FERRAR, NICHOLAS, *The Ferrar Papers, Containing a Life of Nicholas Ferrar; The Winding-Sheet: An Ascetic Dialogue: A Collection of Short Moral Histories; A Selection of Family Letters*, ed. B. Blackstone (Cambridge, 1938).

FLAMINIO, MARCANTONIO, *Carminum Libri IIII* (Florence, 1552).

FLAVEL, JOHN, *Husbandry Spiritualized: Or, The Heavenly Use of Earthly Things* (London, 1669).

FLETCHER, GILES, and FLETCHER, PHINEAS, *Giles and Phineas Fletcher: Poetical Works*, ed. F. S. Boas, 2 vols. (Cambridge, 1908).

Flowers of Kendalls Epigrams, out of sundrie the moste singular authors selected, as well auncient as late writers (Oxford, 1577).

GASCOIGNE, GEORGE, *The Poesies*, ed. J. W. Cunliffe (Cambridge, 1907).

GOODWIN, JOHN, *Redemption Redeemed* (London, 1651).

GOUGE, WILLIAM, *A short Catechisme, wherein are briefly handled the fundamental principles of Christian Religion. Needful to be knowne by all Christians before they be admitted to the Lords Table*, 7th edn. (London, 1635).

GRANADA, LUIS DE, *Le Vray chemin*, tr. F. de Belleforest (Paris, 1579).

—— *Granados Devotion, Exactly Teaching how a man may truely dedicate and deuote himself vnto God: and so become his acceptable Votary*, tr. Francis Meres (London, 1598).

—— *Spiritual and heauenlie Exercises* (London, 1598).

HALL, JOSEPH, *The Collected Poems of Joseph Hall*, ed. A. Davenport (Liverpool, 1949).

HARINGTON, JOHN, *The Letters and Epigrams of Sir John Harington*, ed. N. E. McClure (Philadelphia, 1930).

HARVEY, CHRISTOPHER, *The Synagogue, or The Shadow of The Temple: Sacred Poems and Private Ejaculations in imitation of Mr. George Herbert*, 2nd rev. edn. (London, 1647).

HAYWARD, JOHN, *David's teares* (London, 1622).

HEMMINGE, NICHOLAS, *The Preacher, or Methode of preaching*, tr. John Horsfall (London, 1574).

HERBERT, GEORGE, *The Temple, Sacred Poems and Private Ejaculations*, ed. Thomas Buck (Cambridge, 1633).

—— *The Works of George Herbert*, ed. F. E. Hutchinson, corrected edn. (Oxford, 1945).

—— *The Latin Poetry of George Herbert: A Bilingual Edition*, tr. M. McCloskey and P. R. Murphy (Athens, Oh., 1965).

—— *The Williams MS of George Herbert's Poems: A Facsimile*, introd. by A. M. Charles (Delmar, NY, 1979).

—— *The Bodleian MS of George Herbert's Poems: A Facsimile of Tanner 307*, ed. with introd. by A. M. Charles and M. A. Di Cesare (Delmar, NY, 1984).

HEYWOOD, THOMAS, *Pleasant Dialogues and Dramma's, selected out of Lucan, Erasmus, Textor, Ovid* (London, 1637).

HOWELL, JAMES, *Instructions for Forreine Travell* (London, 1650).

HYPERIUS, ANDREAS, *The Practise of preaching, otherwise called the Pathway to the Pulpit: conteyning an excellent Method how to frame Divine Sermons & to interpret the Holy Scriptures according to the capacitie of the vulgar people. First written in Latin by the learned pastor of Christ Church, D. Andreas Hyperius; and now lately (to the profit of the same Church) Englished by Iohn Ludham, vicar of Wetherffeld* (London, 1577).

JEWELL, JOHN, *The Works*, ed. R. W. Jelf (Oxford, 1848).

LAUD, WILLIAM, *The History of thee Troubles and Tryal of the Most Reverend Father in God, and Blessed Martyr, William Laud, Wrote by Himself* (London, 1695).

LEIGHTON, WILLIAM, *The Teares, or Lamentations of a sorrowfull Soule* (London, 1613).

LLOYD, DAVID, *Memoires of the Lives, Actions, Sufferings & Deaths of those Noble, Reverend and Excellent Personages that suffered Death, Sequestration, Decimation for the Protestant Religion, and the great Principle thereof, Allegiance to their Sovereign, in our late Intestine Wars 1637–1660* (London, 1668).

LOK, HENRY, *Sundry Christian Passions Contained in two hundred Sonnets* (London, 1593).

LUCAS, FRANCISCUS, *In Sacrosancta quatuor Evangelia F. Lucae Brugensis Commentarius, Alia ad S. Scripturae lucem opuscula* (Antwerp, 1606).

MCFARLANE, I. D. (ed.), *Renaissance Latin Poetry* (Manchester, 1980).

MELANCHTHON, PHILIP, *Loci Communes* (Wittenberg, 1521).

—— *Liber Rhetorices Libri Duo*, tr. and ed. Sister J. M. Lafontaine (Univ. of Michigan Ph.D. diss., 1968).

MONTAGU, RICHARD, *A Gagg for the New Gospell? No. A New Gagg for an Old Goose* (London, 1624).

MORE, THOMAS, *The second parte of the confutacion of Tyndale's answere* (London, 1533).

MOURGUES, O. DE (ed.), *Anthology of French Seventeenth-Century Lyric Poetry* (Oxford, 1960).

NORTON, JOHN, *The Orthodox Evangelist or a Treatise wherein many Great Evangelical Truths (Not a few whereof are much opposed and Eclipsed in this perillous houre of the Passion of the Gospel) Are briefly Discussed, cleared, and confirmed. As a further help, for the Begeting, and Establishing of the Faith which is in Jesus* (London, 1654).

NOWELL, ALEXANDER, *A Catechism, or first Instruction and Learning of Christian Religion* (London, 1570).

OLEY, BARNABAS (ed.), *Herberts Remains, Or, Sundry Pieces of that Sweet Singer of the Temple Mr. G. H., sometime Orator of the University of Cambridge, Now exposed to Public Light* (London, 1652).

PARR, ELNATHAN, *Abba Father* (London, 1618).

PEACHAM, HENRY, *The Garden of Eloquence* (London, 1577).

PEMBLE, WILLIAM, *Vindiciae Fidei, or a Treatise of Justification by Faith* (Oxford, 1625).

—— *Vindiciae Gratiae, or, a Plea for Grace* (London, 1627).

—— *Enchiridion Oratorium* (Oxford, 1633).

PERKINS, WILLIAM, *The Arte of Prophesying* (London, 1592).

—— *A Treatise, tending unto a Declaration, whether a man be in the estate of damnation, or in the estate of grace* (London, 1592).

——*An Exposition of the Symbole or Crede of the Apostles* (Cambridge, 1596).

—— *Two Treatises* (London, 1611).

PRYNNE, WILLIAM, *The Perpetuitie of a Regenerate Mans Estate* (London, 1626).

PUTTENHAM, GEORGE, *The Arte of English Poesie*, ed. G. D. Willcock and A. Walker (Cambridge, 1936).

QUARLES, JOHN, *Gods Love and Mans Unworthiness* (London, 1651).

QUINTILIAN, *Institutio Oratoria*, tr. H. E. Butler, 4 vols. (London, 1921).

READING, JOHN, *Davids Soliloquie conteining many comforts for afflicted minds* (London, 1627).

REVSNERI, NICOLAI (ed.), *Aenigmatographia sive sylloge Aenigmatum et griphorum convivalum* (Frankfurt, 1599).

RICH, JEREMIAH, *Mellificium Musarum: The Marrow of the Muses. Or, An Epitome of Divine Poetrie, Distilled into Pious Ejaculations and Solemne Soliloquies* (London, 1650).

ROGERS, RICHARD, *A Garden of Spirituall Flowers* (London, 1609).

ROUS, FRANCIS, *The Diseases of the Time Attended by their Remedies* (London, 1622).

—— *The Onely Remedy, that can cure a people, when all other Remedies faile* (London, 1627).

RUTHERFORD, SAMUEL, *A Survey of the Spiritual Antichrist, Opening the Secrets of Familisme and Antinomianisme in the Antichristian Doctrine of John Saltmarsh, and Will. Del, the Present Preachers of the Army now in England, and of Robert Town; Tob. Crisp, H. Denne, Eaton, and others. In Two Parts* (London, 1648).

SALES, ST FRANÇOIS DE, *An Introduction to the Devoute Life, composed in Frenche by the R. Father in God Francis Sales, bishop of Geneva, and translated into English by I. Y.* (Douai, 1613).

—— *An Introduction to a Devout Life, Translated and Reformed from the Errors of the Popish Edition, To which is perfixed [sic] A Discourse, of the Rise and Progress of the Spiritual Books in the Romish Church*, ed. William Nicholls D. D. (London, 1701).

—— *Letters to Persons in the World*, Library of St. Francis de Sales, i, ed. Revd H. B. Mackey, OSB (London, 1882).

—— *The Catholic Controversy: Treatise Written to the Calvinists of the Chablais*, Library of St. Francis de Sales, iii, ed. Revd H. B. Mackey, OSB (London, 1886).

—— *The Spirit of St. Francis de Sales, by his friend Jean Pierre Camus, bishop of Belley*, tr. J. S. (London, 1910).

—— *Œuvres de Saint François de Sales: Édition complète*, 12 vols. (Annecy, 1912).

SAVONAROLA, JÉRÔME, *Apologeticus De Ratione Poeticae Artis*, in *Compendium philosophia et alia* (Venice, 1534).

—— *De Simplicitate Christianae Vitae* (Strasburg, 1615).

—— *The Felicity of a Christian Life by Hierome Savonarola, in Five Treatises* (London, 1651).

—— *La Fonction de la poésie*, tr. B. Prichard (Lausanne, 1989).

SIDNEY, MARY, and SIDNEY, Sir PHILIP, *The Sidney Psalms*, ed. R. E. Pritchard (Manchester, 1992).

SIDNEY, SIR PHILIP, *The Poems of Sir Philip Sidney*, ed. W. A. Ringler (Oxford, 1962).

—— *An Apology for Poetry or The Defence of Poesy*, ed. G. Shepherd (London, 1965).

—— *Selected Poems*, ed. K. Duncan-Jones (Oxford, 1973).

SOUTHWELL, ROBERT, *Marie Magdalens Funerall Teares* (London, 1594).

TAFFIN, JEAN, *Of The Markes of the Children of God, and of their Comforts in Afflictions*, tr. Anne Locke (Paris, 1609).

Tottel's Miscellany, 1557, Songes and Sonnettes (Leeds, 1966).

VALDÉS, JUAN DE, *Le Cento et Diece Considerationi del Valdesso, tradotte della Spagnola nella Italian lingua* (Basle, 1550).

—— *The Hundred and Ten Considerations of Signior Iohn Valdesso. Written In Spanish, Brought out of Italy by Vergerius, and first set forth in Italian at Basil by Coelius Secundus Curio, Anno 1550. And now translated out of the Italian Copy into English, with notes* (Oxford, 1638).

—— *Trataditos*, ed. E. Boehmer (Bonn, 1880).

—— *XVII Opuscules*, tr. and ed. J. T. Betts (London, 1882).

—— *Juan de Valdés on the Epistle to the Romans*, tr. J. T. Betts (London, 1883).

—— *Diálogo de las Lenguas*, ed. J. Perry (London, 1927).

—— *Diálogo de las lenguas*, ed. J. F. Montesinos (Madrid, 1928).

—— *Las Ciento Diez Divinas Consideraciones: Recension inedita del manuscrito de Juan Sanchez (1558)*, ed. I. T. Idigoras (Salamanca, 1975).

—— *Two Catechisms*, tr. W. B. Jones and C. D. Jones, ed. and introd. J. Nieto (Lawrence, Kan, 1981).

VAUGHAN, HENRY, *The Complete Poems*, ed. A. Rudrum (Harmondsworth, 1976).

WALTON, ISAAK, *The Life of Mr. George Herbert* (London, 1670).

WARD, SAMUEL, *A Collection of such sermons as have been written and published* (London, 1636).

WATSON, THOMAS, *Works*, ed. E. Arber (London, 1870).

WHITLOCK, RICHARD, *Zootomia: Observations on the Present Manners of the English, or A Morall Anatomy of the Living by the Dead* (London, 1654).

WITHER, GEORGE, *The Schollers Purgatory Discovered in the Stationers Common-wealth* (London, 1624).

—— *Halleluiah or Britans second Remembrancer, bringing to Remembrance (in powerfull and Penitentiall Hymnes, Spiritual Songs, and Morall Odes) Meditations advancing the glorie of God, and the Practice of Pietie and Vertue* (London, 1641).

Secondary Material

AMBRUST, C., 'Nineteenth-Century Re-presentations of George Herbert: Publishing History as Critical Embodiment', *The Huntington Library Quarterly*, 53 (1990), 131–51.

ASALS, H. A. R., *Equivocal Predication: George Herbert's Way to God* (Toronto, 1981).

AUSTIN, J. L., *How To Do Things With Words* (Oxford, 1962).

BAKHUIZEN VAN DEN BRINK, J. N., *Juan de Valdés, réformateur en Espagne et en Italie 1529–1541* (Geneva, 1969).

BELL, I., 'Herbert's Valdésian Vision', *ELR* 17 (1987), 303–28.

BINNS, J. W. (ed.), *The Latin Poetry of English Poets* (London, 1974).

BLOCH, C., *Spelling the Word: George Herbert and the Bible* (Berkeley, 1985).

BOASE, A. M., *Poètes anglais et francais de l'époque baroque* (Lille, 1948).

—— *The Poetry of France 1: 1400–1600* (London, 1964).

BRADNER, L., 'New Poems by George Herbert: The Cambridge Latin Gratulatory Anthology of 1613', *Renaissance News*, no. 15 (1962), 208–11.

BURKE, K., *The Rhetoric of Religion: Studies in Logology* (Berkeley, 1970).

CARLTON, C., *Charles I: The Personal Monarch* (London, 1983).

CAVANAUGH, J. C., 'Lady Southwell's Defence of Poetry', *ELR* 14 (1984), 284.

CAVE, T. C., *Devotional Poetry in France c.1570–1613* (Cambridge, 1969).

—— *The Cornucopian Text: Problems of Writing in the French Renaissance* (Oxford, 1979).

CHAN, S., 'The Puritan Meditative Tradition: A Study of Ascetical Piety' (Univ. of Cambridge Ph.D. thesis, 1986).

CHARLES, A. M., *A Life of George Herbert* (Ithaca, NY, 1977).

CHUILLEANDIN, E. NÍ, 'The Debate between Thomas More and William Tyndale, 1528–33: Ideas on Literature and Religion', *JEH* 39 (1988), 382–411.

CLARKE, E., 'Sacred Singer/Profane Poet: Herbert's Split Poetic Persona', in H. Wilcox and R. Todd (eds.), *George Herbert: Sacred and Profane* (Amsterdam, 1995), 23–32.

COHEN, C. L., *God's Caress: The Psychology of Puritan Religious Experience* (Oxford, 1986).

COLLETT, B., *Italian Benedictine Scholars and the Reformation: The Congregation of Santa Giustina of Padua* (Oxford, 1985).

COLLINSON, P., *The Elizabethan Puritan Movement* (London, 1967).

—— 'A Comment: Concerning the Name Puritan', *JEH* 31 (1980), 483–8.

—— *The Religion of Protestants: The Church in English Society, 1559–1625* (Oxford, 1982).

COOK, E., *Seeing Through Words: The Scope of Late Renaissance Poetry* (New Haven, 1986).

COOLIDGE, J. S., *The Pauline Renaissance in England: Puritanism and the Bible* (Oxford, 1970).

COUSINS, A. D., *The Catholic Religious Poets from Southwell to Crashaw: A Critical Study* (London, 1991).

CURTIUS, E. R., *European Literature and the Latin Middle Ages*, W. R. Trask (London, 1953).

D'ANGERS, J. E., OFM, CAP, *L'humanisme chrétien au XVIIe siècle: St. François de Sales et Yves de Paris* (The Hague, 1970).

DAVIS, H., *Worship and Theology in England, 1603–1690* (Princeton, 1975).

DICKSON, D. R., 'Between Transubstantiation and Memorialism: Herbert's Eucharistic Celebration', *George Herbert Journal*, 11 (1987), 1–14.

DOELMAN, J., 'The Accession of King James I and English Religious Poetry', *SEL* 34 (1994), 19–40.

DUBROW, H., and STRIER, R., *The Historical Renaissance: New Essays on Tudor and Stuart Literature and Culture* (Chicago, 1988).

FINCHAM, K. (ed.), *The Early Stuart Church 1603–1642* (London, 1993).

FISH, S. E., *Self-Consuming Artifacts: The Experience of Seventeenth-Century Literature* (Berkeley, 1972).

—— *The Living Temple: George Herbert and Catechising* (Berkeley, 1978).

FLESCH, W., *Generosity and the Limits of Authority: Shakespeare, Herbert, Milton* (Ithaca, NY, 1992).

FRASER, R., *The War Against Poetry* (Princeton, 1970).

FREEMAN, R., *English Emblem Books* (London, 1948).

FREER, C., *Music for a King: George Herbert's Style and the Metrical Psalms* (Baltimore, 1980).

GILLY, C., 'Juan de Valdés: Übersetzer und Bearbeiter von Luthers Schrifte in seinem Dialogo de Doctrina', *Archiv für Reformationsgeschichte*, 74 (1983), 257–305.

GILMAN, E. B., *Iconoclasm and Poetry in the English Reformation: Down Went Dagon* (Chicago, 1986).

GIOVANNOZZI, L., *Contributo all Bibliografia delle Opere del Savonarola: Edizioni dei Secc. XV e XVI* (Florence, 1953).

GOLDBERG, J., *Voice Terminal Echo: Postmodernism and English Renaissance Texts* (New York, 1986).

GRANT, P., *The Transformations of the Word: Studies in Donne, Herbert, Vaughan and Traherne* (Montreal, 1974).

GREEN, I., ' "For Children in Yeeres and Children in Understanding": The Emergence of the English Catechism under Elizabeth and the Early Stuarts', *JEH* 37 (1986), 397–425.

GREENBLATT, S., *Renaissance Self-Fashioning: From More to Shakespeare* (Chicago, 1980).

GREENE, R., *Post-Petrarchism: Origins and Innovations of the Western Lyric Sequence* (Princeton, 1991).

HALEWOOD, W. H., *The Poetry of Grace: Reformation Themes and Structures in English Seventeenth-Century Poetry* (New Haven, 1970).

HAMILTON, R., 'Juan de Valdés and Some Renaissance Theories of Language', *Bulletin of Hispanic Studies*, 30 (1953), 125–33.

HARMAN, B. L., 'George Herbert's *Affliction (i)*: The Limits of Representation', *ELH* 44 (1977), 267–85.

—— *Costly Monuments: Representations of the Self in George Herbert's Poetry* (Cambridge, Mass., 1982).

HILL, C., *Society and Puritanism in Pre-Revolutionary England* (London, 1964).

—— *The Collected Essays of Christopher Hill. Volume II: Religion and Politics in Seventeenth Century England* (Brighton, 1986).

HODGKINS, C., *Authority, Church and Society in George Herbert: Return to the Middle Way* (New York, 1993).

HUEHNS, G., *Antinomianism in English History with Special Reference to the Period 1640–1660* (London, 1951).

HUNTER, J. C., 'Herbert's "The Water-Course": Notorious and Neglected', *Notes and Queries*, 34 (1987), 310–12.

JAMES, F., 'Praedestinatio Dei: The Intellectual Origins of Peter Martyr Vermigli's Doctrine of Double Predestination' (Univ. of Oxford D.Phil. thesis, 1993).

JANELLE, P., *Robert Southwell the Writer: A Study in Religious Inspiration* (London, 1935).

JEANNERET, M., *Poésie et tradition biblique au XVIe siècle* (Paris, 1969).

JONES, R. M., *Mysticism and Democracy in the English Commonwealth* (Cambridge, Mass., 1932).

KERRIGAN, W., and BRADEN, G., *The Idea of the Renaissance* (Baltimore, 1989).

LAKE, P., *Moderate Puritans in the Elizabethan Church* (Cambridge, 1982).

—— 'Popular Form, Puritan Content? Two Puritan Appropriations of the Murder Pamphlet from Mid-Seventeenth-Century London', in A. Fletcher and P. Roberts (eds.), *Religion, Culture and Society in Early Modern Britain: Essays in Honour of Patrick Collinson* (Cambridge, 1994).

LANGER, U., *Divine and Poetic Freedom in the Renaissance: Nominalist Theology and Literature in France and Italy* (Princeton, 1990).

LEVERENZ, D., *The Language of Puritan Feeling: An Exploration in Literature, Psychology and Social History* (New Brunswick, NY, 1980).

LEWALSKI, B. K., *Protestant Poetics and the Seventeenth-Century Religious Lyric* (Princeton, 1970).

LONGHURST, J. E., *Erasmus and the Spanish Inquisition: The Case of Juan de Valdés* (Albuquerque, N. Mex., 1950).

LULL, J., *The Poem in Time: Reading Herbert's Revisions of 'The Church'* (Newark, Del., 1990).

MCCABE, R. A., *Joseph Hall: A Study in Satire and Meditation* (Oxford, 1982).

MACCULLOCH, D., *The Later Reformation in England 1547–1603* (London, 1990).

MCGRATH, A., *The Intellectual Origins of the European Reformation* (Oxford, 1987).

MCNAIR, P., *Peter Martyr in Italy: An Anatomy of Apostasy* (Oxford, 1967).

MADDISON, C., *Marcantonio Flaminio: Poet, Humanist and Reformer* (London, 1965).

MAROTTI, A., *Manuscript, Print, and the English Renaissance Lyric* (Ithaca, NY, 1995).

MARTIN, J., 'Isaak Walton and his Precursors: A Literary Study of the Emergence of the Ecclesiastical *Life*' (Univ. of Cambridge Ph.D. thesis, 1993).

MARTZ, L. L., *The Poetry of Meditation: A Study in English Religious Literature of the Seventeenth Century*, rev. edn. (New Haven, 1962).

—— *The Poem of the Mind* (New York, 1966).

MAYCOCK, A. L., *Nicholas Ferrar of Little Gidding* (London, 1963).

MILLER, E., and DIYANNI, R., *Like Season'd Timber: New Essays on George Herbert* (New York, 1987).

MILLER, P., *The New England Mind: The Seventeenth Century* (New York, 1939).

MINNIS, A. J., *Mediaeval Theory of Authorship* (London, 1984).

MORTIMER, A., 'Words in the Mouth of God: Augustinian Language-Theory and the Poetics of George Herbert', in R. Waswo (ed.), *On Poetry and Poetics* (Zurich, 1985), 31–43.

MOURGES, O. DE, *Metaphysical, Baroque and Précieux Poetry* (Oxford, 1953).

MULLER, R. A., *Christ and The Decree: Christology and Predestination in Reformed Theology from Calvin to Perkins* (Durham, NC, 1986).

NIETO, J., *Juan de Valdés and the Origins of the Spanish and Italian Reformation* (Geneva, 1970).

NOVARR, D., *The Making of Walton's Lives* (Ithaca, NY, 1958).

NUTTALL, A. D., *Overheard by God: Fiction and Prayer in Herbert, Milton, Dante and St. John* (London, 1980).

NUTTALL, G. F., 'The Last of James Nayler: Robert Rich and the Church of the First-Born', *The Friends' Quarterly*, 60 (1985), 527–34.

—— *The Holy Spirit in Puritan Faith and Experience*, new edn. (Chicago, 1992).

OBERMAN, H. A., *Forerunners of the Reformation* (London, 1967).

—— *The Dawn of the Reformation* (Edinburgh, 1986).

ONG, W., *The Presence of Word* (New Haven, 1967).

PAHLKA, W. H., *Saint Augustine's Meter and George Herbert's Will* (Kent, Oh., 1987).

PATRIDES, C. A. (ed.), *George Herbert: The Critical Heritage* (London, 1983).

—— and WADDINGTON, R. B. (eds.), *The Age of Milton* (Manchester, 1990).

PETROCCHI, M., *Storia della spiritualita italiana I* (Rome, 1978).

PRELOWSKI, R., 'The "Beneficio di Cristo" ', in J. A. Tedeschi (ed.), *Italian Reformation Studies in Honour of Laelius Socinus* (Florence, 1965), 23–102.

PRICKETT, S., *Words and 'The Word': Language, Poetics and Biblical Interpretation* (Cambridge, 1986).

RAY, R., 'The Herbert Allusion Book: Allusions to George Herbert in the Seventeenth Century', *Studies in Philology*, 83 (1986), 1–182.

RICART, D., *Juan de Valdés* (Mexico City, 1958).

RIDOLFI, R., *The Life of Girolamo Savonarola*, tr. C. Grayson (New York, 1959).

RUSSELL, C. (ed.), *Origins of the English Civil War* (London, 1973).

SCHOENFELDT, M. C., *Prayer and Power: George Herbert and Renaissance Courtship* (Chicago, 1991).

SHARPE, K., *The Personal Rule of Charles I* (New Haven, 1992).

SHUGER, D. K., *Sacred Rhetoric: The Christian Grand Style in the Renaissance* (Princeton, 1988).

SMITH, N. (ed.), *A Collection of Ranter Writings from the 17th Century* (London, 1983).

—— 'George Herbert in Defence of Antinomianism', *Notes and Queries*, 31 (1984), 334–5.

—— *Perfection Proclaimed* (Oxford, 1989).

STEWART, S., *George Herbert* (Boston, 1986).

STRIER, R., *Love Known: Theology and Experience in George Herbert's Poetry* (Chicago, 1983).

SUMMERS, C. J., and PEBWORTH, T.-L., (eds.), *'Too Riche Too Clothe The Sunne': Essays on George Herbert* (Pittsburgh, 1980).

———— (eds.), *'The Muses Common-weale': Poetry and Politics in the Seventeenth Century* (New York, 1988).

SUMMERS, J., *George Herbert: His Religion and Art* (Cambridge, Mass., 1954).

TAYLOR, M., *The Soul in Paraphrase* (The Hague, 1974).

TEDESCHI, J. A. (ed.), *Italian Reformation Studies In Honour of Laelius Socinus* (Florence, 1965).

TODD, R., *The Opacity of Signs: Acts of Interpretation in George Herbert's 'The Temple'* (New York, 1986).

TRINKAUS, C., *'In Our Image and Likeness': Humanity and Divinity in Italian Humanist Thought*, 2 vols. (London, 1970).

—— and OBERMAN, H. A. (eds.), *The Pursuit of Holiness* (Leiden, 1974).

TUVE, R., *A Reading of George Herbert* (Chicago, 1952).

TYACKE, N., 'Puritans, Arminians and Counter-Revolutionaries', in C. Russell (ed.), *Origins of the English Civil War* (London, 1973).

—— *Anti-Calvinists: The Rise of English Arminianism c.1590–1640* (Oxford, 1987).

VEITH, G. E., JR., *Reformation Spirituality: The Religion of George Herbert* (Lewisburg, Pa., 1985).

—— 'The Religious Wars in George Herbert Criticism: Reinterpreting Seventeenth-Century Anglicanism', *George Herbert Journal*, 11 (1988), 19–33.

WAKEWELD, G. S., *Puritan Devotion: Its Place in the Development of Christian Piety* (London, 1957).

WALL, J. N., *Transformations of the Word: Spenser, Herbert, Vaughan* (Athens, Oh., 1988).

WATTS, T., *Cheap Print and Popular Piety, 1550–1640* (Cambridge, 1991).

WEINBERG, B., *A History of Criticism in the Italian Renaissance* (Chicago, 1961).

WEINER, A. D., *Sir Philip Sidney and the Poetics of Protestantism: A Study of Contexts* (Minneapolis, 1978).

WEINSTEIN, D., *Savonarola and Florence: Prophecy and Patriotism in the Renaissance* (Princeton, 1970).

WENGEN-SHUTE, R. VAN, *George Herbert and the Liturgy of the Church of England* (Oegstgeest, The Netherlands, 1981).

WESTERWEEL, B., *Patterns and Patterning: A Study of Four Poems by George Herbert* (Amsterdam, 1984).

WHITE, H. C., *English Devotional Literature (Prose) 1600–1640* (Madison, 1931).

WHITE, P., *Predestination, Policy and Polemic: Conflict and Consensus in the English Church from the Reformation to the Civil War* (Cambridge, 1992).

WILCOX, H., 'Something Understood: The Reputation and Influence of George Herbert to 1715' (Univ. of Oxford D.Phil. thesis, 1984).

WILCOX, P., 'Restoration, Reformation and the Progress of the Kingdom of Christ: Evangelisation in the Thought and Practice of John Calvin, 1555–64' (Univ. of Oxford D.Phil. thesis, 1993).

YATES, F. A., *The French Academies of the Sixteenth Century* (London, 1947).

ZIM, R., *English Metrical Psalms: Poetry as Praise and Prayer 1535–1601* (Cambridge, 1987).

INDEX OF POEMS

Index of Poems

GENERAL INDEX

Adam 111, 161, 200, 206, 235, 237, 273
Ames, William 196, 204, 209, 210, 266
An Apology for Poetry 9, 25
Anglicanism:
    definitions of 9–10
    and Herbert 14
    reception of *The Temple* 256
antinomianism 196–7, 199, 201, 221
Aquinas 21, 33, 41–3
Aristotle 16–22, 28, 33, 41, 46, 148, 149
Arminian Nunnery, The 223
Arminianism 124, 126, 182–9, 192, 194,
    201, 225–6, 260, 276
Augustine 15
    De Musica 231, 240
    and 'ejaculation' 100–11,
    and rhetoric 28, 44–6, 49, 53–5, 60–6,
        72, 92, 177, 254
    and wordless prayer 116–20, 126, 134, 165

B, *see* Bodleian manuscript
Bacon, Francis 16, 22–3, 244
Bacon, Roger 221–2
Ball, John 208
baptism 10, 49, 191, 202, 252–3, 276–7
Bartas, Guillaume de Saluste Sieur du 3,
    29, 77, 98–9, 131
Barton, William 177
Baxter, Richard 194, 257, 280
Bayly, Lewis 181, 187, 210
Bayne, Paul 201, 202
Bedell, William 211
Beza 2, 76–7, 131–2, 140, 145, 179, 187, 222
Bible, *see* Scripture
biblical allusion:
    I Cor. 1: 18   220
    I Cor. 1: 22–3   188
    Eph. 4: 22–4   195
    Ex. 28   194
    Gen. 32   252–3
    Heb. 4: 10   195
    Isaiah 64: 6   187
    Jeremiah 32: 33   244
    Job 32   146
    John 7: 18   276
    John 14: 6   86

Ps. 3: 4   118
Ps. 6   143, 153
Ps. 31   141–2
Ps. 32   143–4, 166
Ps. 139   145–7
Ps. 51   141–3, 152
Ps. 56: 8   8 118
Ps. 61   155
Ps. 79   140
Ps. 102   151–2
Ps. 123   140
Ps. 130   152
Ps. 143   151
Romans 6   216
Romans 8: 13   190
Romans 8: 26   165
Song of Songs 133
Billy, Jacques de 123
Blois, Louis de 85, 103–6, 134
Bodleian manuscript 48, 97, 160, 195, 235,
    272, 277
Book of Common Prayer 18, 27, 124, 141,
    142, 262
Booke of Martyrs 27, 141
Burton, Henry 187, 208

Calvin 19, 22, 66, 76, 81, 179, 181
    and divine agency 190, 197, 201–2
    and the Psalms 130, 132, 134–5, 138
    and signification 207, 210, 214
Calvinist doctrine:
    assurance 279
    good works 121, 185–90, 260
    holiness 196–7
    mortification 241–2
    perseverance 275–6
    predestination 184
    salvation 266
    sanctification 208, 239
Calvinist poetry 75–7, 140
Cambridge 5, 12, 28, 54, 73, 78, 220, 259
Capel, Richard 225
Carbo, Ludovicus 15, 35, 73
catechisms 208–9
Cave, Terence 21, 75, 139
Ceppède, Jean de 78

295

General Index

Holy Spirit:
and holiness 187, 196, 198–201
and mortification 190–2
and 'motions' 92–6, 164–5, 209, 211, 215
and poetry 57, 98, 80–1
and Reformed theology 18–19
and Savonarola 28, 32, 43
and Valdés 224–5, 227–9
Hoskins, John 22
Howell, James 147
Huehns, Gertrude 196
Hyperius, Andreas 90–3, 174

Ignatian meditation 82
imagination 23, 32, 38, 175, 177
and meditation 77, 81–2, 89, 91, 95, 127–8
inspiration:
of authorship 22, 24, 57–8, 229–30, 251
of speech 16, 45, 84, 227–9
invention 23, 43, 44, 47–51, 61, 205, 228, 251–2
invocation 84–9

James I 2–5, 15, 17, 147, 150, 175, 265
Jeanneret, Michel 142, 145
Jesuit poetic theory 128
justification 25, 74, 186, 195, 207, 246

Keckermann, Bartholomew 55
Knevet, Ralph 8, 175, 231

Langer, Ullrich 22, 278
Laud, William 10, 182–4
Legate, John 9, 256
Leighton, William 4, 129, 262
Lessius 73
Leverenz, David 258
Little Gidding 13, 37, 72, 188
liturgy 176, 177, 194, 262
Lok, Anne 143
Lok, Henry 29, 114, 129, 138
Louis de Blois 85, 103–6, 134
Luis de Granada 103, 106, 134
Lull, Janis 160
Luther 22, 76, 141

Marotti, Arthur 12, 68, 178
Marot–Bèze Psalter 131–4, 136–7, 141
Martin, Jessica 264
Martz, Louis L. 4, 14, 71–113, 127–8, 134, 150, 232
Melanchthon, Philip 76, 224

Melville, Andrew 57
Merritt, Julia 183
middle way 183
see also *via media*
Milton, John 273
Montagu, Richard 182
mortification 189–221, 228–66, 271–6
Mortimer, Anthony 158
'motions':
in *An Introduction to the Devout Life* 92–7, 137–8
mortification and 'motions' 190–218
inspiration and 'motions' 226–7, 273
spiritual and rhetorical 17–23
in spiritual discourse 163–75
Moxon, Joseph 62
mysticism 86, 95, 105, 222

Neo-Latin poetry 76–7, 123
Neoplatonism 39, 40, 69
Nethersole, Francis 5
Nicholls, William 71–2, 95
nominalism 22, 121, 268, 278
Norton, John 196, 197
Novarr, David 264
Nowell, Alexander 208
Nuttall, A. D. 13, 113, 166, 234, 236, 239, 242, 258
Nuttall, Geoffrey 198, 224

Oberman, Heiko A. 201
Ochino, Bernadino 189
Oley, Barnabas 10, 79, 256, 259, 261–3, 271
Orator of the University of Cambridge 4, 5, 28, 54, 78
oratory 35, 44, 60, 64, 67, 91, 268
see also classical rhetoric
Oxford 9, 179, 225
Ozment, Steven 268

Paradise Lost 273
Paradise Regained 216, 233
Parr, Elnathan 102, 211
passions 17, 133–55
Peacham, Henry 23–4
Pemble, William 66, 225–7, 231, 250, 251, 269
perfection 41, 42, 69, 125, 204, 266
Perkins, William 185, 202–6, 210, 212–13, 227, 258
perseverance 19, 42, 182, 186–8, 210, 276–80
Peter Martyr 76, 179